THE POLITICAL WRITINGS OF
JOHN DICKINSON
1764-1774

A Da Capo Press Reprint Series

THE ERA OF THE AMERICAN REVOLUTION

GENERAL EDITOR: LEONARD W. LEVY
Brandeis University

THE POLITICAL WRITINGS OF
JOHN DICKINSON
1764-1774

Edited by
Paul Leicester Ford

DA CAPO PRESS · NEW YORK · 1970

A Da Capo Press Reprint Edition

This Da Capo Press edition of *The Political Writings of John Dickinson, 1764–1774*, is an unabridged republication of the first edition published in Philadelphia in 1895 as Volume XIV of the *Memoirs of the Historical Society of Pennsylvania*. The original edition specified that this work was to be Volume I of the collected *Writings of John Dickinson*, but additional volumes were never published.

Library of Congress Catalog Card Number 70-119061

SBN 306-71950-9

Published by Da Capo Press
A Division of Plenum Publishing Corporation
227 West 17th Street, New York, N. Y. 10011

LIFE AND WRITINGS

OF

JOHN DICKINSON.

ESSE QUAM VIDERI

John Dickinson Esquire

THE WRITINGS

OF

JOHN DICKINSON.

Vol. I.

POLITICAL WRITINGS

1764-1774.

EDITED AT THE REQUEST OF THE HISTORICAL SOCIETY
OF PENNSYLVANIA,

By PAUL LEICESTER FORD.

PHILADELPHIA :
THE HISTORICAL SOCIETY OF PENNSYLVANIA.
1895.

At a meeting of the Historical Society of Pennsylvania, held May 6, 1889, it was

Resolved, That the President of the Society appoint a committee to collect the published and unpublished correspondence and writings of John Dickinson, with a view of including them in the Memoirs of the Society, and that CHARLES J. STILLÉ, Esq., LL.D., be invited to edit the same. Subsequently the writing of the Life of Dickinson was undertaken by DR. STILLÉ, and the editing of the Writings of Dickinson by MR. FORD.

To

MY BROTHER,

WORTHINGTON CHAUNCEY FORD,

WHOSE SCHOLARLY PUBLICATIONS AND ADVICE

HAVE SO OFTEN AIDED

THE EDITOR,

THIS COLLECTION IS DEDICATED.

PREFACE.

JOHN DICKINSON has been aptly termed the "Penman of the Revolution." In the literature of that struggle, his position is as pre-eminent as Washington in war, Franklin in diplomacy, and Morris in finance. From no other leader of that movement originated a series of arguments of half the number, importance or popularity. In 1765 his pen produced the "Declaration of Rights" of the Stamp Act Congress, the first American state paper that can claim the slightest element of nationality. His "Letters of a Farmer" ran through the colonies like wildfire, furnishing a common fighting ground to all and so leading the way to union. The "Liberty Song," sung and re-sung, with its line "By uniting we stand, by dividing we fall," still further pointed the path that led to the first Congress. For that body he drew the famous "Petition to the King" and "the Address to Inhabitants of Quebec," being the only member to whom was assigned the framing of two papers. In the Continental Congress he drew the "Second Petition to the King," offering for the last time the olive branch; while at the same time writing the "Declaration upon taking up Arms," so cheered by the Continental batallions. But for his disapproval of a Declaration of Independence at the time it was moved, he would have been the framer of the vindication of that step. And his pen prepared the draft of the Articles of Confederation, which welded a people into a league, if not a nation.

But more than the Revolution can be traced in these volumes. Here is epitomized as well the story of Ameri-

can history in the period of its greatest development.
The chief struggle for ten years was to unite a people ; for
another ten, to form a nation ; then for twenty years a long
struggle for that nation to acquire and maintain a position
with other nations.　Of all this, Dickinson's writings form
an important part.　Opening with a dispute which concerned the local politics of a single province, they quickly
pass to the stage of the action of an individual colony on a
question of common concern.　Following these come writings that received the approval of seven colonies.　Then
those that twelve assented to.　Finally are those which
were adopted by the whole thirteen, and the union of
Americans for opposition to a common enemy, was completed.　Union of feeling having been obtained, the question of the legal relation of these separate colonies, or
states, to each other became important.　Here too, Dickinson exercised much influence.　In his own state, he
wrote concerning the local government.　In Congress he
drew the first band of union.　At Annapolis he signed the
call for a general convention to frame a new government.
His part in the Federal Convention was prominent and
material.　His writings in support of the government there
framed aided its adoption.　Nationality having been obtained, he turned his pen to the relations of America to
Europe.　And though he did not live to see the third
stage of the epoch ended, and his country so established
both internally and externally, that forty years of peaceful
development succeeded, yet he lived long enough to have
been able to feel that he and his contemporaries had not
labored in vain, but had been instruments in the accom-
plishment of a great movement.

Though Dickinson's writings were so popular in their
day, but one collection of them has ever been made.　This
consisted of a selection, edited by Dickinson himself, and
published in 1801, a re-issue of which was made in 1814.

In this was printed his "Speech" of 1764, the "Regulation of the Colonies," the Stamp Act Congress "Resolutions," the "Address to Barbadoes," the "Farmer's Letters," the "Essay" of 1774, the "Addresses" and "Petitions" of the Congresses of 1774 and 1775, the Congressional Address of 1779, and the two series of the Letters of Fabius. Thus more than two-thirds of his writings were omitted, and have remained unknown.

Believing that Dickinson's position and influence have been slighted by this suppression, the editor began the preparation for a new edition of his writings over five years ago. After advancing some ways in the work, he learned of a similar labor being planned by the Historical Society of Pennsylvania, and only too gladly merged his individual attempt with theirs. He has endeavored to make the present collection contain all that is extant of Dickinson's writings, but has, unfortunately, not been able to obtain access to or copies of some of the Dickinson papers in the possession of a descendant. Aside from this hiatus, other omissions probably occur. After a careful study of over two thousand issues of the newspapers printed in Pennsylvania between 1762 and 1777, the editor is convinced, from his knowledge of Dickinson's style, that he was a constant writer for the press, and that a number of the broadsides of the period were also written by him. But deeming his personal opinion on this matter insufficient evidence to warrant the inclusion of such articles and broadsides in this collection, the editor has omitted all that he could not in some other way verify. Fortunately most of the pieces so omitted are of comparatively small moment ; and the editor believes that the present edition includes all that is essential and important of Dickinson's works. The first two volumes will contain his political writings, and a third will be devoted to his correspondence.

The editor is under special obligations to Dr. Charles J.

Stillé, author of the very valuable *Life of John Dickinson*, which constitutes the first volume of this series ; to Miss Frances A. Logan, a collateral descendant of Dickinson ; to Mr. Frederick D. Stone, librarian of the Historical Society ; and to that Society, for their aid in the preparation of this edition. He also gives thanks for assistance to Dr. S. A. Green, Mr. A. P. C. Griffin, and Mr. Lindsay Swift, of Boston ; Mr. E. M. Barton, of Worcester ; Mr. Wilberforce Eames, Mr. Charles L. Woodward, Mr. William Kelby, and Dr. Thomas Addis Emmet, of New York ; Mr. Charles R. Hildeburn, and Mr. Bumford Samuels, of Philadelphia ; and Mr. S. M. Hamilton, of Washington. Last he must record the aid given by two now passed away, Dr. J. S. H. Fogg, and Dr. George H. Moore, to both of whom American history owes so much.

PAUL LEICESTER FORD.

January 29, 1894.

PREFACE.*

The present age has been witness to as great political phenomena, as have appeared in the history of the world.

Among other events, we have seen *America*, in a dignified progression, from resentment of injuries to remonstrances, from remonstrances to arms, and from arms to liberty—after a vicissitude of fortunes delivered from despotism, and establishing her freedom in a republican form of government, on the pure and just principles of *popular representation* and *federal union*, delineated in these writings.

Throughout the course of these contests, the friends of liberty in *Great-Britain*, many of them peers or members of the house of commons, of the highest characters, were warm advocates for THE JUSTICE OF OUR CAUSE.

In the year 1774, the earl of *Chatham*, in a speech worthy of his distinguished talents and illustrious reputation, said—"If we take a transient view of those motives, which induced the ancestors of our fellow subjects in *America*, to leave their native country, to encounter the innumerable difficulties of the unexplored regions of the Western world, our astonishment at the present conduct of their descendants will naturally subside. There was no corner of the globe to which they would not have fled, rather than submit to the slavish and tyrannical spirit, which prevailed at that period in their native country; and viewing them in their original, forlorn, and now flourishing state, they may be cited as illustrious in-

*To the edition of 1801. The original MS. in Dickinson's handwriting is still in existence.—*Editor.*

(xiii)

stances to instruct the world—*what great exertions man-kind will make, when left to the free exercise of their own powers.*

"It has always been my fixed and unalterable opinion, and I will carry it with me to the grave, that *this country* had no right whatever to tax *America.* It is contrary to all the principles of justice and civil policy: it is contrary to that essential, unalterable right in nature, ingrafted into the *British* constitution as a fundamental law, that *what a man has honestly acquired is absolutely his own,* which he may freely give, but which cannot be taken from him without his own consent.

"Pass then, my lords, instead of these harsh and severe edicts, an amnesty over their errors; by measures of lenity and affection, allure them to their duty; act the part of a generous and forgiving parent. *A period may arrive,* when this parent may stand in need of every assistance, she can receive from a grateful and affectionate offspring."

Soon afterwards, in a confidential letter to a friend, he writes—"Every step on the side of government in *America,* seems calculated to drive the *Americans* into open resistance, vainly hoping to crush the spirit of liberty in that vast continent, at one successful blow; but millions must perish there, before the seeds of freedom will cease to grow and spread, in so favourable a soil; and in the mean time, devoted *England* must sink herself, under the ruins of her own foolish and inhuman system of destruction. It is plain, that *America* cannot bear chains. Would to heaven it were equally plain, that the oppressor, *England,* is not doomed one day to bind them round her own hands, and wear them patiently.

"*Luxuria incubuit, victumque ulciscitur orbem—sævior armis.*

"Happily, beyond the *Atlantic,* this poison has not reached the heart. When then will infatuated administration begin to fear that freedom they cannot destroy, and which they do not know how to love?''

In another letter, he says—''I have not words to express my satisfaction, that the congress has conducted this most arduous and delicate business with such manly wisdom and calm resolution, as does the highest honour to their deliberations. Very few things are contained in their resolves, that I could wish had been otherwise. Upon the whole, I think it must be evident to every unprejudiced man in *England*, who feels for the rights of mankind, that *America*, under all her oppressions and provocations, holds forth to us the most fair and just opening, for restoring harmony and affectionate intercourse, as heretofore. I trust, that the minds of men are more than beginning to change on this great subject ; and that it will be found impossible for freemen in *England*, to wish to see three millions of *Englishmen*, slaves in *America*.''

In the beginning of the year 1775, soon after the *American* papers had beed laid before the peers, he made another speech becoming his splendid fame. These were some of his expressions—''This universal opposition to your arbitrary system of taxation, might have been foreseen ; it was obvious from the nature of things, and from the nature of man, and *above all*, from the confirmed habits of thinking, from the spirit of WHIGGISM flourishing in *America*. The spirit which *now* pervades *America*, is *the same* which formerly opposed loans, benevolences, and ship-money in this country ; is *the same spirit* which roused all *England* to action at the revolution, and which established at a remote æra, your liberties, on the basis of that grand fundamental maxim of the constitution, that no subject of *England* shall be taxed, but by his own consent.

''To maintain this principle, is the *common cause* of the WHIGS, on the other side of the *Atlantic*, and on this. *It*

is liberty to liberty engaged.   In this great cause they are
immoveably allied.   It is the alliance of *God* and *nature*,
immutable, eternal, fixed as the firmament of heaven.*

"As an *Englishman*, I recognize to the *Americans*, their
supreme unalterable right of property.   As an *American*, I
would equally recognize to *England*, her supreme right of
regulating commerce and navigation.   This distinction is
involved in the abstract nature of things; property is private, individual, absolute: the touch of another annihi-
lates it.   Trade is an extended and complicated consideration; it reaches as far as ships can sail, or winds can blow;
it is a vast and various machine.   To regulate the numberless movements of its several parts, and combine them
into one harmonious effect, for the good of the whole, requires the superintending wisdom and energy of the supreme power of the empire.

* "*Arbitrary taxation* is plunder authorized by law; it is the support
and the essence of tyranny; and has done more mischief to mankind,
than those other three scourges from heaven, famine, pestilence, and the
sword.

"I need not carry your lordships out of your own knowledge, or out
of your own dominions, to make you conceive what misery this right of
taxation is capable of producing in a provincial government.

"We need only recollect, that *our countrymen* in *India* have, in the
space of five or six years, in virtue of this right, destroyed, starved and
driven away more inhabitants from *Bengal*, than are to be found at present in all our *American* colonies.—This is no exaggeration, my lords,
but plain matter of fact."

SHIPLEY, bishop of *St. Asaph*, against the bill for altering the
     charter of *Massachusetts, &c.*

"We seem not to be sensible of the high and important trusts, which
Providence has committed to our charge.   The most precious remains of
civil liberty, that the world can now boast of, are now lodged in our
hands, and GOD forbid, that we should violate so sacred a deposite.

"By enslaving your colonies, you not only ruin the peace, the commerce, and the fortunes of both countries; but you extinguish the fairest
hopes, shut up the last asylum of mankind.

"I think, my lords, without being weakly superstitious, that a good
man may hope, that heaven will take part against the execution of a
plan, which seems big not only with mischief, but *Impiety*."   *Idem.*

"On this grand practical distinction, then, let us rest : taxation is theirs, commericial regulation is ours. As to the metaphysical refinements, attempting to shew, that the *Americans* are equally free from legislative controul, and commercial restraint, as from taxation, for the purpose of revenue, I pronounce them futile, frivolous, and groundless.

"When your lordships have perused the papers transmitted to us from *America*, when you consider the dignity, the firmness, and the wisdom with which the *Americans* have acted, *you cannot but respect their cause.*

"History, my lords, has been my favourite study, and in the celebrated writings of antiquity, have I often admired the patriotism of *Greece* and *Rome:* but, my lords, I must declare and avow, that in the master states of the world, I know not the people or the senate, who, in such a complication of difficult circumstances, can stand in preference to the delegates of *America*, assembled in general congress at *Philadelphia.* I trust, it is obvious to your lordships, that all attempts to impose servitude upon such men, to establish despotism over such a mighty continental nation, must be vain."

Lord *Chatham* was ably supported by his friend, the excellent lord *Camden*, who among other things said— "When the famous *Selden* was asked, ' by what statute *resistance to tyranny* could be justified?' his reply was—'it is to be justified by the *custom of England*, which is part of *the law of the land.*'

"I will affirm, my lords, not only as a statesman, a politician, and a philosopher, but as a common lawyer, that you have no right to tax *America.* No man, agreeably to the principles of natural and civil liberty, can be divested of any part of his property, without his consent ; and *whenever oppression begins, resistance becomes lawful and right.*"

In the year 1777, lord *Chatham* moved an amendment to a proposed address, recommending measures of accommodation, and an immediate cessation of hostilities, as necessary for effectuating that purpose, which "he supported with all the energy and eloquence, which had formerly produced such mighty effects ; and which must now have roused the nation from its death-like torpor, had this been within the compass of human virtue or human ability."

After some weighty observations respecting the conduct of ministers he proceeded thus—"You may swell every expence, and strain every effort, accumulate every assistance, and extend your traffic to the *shambles* of every *German* despot, your attempts will be forever vain and impotent.—But, my lords, where is the man, that in addition to the disgraces and mischiefs of the war, has dared to authorize and associate to our arms the *tomahawk* and *scalping-knife* of the savage? To call into civilized alliance, the wild and inhuman inhabitant of the woods? To delegate to the merciless Indian, the defence of disputed rights, and to wage the horrors of his barbarous warfare against our brethren? These enormities cry aloud for redress and punishment.*

*The *American secretary*, in a letter to general *Carlton* dated *Whitehall,* March 26th, 1777, says: "As this plan cannot be advantageously executed without the assistence of *Canadians* and *Indians,* his majesty *strongly recommends* it to your care, to furnish both expeditions with good and *sufficient bodies of these men :* and I am happy in knowing, that your influence among them is so great, that there can be no room to apprehend you will find it difficult to fulfil his majesty's *intentions.*"

In the "Thoughts for conducting the war from the side of *Canada,*" by general *Burgoyne,* that general desired "*a thousand or more savages.*"

Colonel *Butler* was desired to distribute [the king's bounty-money among *such of the savages* as would join the army; and after the delivery of *the presents,* he asks for £4011, *York* currency, before he left *Niagara.* He adds, in a letter that was laid on the table, in the house of commons, "I flatter myself, that you will not think of expence, however high, to be useless, or given with too lavish hand. I waited seven days to *deliver them the presents,* and GIVE THEM THE HATCHET, WHICH THEY AC-

"It is not, my lords, a wild and lawless banditti whom we oppose : *the resistance of America, is the struggle of free and virtuous patriots.*"

It is remarkable, that this great and good man, in the year 1775, not only lays the *justice of American claims*, on the same eternal and immutable foundations contended for in the following "*Essay on the constitutional power of Great-Britain over the colonies in America,*" published at *Philadelphia* in the preceding year, 1774, but makes the same *comparison* that was made in *that Essay*, between the opposition of *America* to *British* measures, and the opposition of *Britain*, to the measures of the *Stuarts*, respecting loans, benevolences, and ship-money ; and also makes the same *distinction* between taxation and regulation of commerce, that is asserted in *that Essay* and inforces that distinction by the same *arguments* which in the *Essay* are employed on that subject. He likewise insists, as is urged in *that Essay*, that the *admission of an authority to regulate commerce*, does not imply the concession of an authority to legislate, for the purpose of taxation. He, also, called the public attention to the *extraordinary case*, which is stated in that *Essay*—that a period may arrive, when the parent will stand in need of the assistance of her offspring.

Thus has the *justice* of our cause been maintained by the best and wisest men in *Britain*, not only by those beforementioned, but by multitudes of others.

CEPTED, and PROMISED TO MAKE USE OF IT. This letter is dated *Ontario*, July 28th, 1777.

In another letter, colonel *Butler* says, "The *Indians* threw in a heavy fire on *the rebels*, and made *a shocking slaughter* with their *spears and hatchets*. The success of this day, will plainly shew the utility of your excellency's constant support of my *unwearied endeavours* to *conciliate to his majesty so serviceable a body of* ALLIES." This letter is to sir *Guy Carlton*, and dated, camp before *Fort Stanwix*, August 15th, 1777. In another letter he says, "*many of the prisoners* were, *conformably to the* Indian *custom*, AFTERWARDS KILLED." More on this subject may be seen in general *Burgoyne's* proclamation, proceedings in parliament, &c.

Of what *importance* our successful opposition has been, and is now thought on the other side of the *Atlantic*, we may judge from the following declaration of that honest, benevolent, and enlightened statesman *Charles Fox*, in the house of commons—"THE RESISTANCE OF THE AMERICANS TO THE OPPRESSIONS OF THE MOTHER COUNTRY, HAS UNDOUBTEDLY PRE-SERVED THE LIBERTIES OF MANKIND."

What political event, in the annals of the world, can be more worthy of being commended to the attention of na-tions!

We now behold the sun of liberty illumining *Europe;* and we have reason to believe, that its rays will reach to other quarters of the globe, beaming with a benign influ-ence on the human race.

With such knowledge of facts, and with such hopes of the future, every *American* who loves his country, must be pleased to trace our momentous controversy with *Great-Britain*, from its commencement in her injustice, to its termination in our independence; and every friend to man-kind must rejoice, in contemplating the actual and prob-able consequences of our revolution to other nations.

If this intelligence should be conveyed in narratives, written in coolness and leisure, after the agitation of events had subsided, no doubt it would be agreeable : but, this collection offers to our fellow-citizens, in a series from the beginning of the year 1764, writings composed and published in the midst of the arduous contention, while *Britain* with insulting pretensions, and relentless cruelties, was practising every artifice, and straining every nerve, by statutes and by swords, to bend or break us into bondage : and the editors think it their right and duty, to insert some testimonies concerning several of these writings, to shew the sentiments that were entertained of them at the times when they were published, or soon after.

CONTENTS.

(xxi)

A SPEECH

ON A

PETITION FOR A CHANGE OF GOVERNMENT

OF THE

COLONY OF PENNSYLVANIA.

BY

JOHN DICKINSON.

WITH A PREFACE BY
REV. WILLIAM SMITH.

———

MAY 24, 1764.

NOTE.

THE supply bill passed by the Pennsylvania Assembly in the spring of 1764 was the immediate cause of the controversy which occasioned this speech; but the real matter at issue was of long and serious standing, having been practically the main political question for many years in Pennsylvania, and therefore needless to touch upon here. In June, 1763, Sir Jeffrey Amherst had informed the Governor of the Colony, of the danger of the Indian outbreak, later known as Pontiac's conspiracy, and asked an immediate calling of the Assembly to vote the troops and supplies necessary to quell it. Among other acts voted in pursuance of this, was one granting "his Majesty the sum of fifty-thousand Pounds," to which the Governor refused to assent, being bound by his instructions from the Proprietors. (*Minutes*, v, 325-6.) The Assembly at once appointed a committee "to draw up and bring in certain resolves upon the present Circumstances of this Province." A new supply bill was also framed, to which the Governor again refused his assent, and to which the Assembly resolved unanimously to adhere; and a message was drawn and sent to the Governor explaining the reasons for their action. (*Minutes*, v, 329-30.) This in turn produced another message from the Governor, and a counter message from the Assembly, leaving each side determined to maintain its position. The committee on resolutions therefore promptly introduced (March 24, 1764), these resolves, the first twenty-six being a justification of the Colony and Assembly, and the final one being:

"That this House will adjourn, in order to consult their constituents, whether an humble address should be drawn up, and transmitted to his Majesty, praying that he would be graciously pleased to take the people of this province under his immediate protection and government, by compleating the Agreement heretofore made with the first Proprietary for the Sale of the Government to the Crown, or otherwise as his Wisdom and Goodness shall seem meet."

The Assembly "*ordered*, that the foregoing resolves be made public," and then adjourned till the following May. On re-assembling a number of petitions to the King asking him to change the colony from a proprietary to a royal one were laid before the Assembly, with the request that they should be transmitted to the King. The question was therefore put "whether a committee shall now be appointed to prepare and bring in a Draft of a Petition from this House, to accompany the afore mentioned Petitions to his Majesty for a Change of the Government of this Province?" This resolution was carried by "a great majority," a committee named to prepare a petition, and a draft, drawn by Franklin (Franklin's *Writings*, III, 303), was reported on the same day (May 23). This was debated on the next day, when Dickinson delivered the following speech, which sufficiently details the subsequent proceedings. Galloway (note in *Speech* as printed) stated that :

During the Time of the Debates respecting the Change of Government, Mr. Dickenson seldom attended, and was absent when the important one came on, which issued in the Resolve, to adjourn and consult the People. At the next Meeting several Motions were made to bring this Resolution to an Issue, and after great Deliberation, it was resolved by a Majority of 27 to 3, that a Committee should be appointed to bring in the Petition to his Majesty to resume the Powers of Government. But at none of these Debates and Resolutions was Mr. Dickenson present, tho' he well knew, or least had great Reasons to Expect this Business was in continual Agitation.

During this Time, and the Recess of the Assembly, Mr. Dickenson employed himself in collecting his Sentiments in Opposition to the Measure, and in forming his Thoughts into the best Order, and dressing them in the best Language his Abilities were capable of. And upon the first reading of the Petition, and not till then, had he in all this Time, entered into the Debate, or publickly deliver'd his Opinion respecting the intended Change.

After a Measure is resolved on in a House of legislature, it is well known to be contrary to all Rule and Order, to object to the Measure ; otherwise publick Business cou'd never be brought to an Issue. Members may speak to the Mode, but not object against the Thing resolved on. But this Rule, so necessary in public Transactions, was sacrificed either to Mr. Dickenson's Indolence in not attending, or to his Industry in forming his Speech, For he was permitted to object to the Design itself.

In the Debate on the first reading of the Petition, he attempted to deliver his Objections against the Measure, ore tenus; But finding

every thing he offer'd judiciously and sensibly refuted by several
Members, he was obliged to retreat to his Speech, in writing, which
after a short Introductory Apology, he read in his place, in a Manner
not the most deliberate.

This unparliamentary Mode of Proceeding, and the Difficulty of Retaining in the Memory so long and elaborate a Performance, obliged,
and indeed justified the Gentleman, the Author of the following
Speech, in taking short Notes, from which, after Mr. Dickenson had
concluded, he rose to answer the Objections offer'd against the Petition. But the Speaker being exceedingly indisposed, the Debate was
adjourn'd till next Day.

Before the Adjournment, Mr. Dickenson was requested by several
members, and informed by the Speaker, that he ought to leave his
Speech on the Table for the Perusal and Consideration of the House.
But this he several times evaded, alleging in Excuse, that it was too
incorrect and indigested ; altho' he was repeatedly informed that none
wou'd examine it with a View to make any critical observations on the
Stile or Method, but only to make themselves acquainted with the
Substance. At length he was prevail'd on to promise in the most solemn Manner, that he would deliver it to Mr. Galloway that Evening.
That Gentleman called on him at the Time appointed, but Mr. Dickenson continuing in the same Humour, declined delivering it. Nor
did he give the Members an Opportunity of perusing it, until the Debate was over, and the Question called for whether the Petition shou'd
be transcribed for a third Reading. Which passed in the Affirmative
by the Votes of all the Members who rose on the former Question.
All that Mr. Dickenson had either said or read, not having the Success
of altering the Opinion of a single Member.

Nor did the Speech then remain long upon the Table, for Mr. Dickenson immediately after, got it into his Hands again, and carried it
out of the House. What has been done with it since, to whose Care
and Correction it has been committed, and by whom, and with what
Views it has been published, the Preface attending it sufficiently demonstrates.

However, since the Art and Dress in which it now appears to the
Public, is very different from that in which it appeared in the House,
renders it little less than necessary, that the Public shou'd know the
Arguments and Reasons which prevailed on the Members to retain
their former Resolution, of prosecuting the Petition to the Crown ; the
following Speech, in Substance the same that was offered by Mr. Galloway, in Answer to Mr. Dickenson, taken from the short Notes, and
put into Order, is submitted to the Consideration of the Lovers and
Supporters of public Liberty, Order, and good Government.

Dickinson's *Speech* was at once put in type, with the addition of a preface by the Rev. William Smith, and the *Pennsylvania Journal* of June 28, 1764, announced that:

To Morrow will be published and to be sold by
WILLIAM BRADFORD
At his Book Store adjoining the *London* COFFEE-HOUSE.
A
SPEECH
Delivered in the HOUSE OF ASSEMBLY of the Province
of *Pennsylvania*, May 24th, 1764.
By John Dickinson, Esq.

As printed, it made a pamphlet of thirty pages, the preface filling an additional thirteen. The title was:

A / Speech, / Delivered in the House of Assembly of the Province of / Pennsylvania, May 24th, 1764. / By John Dickinson, Esq ; / One of the Members for the County of Philadelphia. / On Occasion of a Petition, drawn up by Order, and then / under Consideration, of the House; praying his Majesty for a / Change of the Government of this Province. / With a Preface. / Certe ego libertatem, quæ mihi a Parente meo tradita est, experiar; verum / id frustra, an ob rem faciam, in vestra manu situm est, Quirites. / Sall. Bel. Jugurth. in Orat. Memmii. / As for me, I will assuredly contend for that glorious plan of Liberty / handed down to us from our ancestors; but whether my Labours / shall prove successful, or in vain, depends wholly on you, my dear / Countrymen ! / Philadelphia : / Printed and Sold by William Bradford, at his / Book-Store adjourning the London Coffee-House. / M,DCC,LXIV.

A second edition was printed only three weeks later (pp. xv, 30), with the following title:

A / Speech, / Delivered in the House of Assembly of the Province of / Pennsylvania, May 24th, 1764. / By John Dickinson, Esq ; / One of the Members for the County of Philadelphia. / On Occasion of a Petition drawn up by Order, and then / under Consideration, of the House ; praying his Majesty for a / Change of the Government of this Province. / With a Preface. / The Second Edition. / . . . . . / Philadelphia : / Printed and Sold by William Bradford, at his / Book-Store adjoining the London Coffee-House. / M,DCC,LXIV.

This edition was translated into German and printed as:

Eine / Rede, / gehalten / in dem Hause der Assembly der Provinz / Pennsylvanien, am 24ten May, 1764. / Von / Herrn John Dickinson / einem der Mitglieder des Hauses für / Phila-

delpbia Caunty. / 1Bey Gelegenbeit einer Uittscbrift, die auf
1Besebl des / 1bauses ausgesetzt, und damals in Ueberlegung
genom/men war, worin Eine 1Bönigliche Majestät um eine / Ver=
änderung des Governments dieser Proving er=/sucbt wird. / Mit
einer Uorrede. / . . . / Aus dem Englischen übersetzt, nach der
zweyten Auflage. / Philadelphia, Gedruckt und zu finden bey
1benrich Miller, in der Zweyten=Strasse. [1764.] 8vo. pp. xvi, 35.

The speech was also printed in London (pp. xv, 31), as follows :

    A /Speech, / Delivered In / the House of Assembly / Of the Province
of Pennsylvania, / May 24th, 1764. / By John Dickinson, Esq ; / One
of the Members for the County of *Philadelphia.* / On Occasion of a
Petition drawn up by Order, and then / under Consideration of the
House ; praying his *Majesty* for / a Change of the *Government* of this
Province. / With / A Preface. / *Certe ego libertatem, quæ mihi a
Parente meo tradita est, experiar verum | id frustra, an ob rem faciam,
in vestra manu situm est, Quirites.* / Sall. Bell. Jugurth. in Orat.
Memmii / As for me, I will assuredly contend for that glorious plan
of *Liberty* / handed down to us from our ancestors ; but whether my
Labours / shall prove successful, or in vain, depends wholly on you,
my dear / Countrymen ! / Philadelphia Printed : / London, / Re-Printed
for J. Whiston and B. White, in *Fleet-street.* / M.DCC.LXIV. /

This edition is reviewed in the *Monthly Review,* XXXI, 318, and the
Critical Review, XVIII, 316. The speech was also included in *The Political Writings of John Dickinson* (I, 1), where a few slight changes were
made in the text, which are noted in the present republication. The
speech called forth two replies :

    The / Speech / Of / Joseph Galloway, Esq ; / One of the Members for
Philadelphia County : / In Answer / To the Speech of John Dickinson,
Esq ; / Delivered in the House of Assembly, of the / Province of Penn-
sylvania, May 24, 1764. / On Occasion of a Petition drawn up by
Order, and / then under the consideration of the House ; / praying his
Majesty for a Royal, in lieu of / a Proprietary Government. / Audi et
alteram Partem. / Philadelphia : / Printed and sold by W. Dunlap,
in Market-street. / MDCCLXIV. 8vo. pp. xxxv, (5), 45.

    The / May Be / Or Some / Observations / Occasion'd by reading a
Speech deliver'd in / the House of Assembly, the 24th of May / last,
by a certain eminent Patriot. / . . . . . / Philadelphia : / Printed by
Anthony Armbruster, in Arch-street. [1764.] Sm. 8vo. pp. 7.

These in turn produce the replies of Dickinson, printed *post,* and the
controversy was further continued in the *Pennsylvania Gazette,* Feb. 28 ;
March 14 ; and April 4, 1765.

               EDITOR.

A

SPEECH,

Delivered in the House of Assembly of the Province of
Pennsylvania, *May* 24th, 1764.

By JOHN DICKINSON, Efq;.

One of the Members for the County of *Philadelphia.*

On Occafion of a PETITION, drawn up by Order, and then
under Confideration, of the *Houfe*; praying his *Majefty* for a
Change of the *Government* of this *Province.*

With a PREFACE.

---

*Certe ego libertatem, quæ mibi a Parente meo tradita eft, experiar; verum
id fruftra, an ob rem faciam, in veftra manu fitum eft, Quirites.*
SALL. Bel. Jugurth. in Orat MEMMII.

As for me, I will affuredly contend for that glorious plan of *Liberty*
handed down to us from our anceftors; but whether my Labours
fhall prove fuccefsful, or in vain, depends wholly on you, my dear
Countrymen!

PHILADELPHIA:

Printed and Sold by WILLIAM, BRADFORD, at his
Book-Store adjoining the *London* Coffee-Houfe.
M,DCC,LXIV.

PREFACE.*

To understand clearly the nature of that dispute which led the Assembly to those measures, which are so justly animadverted on in the following excellent speech, it will be proper to look a few years backward.

In the year 1759, Governor *Denny*, whose administration will never be mentioned but with disgrace in the annals of this province, was induced, by considerations to which the world is now no stranger, to pass sundry acts, contrary to his duty, and to every tie of honor and justice. On the 2d of September, 1760, his late Majesty in council repealed six of these acts; and in regard to the seventh (which was an act for granting to his Majesty one hundred thousand pounds, by a tax on all estates, real and personal, &c.) the Lords of his Majesty's most honorable privy Council declared it their opinion "that the said act was fundamentally WRONG and UNJUST, and ought to be repealed, unless six certain amendments were made therein."

Benjamin Franklin and Robert Charles, Agents for the Province, undertook that, in case the act might be left unrepealed, "the Assembly of Pennsylvania would prepare and pass an act for making the amendments proposed by the Lords of the Council, and to indemnify the Proprietaries from any damage they might sustain by such act not being prepared and passed." This stipulation was signed by the hands of the said agents, and the Proprietors for the sake of peace accepted of it. [iv]

But, notwithstanding the solemnity of this agreement, the Assembly in framing the late *Supply-Bill*, insisted upon explaining the 2d and 3d articles of the stipulation in their own way, and inserting them in the bill in different words from those made use of by the Lords of Council, and signed by their

* This preface was written by Rev. William Smith.

(11)

own agents. The Governor, on the contrary, thought that no words could be so proper to convey the meaning of the Lords of Council and prevent disputes, as those which their lordships themselves had made use of, and that he could neither in decency or duty depart from them.

Hereupon messages ensued, and the Assembly, among other vehement and warm resolves, broke up with the following most extraordinary one, *viz.*

"That this House will adjourn, in order to consult their constituents, whether an humble address should be drawn up, and transmitted to his Majesty, praying that he would be graciously pleased to take the people of this Province, under his immediate protection and government, &c."*

What methods were taken, during this adjournment, to lead a number of rash, ignorant and inconsiderate people into petitions, the evil tendency of which they did not understand, is an enquiry not suitable to the present occasion. It is enough to say that, after incredible pains, in a province containing near THREE HUNDRED THOUSAND SOULS, not more than 3500 could be prevailed upon to petition for a change of government; and those very generally of a low rank, many of whom could neither read nor write.†

The wiser and better part of the Province had far different notions of this measure. They considered that the moment they put their hands to these petitions, [v] they might be surrendering up their birth-right, and putting it in the power of a few men, for the sake of gratifying their own ambitious projects and personal resentments, to barter away that glorious plan of public liberty and charter privileges, under which this Province has risen to the highest degree of prosperity, with a rapidity almost unparalleled in history.

Though the ill-success of these petitions must have been very mortifying to the projectors of them, yet the Assembly were at all hazards to be persuaded to make them the foundation of a petition to the King for a change of government. It was in vain to urge the smallness of the numbers who signed

* See Galloway's *Speech*, xix.—*Ed.*   † *Ibid*, xx.—*Ed.*

the petitions; the high veneration in which our present constitution hath long been held by good men of every denomination, and the multitudes of industrious people whom even the very fame of it hath invited among us, from almost every part of the world. These considerations were but slight bars to men actuated by ambition and resentment; men who have long found their own importance to consist in fomenting the divisions of their country, and now hope to aggrandize themselves by bringing about the proposed change, whatever may be its consequences to others. They therefore found means to carry their petition thro' the House, but not without the most spirited testimony against it, from a NOBLE FEW, a PATRIOT MINORITY, whose names will be mentioned with honor, so long as any remembrance is left of the present boasted LIBERTIES of PENNSYLVANIA.

At the head of these FEW, the worthy author of the following SPEECH signalized himself. Having devoted to a severe course of study those years which too many give to dissipation and pleasure, he shewed himself, at his first entrance on public life, possessed of a knowledge of the laws and constitution of his country, which [vi] seldom falls to the share even of grey hairs. Alike independent in spirit and in fortune, removed as far as any man can be from all connections with the Proprietors or their immediate friends, and following only the unbiassed dictates of his own heart, he could not be a silent spectator while the most distant attempt was made upon that constitution, for which our fathers planted a wilderness, and which is derived to us by the FAITH OF CHARTERS, and SANCTITY OF LAWS!

This SPEECH was delivered on the 24th of May, and the late Speaker, Mr. Norris, with the four members under mentioned, are said to have declared to Mr. Dickinson, that he had fully spoke their sentiments, in his own. The next day in the afternoon, Mr. Dickinson *moved* that the further consideration of the matter should be adjourned to the following morning. But it was voted by a great majority (Mr. Dickinson, Mr. Joseph Richardson, Mr. Isaac Saunders, and Mr. John Montgomery being for the negative) that the PETITION as then drawn, should be transcribed, in order to be signed by the Speaker; which was ordered accordingly.

Mr. Dickinson having then digested the heads of his speech into the nature of a *Protest,** in which he was joined by Mr. Saunders and Mr. Montgomery,† offered it to be entered in the minutes; but it was refused.

Mr. Norris, the Speaker, who, from the nature of his office, could not join in the *Protest* or take any part in the debate, finding matters pushed to this extremity, informed the House, in a very solemn and affecting manner, "That for thirty years past he had had the honour of serving as a Representative of the people of this Province, and near half that time as Speaker.————That, in these offices, he had uniformly endeavoured, accord-[vii]ing to the best of his judgment, to promote the public good.————That the subject of the present debate was a matter of the utmost importance to the Province.————That as his sentiments on the occasion were very different from those of the *majority*, and his seat in the chair prevented him from entering into the debate, he therefore *prayed* the House, That if, in consequence of their order, his duty should oblige him to sign the *Petition* as Speaker, he might be permitted to offer his sentiments on the subject before he signed, and that they might be entered on the minutes;" which was granted accordingly.

The House then adjourned to the next morning, and when they met, the Clerk delivered the members a letter from the Speaker, acquainting them that his indisposition prevented his further attendance, and praying them to choose a new Speaker. Thus this aged member and faithful servant of the House, as if foreseeing troubles to come, chose to retire, and leave them to those whose temper they better suited.

Benjamin Franklin, Esq., was *accordingly* chosen *Speaker*, and in the afternoon of the same day, signed the *Petition*, as one of his first acts, an act which————but posterity will best be able to give it a name!

As these transactions could not fail of being very interesting to the good people of this Province, it is not to be wondered

* Printed *post.—Ed.*   † See their letter below.

that they expressed an earnest desire to see the following *Speech*, that they might be able to form some knowledge of what was intended ; for their own Representatives did not think proper to let the contents of their petition for the proposed change be known ; though upon this single stake, so far as depended upon them, they have risked our whole constitution. On the 6th of June, therefore, a great number of the principal Gentlemen of *Philadelphia* applied to Mr. Dickinson for a copy of his speech, by letter as follows, *viz.* [viii]

PHILADELPHIA, *June 6th,* 1764.

Sir, We whose names are underwritten, citizens of Philadelphia, acknowledge the obligations that the good people of this Province are under to you, for your spirited defence of our charter privileges, which we apprehend are greatly endangered by some late proceedings, particularly the setting on foot a petition to his Majesty for a change of government. We are surprised that our representatives, who ought to be guardians of the constitution, do not check rather than encourage this unseasonable application of a few (comparatively) of the people of this extensive Province. We hereby testify our sincere gratitude to you, sir, and the other patriot members that appeared on the side of our Charter and Privileges, and request a copy of the speech you delivered on that occasion in the House, as we are persuaded that the publication thereof would be of great utility and give general satisfaction. We beg leave to assure you of our regard, and are

Sir, Your most obedient humble servants.

About the same time Mr. Saunders and Mr. Montgomery, earnestly desirous that their names might be joined with Mr. Dickinson's through this whole affair, sent him the following letter :

Sir, As we are informed that a number of the principal gentlemen of the city of Philadelphia intend applying to you to have your speech, which was delivered a few days ago in the House of Assembly, against the measures proposed for a change of government, published, and as we are of opinion the publication thereof, together with the reasons on which our protest is founded, may be of considerable service, we judge it proper (in case you are of the same opinion of making them public) that you should signify to the public how heartily we have concurred with you in the same sentiments, set forth in your speech, and in disapprobation of the late resolves of the House ; this we judge a piece of justice due to ourselves, lest we incur, from our constituents, the imputa-

tion of betraying or sacrificing their essential rights and privileges which
we meant to defend.   We likewise authorize you hereby to affix our
names to the dissent and protest,* which the House refused entering on
their minutes.   We are respectfully,

Sir, Yours, &c.,

ISAAC SAUNDERS,

JOHN MONTGOMERY. [ix]

Having thus given a faithful account, both of the occasion of
this Speech, and of its publication, it would be almost impossible not to quote a few passages from former Assemblies, to
shew in what high terms, even of rapture and admiration, they
continually mentioned our present constitution and plan of
government.

" We hope, say they,† the people of Pennsylvania will never
be wanting to acknowledge the great wisdom and singular
goodness of our late honourable Proprietor, from whom we
derive the privileges of our annual elections, as well as many
other immunities which have so manifestly contributed to the
prosperity of the Province, &c."   Again,

" When ‡ we commemorate the many blessings bestowed on
the inhabitants of this colony, the *religious* and *civil liberties* we
possess, and to whom these valuable blessings, under God and
the King, are owing, we should be wanting to ourselves, and
them that we represent, did we not do justice to the memory of
thy worthy ancestor."

" Our § happy constitution, secured to us by the wisdom and
goodness of our first Proprietary and founder of this province,
so happily continued to us under the government of his honourable descendants, justly entitle them to our affection and zeal
for their honor and interest."

But it would be endless to quote all that has been said by our
Assemblies, in favour of the constitution of this province, and
its worthy founder. The sum of the whole, when taken from
the minutes, and thrown together in their own express words,
is nothing less than what follows.

* As all the arguments in this *Protest* are to be found more at large
in the following Speech, it is not printed here, but will be published by
itself in the newspapers.

† Assembly 1730.

‡ Address to the honourable JOHN PENN, Esq., 1764.

§ Assembly 1738.

WILLIAM PENN,
[1] A man of principles truely humane,
an Advocate for [x]
RELIGION and LIBERTY,
[2] *Possessing* a noble spirit
That exerted itself
For the good of mankind,
WAS
[3] The great and worthy founder
Of
PENNSYLVANIA.
To its inhabitants, by CHARTER,
[4] He granted and confirmed
[5] Many singular PRIVILEGES and IMMUNITIES,
[6] CIVIL and RELIGIOUS ;
[7] Which he continually studied
to preserve and defend for them,
Nobly declaring
[8] That they had not followed him so far
To lose a single tittle
Of the GREAT CHARTER
To which all *Englishmen* were born !
For these Services,
[9] Great have been the acknowlegements
Deservedly paid to his MERIT ;
[10] And his MEMORY
Is dear to his people,
Who have repeatedly confessed
That,
[11] Next to divine Providence,
[12] Their Happiness, Prosperity and Increase
[13] Are owing
To his wise conduct and singular goodness,

[1] Minutes 1734.
[2] Minutes 1740.
[3] Minutes 1738, 1740, 1745.
[*] Minutes 1755.
[5] Minutes 1730.
[6] Minutes 1734.
[7] Minutes 1735.
[8] Minutes 1756.
[9] Minutes 1740.
[10] Minutes 1719.
[11] Minutes 1725.
[12] Minutes 1731.
[13] Minutes 1734.

" Which deserve ever to be remembered,
With
GRATITUDE and AFFECTION,
BY PENNSYLVANIANS. [xi]

Were it intended to write the highest encomium on the constitution of this country, and to erect the most lasting monu-
ment to the memory of its illustrious founder, a more noble
inscription could hardly be devised than what is contained in
the foregoing minutes of Assembly; and a time may come
when impartial posterity, notwithstanding the present ingrati-
tude of a *few*, may perhaps adapt it for this purpose.

As to the wild measures now on foot, they will undoubtedly
destroy themselves by their own violence; and it would be
impossible to add anything that can more expose their rashness
than what is contained in the following Speech. The Proprietors hold *their Right* by that charter under which ours is derived. Can the latter in law or equity be deemed more sacred
than the former? Have the Proprietors, by any act of theirs,
forfeited the least tittle of what was granted them by his Majesty's royal ancestors? Or can they be deprived of their
charter rights without their own consent? Have they not
constantly sheltered themselves under the wing of government,
and received the approbation of his Majesty's first servants in the
law to every material *Instruction* sent to their governors here?

In the present dispute nothing has been insisted upon on the
part of our Governors but a strict adherence to what has been
solemnly determined by his Majesty in Council.

Indeed we have every way the worst of this whole business.
If a change were to take place, the Proprietors before they resign their charter, would certainly obtain a full equivalent for
their *Rights of Government*, and likewise have all their *Rights
of Property* secured to them by laws which we could not dispute. Such a change, were they inclined to it, could certainly
be of very little prejudice to them; but with respect to us the
case is quite different. Instead of securing anything in rever-
sion or exchange, our representatives, by their present petition,

" Minutes 1732.

seem (so far at least as depends on them) to have offered up our whole charter rights, leaving it to the grace of others to return us any part, or indeed no part of them, according as it may be thought proper. But, thanks be to God, this is a power with which our representatives were never vested by us; and therefore the act they have committed is VOID in itself. Nor is there any doubt but an immense majority of the good people of this Province will still be found ready, at a proper time, to vindicate their charter rights, and to let the world know that they hold those men unworthy of all future trust, who could wantonly sport with things so sacred.

Former Assemblies made it an article of impeachment against one of the most considerable * men of this Province " That he had contrived to violate (only) a part of the constitution of this government." But what would they have thought of an attempt to violate the whole?

We know it will be replied, that the change now proposed is not a violation of this kind, and that our privileges might be preserved in virtue of our *Laws*, even if our charter were given up. But a sufficient answer is given to this in page the 11th and 12th of the following [xii] *Speech;* and indeed it is astonishing that this argument could ever be made use of to impose upon any person, when it is well known that the chief privileges, by which the constitution of this province is distinguished, depend upon our charter alone, and upon no positive law whatever.

And here, let no wrong construction be put upon this defence of the particular constitution of *Pennsylvania.* Those who now contend for it, have the highest veneration for the dignity and authority of the Crown. They think themselves as much under its immediate protection as any of his Majesty's subjects on this continent are; and it is well known, that they have on all occasions been among the first of those who have appeared in defence of the just rights of our gracious Sovereign.

They think it may be said, without giving the least offence, that the inhabitants of this Province enjoy certain privileges

* James Logan, Esq.

which are not to be found in the governments around them, and which they could not have the least hopes of preserving in case of any change of our present constitution. Multitudes of people have chosen a settlement in this Province, preferable to all others, on account of these privileges, and they now think that they have a right to the perpetual enjoyment of them ; as they are in no case inconsistent with good order or the public good. Many private corporations in his Majesty's dominions enjoy singular immunities upon the like foundation ; and those bodies have never been thought undutiful for adhering tenaciously to their rights, from age to age. Certainly we may be considered in a something higher light than Corporate Bodies of this kind.

Having swelled this preface to a much greater length than was at first intended, we shall only offer one remark more, upon the terms in which the *Petition* of our Assembly is said to be drawn up. We have heard that this Province is described in it as a scene of *riot, violence and confusion ;* but yet one can hardly judge it possible, that our representatives could venture to approach the royal ear with such an unjust account of their constituents. Nevertheless we have a right to insist on a copy of this petition from the committee in whose hands it is, that if we lie under any accusations in it, we may have an opportunity to answer them. This is so reasonable, that we are persuaded it cannot be refused, especially in a matter wherein we may be greatly affected.

We would only observe that the present is not a time for divisions of any kind in his Majesty's colonies ; but for the closest union among ourselves, that we may be able, by decent and just representation of the state of our country, to save it from burthens which it cannot bear, and to encourage it in those improvements whereof it is capable. Let it be remembered how little we have got by bringing our party quarrels before the Crown these many years past ; most certainly nothing but shame to ourselves, and a load of expense to our country, which, however beneficial it may have been to the *Agents* employed, has not been of the least service to the public.

THE SPEECH

OF

JOHN DICKINSON, ESQ., &c.

Mr. Speaker,*

When honest men apprehend their country to be injured, nothing is more natural than to resent and complain: but when they enter into consideration of the means for obtaining redress, the same virtue that gave the alarm, may sometimes, by causing too great a transport of zeal, defeat its own purpose; it being expedient for those who deliberate of public affairs, that their minds should be free from all violent passions. These emotions blind the understanding: they weaken the judgment. It, therefore, frequently happens, that resolutions formed by men thus agitated, appear to *them* very wise, very just, and very salutary; while others, not influenced by the same heats, condemn those determinations, as weak, unjust and dangerous. Thus, Sir, in councils it will always be found useful, to guard against even that indignation, which arises from integrity.

More particularly are *we* bound to observe the utmost caution in our conduct, as the experience of [2] many years may convince us, that all our actions undergo the strictest scrutiny. Numerous are the instances, that might be mentioned, of rights vindicated and equitable demands made in the province, according to the opinions entertained here, that in *Great Britain*, have been adjudged to be illegal attempts, and pernicious pretensions.

* Isaac Norris, Esquire. *Note in Writings.*

(21)

These adjudications are the acts of persons vested with such dignity and power, as claim some deference from us: and hence it becomes not unnecessary to consider, in what light the* measures now proposed may appear to those, whose sentiments from the constitution of our government, it will always be prudent to regard.

But on this important occasion, we ought not to aim only at the approbation of men, whose authority may censure and control us. More affecting duties demand our attention. The honor and welfare of *Pennsylvania* depending on our decisions, let us endeavour so to act, that we may enjoy our own approbation, in the cool and undisturbed hours of reflection: that we may deserve the approbation of the impartial world; and of posterity who are so much interested in the present debate.

No man, Sir, can be more clearly convinced than I am of the inconveniences arising from a strict adherence to proprietary instructions. We are prevented from demonstrating our loyalty to our excellent Sovereign, and our affection to our distrest fellow-subjects, unless we will indulge the Proprietors, with a distinct and partial mode of taxation, by which they will save perhaps four or five hundred pounds a year, that ought to go in ease of our constituents. [3]

This is granted on all sides to be unequal; and has, therefore, excited the resentment of this House. Let us resent—but let our resentment bear proportion to the provocation received; and not produce, or even expose us to the peril of producing, effects more fatal than the injury of which we complain. If the change of government now

* The controversy between the Province and the Proprietaries, was,—Whether the estates of the Proprietaries should be taxed as the estates of other persons were. The Proprietaries claimed an exemption, and were supported in their claim by the *British Ministers*. The Assembly took this opportunity to attempt a change of the Government from proprietary to royal. *Note in Writings.*

meditated, can take place, with all our privileges preserved, let it instantly take place : but if *they* must be
consumed in the blaze of royal authority, we shall pay too
great a price for our approach to the throne ; too great a
price for obtaining (if we should obtain) the addition of
four or five hundred pounds to the proprietary tax ; or, indeed, for any emolument likely to follow from the change.

I hope I am not mistaken when I believe that every
member in this House feels the same reverence that I do
for these *inestimable rights.* When I consider the spirit
of liberty that breathes in them, and the flourishing state
to which this province hath risen in a few years under
them, I am extremely desirous that they should be transmitted to future ages ; and I cannot suppress my solicitude
while steps are taking that tend to bring them all into
danger. Being assured that this House will always think
an attempt to change this government too hazardous, unless these privileges can be *perfectly secured*, I shall beg
leave to mention the reasons by which I have been convinced that such an attempt ought not *now* to be made.

It seems to me, sir, that a people who intend an innovation of their government ought to chuse the most proper
time, and the most proper *method*, for accomplishing their
purposes ; and ought seriously to weigh all the probable
and possible *consequences* of such a measure. [4]

There are certain periods in public affairs when designs
may be executed much more easily and advantageously
than at any other. It hath been by a strict attention to
every interesting circumstance, a careful cultivation of
every fortunate occurrence, and patiently waiting till they
have ripened into a favourable conjecture, that so many
great actions have been performed in the political world.

It was through a rash neglect of this prudence, and too
much *eagerness* to gain his point, that the Duke of *Monmouth* destroyed his own enterprise and brought himself

dishonourably to the block, though everything then verged towards a revolution. The Prince of Orange, with a *wise delay*, pursued the same views and gloriously mounted a throne.

It was through a like neglect of this prudence that the commons of *Denmark*, smarting under the tyranny of their nobility, in a fit of revengeful fury *suddenly* surrendered their liberties to their king; and ever since, with unavailing grief and useless execrations, have detested the *mad moment* which slipt upon them the shackles of slavery, which no struggles can shake off. With *more deliberation*, the *Dutch* erected a stadholdership, that hath been of signal service to their state.

That excellent historian and statesman, *Tacitus*, whose political reflections are so justly and universally admired, makes an observation in his third annal that seems to confirm these remarks. Having mentioned a worthy man of great abilities, whose ambitious ardour hurried him into ruin, he uses these words, "*quod multos etiam bonos pessum dedit, qui spretis quæ tarda cum securitate, præmatura vel cum exitio properant.*" "Which misfortune hath happened to many good men, who despising [5] those things which they might *slowly* and *safely* attain, seize them too hastily, and with fatal speed rush upon their own destruction."

If then, Sir, the best intentions may be disappointed by too rapid a prosecution of them, many reasons induce me to think, that this is not the *proper time* to attempt the change of our government.

It is too notorious and too melancholy a truth, that we now labor under the disadvantage of royal and ministerial displeasure. The conduct of this province during the late war, has been almost continually condemned at home. We have been covered with the reproaches of men, whose stations give us just cause to regard their reproaches. The last letters from his majesty's secretary of state prove, that the reputation of the province has not yet revived. We are therein expressly charged with double dealing, disrespect for his Majesty's orders, and in short, accusations, that shew us to be in the utmost discredit. Have we the least reason to believe, when the transactions of this year and the cause of our application for a change, are made known to the king and his ministers, that their resentment will be waived? Let us not flatter ourselves. Will they not be more incensed when they find the public service impeded, and his majesty's dominions so long exposed to the ravages of merciless enemies, by our inactivity and obstinacy, as it will be said? For this, I think, hath been the constant language of the minority on the like occasions. Will not their indignation rise beyond all bounds when they understand that our hitherto denying to grant supplies, and our application for a change, proceed from the governor's strict adherence to the terms of the stipulations, so solemnly made, and so repeatedly approved, by the late and present King? [6]

But I may perhaps be answered, "that we have agreed to the terms of the stipulations, according to their true meaning, which the governor refuses to do." Surely, Sir, it will require no slight sagacity in distinguishing, no common force of argument, to persuade his Majesty and his Council, that the refusal to comply with the true meaning of the stipulations proceeds from the Governor, when he insists on inserting in our bill the very words and letters of those stipulations.

"But these stipulations were never intended to be inserted *verbatim* in our bills, and our construction is the most just." I grant it appears so to *us*, but much I doubt whether his Majesty's Council will be of the same opinion. That Board and this House have often differed as widely in their sentiments. *Our* judgment is founded on the

knowledge we have of facts, and of the purity of our intentions. The judgment of *others*, is founded on the representations made to them of those facts and intentions.
These representations may be unjust; and, therefore, the
decisions that are formed upon them may be erroneous. If
we are rightly informed, we are represented as the mortal
enemies of the proprietors, who would tear their estates to
pieces unless some limit was fixed to our fury. For *this
purpose* the second and third articles of the stipulations
were formed. The inequality of the mode was explained
and enlarged upon by the provincial counsel; but in vain.
I think, I have heard a worthy member who lately returned from *England* mention these circumstances.

If this be the case, what reasonable hope can we entertain of a more favourable determination *now?* The Proprietors are still living. Is it not highly probable that
they have interest enough, either to prevent the change or
to make such terms as will fix upon us *forever* those demands that appear so ex- [7] tremely just to the *present Ministers?* One of the Proprietors appears to have great inti-
macy and influence with some very considerable members
of his Majesty's Council. Many men of the highest character, if public reports speak truth, are now endeavouring
to establish proprietary governments, and, therefore, probably may be more readily inclined to favour proprietary
measures. The very gentlemen who *formed* the articles
of the stipulations *are now in power*, and, no doubt, will
inforce their *own acts* in the strictest manner. On the
other hand, every circumstance that now operates against
us, may in time turn in our favour. We may, perhaps,
be fortunate enough, to see the present prejudices against
us worn off; to recommend ourselves to our Sovereign and
to procure the esteem of some of his ministers. I think I
may venture to assert that such a period will be infinitely
more proper than the present, for attempting a change of
our government.

With the permission of the House, I will now consider the *manner* in which this attempt is carried on; and I must acknowledge that I do not in the least degree approve of it.

The time may come when the weight of this government may grow too heavy for the shoulder of a subject, at least too heavy for those of a woman, or an infant. The proprietary family may be so circumstanced as to be willing to accept of such an equivalent for the government from the crown, as the crown may be willing to give. Whenever this point is agitated, either on a proposal from the crown or proprietors, this province may plead the cause of her privileges with greater freedom and with greater probability of success than at present. The royal grant, the charter founded upon it, the public faith pledged to the adventurers for the security of those rights to them and their poste- [8] rity, whereby they were encouraged to combat the dangers, I had almost said, of another world; to establish the British power in remotest regions, and add inestimable dominions with the most extensive commerce to their native country; the high value and veneration we have for these privileges, the afflicting loss and misfortune we should esteem it, to be deprived of them, and the unhappiness in which his Majesty's faithful subjects in this province would thereby be involved; our inviolable loyalty and attachment to his Majesty's person and illustrious family, whose sovereignty hath been so singularly distinguished by its favourable influence on the liberties of mankind.—All these things may then be properly insisted on. If urged with that modest heart-felt energy, with which good men should always vindicate the interests of their country, before the best of sovereigns,* I should not despair of a gracious attention to our humble

* The preceding six words are struck out in *Writings.—Ed.*

requests.   Our petition in such a case, would be simple, respectful and perhaps affecting.

But in the present mode of proceeding, it seems to me, that we preclude ourselves from every office of decent duty to the most excellent of Kings, and from that right of earnestly defending our privileges, which we should otherwise have.   The foundation of this attempt, I am apprehensive, will appear to others, *peculiarly unfortunate*.   In a sudden passion, it will be said, against the Proprietors, we call out for a change of government.   Not from reverence for his Majesty, not from a sense of his paternal goodness to his people, but because we are angry with the Proprietors, and tired of a dispute founded on an order approved by his Majesty and his royal grandfather. ::

Our powerful friends on the other side of the *Atlantic*, who are so apt to put the kindest constructions on [9] our actions, will, no doubt, observe "that the conduct of the people of *Pennsylvania* must be influenced by very extraordinary councils, since they desire to come *more immediately* under the King's command, BECAUSE they will *not obey* those royal commands which have been already signified to them."

But here it will be said, nay it has been said, and the petition before the House is drawn accordingly, "we will not alledge this dispute with the Governor on the stipulations, but the general inconveniences of a proprietary government as the cause of our desiring a change."   'Tis true we may act in this artful manner, but what advantages shall we gain by it?   Though *we* should keep the secret, can we seal up the lips of the Proprietors?   Can we recall our message to the Governor?   Can we annihilate our own resolves?   Will not all—will not any of these discover the *true cause* of the present attempt?

Why, then, should we unnecessarily invite fresh invectives in the very beginning of a most important business, that, to be happily concluded, requires all the favour we can procure and all the dexterity we can practice?

We intend to surround the throne with petitions that our government may be changed from proprietary to royal: at the same time we mean to preserve our privileges: but how are these two points to be reconciled?

If we express our desire for the preservation of our privileges, in so general or faint a manner as may induce the King to think they are of no great consequence to us, it will be nothing less than to betray our country. [10]

If, on the other hand, we inform his Majesty "that though we *request* him to change the government, yet we *insist* on the preservation of our privileges," certainly it will be thought an unprecedented stile of petitioning the crown, that humbly asks a favour and boldly prescribes the terms on which it must be granted.

How then shall we act? Shall we speak, or shall we suppress our sentiments? The first method will render our request incoherent: the second will render it dangerous. Some gentlemen are of opinion that these difficulties may be solved by intrusting the management of this affair to an Agent; but I see no reason to expect such an effect. I would first observe that this matter is of too prodigious consequence to be trusted to the discretion of an Agent. But if it shall be committed by this House, *the proper guardian of the public liberties*, to *other* hands, this truth must at some time or other be disclosed: "that we will never consent to a change unless our privileges are preserved." I should be glad to know with what finesse this matter is to be conducted. Is the agent to keep our petition to the crown in his pocket till he has whispered to the ministry? Will this be justifiable? Will it be decent? Whenever he applies to *them*, I presume, they will desire to know his authority for making such an application. Then our petition must appear; and whenever

it does appear, either at first or last, *that*, and the others
transmitted with it, I apprehend, will be the foundation
of any resolutions taken in the King's Council.

Thus, in whatever view this transaction is considered,
shall we not still be involved in the dilemma already mentioned, "of begging a favour from his Majesty's goodness,
and yet showing a distrust that the royal hand, stretched
out at our own request for our relief, may do us an
injury?" [11]

Let me suppose, and none can offer the least proof of
this supposition being unreasonable, that his Majesty will
not accept of the government, clogged, as it will be said,
with privileges inconsistent with the royal rights: how
shall we act then? We shall have our choice of two
things : one of them destructive, the other dishonourable.
We may either renounce the laws and liberties framed and
delivered down to us by our careful ancestors : or we may
tell his Majesty with a surly discontent, "that we will not
submit to his *implored protection*, but on such conditions
as we please to impose on him." Is not this the inevitable and dreadful * alternative, to which we shall reduce
ourselves?

In short, Sir, I think the farther we advance in the path
we are now in, the greater will be the confusion and
danger in which we shall engage ourselves. Any body of
men acting under a charter, must surely tread on slippery
ground when they take a step that may be deemed a surrender of that charter. For my part, I think the petitions
that have been carried about the city and country to be
signed, and are now lying on the table, can be regarded in
no other light than as a surrender of the charter, with a
short indifferent hint annexed of a desire that our privileges may be spared if it shall be thought proper. Many

* "and dreadful" struck out in *Writings.*—*Ed.*

striking arguments may, in my opinion, be urged, to prove that any request made by this House for a change may, with still greater propriety be called a surrender. The common observation "that many of our privileges do not depend on our charter only, but are confirmed by laws approved by the Crown," I doubt will have but little weight with those who will determine this matter.

It will readily be replied, "that these laws were founded on the charter; that they were calculated for a proprietary government, and for no other, and ap- [12] proved by the Crown in that view alone ; that the proprietary government is now acknowledged by the people living under it to be a bad government, and the Crown is intreated to accept a surrender of it : that, therefore, by abolishing the proprietary government, everything founded upon it must of consequence be also abolished."

However, if there should be any doubts in the law on these points, there is an easy way to solve them.

These reflections, Sir, naturally lead me to consider the *consequences* that may attend a change of our government, which is the last point I shall trouble the House upon at this time.

It is not to be questioned, but that the Ministry are desirous of vesting the immediate government of this Province advantageously in the Crown. 'Tis true, they don't chuse to act arbitrarily, and tear away the present government from us without our consent. This is not the age for such things. But let *us* only furnish them with a pretext, by pressing petitions for a change ; let us only relinquish the hold we now have, and in an instant we are precipitated from that envied height where we now stand. The affair is laid before the Parliament, the desires of the Ministry are insinuated, the rights of the Crown are vindicated, and an act passes to deliver us at once from the government of Proprietors, and the privileges we claim under them.

Then, Sir, we, who *in particular* have presented to the authors of the fatal change this *long-wished* for opportunity of effecting it, shall, for *our assistance*, be entitled to their thanks—*Thanks!* which I am persuaded every worthy member of this House would *abhor* to deserve and would *scorn* to receive. [13]

It seems to be taken for granted that by a change of government we shall obtain a change of those measures which are so displeasing to the people of this Province—that justice will be maintained by an equal taxation of the proprietary estates—and that our frequent dissentions will be turned into peace and happiness.

These are effects indeed sincerely to be wished for by every sensible, by every honest man; but reason does not always teach us to expect the warm wishes of the heart. Could our gracious Sovereign take into consideration the state of every part of his extended dominions, we *might* expect redress of every grievance; for with the most implicit conviction, I believe he is as just, benevolent and amiable a Prince as heaven ever granted in its mercy to bless the people. I venerate his virtues beyond all expression. But *his* attention to our particular circumstances being impossible, we must receive our fate from ministers; and from *them* I do not like to receive it.

We are not the subjects of ministers; and, therefore, it is not to be wondered at if they do not feel that tenderness for us that a good prince will always feel for his people. Men are not born ministers. Their ambition raises them to authority, and when possessed of it, one established principle with them seems to be, "never to deviate from a precedent of power."

Did we not find in the late war, though we exerted ourselves in the most active manner in the defence of his Majesty's dominions, and in promoting the service of the Crown, every point in which the Proprietors thought fit to make any opposition, decided against us? Have we not also found, since the last disturbance of the public peace by our savage enemies, the conduct of the late Governor highly applauded by the ministry, for his adher-[14]ence to those very stipulations now insisted on, and ourselves subjected to the *bitterest reproaches*, only for attempting to avoid burthens, that were thought extremely grievous. Other instances of the like kind I pass over to avoid a tedious recapitulation.

Since then the gale of ministerial favour has in *all seasons* blown propitious to proprietary interests, why do we now fondly flatter ourselves that it will *suddenly* shift its quarter? Why should we with an *amazing credulity* now fly for *protection* to *those* men, trust *everything* to *their* mercy, and ask the most distinguishing *favours* from *their* kindness, from whom we complained a few months ago that we could not obtain the most reasonable requests? Surely, Sir, we must acknowledge one of these two things: either, that our *complaint* was then *unjust*, or, that our *confidence* is now *unwarranted*. For my part, I look for a rigid perseverance in former measures. With a new government I expect new disputes. The experience of the royal colonies convinces me that the immediate government of the Crown is not a security for that tranquility and happiness we promise ourselves from a change. It is needless for me to remind the House of all the frequent and violent controversies that have happened between the King's Governors in several provinces and their Assemblies. At this time, if I am rightly informed, *Virginia* is struggling against an instruction relating to their paper currency,* that will be attended, as that colony apprehends, with the most destructive consequences if carried into execution.

Indeed, Sir, it seems vain to expect, where the spirit of

* "relating to their paper currency" omitted in *Writings.—Ed.*

liberty is maintained among a people, that public contests
should not *also* be maintained. Those who *govern*, and
those who *are governed*, seldom think they can gain too
much on one another. Power is like the *ocean*, not easily
admitting limits to be fixed in it. It must be [15] in
motion. Storms, indeed, are not desirable, but a long dead
calm is not to be looked for, perhaps, not to be wished for.
Let not *us* then, in expectation of *smooth seas* and an *undisturbed course*, too rashly venture our *little vessel* that hath
safely sailed round *our own well known* shores, upon the
midst of the *untry'd deep*, without being first fully convinced that her *make* is strong enough to bear the *weather*
she may meet with, and that she is well *provided* for so
long and so dangerous a voyage.

No man, Sir, amongst us hath denied, or will deny,
that this Province must *stake* on the event of the present
attempt, liberties that ought to be immortal—*Liberties!*
founded on the acknowledged rights of human nature and
restrained in our mother-country, only by an unavoidable
necessity of adhering in some measure to long-established
customs. Thus hath been formed between old errors and
hasty innovations an entangled chain, that our ancestors
either had not moderation or leisure enough to untwist.

I will now briefly enumerate, as well as I can recollect,
the particular privileges of Pennsylvania.

In the first place, we here enjoy that best and greatest
of all rights, *a perfect religious freedom.*

Posts of honour and profit are unfettered with *oaths* or
tests, and, therefore are open to men whose abilities, strict
regard to their conscientious persuasion, and unblemished
characters qualify them to discharge their duties with
credit to themselves and advantage to their country. Thus
justice is done to merit, and the public loses none of its
able servants.*

* This sentence is omitted in *Writings.—Ed.*

The same wisdom of our laws has guarded against the absurdity of granting greater credit even to villains, [16] if they will swear, than to men of virtue, who from religious motives cannot. Therefore, those who are conscientiously scrupulous of taking an oath, are admitted as witnesses in criminal cases. Our legislation suffers no checks from a council instituted * in fancied imitation of the House of Lords. By the right of sitting on our own adjournments, we are secure of meeting when the public good requires it: and of not being dismist when private passions demand it. At the same time, the strict discharge of the truth committed to Us, is inforced by the short duration of our power, which must be renewed by our constituents every year.

Nor are the people stript of all authority in the execution of laws. They enjoy the satisfaction of having some share, by the appointment of provincial commissioners, in laying out the money which they raise, and of being in this manner assured that it is applied to the purposes for which it was granted. They also elect sheriffs and coroners, officers of so much consequence in every determination that affects honour, liberty, life or property.

Let any impartial person reflect how contradictory some of these privileges are to the most ancient principles of the English constitution, and how directly opposite other of them are to the settled prerogatives of the crown, and then consider what probability we have of retaining them on a *requested*† change: that is of continuing in fact a proprietary government, though we humbly pray the King to change this government. Not unaptly, in my opinion, the connection between the proprietary family and this Province may be regarded as a marriage. Our privileges

---

* Appointed by the Crown. *Note in Writings.*

†*Imperium facile iis artibus retinetur, quibus initio partum est.* Sall. Bell. Catalia.

may be called the fruits of that marriage. The domestic
peace of this fa-[17] mily, it is true, has not been unvexed
with quarrels and complaints. But the pledges of their
affection ought always to be esteemed: and whenever the
parents on an *imprudent request* shall be *divorced*, much I
fear that their *issue* will be declared *illegitimate. This* I
am well persuaded of, that surprizing must our behaviour
appear to all men, if in the instant when we apply to his
Majesty for relief from what we think oppression, we
should discover a resolute disposition to deprive him of the
uncontroverted prerogatives of his royal dignity.

At this period when the administration is regulating
new colonies, and designing, as we are told, the *strictest
reformations** in the old, it is not likely that they will
grant an invidious distinction in our favour. Less likely
is it, as that distinction will be liable to so many, and
such strong *constitutional* objections; and when we shall
have the weight both of the clergy and ministry, and the
universally received opinions of the people of our mother
country to contend with.

I mean not, Sir, the least reflection on the church of
England. I reverence and admire the purity of its doctrine and the moderation of its temper. I am convinced
that it is filled with learned and with excellent men : but
all zealous persons think their own religious tenets the
best, and would willingly see them embraced by others.
I, therefore, apprehend that the dignified and reverend
gentlemen of the church of *England* will be extremely desirous to have *that* church as well secured, and as much
distinguished as possible in the American colonies : especially in those colonies where it is overborne, as it were,
by dissenters. There never can be a more critical opportunity for this purpose than the present. The cause of the

---

*Some late Acts of Parliament shew what strict reformations are to be
made in the Colonies.

church will besides be con- [18] nected with that of the crown, to which its principles are thought to be more favourable than those of the other professions.

We have received certain information that the conduct of this Province, which has been so much censured by the ministry, is attributed to the influence of a society, that holds warlike measures at all times to be unlawful.* We also know that the late tumultuous and riotous proceedings, which are represented in so strong a light by the petition, now before the House, have been publicly ascribed to the influence of another society. Thus the blame of everything disreputable to this province is cast on one or the other of these dissenting sects. Circumstances! that, I imagine, will neither be forgot nor neglected.

We have seen the event of our disputes concerning the *Proprietary* interests; and it is not to be expected that our success will be greater when our opponents become more numerous, and will have more dignity, more power, and, as they will think, more law on their side.

These are the dangers, Sir, to which we are now about to expose those privileges in which we have hitherto so much gloried. *Wherefore?* To procure two or three, perhaps four or five hundred pounds a year (for no calculation has carried the sum higher), from the Proprietors, for two or three or four or five years, for so long and something longer, perhaps, the taxes may continue.

But are we sure of gaining this point? *We are not.* Are we sure of gaining any other advantage? *We are not.* Are we sure of preserving our privileges? *We are not.* Are we under a necessity of pursuing the measure proposed at this time? *We are not.* [19]

---

* In the *Writings* this is altered to read: "is attributed to the influence of one religious society" and the remainder of the sentence is omitted.—*Ed.*

Here, Sir, permit me to make a short pause. Permit me to appeal to the heart of every member in this House, and to entreat him to reflect how far he can be justifiable in giving his voice, thus to hazard the liberties secured to us by the wise founders of this Province; peaceably and fully enjoyed by the present age, and to which posterity is so justly entitled.

But, Sir, we are told there is no danger of losing our privileges if our government should be changed, and two arguments are used in support of this opinion. The first is, "That the government of the Crown is exercised with so much lenity in *Carolina* and the *Jerseys*." I cannot perceive the least degree of force in this argument. As to *Carolina*, I am not a little surprized, that it should be mentioned on this occasion, since I never heard of one privilege that colony enjoys more than all the royal governments in *America*. The privileges of the *Jerseys* are of a different nature from many of which we are possest; and are more consistent with the royal prerogative.

Indeed I know of none they have, except that * *Quakers* may be witnesses in criminal cases, and may bear offices. Can this indulgence shewn to them for a particular reason, and not contradictory to the rights of the crown, give us any just cause to expect the confirmation of privileges directly opposite to those rights, and for confirming which no such reason exists. But, perhaps, the gentlemen who advance this argument mean that *we* shall purchase a change at a cheap price if we are only reduced to the same state with the *Jerseys*. Surely, Sir, if this be their meaning, they entirely forget those extraordinary privileges which some time ago were mentioned. [20]

How many must we in such a case renounce? I apprehend it would prove an argument of little consolation to these gentlemen if they should lose three-fourths of their

* In *the Writings* "the People called" is added here.—*Ed.*

estates, to be sold, that they still remain as rich as their neighbors, and have enough to procure all the necessaries of life.

It is somewhat remarkable that this single instance of favour, in permitting an affirmation instead of an oath, in a single province, should be urged as so great an encouragement to us, while there are so many examples of another kind to deter us. In what *royal government* besides the *Jerseys* can a *Quaker* be a witness in criminal cases, and bear offices? * *In no other.* What can be the reason of this distinction in the *Jerseys?* Because in the infancy of that colony, when it came under the government of the crown, there was, as appears from authentic vouchers, an ABSOLUTE NECESSITY from the scarcity of other proper persons, to make use of the people called *Quakers* in public employments. Is there such a necessity in this Province? Or can the ministry be *persuaded* that there is such a necessity? No, Sir, those from whom they will receive information will grant no such thing; and, therefore, I think there is the *most imminent danger*, in case of a change, that the people of *this society* will lose the exercise of those rights, which, though they are entitled to as men, yet such is the situation of human affairs, they with difficulty can find a spot on the whole globe where they are allowed to enjoy them. It will be an argument of some force, I am afraid, that the church of *England* can never expect to raise its head among us, while we are encouraged, as it will be said, in dissension; but if an *oath* be made necessary for obtaining offices of honour and profit, it will then be expected that any Quakers [21] who are tempted to renounce their principles, will undoubtedly make an addition to the established church.

If any other consideration than that which has been

---

*It is said that a Quaker was lately committed to gaol in New York, because he would not swear in a criminal case.

mentioned was regarded in granting that indulgence in the *Jerseys*, though no other is expressed, it seems not improbable that the nearness of this Province might have had some weight, as from its situation it afforded such strong temptations to the inhabitants of the *Jerseys* to remove hither had they been treated with any severity.

Their government, in some measure, was formed in imitation of our government; but when this is altered, the *English* constitution must be the model by which it will be formed.

Here it will be said, "this cannot be done but by the Parliament; and will a British Parliament do such an act of injustice as to deprive us of our rights?" This is the second argument used to prove the safety of the measures now proposed.

Certainly the *British* Parliament will not do what they think an unjust act: but I cannot persuade myself that *they* will think it unjust to place us on the same footing with themselves. It will not be an easy task to convince them that the people of *Pennsylvania* ought to be distinguished from all other subjects under his Majesty's *immediate* government, or that such a distinction can answer any good purpose. May it not be expected that they will say: "No people can be freer than ourselves; everything "more than we enjoy is licentiousness, not liberty: any "indulgences shown to the colonies heretofore were like "the indulgences of parents to their infants; they ought "to cease with that tender age, and, as the colonies grow "up to a more vigorous state, they ought to be carefully "disci [22] plined, and all their actions regulated by strict "laws. Above all things, it is necessary that the preroga- "tive should be exercised with its full force in our Amer- "ican provinces, to restrain them within due bounds and "secure their dependance on this kingdom."*

* The subsequent conduct of *Great Britain*, has fully evinced her resolution to adhere to such political maxims as these. *Note in Writings.*

I am afraid that this will be the opinion of the Parliament, as it has been, in every instance, the undeviating practice of the ministry.

But, Sir, it may be said "these reasons are not conclu-"sive, they do not demonstratively prove that our privi-"leges *will be* endangered by a change." I grant the objection : but what stronger reasons, what clearer proofs are there that they *will not be* endangered by a change.

They are safe now ; and *why* should we engage in an enterprise that will render them *uncertain?* If nothing will content us but a revolution brought about by ourselves, surely we ought to have made the strictest enquiries what terms we may expect, and to have obtained from the ministry some kind of security for the performance of those terms.

These things might have been done. They are not done. If a merchant will venture to travel with great riches into a foreign country, without a proper guide, it certainly will be adviseable for him to procure the best intelligence he can get of the climate, the roads, the difficulties he will meet with, and the treatment he may receive.

I pray the House to consider, if we have the slighest security that can be mentioned, except opinion (if that is any) either for the preservation of our present privileges, or gaining a single advantage from a change. [23] Have we any writing? have we a verbal promise from any Minister of the Crown? We have not. I cannot, therefore, conceal my astonishment, that gentlemen should require a less security for the invaluable rights of *Pennsylvania* than they would demand for a debt of five pounds. Why should we press forward with this unexampled hurry when no benefit can be derived from it? Why should we have any aversion to deliberation and delay when no injury can attend them?

It is scarcely possible, in the present case, that we can spend too much time in forming resolutions, the consequences of which are to be *perpetual*. If it is true, as some aver, that we can *now* obtain an advantageous change of government, I suppose that it will be also true next week, next month, and next year; but if *they* are mistaken it will be early enough whenever it happens to be disappointed and to repent. I am not willing to run risques in a matter of such prodigious importance on the credit of *any man's opinion*, when by a small delay, that can do no harm, the steps we are to take may become more safe. *Gideon*, though he had conversed with an "angel of the Lord," would not attempt to relieve his countrymen, then sorely opprest by the *Midianites*, least he should involve them in greater miseries, until he was convinced by two miracles that he should be successful. I do not say we ought to wait for *miracles*, but I think we ought to wait for something which will be next kin to a miracle; I mean, some *sign* of a *favourable disposition* in the *ministry* towards us. I should like to see an *olive leaf* at least brought to us, before we quit the *ark*.

Permit me, Sir, to make one proposal to the House. We may apply the Crown now, as freely as if we were under its immediate government. Let us desire his Majesty's judgment on the point * that has occasioned this unhappy difference between the two branches of the [24] legislature. This may be done without any † violence, without any hazard of our constitution. We say the justice of our de-

---

* This point was one of the stipulations approved by the Crown, in favour of the proprietors, with respect to the taxation of their estate. The governor, one branch of the legislature, insisted upon inserting in the bill then under consideration, the words of the stipulation ; and thus adhered to the stipulation. The house of assembly, the other branch of the legislature, insisted upon taxing the proprietary estate, without being thus bound. *Note in Writings.*

† Nihil vi, nihil secessione opus est. Sall. Bell. Jugurth.

mands is clear as light; every heart must feel the equity of them.

If the decision be in our favour, we gain a considerable victory; the grand obstruction of the public service is removed, and we shall have more leisure to carry our intentions coolly into execution. If the decision be against us, I believe the most zealous amongst us will grant it would be madness to expect success in any other contest. This will be a single point, and cannot meet with such difficulties as the procuring a total alteration of the government. Therefore, by separating it from other matters we shall *soon* obtain a determination, and know *what chance* we have of succeeding in things of greater value. Let us try our fortune. Let us take a cast or two of the dice for smaller matters before we dip deeply. Few gamesters are of so sanguine a temper as to stake their *whole wealth* on *one* desperate throw at first. If we *are* to *play* with the *public happiness*, let us act at least with *as much* deliberation as if we were *betting* out of our private purses.

Perhaps a little delay may afford us the pleasure of finding our constituents more unanimous in their opinions on this interesting occasion: and I should chuse to see a vast majority of them join with a calm resolution in the measure before I should think myself justifiable in voting for it, even if I approved of it.

The present question is utterly foreign from the purposes for which we were sent into this place. There was not the least probability at the time we were elected that this matter could come under our consideration. We are not debating how much money we shall [25] raise, what laws we shall pass for the regulation of property, nor on anything of the same kind that arises in the usual parliamentary course of business. We are now to determine WHETHER A STEP SHALL BE TAKEN THAT MAY PRODUCE AN ENTIRE CHANGE OF OUR CONSTITUTION.

In forming this determination one striking reflection should be preserved in our minds; I mean, "that we are the servants of the people of *Pennsylvania*"—of *that people* who have been induced by the excellence of the present constitution, to settle themselves under its Protection.

The inhabitants of remote countries, impelled by that love of liberty which allwise Providence has planted in the human heart, deserting their native soils, committed themselves with their helpless families to the mercy of winds and waves, and braved all the terrors of an unknown wilderness in hopes of enjoying in these woods the exercise of those invaluable rights which some unhappy circumstance had denied to mankind in every other part of the earth.

Thus, Sir, the people of *Pennsylvania* may be said to have *purchased* an inheritance in its constitution, at a prodigious price; and I cannot believe, unless the strongest evidence be offered, that they are now willing to part with that which has cost them so much toil and expence.

They have not hitherto been disappointed in their wishes. They have obtained the blessings they sought for.

We have received these seats by the free choice of this people under this constitution; and to preserve it [26] in its utmost purity and vigour, has always been deem'd by me a principal part of the trust committed to my care and fidelity. The measure now proposed has a direct tendency to endanger this constitution, and, therefore, in my opinion, we have *no right* to engage in it without the *almost universal consent of the people* exprest in the plainest manner.

I think I should improperly employ the attention of this House if I should take up much time in proving that the deputies of a people have not a right, by any law divine or human, to change the government under which their authority was delegated to them, without such a consent as has been mentioned.—The position is so consonant to natural justice and common sense, that I believe it never has been seriously controverted. All the learned authors that I recollect to have mentioned this matter speak of it as an indisputable maxim.

It may be * said, perhaps, in answer to this objection, "that it is not intended to change the government, but the governor." This, I apprehend, is a distinction only in words. The government is certainly to be changed from proprietary to royal, and *whatever may be intended*, the question is, whether such a change will not expose our present privileges to danger.

It may also be said "that the petitions lying on the table are a proof of the people's consent." Can petitions so industriously carried about, and after all the pains taken, signed only by about thirty-five hundred persons, be look'd on as the *plainest expression of the almost universal consent* of the many thousands that fill this Province? No one can believe it. [27]

It cannot be denied, Sir, that much the greatest part of the inhabitants of this Province, and among them men of large fortunes, good sense, and fair characters, who value very highly the interest they have in the present constitution, have not signed these petitions, and, as there is reason to apprehend, are extremely averse to a change at this time. Will they not complain of such a change? And if it is not attended with all the advantages they now enjoy, will they not have reason to complain? It is not improbable that this measure may lay the foundation of more bitter and more lasting dissentions among us than any we have yet experienced.

Before I close this catalogue of unhappy consequences,

* This was frequently said in the House.

that I expect will follow our request of a change, I beg leave to take notice of the *terms* of the petition that is now under the consideration of the House.

They equally excite in my breast—surprise, and grief, and terror. This poor Province is already sinking under the weight of the discredit and reproaches that, by *some fatality*, for several years past have attended our public measures; and we not only seize this unfortunate season to engage her in new difficulties, but prepare to pour on her devoted head a load that must effectually crush her. We inform the King by this petition that *Pennsylvania* is become a scene of confusion and anarchy: that armed mobs are marching from one place to another: that such a spirit of violence and riot prevails as exposes his Majesty's good subjects to constant alarms and danger: and that this tumultuous disposition is so general that it cannot be controuled by any powers of the present government; and that we have not any hopes of returning to a state of peace and safety but by being taken under his Majesty's immediate protection. [28]

I cannot think this a proper representation of the present state of this Province. Near four months are elapsed since the last riot, and I do not perceive the least probability of our being troubled with any more. The rioters were not only successfully opposed, and prevented from executing their purpose, but, we have reason to believe, that they were convinced of their error, and have renounced all thoughts of such wild attempts for the future. To whose throat is the sword now held? What life will be saved by this application? Imaginary danger! Vain remedy! Have we not *sufficiently felt* the effects of royal resentment? Is not the authority of the Crown *fully enough exerted* over us? Does it become *us* to paint, in the strongest colours, the folly or the crimes of our *countrymen?* To require unnecessary protection against men who intend us no injury, in such *loose* and *general* expressions *as may produce even the establishment of an armed force among us?*

With unremitting vigilance, with undaunted virtue, should a free people *watch* against the encroachments of power, and *remove* every pretext for its extension.

We are a dependant colony ; and we need not doubt that means will be used to secure that dependance. But that we ourselves should furnish a reason for settling a *military establishment* upon us, must exceed the most extravagant wishes of those who would be most pleased with such a measure.

We may introduce the innovation, but we shall not be able to stop its progress. The precedent will be pernicious. If a specious pretence is afforded for maintaining a small body of troops among us now, equally specious pretences will never be wanting hereafter for adding to their numbers. The burthen that will be imposed on us for their support is the most trifling [29] part of the evil. The poison will soon reach our vitals. Whatever struggles we may make to expell it,

Hæret lateri lethalis arundo—

The dart with which we are struck will still remain fixed—too firmly fixed, for our feeble hands to draw it out. Our fruitless efforts will but irritate the wound, and at length we must tamely submit to—I quit a subject too painful to be dwelt upon.

These, Sir, are my sentiments on the petition that has occasioned this debate. I think this neither the *proper season* nor the *proper method* for obtaining a change of our government. It is *uncertain* whether the measures proposed will place us in a better situation than we are now in, with regard to the point lately controverted; with respect to other particulars, it may place us in a worse. We shall run the *risque* of *suffering* great *losses.* We have *no certainty* of *gaining* anything. In seeking a *precarious*, *hasty*, *violent* remedy for the present *partial* disorder, we are *sure* of exposing the *whole body* to danger. I cannot perceive the necessity of applying such a remedy. If I did, I would with the greatest pleasure pass over to the opinion of some gentlemen who differ from me, whose integrity and abilities I so much esteem, that whatever reasons at any time influence me to agree with them, I always receive a satisfaction from being on their side. If I have erred now, I shall comfort myself with reflecting that it is an *innocent error*. Should the measures pursued in consequence of this debate be opposite to my opinion, and should they procure a change of government with all the benefits we desire, I shall not envy the praise of others, who by their *fortunate* courage and skill have conducted us unhurt, through the midst of such threatening dangers, to the wished for port. I shall cheer- [30] fully submit to the censure of having been *too apprehensive* of injuring the people of this Province. If any severer sentence shall be passed upon me by the worthy, I shall be sorry for it; but this truth I am convinced of, that it will be much easier for me to bear the unmerited reflections of *mistaken zeal* than the just reproaches of a *guilty mind*. To have concealed my real sentiments, or to have counterfeited such as I do not entertain, in a deliberation of *so much consequence* as the present, would have been the *basest hypocrisy*. It may, perhaps, be thought that this, however, would have been the most *politic* part for me to have acted. It might have been so. But if *policy* requires, that our words or actions should *belye* our hearts, I thank God that I *detest* and *despise* all its *arts* and all its *advantages*. A good man *ought* to serve his country, even though she *resents* his services. The great reward of honest actions is not the fame or profit that follows them, but the *consciousness* that attends them. To discharge on this important occasion the *inviolable duty* I owe the public, by obeying the *unbiassed dictates* of my *reason* and *conscience*, hath been my sole view; and my only wish now is that the resolutions of this House, whatever they are, may promote the happiness of *Pennsylvania.*

FINIS.

A PROTEST

AGAINST A

RESOLUTION OF THE ASSEMBLY OF PENNSYLVANIA

FOR PETITIONING THE KING

TO CHANGE THE COLONY OF PENNSYLVANIA

FROM A

PROPRIETARY TO A ROYAL GOVERNMENT.

BY

JOHN DICKINSON.

———

MAY 28, 1764.

NOTE.

IN spite of Dickinson's *Speech*, the Pennsylvania Assembly voted, on May 24, to petition the crown to make the colony a royal one. Four days later " Mr. Dickinson having then digested the heads of his speech into the nature of a *Protest*, in which he was joined by Mr. Saunders and Mr. Montgomery, offer'd it to be entered in the minutes; but it was refused." (Smith's *Preface, ante*, p. 14.) "It being moved by some Members, that they should be admitted to enter their Reasons, by way of Protestation against a late Measure resolved on by a Majority of the House, the Question was put, and carried in the Negative--Yeas, Three, Mr. Dickinson, Mr. Saunders, and Mr. Montgomery;—Nays, Twenty-four." (*Votes and Proceedings*, V, 349). Franklin, in his preface to Galloway's *Speech*, (p. xxxiv) gives the reasons of the majority for declining to allow it. Refused an entry in the *Votes*, it was printed in the *Pennsylvania Gazette* of July 26, 1764, with a prefatory note, which is here reprinted.   EDITOR.

PREFACE.

PHILADELPHIA, July 26.

MR. HALL,

As Mr. DICKINSON'S Speech, that was lately published, has been so generally admired, you could hardly render a more acceptable Service to your Readers, than by inserting it in your News-Paper; but as it might probably be too long to obtain a Place there entire, I herewith send you the Substance of it, which was digested into the Nature of a Protest by Mr. Dickinson himself, when he found that the House could by no means be prevailed on to lay aside their Petition for a change of Government. This Protest Mr. Dickinson, with some other Members, prayed the House (though in vain) to enter on their Minutes.

(55)

THE PROTEST.

We —— dissent from, and protest against, the above mentioned Resolution, for the following Reasons :

Because we think a Change of our Government is a Matter of such vast Importance to the good People of this Province, and so foreign from the Purposes for which we receive our Seats in this House, that it ought not to be attempted without the almost universal Consent of the People; of which Consent, we have not now any Evidence, unless the Petitions lying on the Table, and signed only by about Thirty-five Hundred Persons, though not addressed to us, nor requesting us at this Time to make such an Attempt, can be looked on as such Evidence. On the Petition of so inconsiderable a Number, We do not think this House has a Right to deprive so many thousand Inhabitants of this Province of their present Government, or to take any Step that may produce such a Consequence.

Because it appears from the Letters of the Secretaries of State, lately laid before this House, that this Province at present labours under the heavy and deplorable Misfortune of having incurred, in a very high Degree, the Displeasure of our most Excellent Sovereign, and therefore at present may be regarded in a very unfavorable Light.

Because We apprehend, if his Majesty shall be pleased to determine, that the Governor, in his Controversy with this House, has discharged his Duty to the Crown, by strictly observing Stipulations approved by his Majesty, and his royal Grandfather, that the Conduct of this House on the present Occasion will add to the Resentment already

(57)

entertained, and that the Controversy above mentioned will be thought an unjustifiable Foundation for the present Attempt.

Because We apprehend there will be a great Danger of our not retaining the Privileges this Province now enjoys, when the King shall take the Government immediately into his own Hands, on the Request of the Representatives of the People.

Because We apprehend, that such a Request may be regarded in his Majesty's Council, as a Surrender of our present Constitution; at least it may be consider as the Request of the whole Province (though we are not desired to make such a Request even by the Petitions now lying before this House) that the Proprietary Government may be abolished, and therefore may be thought a sufficient Reason for his Majesty and his Parliament to form a new Government for this Province, and that thus the civil and religious Liberty, of which the People are now possessed, may be greatly lessened and restrained.

Because We think that the Conduct of this Province, which hath brought upon it his Majesty's Resentiment, being, as we are informed and believe, attributed by his Majesty's Council to the Influence of one Sect of Dissenters, and the Blame of the late Tumults and Disorders among us being cast on another Sect of Dissenters, great Reason will therefore be afforded to his Majesty and his Parliament, if a Change of our Government is made before the Conduct of the People so censured can be properly vindicated, to lay some uncommon Restrictions on Persons of such particular Professions, who may, under the Misrepresentations made of their Behaviour, for a Time, appear criminal.

Because We apprehend that the Petition, now ordered to be signed by the Speaker, is extremely reproachful and injurious to the People of Pennsylvania, by representing the

Province at this Time in a State of Confusion and Anarchy, through Multitudes of tumultuous and riotous Insurgents.

Because We think the Petition will be extremely danger- ous, not only to the peculiar Privileges of this Province, but to the common Liberty we are entitled to with the rest of his Majesty's Subjects, the Petition being so worded that, in our Opinion, it may be construed as calling on the Crown to restore Peace and Security to us, even by the Establishment of an armed Force.

Because We think that this important Matter has not been considered and debated with that Deliberation that its Consequence to our Constituents demands, and no In- convenience, that we know of, can arise from bestowing a little more Time on the Consideration of a Measure, the Consequences of which are to be perpetual.

Lastly, because We think that the necessary Precautions have not been taken by this House to procure a happy Determination of a Measure so deeply affecting the valu- able Rights of the People of Pennsylvania. Before any Petition to the Crown should be agreed to by this House, it is our firm Opinion the Sentiments of the King or the Ministry should have been known, with respect to the Ad- vantages we may gain, or the Disadvantages we may suffer from the Measure proposed; and some kind of Security should have been obtained for saving to the Inhabitants of this Province the Blessings they now enjoy—Till these things are done, we think no Step ought to be taken by this House that may expose to Hazard the Continuance of these Blessings to the present and succeeding Ages.

Influenced by these and other Reasons, we declare our Disapprobation of the Petition now voted for. To obey the Dictates of our Consciences and Judgment; to dis- charge the sacred Duty we owe to our Constituents; and to promote the Happiness of Pennsylvania, has been our Aim and Endeavour. As our Opinion hath been overruled, and Measures pursued which we apprehend may be injurious to our Country, We pray God that this Province may never have too fatal Cause to think that we are right.

A PETITION

TO THE

KING

FROM THE

INHABITANTS OF PENNSYLVANIA.

DRAWN BY

JOHN DICKINSON.

————

JULY, 1764.

NOTE.

DEFEATED by the votes of the Assembly from an official protest against petitioning the King to change the government of the province, the opponents of that measure united on the following petition, drawn by Dickinson, which was printed as a broadside, and circulated thoughout the colony for signatures. The head lines were:

To the / King's Most Excellent / Majesty in Council, / the Representation and Petition of / Your Majesty's dutiful and loyal Subjects, / Freeholders and Inhabitants of the Province of Pennsylvania. [Fo. pp. 2.]

An edition in German was also printed, with the title of:

Seiner Königlichen Erhabensten Majestät / im Hohen Rath, / nahe sich / Diese demüthigste Vorstellung und Bitte / von / Seiner Majestät gehorsamst-getreuen Unterthanen, den freyen / Einwohnern der Provinz Pennsylvanien. [Fo. pp 2.]

This petition was analysed and answered in Franklin's preface to Galloway's *Speech* (p. xxvii.). EDITOR.

(63)

To the King's Most Excellent Majesty in Council, the Representation and Petition of Your Majesty's dutiful and loyal Subjects, Freeholders and Inhabitants of the Province of Pennsylvania.

Most humbly sheweth,
   That having received certain information that the Assembly of this Province, during their last sitting, had drawn up a PETITION to your Majesty, setting forth among other things, " 'That mischievious disagreements subsist in this government, which proceed, as they conceive, from the very Nature of it; and that a Spirit of Violence, Riot and Confusion prevails among us, which cannot be controlled by the present Powers of Government and renders a Change of the same necessary:"—Sundry Magistrates and reputable Freeholders alarmed at the Nature of this Petition, and considering the whole Province as deeply affected by it, did (in Behalf of themselves and others) apply to the Speaker of Assembly for a Copy of the same, and to know whether the House intended to transmit it to England, without communicating its Contents to their Constituents, and obtaining their fullest and most explicit Consent therein.

   That they were informed by the Speaker, that the Petition had already been transmitted to be laid before your Majesty, and no Copy of it could be given without the Leave of the House, at their Meeting in September next; when we apprehend it might be too late for us to submit our Sense of this Matter to your Majesty; and therefore we beg to Leave in all humble Duty, *to represent—*

(65)

That as there is no civil Happiness on Earth which we should esteem equal to that of being under your Majesty's immediate Government, if our remote Situation could permit such a Blessing; yet we and all your American Subjects must be governed by Persons authorized and approved by your Majesty, on the best Recommendation that can be obtained of them, we cannot perceive our Condition in this Respect to be different from our Fellow Subjects around us, or that we are thereby less under Majesty's particular Care and Protection than they are; since there can be no Governor of this Province, without your Majesty's immediate Approbation and Authority.

That the particular Mode or Frame of Government which we enjoy under your Majesty in this Province (as derived to us by the Charter of your Royal Ancestor King Charles the Second, and delivered to us by our wise Founder, William Penn, Esq.;) is held in the highest Estimation by good Men of all Denominations among us, and hath brought Multitudes of industrious People from various Parts of the World, who trusting in the perpetual Enjoyment of the inestimable Privileges it gives them, have, at their own Expence, settled this Colony, and raised it, in a few Years, to be one of the most flourishing in your Majesty's American Dominions; cheerfully embracing every Opportunity of manifesting their Loyalty and Affection to your Majesty's Royal Person and Family.

That such disagreements have arisen in this Province we have beheld with Sorrow, but as others around us are not exempted from the like Misfortunes, We can by no Means conceive them incident to the Nature of our Government, which hath often been administered with remarkable Harmony; and your Majesty, before whom our late Disputes have been laid, can be at no Loss, in your great Wisdom, to discover whether they proceed from the above Cause, or should be ascribed to some other.

That this Province (except from the Indian Ravages) enjoys the most perfect internal Tranquility; and a Spirit of Riot and Violence is so foreign to the general Temper of its Inhabitants, that there are as few instances of any Disturbance of this kind to be met with among them since the first Settlement of the Colony, as perhaps the like number of People in any part of the World: That where such disturbances have happened, they have been speedily quieted; the civil Powers have been supported; and tho' there are perhaps Cases in all Governments, where it may not be possible speedily to discover Offenders, yet we know of no instance among us where Persons legally accused or Convicted, have been screen'd from the Public Justice; and if the executive Part of our Government should seem in any case too weak, we conceive it is the Duty of the Assembly, and in their Power, to strengthen it, without representing us in a Light that might undeservedly subject us to your Majesty's Royal Displeasure, which we deem the greatest of all Misfortunes.

We therefore most humbly pray—That your Majesty would be graciously pleased, wholly to disregard the said Petition of the Assembly, as exceedingly grievous in its Nature; as by no means containing a proper Representation of the State of this Province; and as repugnant to the general Sense of your numerous and loyal Subjects in it; there being but few of them (comparitively speaking) who could by any means be prevail'd on to give the least countenance to this Measure.

A REPLY

TO THE

SPEECH

OF

JOSEPH GALLOWAY.

BY

JOHN DICKINSON.

———

SEPTEMBER 4, 1764.

NOTE.

THE personalities in Galloway's *Speech* in reply to Dickinson irritated the latter so greatly, that he challenged him to a duel, which Galloway declined. Dickinson then wrote the following pamphlet, published in the second week of September, 1764, with the title :

A / Reply / To a Piece called / The / Speech / Of Joseph Galloway, Esquire. / By / John Dickinson. / "Yes, the last pen for freedom let me draw, / When truth stands trembling on the edge of law ; / Here, last of Britons ! Let your names be read ; / Are none, none living? Let me praise the dead, / And for that cause which made your fathers shine, / Fall by the votes of their unhappy line." / Pope./ Philadelphia : / Printed and Sold by William Bradford, / At his Book-Store, in Market-street, adjoining the / London Coffee-House, M,DCC,LXIV. [8vo. pp. iv, 45, xii.]

A London reprint was issued with the title of :

A / Reply / to / a piece / called the / Speech / of / Joseph Galloway, Esq; / By John Dickinson. / . . . . . / Philadelphia Printed : / London, / Re-Printed for J. Whiston, and B. White, in Fleet-street. / MDCCLXV. [8vo. pp. iv, 62, (1).]

It was noticed in the *Monthly Review*, XXXII. 67 ; and the *Critical Review*, XVIII, 197.

EDITOR.

(71)

For The Honble Thomas Penn Esqr

A

R E P L Y

To a PIECE called

T_H E

S P E E C H

Of JOSEPH GALLOWAY, Efquire

B Y

JOHN DICKINSON,

" YES, the laft pen for freedom let me draw,
When truth ftands trembling on the edge of law ?
Here, laft of Britons! Let your names be read;
Are none, none living? Let me praife the *dead*,
And FOR THAT CAUSE which made *your fathers* fhine,
Fall by the votes of their unhappy line."
POPE.

PHILADELPHIA:

Printed and Sold by WILLIAM BRADFORD,
At his BOOK-STORE, in *Market-ftreet*, adjoining the
LONDON COFFEE-HOUSE, M,DCC,LXIV.

PREFACE.

---

*The Pamphlet called " The Speech of Joseph Galloway, Esquire"
was published on Saturday the 11th day of* August.—*The next
day I left Town to attend the Courts in the* Lower Counties, *and
did not return till the 26th.—The following Reply was written in
the small intervals I could spare from the Hurry of the Courts at*
Dover *and* New-Castle, *and these frequently interrupted.—The
Court for* Chester *County began the 28th, and held till the 31st
day of August; and* Philadelphia *County Court began yesterday,
so that it has been impossible for me to prepare this Piece for the
Public, in the Manner I wish'd to do.*

*I hope the Reader will therefore be so kind, as to excuse any In-
accuracies that may be discovered; which I should have carefully
endeavoured to correct, if my Business had not prevented me.*

Philadelphia, September 4th, 1764.

(75)

CONTENTS.

(76)

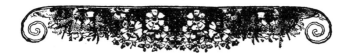

A REPLY, &c.

Two reasons induce me to address the public at present. The one is, to clear a few plain arguments on a matter of the utmost consequence, from the objections lately made against them, in a piece call'd " *The Speech of Joseph Galloway, Esq.; &c.*" The other is, to answer the unjust accusations contain'd in that piece.

To act honestly, and to be traduc'd, hath been the fate of many men. To bear slanders with temper, and to entertain a proper pity or contempt, for their weak or wicked authors, has been the lot of few. I will endeavour to imitate their example: and by proposing it to myself, I hope I shall be able so far to suppress the resentment naturally arising from a sense of unprovok'd injuries, that my vindication may be presented not unacceptably, nor uselessly, to candid minds.

Could I be convinced, that men of sense or virtue, would be persuaded or pleased, by wild declamation or illiberal reflections, I might perhaps be induced to defend myself, in the same shattered style and abusive lan- [2] guage, with which I have been attacked: but as these must always offend the wise and good, whose approbation only is worth wishing for, to Mr. *Galloway* I resign the undisputed glory of excelling in his *favorite* arts—of *writing confusedly*, and *railing insolently*.

Presumptuous indeed must I appear, should I venture into these lists, against a person who wields the weapons

(77)

of wordy war—*the only weapons he dares to wield*—with
so peculiar a dexterity in his exercise, as to feel no kind
of restraint either from *sense* or *truth;* the regularity of
whose sober discipline would prove, I presume, too great
a confinement to this advocate of *freedom.*

When I perceived, that Mr. *Galloway* was hardy enough
to obtrude on the public a *pretended speech*, of which he
never spoke one sentence in the House, I was not surprised to find, that a person who treated his own character
with such licence, should not be unsparing of others. But
—*why* he should engage in the *preposterous* project—*why*
he should so industriously endeavour to exhibit me as a
villain to my country, for speaking my sentiments in that
place where my country had commanded me to speak them
—*why* he has wantonly wounded a man, who never designed or wished *him* an injury; but has always, as far as
his power extended, rendered him all the offices of civility
—for *what reasons*, I say, he has thus violated the laws
of *humanity* and *decency*, his own heart is best able to
decide—The public, with which he endeavours to establish his character, by destroying *that of another*, may perhaps be able to guess the *secret causes*, by which he has
been transported into such unjustifiable excesses of rage
and rancour against *me*—For my part, I shall avoid
an enquiry, that would only lead me, I fear, to a painful
discovery of the *depravity*, to which the human mind is
subject. [3]

Leaving then to the impartial world the judgement to be
passed on Mr. *Galloway's* conduct—Leaving to *him* the
enjoyment of the *solid satisfaction*, that must arise from
the meritorious exploit of stabbing publicly a reputation,
which has hitherto escaped his *insidious attempts*, I shall
endeavour to perform the task imposed on me by his
cruelty, and to defend myself from those darts, which with
unfriendly hands he has aim'd at *my heart.*

When the change of our government, after the adjournment of the assembly in *March* last, came to be the general subject of conversation, the importance of the measure
filled my mind with the greatest anxiety. A severe fit of
sickness had prevented my attendance when the resolves
were past: but I considered that at the next meeting of the
House, the duties of the post which my country had assign'd me, would call upon me to act a part of more consequence, than perhaps would ever fall to my share again,
in the whole course of my life. Mindful of the trust committed to me, I endeavour'd to understand a matter on
which so much depended.

I soon perceiv'd, that if a change took place, there were
two things to be wish'd for, which there appear'd to me no
probability of obtaining. The first was, that the *point* on
which we lately differ'd with the governor, and *some others*
which have been earnestly urg'd by former assemblies,
should be determin'd in our favour. The second was, that
our *privileges should be perfectly secured.*

But insurmountable obstructions seem'd to present
themselves, *at this time,* against these attempts. * "What
"reasonable hopes of success can we entertain, of having
"these points decided in our favour, while those [4] min-
"isters who so repeatedly and warmly have approv'd of
"the proprietors insisting on them, are still in power?"
Our danger not only is, that these points will not be decided for us; but, if the proprietors, tired and incensed,
should think proper to surrender the government and
make their own terms with the crown, is it not highly
probable, that they have interest enough to make the
change in such a manner as will fix upon us *forever,* those
demands which appear so extremely just to the present
ministers? Add to this, the "deplorable misfortune under
"which we now labour, of having incurr'd the displeasure

* Speech, page 6.

"of his majesty and his ministers." These reflections in-
duc'd me to think and to say—that *this* is not the proper
time to attempt a change of our government.

Mr. *Galloway*, by way of prelude to his answer to these
observations, endeavours to shew that I have contradicted
myself: but this *supposed* contradiction is founded on a
supposed concession, which I never made—"*of the necessity of a change.*" My *approbation* of a change, if we
can enjoy all the advantages we now do, is call'd, "*a
confession that a change is necessary.*" But certainly it
would have been more natural to construe it as it was
intended, and as the sense requires—"that, *if we are to
lose nothing by the change*, I am as willing to be under
the immediate government of the crown, as of the proprietors."

After this unsuccessful attempt to raise a contradiction,
Mr. *Galloway* takes the trouble of attacking the "inap-
posite instance," as he calls it, relating to the Duke of
Monmouth. This instance was mentioned to confirm a
preceding observation; and Mr. *Galloway*, in attempting
to answer it, *unluckily for himself*, points out and enforces
the very truth for which it was adduced. He says, "the
duke failed, and no wonder; for he [5] landed at a *time*
"when the king was supported in the warmest manner by
"the parliament, and no one circumstance to promise
him success." Thus, I say,—"our attempt is made at
a *time* when the proprietors are supported in the warmest manner by the crown, and its ministers; and no one
circumstance to promise us success."—But, suppose the
duke had waited till the parliament did *no longer* support the King; but, when they and the whole nation, in
the utmost dread of popery and arbitrary power, were
looking round with impatient terror for a deliverer, and
when many circumstances promised that nobleman success;
is it evident that he would not *then* have succeeded, or

that he would have been taken and put to death? Or, if King *William* had made his attempt, before the nation was properly alarmed, is it certain that the revolution would have been accomplished with such amazing facility? Rashness ruined the one. Caution crowned the other. This is all I intended to prove.

Mr. *Galloway* then proceeds, and *supposes* that all the determinations of the ministry, were mistakes occasioned by proprietary misrepresentations. He then *supposes* that these determinations were solely owing to the influence of two friends of the proprietors, lately deceased: And lastly, he *supposes* that now there will be a *total* alteration in ministerial resolutions.

These *suppositions*, I acknowledge, are as good securities as any we have, that the grand points controverted between us and the proprietors, will, in any case of a change, be decided in our favour, or that our privileges will be preserved. But still they seem to be too sanguine. Let us remember with what *unanimity* the ministry at different times have expressed their resentment of our conduct; and, that it is only *guess-work* to imagine, their resolutions were dictated by two men. [6]

Of one thing we are *sure*—that we are in the utmost *discredit* with the king and his ministers. The late resolves prove it. Mr. *Galloway*, however, flatters himself, "that the prejudices against us are not so ineradicably "fixed, but they may be easily overcome, and the province "restored to her former credit." Happy should I be, if I could perceive the least prospect of so great a blessing. By *what means* these prejudices are to be overcome, we are not informed; nor can I conceive. Men of great abilities, and of the most perfect acquaintance with our public affairs, have been employed to remove the force of these misrepresentations, as they are called. Mr. *Franklin* and Mr. *Charles*, our Agents, spent several years in combating these prejudices; and, even Mr. *Galloway* himself, as I have been told, *elucidated* the justice of our cause with his usual *perspicuity* in realms of writing. Yet after all these great labours, his majesty and his ministers still retained their former sentiments. Hence, I fear, that any future efforts for this purpose, "*will be *swallowed up, and sacrificed* (as Mr. *Galloway* most elegantly expresses it) at *the shrine of proprietary instructions, and the measures of power.*" In short, that they will be but † "*ideal shadows,*" and *chimerical notions.*"

In confident expectation of these improbabilities, Mr. *Galloway* is willing to risque the *perpetuating* those demands, which have been constantly made by the proprietors—at a *time*, when *we are certain* that the crown and its ministers look on these demands as highly just and reasonable.

One of his arguments for our riding post in this affair is "that there are many new colonies to be [7] settled now, "and that it would discourage *these* settlements, if *our* privileges were to be taken away."

'Tis true it will convince the emigrants, they are not to have such privileges as were granted to *us;* or if they *have*, and shall hereafter *petition for a change*, that they will be taken from them.

But this information, I imagine, will be no discouragement.—There is not the same ‡ reason to grant, nor to wish for privileges now, that existed in the persecuting day of *Charles* the second. Grants of land on small quit-rents—furnishing the necessaries of life for the first outset—bounties on labour—and immunities from taxes for

* Pretended speech,—page 30.

† *Qu.* What *Idea* can be formed of an "*ideal shadow?*" and what may be the meaning "*of the shrine of the measures of power?*"

‡ *America* was then so little known, that it was thought the severest kind of banishment to send people over to the colonies.

some years—with the common liberties of other English subjects—will do the business, without the privileges of *Pennsylvania.*

Mr. *Galloway,* before he quits * "this wise policy of settling the extensive newly acquired dominions" as he expresses himself, takes the opportunity of making an *historical flourish*—but unfortunately furnishes " † irrefragable demonstrations" that he is utterly unacquainted with the subject, on which he speaks.

Mr. Franklin read in the House, a short extract from Lord *Clarendon's* life, relating to *Barbados.* Mr. *Galloway* catches it as it fell from the learned member, and now confidently asserts—"that the colony of *Barbados* had, in the opinion of the ablest council, *forfeited her charter privileges.*—And yet upon this policy only, her privileges were preserved."

He refers to Lord *Clarendon's* life, for this curious anecdote. What then must a man think of Mr. *Gal-* [8] *loway,* who looks into the book, and finds—that the colony of *Barbados* did not forfeit any right, that such an opinion was never given—and that there is not a word relating to her *charter privileges.* Yet this is the truth.

The fact was this. *Charles* the first granted the island of *Barbados* by patent to the earl of *Carlisle*—he died—his son leased it to lord *Willoughby* for twenty-one years; appointing him governor, and reserving a moiety of the profits to himself—the civil war broke out—ended—*Charles* the second was restor'd—there being eight or nine years of lord *Willoughby's* lease to come, he pray'd the king to give him a commission to be governor for that time—But the island was now much changed—it was compleatly settled during the troubles and *chiefly by officers of the king's army*—so that now it was of another

---

* Pretended Speech—page 21.   † Id., pa. 73.

consideration and value than it had been—*the king's cus-toms* yearly amounted to *a very large sum*—The planters were greatly alarmed at the thought of * "depending on "the earl of *Carlisle* and lord *Willoughby* for the enjoy-"ment of their estates, which they had hitherto look'd "upon as their own." They applied to the king, † "praying that they may not be opprest by those two "lords. They pleaded, that they were the king's subjects; "that they had repaired thither as to a *desolate place*, and "had by their industry obtained a livelihood there, *when* "*they could not with a good conscience stay in England.* "That if they should be now left to those lords to *ransom* "themselves and *compound for their estates*, they *must leave* "*the country;* and the plantations would be *destroyed*, "which yielded his majesty so good a revenue."

They further ‡ "positively insisted, that the charter "granted to the earl of *Carlisle* was *void in point of law;* "[9] and prayed that his majesty would give them leave "to prosecute in his name in the exchequer, and at their "own charge, to repeal that grant; by which they should "be freed from the *arbitrary power and oppression* which "would be exercised upon them under the colour of that "charter; and his majesty might receive *a great benefit to* "*himself*, by taking the sovereignty into his own hands, to "which it belonged—and in that case, they offered to "make *as great an imposition* of taxes as the plantation "would bear; for the support of the king's governor, and "such other uses, as his majesty should think fit to di-"rect."

Upon this, the king § "referr'd the consideration of the validity and legality of the patent, to his council at law; who upon full deliberation, after the hearing of all parties,

* Lord Clarendon's Life—vol. iii, pa., 933.
† Idem, 934.   ‡ Idem, 937.
§ Lord Clarendon's Life, iii. vol., pa. 938.

returned their opinion, *that this patent was void, and that his majesty take the same into his own power ;*" not that "the *colony had forfeited their charter privileges.*"

On this report, the determination was formed in the king's council. And what does this case prove—but that the crown would not deprive the *proprietors* of *Barbados* of their charter, tho' the people earnestly requested it—tho' *that* people were faithful subjects, who had distinguished their loyalty by suffering in the royal cause—tho' a very great benefit would accrue to the crown—tho' a large salary was to be settled on the king's governor —and lastly, tho' the patent was absolutely ILLEGAL and VOID.

If in *such a case*, the needy and unprincipled *Charles* would not seize upon the interests of the *proprietors* of *Barbados*, can it be conceived that his present majesty will snatch from the proprietors of *Pennsylvania*, without [10] their consent, the charter that was granted in consideration of the services performed by their brave and loyal ancestor.

I think every man in the province, *except* Mr. *Galloway*, will immediately discover whether the case he has quoted will strengthen his reasoning or mine.

Another of Mr. Galloway's arguments is—that the "proprietary estate is daily increasing, and thus their "influence will increase; and, therefore, they will be "more likely in future to oppose with success any meas-"ures that may be taken against their opposition."

To finish this argument, he closes it with an *imaginary contradiction* of mine, in my saying, "This is not the "proper time for a change," and afterwards declaring, "that we are not to expect more success, because the *pro-*"*prietaries* will have more dignity, more power, and, as "they will think, more law on their side."

Mr. *Galloway* certainly takes delight in mistakes, or he

would never have committed so gross an error as he has done here. I said—it could not be expected that our success would be greater when our "opponents become "more *numerous* and will have more dignity, more power, "and, as they will think, more law on thei*ẞ* side." This was intended to prove, that we might find it more difficult after a change to contend for the preservation of our privileges with the *crown* and the *clergy* (the *opponents* here meant) than with the proprietors. But Mr. *Galloway*, with great address, by changing the word *opponents* for *proprietaries*, creates a contradiction for his own *diversion*, and the *deception* of his readers. [11]

However—let it be supposed "that the proprietary estate and influence will greatly increase, and that they become the richest subjects in *England*." I most sincerely wish they may, since the* increase of their wealth must arise from the increase of the wealth and prosperity of *Pennsylvania*. These, I presume, are not things to be dreaded. *Our* power and influence must increase with *their* power and influence—and, therefore, it seems we shall always be as able to cope with them, as we are now —especially if it be considered that a *family* is more liable to accidents than a *people*.

Mr. *Galloway* endeavours to shew, that the conduct of the proprietors has not been constantly approved by the crown and ministry, because five of the thirteen acts opposed by the proprietors, were confirmed.

But granting that the riches of the proprietary family shall increase in a greater proportion than the riches of this province—can it be imagin'd, that they will obtain any *undue influence* over the crown and it's ministers? can it be believed, that the king and parliament will suffer two or three subjects to tyrannise over a dependant colony,

* Pretended Speech, pa. 14, 15, 17.

in whose welfare *Great-Britain* is so much interested? To reduce us to the most abject state of slavery?

The supposition is too monstrous to be admitted—and I should be surprized to hear such language from any person, but one who thinks and writes in Mr. *Galloway's* shambling way. He* shudders at my saying [12] "the "parliament may perhaps be induced to place *us* in the "*same state* with the *royal governments*"—and yet he supposes, they will tamely tolerate our being made *slaves.*

But this opposition, even by Mr. *Galloway's* acknowledgment, did not proceed from any private interest of the proprietors that was affected by these Bills. They were opposed, says he,† "as inconsistent with the royal prerogative"—And surely such an opposition could not be much disapproved of by the crown, as the ministry have declared‡ "that his majesty's royal prerogatives were not to be trusted to the feeble hands of private individuals; who were ever ready to sacrifice them to their private emolument."

If our proprietors are to become such great and dreadful men—if their influence is to grow superior to justice and reason—I cannot conceive how the king's *appointment* of governors can secure us from them, any more than his *approbation.*

If that influence shall ever be so exorbitant as it has been described, will it not prevail in the nomination of governors? Or in determining their conduct? Can even Mr. *Galloway* think that the king's *appointment* will protect us against this influence? If he does, I will answer him in his own words—and if they do not convince *him,* surely he will not be so unreasonable as to expect, that they should convince *any one else.*

"§ Let us but consider that the experience of ages fully

* Pretended Speech, pa. 7.   † id., pa. 25.
‡ id., pa. 23.   § id., pa. 10.

"demonstrates wealth to be the parent of power, and the
"*nurse* of influence, and that an increase of wealth will as
"naturally *beget* an increase of power and influence, as an
"increase of velocity in the *falling stone* will produce
"more certain death."

"Let us but take a view of the proprietary estate, what
"it was fifty, what twenty years ago, and what it is now,
"and we must be convinced *that nothing can prevent* their
"being the richest *subjects in the English nation; and*
"*therefore subjects of the greatest influence and power*, and
"*more likely in future to oppose with success* any measures
"that may be taken against their oppression. Are we to
"expect the same cause will not produce the same effect,
"and that [13] wealth by some MAGIC CHARM in future,
"will, instead of producing power and influence, bring
"forth its contraries? *As vain and chimerical* as the ex-
"pectation of a future Messiah to the deluded Jews."

If there is any force in these arguments of Mr. *Galloway*—if property, from natural causes, produces power,
and cannot fail of having this effect—how vain and ridiculous is it to request the crown—to* " *separate power from
property?*" Yet this forsooth ! is *all Mr. Galloway*, or
the assembly according to his explanation, desires of his
majesty.

Certainly the meaning cannot be, that the king should
take away their estates from the proprietors—this would be
too glaringly unjust. What then can Mr. *Galloway* mean,
when he desires "that the king may separate power and
property," which he declares—and, with prodigious labour, strives to prove—"*inseparable?*" *If he means anything*, I imagine, I have discovered his meaning—and,
tho' Mr. *Galloway* has, in his performance, said many
things that have *surprized* me—yet this is so superlatively

* Pretended Speech, page 8—*et alibi.*

extraordinary, that I would not admit the following construction, unless his intention was too evident to allow of any doubt. I did not think him capable of such designs. I entertained a better opinion of his loyalty. In short, he plainly means—*as he has declared it cannot be done any other way*—that his Majesty shall turn MAGICIAN —and contrive* "some "MAGIC CHARM, whereby wealth instead of producing "power and influence shall bring forth *its* contraries"—*their* contraries I suppose it should be.

This dread of future injuries being removed—or at least the vanity of attempting their removal, [14] on Mr. *Galloway's own principles* being proved—I return to the present situation of affairs.

It is universally believed, that the present ministry are desirous of vesting the government of this province advantageously in the crown. Mr. *Franklin* has frequently said it. If this be the case, how fair an opportunity is presented to the proprietors of gratifying their resentment, if they entertain any against the province, and securing their interest at the same time by entering into a contract with the crown, and fixing, by an act of parliament, those points in which the ministry have constantly supported them—*upon all succeeding ages?*

Many words are unnecessary in so clear a case as this is. Mr. *Galloway* allows, the proprietors have some sense, and that they understand their own interest. The sentiments of the ministry have been declared in their favor. From thence I think it may be taken for granted, that the proprietors either will not consent to a change—or that their consent will be founded on a perfect security given them for their demands, which appear so just to the king and ministry. What may facilitate this measure is, the

* Pretended Speech, pa. 11.

proposal of the assembly—* "that a *full equivalent* "be made to the proprietors" upon their parting with the government. How far these words may be construed to extend, will appear from this consideration. With the *approbation of the crown* the proprietors now insist on certain points which, in their opinion, tend to promote their interests. This, the authority vested in them at present, enables them to do. If they are divested of this authority, without any stipulations for securing their interests *hereafter*, as well as they are at *this time*, it will be said that a *full equivalent* is not made for the power they resign. This security will therefore without [15] doubt, be required —and that requisition may not appear so unreasonable in *Great-Britain* as it does here.

This *full equivalent* comprehends something more than the settlement of these points. The government of itself is very valuable—and surely we shall not desire the king to pay the equivalent out of his own pocket. If the change therefore is made, I don't question but it will be thought highly reasonable—*that we should pay for the blessing, which we so earnestly request.*

The situation of our affairs being such as has been described, I could not perceive any necessity "impelling" us to seize this unhappy period, to plunge this province into convulsions, that might while she was thus disordered, be attended with the worst consequences. A gentler remedy appeared to me a properer remedy.

But here Mr. *Galloway* exclaims—"Shall we pati- "ently wait until proprietary influence shall be at end? "Shall we submit to proprietary demands?" By no means! What I desire, is, vigorously to oppose those demands; and to try the force of that influence, WITHOUT RISQUING TOO MUCH IN THE CONTEST.

* Pretended Speech, pa. 5.

I THEREFORE made a proposal to the House, of a very moderate nature, which I had the pleasure of finding highly approved by a * gentleman, whose acknowledged integrity, patriotism, abilities, and experience will always give weight to his sentiments, with every impartial person. The proposal was—"that we should desire his majesty's judgment, on the point that occasioned the late unhappy difference between the two branches of the legislature." By taking this step, we should have discovered the sense of the ministry on our [16] late disputes—on other important points which have been controverted with our governors—and respecting our privileges.

Thus we should have known what success would attend us in any future attempt to effect a change—and what method would be most agreeable to his majesty. But in the present mode of proceeding we have acted with great zeal, I grant—but we are quite ignorant what the event will be, and whether the censures bestowed on the proprietors, may not be thought in *Great Britain* to be aimed through *them*, at the king. In short, we embark in an enterprize of the highest importance; and then look about us to see how it may be carried on. Instead of wandring through a storm in the dark, with so sacred a charge in our custody—I thought it would have been better to have waited, 'till the tempest was a little abated—or, at least, to have procured some *light* to guide us through the surrounding dangers.

I shall now consider the *manner* in which the present attempt to change our government is made.

Mr. *Galloway* makes this general objection with great warmth to my arguments, "that they are conjectural and "suppositious."

His resentment was to be expected. How absurd must

* The late speaker.

the language of *diffidence* appear to one, who never doubted—the force of his own sagacity? To one who, castigated, but not convinced, by a discovery of his *re-peated errors*, still dares to decide positively in things he does not understand—and drives boldly through *public affairs*, like a *magnanimous bug** through the blaze that has so often scorcht its wings—how contemptible in *his* eyes, must be the man, who modestly [17] pursues a train of enquiry, on the unformed events of futurity—and in his researches after truth, admits a possibility of her escaping him?

Mr. *Galloway*, with a spirit of divination, *unassisted by the common modes of reasoning*—penetrates into the region of contingencies—and fixes with *infallible confidence*, the uncertainties of the times to come,—Far different was the method, which the humble subject of his wrath and reproaches found it proper to pursue. Filled with anxious fears for the welfare of his country—*hesitating and apprehensive*,—it was his endeavour to form a † judgment of things that may *hereafter* happen, from an attentive consideration of *present circumstances* and *past transactions*— the only methods to be practised by those whose disquisitions are not aided by such "‡ active blood" as Mr. *Galloway's* to whom hesitation appears ridiculous, and apprehension absurd! And no wonder—for if any mistake is committed, all the injury that follows, is—only the trifling loss of the PRIVILEGES OF PENNSYLVANIA.

But though Mr. *Galloway* pierces through *futurity* with

---

* "Yet let me flap this *bug* with *mealy wings*." Pope.

† It is somewhat remarkable, that Mr. *Galloway* should with anger make an objection to my arguments, that must in the opinion of every person but himself, operate with equal force against his own. Are not his arguments "conjectural and suppositious?" What proof is there, that any thing will be determined, according to his presumptions and and guesses?

‡ Pretended speech, page 44.

such superior intuition, yet he is subject to a mere mortal frailty in considering *present* things.   Hence he *confounds* those arguments I used with respect to the *manner* of attempting a change of our government, with the arguments I offered concerning the *time*, and does not seem sensible of his mistake.

By way of explanation and introduction to what I said on the *manner* of this attempt, it was *premised*—that [18] some event, arising from the circumstances of the proprietary family, or an act of the crown, might hereafter present us with a more *happy method* of vindicating our rights and privileges than the present.   Upon this Mr. *Galloway* very *gravely* runs into a calculation of the lives of the proprietors and their families—and proves *to his own satisfaction*, that their descendants * *"even they, and every of them"* will always be wicked and cunning.   One virtue, however, he must allow them, to take off the force of my observation—and that is—*a most uncommon harmony among themselves.*   Yet, after spending four pages on this curious digression, Mr. *Galloway* himself must grant—that some *act* of the crown, or a *multitude* of proprietors (as it happened in *Carolina*), or a *dissention* between them, tho' few, will be such a circumstance as will produce the conjuncture I mentioned.   But I will waive these probabilities.   I will indulge Mr. *Galloway* so far as to suppose they are too uncertain or remote to be expected or regarded.   What will this concession prove? That none of those occurrences will afford a favourable mode of making the attempt.   But does it prove the present mode to be a good one? or that any necessity is so urgent as to force us to make use of it, tho' a bad one. By no means!   If I should see a man about to pass a

---

* Pretended Speech, pa. 15, line 18.   "They and every of them" a strong and beautiful expression frequently occurring in *Jacob's law dictionary*, and in any book of *precedents*.

broad, deep* river, over which I had reason to think he
could not swim, would it be an unwise or an unkind act
in me to advise him to walk along the bank, and endeavour to find a bridge, or a narrower or shallower place
—tho' I had no certainty that there was such a bridge
or such a place? Or would this be acknowledging that he
was under a *necessity* of passing the river? My advice
would at least have a *chance* of saving him, and could
do him no harm—for, after being disappointed in his
search, he might return to [19] the spot where I found
him—and *would be at liberty to drown himself at last.*

Mr. *Galloway* mixes all points so confusedly together,
that he not only leads himself into a variety of errors, but
renders it very difficult for another, in answering, to reduce into any order what he has so loosely scattered about.
This I shall, however, endeavour to do.

Had he attended to the objections against the *manner*
of the present attempt, he might have perceived that
they were *three.* The first was—that the circumstances
attending this proceeding might cause others to attribute
it to such passions as are always disgraceful to public
councils and destructive to the honor and welfare of a
people. It certainly will be admitted that all reproaches
of this kind ought to be carefully guarded against—especially by a *dependent colony*, whose conduct has been
frequently and severely reprehended.

Mr. *Galloway*, however, usurps, in his private room,
among his chairs and tables, the *absurd license* of railing
at me on this occasion for speaking my sentiments with
freedom—tho' I spoke in a public council—as the representative of a free people—on a subject in which their reputation and happiness were intimately concerned. Any man
who thinks, will instantly perceive—that it was my *duty*

*Pretended speech, pa. 14.

to mention everything that I apprehended would tend to secure these blessings. When the assembly was deliberating on a step that seemed to me likely to bring discredit and loss upon us, would it have become me to have suppressed my opinion? No! But it would have pleased Mr. *Galloway* and some others—

Great reward for having been a villain!

I SAID—''Our messages to the governor and our re-''solves would discover the *true cause* of the present [20] ''attempt ''—Mr. *Galloway* grants it; and appeals to those resolves for my confusion. How is this charge supported? Why, the resolves mention—''public houses—commissions to judges during pleasure—and the great danger of a military force in a proprietary government'' as grievances. In like manner they mention the point lately controverted. Very well! The *contents* of the resolves are *now proved*—But there still remains one point slipped over in silence—*Why* were these resolves *now* made? The increase of public houses had frequently been complained of before.—Commissions during good behaviour have always been wished for.—The establishment of a military force has been often attempted in the midst of war, when it was vastly more necessary than at this time.—But never 'till *now* has there been an attempt to change the government. More observations I think unnecessary. Impartial persons who read the messages and resolves—and consider *some other circumstances* generally known—will be able to discover the TRUE CAUSE of the present attempt—and to judge whether it may be justly attributed to passion of *any kind.* If his majesty and his ministers, whose present opinion of us is allowed to be extremely unfavorable, should be induced by our late behaviour to think us a rash, turbulent people—it will be a misfortune to be deplored by all lovers of their country.

The second objection against the *manner* of proceeding,

was the *inconsistency* in which we should be involved.
This inconsistency is twofold.   In the first place, our dissention with the governor, and this extraordinary attempt
in consequence of it, may be thought by the king and the
ministry to have arisen on a matter already determined by
the crown.   Hence our *unwillingness* to comply with the
royal pleasure, signifyed to us on this head may be called
a very *improper foundation* of a re-[21]quest "to be more
immediately subjected to the royal pleasure."   But this
objection is easily obviated by *supposing* that the king and
ministry will exactly agree with the assembly in constru-
ing the controverted stipulation.   I sincerely hope they
may; as our construction appears to me extremely reasonable and equitable.   But, of this agreement in sentiments
I desired to have some proof before we proceeded any
further.   We have frequently been disappointed in our
warmest expectations.   In public as well as in private life,
he that never doubts, will often be wrong.

In this second place—there appeared to me an *inconsistency*, in requesting a change of government from the
king—and yet insisting on the preservation of privileges
derogatory of the royal rights.

We certainly prefer in our minds one of these things to
the other.—Either to continue as we are—or to change,
tho' we lose our privileges.   If his majesty will not accept of the government in the same state in which it has
been held by the proprietors, what shall be our choice?
I don't imagine that even Mr. *Galloway*, tho' he ven-
tures to say * "We have no cause to dread a change if
all my fears should prove realities," will dare to propose
a direct renunciation of our rights.   Trifling as *he* seems
to think them—willing as *he* is to expose them to hazard on guesses and surmises—they are yet held in too

* Pretended speech, pa. 21.

much veneration by the good people of *Pennsylvania*—
for him to *declare* his *contempt* of them. If then his
majesty shall be so "*unreasonable*" as to insist upon exercising his authority, in case of a change, as fully in this
province as in any other under his immediate government.
—and we insist that he shall not; the bargain breaks
off—"and the worst consequence is (according to Mr.
Galloway) [22] that we must then remain (as I would have
us remain) in our present situation." A much worse consequence, in my opinion, will follow. May we not *again*
be reproached with *double dealing* and *deceit?*—The assembly's petition to the crown draws a high coloured picture of our present distresses.—But let me suppose Mr.
Galloway deputed to plead the public cause—an office
which I have some reason to think would, by no means,
be disagreeable to him!—*"*If the royal ear is not deaf*
"*—if it will hear*"—these are the pleasing—the descrip-
tive—and convincing strains, in which "that Ear" will
be addressed.

Most gracious sovereign! "The rights of the people of
"*Pennsylvania*—† *the most scandalous and corrupt of all*
"*your subjects*—‡ are fading and expiring under the bale-
"ful influence of proprietary ambition and power—§ our
"liberties are daily consuming before them — ‖ our
"privileges are *swallowed up* and sacrificed at the *shrine*
"of proprietary instructions and the measures of power—

---

* A beautiful and striking repetition in the pretended speech, pa. 11.

† Id., pa. 19, at the bottom.—This expression is strictly agreeable
to Mr. *Galloway's* argument.—For if the corruption of the people in
this province is one reason of his desiring a change, he must say we are
more corrupt than his majesty's subjects in the rest of his dominions;
otherwise we request a government under which the people are as bad as
ourselves ; and, therefore, the change can be no service to us.

‡ Pretended speech, pa. 4, line 4.

§ Id., pa. 41, 6 lines from the bottom.   ‖ Id., pa. 30, line 6.

"*they are now but ideal shadows and chimerical no-
"tions—†indeed our *liberties are lost*—and ‡we shall
"soon be reduced to the servile condition of the par-
"liament *of* Paris, or of the worst *of* slaves of the most
"absolute monarch.—§ The fever of ambition and ar-
"bitrary power is raging with unremitting violence in
"the *foul* and *active blood*, WITH MANY OTHER PARTS Of
"our *political institution*, so that its *conduct* and *beha-* [23]
"*viour* ‖ is not *animated* and *directed* as THEY ought
"to be.   The *effect* thereof has *nearly* destroyed the
"powers of LIFE and *living* motion, and nature is *no*
"*longer* capable of struggling for relief.   We, therefore,
"pray your majesty that you and the ¶virtuous minister
"on whom you much rely will make **WEAPONS out of
"the *old contract* between the crown and our first pro-
"prietor—out of the *opinion* of some very great men,
"your servants—and out of the *quit rents* in the lower
"counties, to be used for the restoration of our liberties
"—under ††*which circumstances* it will be the highest
"*presumption* to oppose the *resumption* of the nomina-
"tion *of* the governor *of* this province, which is all the
"change we intend you shall make.—Proprietary in-
"structions, *with which your majesty is well acquainted*,
"and private interest have imposed ‡‡*thraldom* and *bond-*
"*age* upon us.   §§ The stream of justice is not only be-
"come *turbid* but *thick*, so that it can no longer *discharge*
"*its duty*.   Security of life and estate is become an empty
"name, and the *spirit* of liberty, distrest, *and worn out* by
"ineffectual efforts for her preservation, is *verging* fast to

* Pretended speech.   † Id., pa. 19, line 11, and pa. 18, line 5.
‡ Id., pa. 19 and 29.   ⸸ Id., pa. 44, passim.
‖ Id., pa. 43, line 12, from the bottom—id., pa. 29, last line.
¶ Id., pa. 8.   ** Id., pa. 43, throughout—and two lines of pa. 44.
†† Id., pa. 43, 3d line from the bottom.
‡‡ Id., pa. 44, line 4.   §§ Id., ib., passim.

"a *dissolution.* Nothing but a medicine administered *to* "*this spirit* by your royal hands can possibly revive or "restore her. This medicine we now attempt to obtain "before the MIDNIGHT GLOOM approaches and FATAL "DEATH puts an end to our struggles." When his majesty shall be so happy as to hear this eloquent address, how much must his *pity* be excited! If he understands it, and shall be pleased to express his willingness to take us under his immediate care and protection, in the *same manner* with the rest of his subjects—how must he be surprised at our refusing, or even hesitating to accept [24] that which we have so warmly requested—unless particular points are granted to us? How must he be *astonished* to find that we are more afraid of being placed upon a footing with other *Englishmen* under his dominion, than of the * MIDNIGHT GLOOM and FATAL DEATH which are hastening to overtake us? With what justice may his gracious majesty tell us, "that we have endeavoured to impose on him, by representing ourselves as an oppressed, miserable people, standing on the brink of destruction; when, upon his hearing our cries for assistance and safety, —mercifully stretching out his hand to relieve us, and offering us to partake of the *same happiness* enjoyed by the rest of his subjects, we reject his *implored protection*— and thereby prove the falsehood and absurdity of our pretences?"

Thus, by *requesting a change*, we lay ourselves under the inevitable necessity, either of quietly giving up our rights and privileges, in order to maintain a *consistency* in our conduct; or of incurring the severe censure above mentioned—unless the king will be so *good natur'd*, in consideration of the *infinite pains* we have taken to recom-

---

* *Quære*—What Mr. *Galloway* means by "midnight gloom?" "And what is a death not fatal?"—As he makes a distinction between "fatal death" and some other "death."—

mend ourselves to his favor—as to be contented with the *same share of power* in this province; which his two subjects *Thomas* and *Richard Penn* now have.

My third objection against the *manner* of the present attempt to alter our government was—"that it might be "deemed in *Great Britain* a surrender of our charter—or "at least a sufficient foundation for the parliament's pro-"ceeding to form a new constitution for us."—[25]

No person can *surrender* what he has not. This term, therefore, when applied to the people of *Pennsylvania*, means a giving up of the peculiar rights derived to *them*, under their charter.

They can not surrender what belongs to others—and therefore *their* act can not take away the rights of the proprietors. But should the proprietors, enraged at our behaviour, and fatigued with disputes, make their own terms with the crown, and give up the royal charter—then the *surrender* may be said to be compleated.

Mr. *Galloway* says,—the petitions can not be thought in any manner to surrender our privileges—because "they "*request* the enjoyment of those privileges." But, if it be considered, that to procure peace and safety, is the design of forming societies, and of establishing governments—and that these petitions expressly declare . . . * "there "is no peace and safety among us, and that we have "no hopes of either being restored but by the change for "which we pray." Certainly, if we are thought to be in our senses, it will be concluded that we intend to *surrender intirely* a government, which does not answer the ends of government—even tho' we should be deprived of *some agreeable things* tacked to it—For who but a *Bedlamite* would shiver in a thin silk coat, in the midst of winter, only because it had a fine lace upon it?—

* Pretended speech, pa. 18, 36, et alibi.

It may seem therefore a reasonable construction of these petitions to understand them in this sense—"that the "petitioners will be much obliged to his majesty, if he "will be so good as to put the lace on warmer coats for them "—but, if he will not condescend to do that, he may keep "the lace for his trouble—provided he will furnish them "coats of good *English broad cloth.*" [26]

Let it however be supposed—that our petitions, with a resignation of the charter by the proprietors can not be called a *surrender* of our privileges, in strictness of law —and that the matter comes to be settled by the parliament.

Here Mr. *Galloway* launches out on a flood of words. —Here he overwhelms me with his "*irrefragable demonstration* "—* "Will the king, lords and commons (says he) "be the dupes of the ministry; and, without considera- "tion—† without the least reason, in an instant pass a law "—*to blast our liberties*—to ‡*take away our rights*, and "§*deprive an affectionate people of new privileges?*" ‖Will they act so black—so base so unjust a—part?

INCONSISTENCY! that would be astonishing in any man, but him who is the author of it!

How can the king and parliament be *unjust*, in saving us from *midnight gloom* and *fatal death?* How can they blast those liberties "*which are ¶already lost?*"—Take away our rights, when **security of life and estate is now become an empty name among us?* "Or deprive us of "our privileges, ††*which are long since swallowed up and "sacrificed at the shrine of proprietary instructions, and the "measures of power*, and so turn'd into *ideal shadows?*"

* Pretended speech—pa. 23.   † Id. pa. 24.
‡ Id. pa. 22.   7th line from the bottom.
§ Id. pa. 21.   4th line from the bottom.
‖ Id. pa. 25.   ¶ Id. pa. 19, line 11, pa. 18, line 5.
** Id. pa. 44.   †† Id. pa. 30.

Cunning and cruel king! to *strip* thy subjects of that which they *have not.** "Look history through," it cannot furnish an instance of such royal craft and unkindness, except that recorded by Sir *Richard Blackmore*, of an ancestor of prince *Voltiger.*[27]

> *A painted vest prince* Voltiger *had on,*
> *Which from a naked Pict, his grandsire won.*

I will not pursue this point any farther. I will suppose in Mr. *Galloway's* favour, that what he calls his speech was so long, and took so much time in making, that he forgot in forming one part, what he had written in another.

To attend him still farther in his political rambles, for some respect is due, to be sure, to † "one of the happy instruments of relieving his country," and its ‡ "long supporter," I will grant out of *complaisance* to him, in order to give his argument its *fullest force*, that he has told a great many *falsehoods*—that we are not in the deplorable condition *he* has represented us—and that our liberties, rights and privileges which he has taken so much pains to blast, are still fresh and flourishing.

Why then (says he) it will be unjust in the king and parliament to deprive us of them ; and we have § "irrefragable proofs" of the justice of the house of commons, *because* in the years 1718 and 1748, they would not pass an act to give royal instructions the force of laws in *America.*

Thus he concludes, that because the house of commons would not make the king *absolute monarch* of *North America*, which would have been injurious to the rights

---

* A fine expression in pretended speech pa. 9, line 1.

† Pretended speech, pa. 27.

‡ D. pa. 2. Quære, If this term is applicable to Mr. *Galloway*, who is a *short* man ?

§ Id. pa. 26.

of *Great Britain*—THEREFORE, they will not allow him to exercise in *one province* that authority, which he exercises in every other part of his dominions.——*Truly*, an uncommon, but not a very syllogistical method, of arguing! [28]

Let Mr. *Galloway*, when he shall be employed in "supporting the expiring liberties of his country," step into the *British* senate—and endeavour to convince *them* of this injustice.

When he has made a *speech* for this purpose, suppose some unconverted member should thus address him.— "Sir, we are perfectly satisfied in *what rank* we are to place your abilities—the "*proofs* are *irrefragable*"—but as to the point you have insisted on, you do not seem to express yourself with *clearness.* You speak of an *impelling necessity* to come under the king's immediate government,"—and yet you say it will be "unjust to bring you under it, on the same conditious with his other subjects." I should, therefore be glad to have a short, plain answer to this question.—*Are the inhabitants of Pennsylvania more or less happy than the inhabitants of the royal governments?*"

How will our deputy extricate himself from this dilemma? If we are more happy, *why* do we *desire* a change—or why does Mr. *Galloway* talk of the "expiring liberties of his country?" If we are less happy— *why* do we *dread* it? Why are we unwilling to become in *every respect* like those who are happier than ourselves? Or where is the *injustice* of placing us in the same situation.

Before I quit this point, I must make one observation more, to shew by Mr. *Galloway's* contradiction of himself (though I am almost tired with taking notice of his contradictions) that notwithstanding the rage with which he has asserted the contrary—he really thinks our privileges will be indangered, if the parliament should take the change of our government into their consideration. [29]

He employs many pages to prove there is *no danger*, tho' the affair should come before the parliament.—Yet, speaking of a change in the case of an infant proprietor, he says—* "Is it to be by a *parliamentary enquiry*, and an act of the *British legislature*, in consequence of such enquiry? If *it is*, the *rights* of the *people* may be *involved* in the *enquiry*, which the *mode intended* by the house is *calculated* to avoid. *Hence* it appears, that this period of all others, will be attended with most difficulty to the crown, and *danger* to our *privileges*."

Thus he acknowledges, that the house of assembly, in making the present attempt, have endeavoured to avoid a parliamentary enquiry, *because* the *rights* of the *people* would be *involved* in it, to the *danger* of our *privileges*.—

Upon the whole that has been said with regard to a change—and the *safety* or the *danger* of the measure I thus conclude.

If it *cannot* be accomplished—the *manner* in which it has been attempted will load this province with new disgrace. If it *is* accomplished, we are utterly ignorant *how* it will be. The fate of our privileges, and the great points controverted between us and the proprietors, are now to be *everlastingly* determined. Many unhappy circumstances attend us in the enterprize.

HERE then I fix the argument. On *this point* I rely. Whatsoever may be the force of the reasonings on either side—however probable or improbable the success may be —yet after placing everything in the strongest light against myself—*it must be granted*—that the event is *undoubtedly uncertain*—and that the persons desiring a change know *no more*, what [30] will be the consequences—than they know what will be the figure of next year's clouds.

* Pretended speech, pa. 16.

A measure in which the happiness of so many thousands is involved, ought not therefore to have been pursued in so hasty and unguarded a manner. *Precautions* should have been taken. *Securities* should have been obtained. This was—this is—*my firm opinion*—and should a change be happily obtained, without injuring a single privilege, or settling a single point against us—should the conduct of the assembly and the people in this affair be *intirely approved* by his majesty and his ministers—I shall always *rejoice*—that I was not concerned in exposing the *inestimable interests* of my country to HAZARD.

I proceed to other points. Mr. *Galloway* takes great pains to prove that the * "representatives of a people have a right to change the constitution without the [31] consent of the people," *because* "almost every government in the civilized world has been changed"—*by force and injustice:*

* " It can never be thought that the people intrust any representatives with their capital privileges farther than to use their best skill to secure and maintain them. They never so delegated or impowered any men, that *de jure* they could deprive them of that qualification ; and *a facto ad jus non valet argumentum :* For the question is not, what may be done ? But what ought to be done ? Overseers and stewards are impowered, not to alienate, but preserve and improve other men's inheritances. No owners deliver their ship and goods into any man's hands to give them away, or run upon a rock ; neither do they consign their affairs to agents or factors without limitation : All trusts suppose such a fundamental right in them that give them, and for whom the trusts are, as is altogether indissolvable by the trustees. The trust is, the liberty and property of the people ; the limitation is, that it should not be invaded, but be inviolably preserved, according to the law of the land."—WILLIAM PENN'S works, I. vol., pa. 682, &c.

When *Henry* the *Fourth of France* and his minister, the duke of *Sully,* formed the glorious and benevolent scheme of giving peace and happiness to *Europe* by reducing it into a kind of great commonwealth, which was to be effected by *changing the government of several states ;* such was their regard to the first principles of justice and the rights of mankind that it was determined, that no step should be taken *without carefully and deliberately consulting the people of the several nations,* who would be affected by their measures.—Sully's Memoirs, V. vol

Because "the revolution was brought about"—*with such universal consent, that King William was established on the British throne, without fighting a battle:* Because "the first frame of our government was altered"—*being found impracticable, and that its* *privileges could scarcely be exercised or enjoyed:*" *Because* "six parts in seven of the assembly, have a right to alter the charter," *by a law with the Governor's assent:* Because he dignifies himself and those who join with him with the title of "long supporters and lovers of their country"—and charges *with great truth, to be sure, all who differ in opinion from them* "*with being the friends of arbitrary power?*"

In the *same striking* method of arguing, he attempts to prove—*that* the petition for a change ought not to alarm a free people, *because*, "though it calls for a military es-"tablishment among us," yet this is only shewing our desire, that a military force *may* be fixed, which, "already "is fixed:" Or in other words, it is only discovering our *hearty approbation* of a *disagreeable measure* "—*that*" † a military establishment is already *established* (to use his own words) *because* there are *some* soldiers in garrison at our advanced forts—for *these* he certainly means by "the military establishment already established," or nothing—*that* a military force in a *dependant colony*, lodged in the hands of the *king*, is *less dangerous* to liberty, than in the hands of a *subject*—*that* it is the strongest evidence of the *prudence* and *public spirit* of *such* a *colony*, to represent themselves as a sett of *ruffians* among whom there is no safety for men of virtue, nor any respect for government, but all things are involved in *anarchy*—and therefore humbly to [32] pray, that his majesty will be pleased to send over some regiments to instruct them in the *gentle lessons* of *duty* and *obedience*—*that* this will not

* Pretended speech, pa. 33.

† Pretended speech, pa. 40, lines 7, 8.

furnish a pretence to send over *more regiments*, than are desired—nor to make us *pay* for these blessings *of swords and bayonets*, which we have *requested*—or if these inconveniences should follow,—*that* they will be greatly overballanced by the advantages of the civil war that would probably ensue, if these troops should be employed, as Mr. *Galloway* would wish them to be.

These are his arguments, and the tendency of them, on these points. Arguments!—Yielding such ample room for the entertainment of the public, that I hope some gentleman who has more leisure than I have, will divert the world with the strictures upon them they deserve. I pass on to matters, in which I am more particularly concerned —I mean to answer those charges, which Mr. *Galloway* has made against me.

The first of these, is "that my late conduct has been in-
"fluenced by a restless thirst after promotion; a fondness
"to serve the purposes of power from an expectation of
"being rewarded with posts of honour and profit."

In answering such a charge as this Mr. *Galloway* might perhaps have some advantage over *me*.

'Tis true, I cannot boast of being *a "long supporter of the rights of the people," since it is but lately that my youth has been favoured with any public marks of their approbation. I have not heated the minds of men with inflamatory harangues—and while they have been weakly wondering at my public [33] spirit, found myself *rewarded in gold* for the breath I have wasted. I have not *every year* since I have been a representative given myself an *office of profit*—so far from it that I have not taken *even a single farthing* for my wages during the whole time I have been in the Assembly, nor in my whole life touched a mite of public money. I have not enriched myself with a *most lucrative post*, torn from the *old age* of a worthy man,

* That is, in Mr. *Galloway's* sense of this expression.

who was grey-headed long before my birth. I have not, while the * " *shop* was open for the sale of laws, and good substantial purchases might have been made "—wasted the public wealth, in buying at an exorbitant price, those that would not last a *twelve month.* I have not *lined* my pockets, and the pockets of all my dependants, with the spoils of my country, infamously plundered in *vile jobs,* while with unbounded confidence she trusted her stores to my faith. I have not bought with the public money *commissions of judges* in all the courts where I practice for *my most intimate friends.* I have not attempted to abolish that sacred right of *englishmen,* the right of trial by a jury. I have not *juggled in dirty cabals,* about the offices of *chief justice* and *attorney general*—with *competent salaries to be annexed to them.* I have not taken raw councils in *taverns,* for regulating the conduct of *Pennsylvania.* In short, I have not in all my *public conduct* had an eye to my *private emolument*—and, therefore, I have not the consolation to reflect, that I found this province in credit, and that, while I have been *druming—merely for her good, as I pretended—my* interests have † *advanced* as *her* interests have *declin'd,* [34] and that I am now possest, *by my popularity alone,* of a considerable estate, while *she* is sunk into disgrace.

I cannot boast indeed of such exploits as these—and I sincerely pray, that my mind may be never tainted with the base ambition of rising by *sordid practices.* No digni-

* Preface to pretended speech, pa. 4, line 13.

† This was the fate of unhappy *Athens;* which saw her pretended patriots thriving in proportion to her misfortunes.

"Cast your eyes, I beseech you, upon those men, to whom you owe these rare monuments of their administration. Some of them were raised from poverty to affluence, others from obscurity to splendor ; some have built magnificent houses, others have acquired large tracts of valuable lands ; and the lower the fortune of the state has fallen, the higher has that of much people risen."—*Demosthenes* in the second *Olynthian.*

ties can adorn his character, who has attained them by *meanness.*

With *equal scorn* do I behold him, who endeavours to recommend himself, either to *men of power*, or to the *public*, by flattering their passions or errors, and by forfeiting his honor and integrity.

The good man who is guided through life by his conscience and reason, may in *particular instances*, offend even honest and wise men—but his *virtue* will naturally produce an *uniformity* in his conduct *upon the whole*, that will discover his probity, and procure him the general approbation of the worthy.

These sentiments perhaps may prove destructive to one, who designs to establish his reputation and felicity on the basis of a party—*since it is highly improb-[35]able, *that*

* This sentiment is so strongly confirm'd by a beautiful passage in SULLY's memoirs, that is is hoped the inserting it will afford pleasure to every one who reads it.

The duke of SULLY being a *Protestant*, was appointed by his master, *Henry* the *fourth* of *France*, to preside in a general assembly of the *Protestants*, which was called to meet at *Chatellerant.* . . . The duke was *their faithful friend* through his whole life, and strictly attached to them by *principle;* but the warmth of their temper led them in to many things, *in this assembly*, in which he could not join with them . . . without offering violence to his own sentiments . . . and integrity . . .

The following is the account he gives of his conduct. " A *common* "*prejudice* prevails among all sorts of religion ; a man is never supposed "to be a *sincere professor* of the one he has embraced, unless he supports "it *obstinately*, even in *such points* where it is most *visibly wrong.*"

The same remark may perhaps be found true in all parties. "Upon "this footing, I confess, the method I was determined to pursue, might "from *some persons*, draw upon me the epithets of *false brother, deserter*, "and if they please, *traytor* : However, it was not the approbation of "*such as those*, that I proposed to obtain, but of persons, who *of what-* "*ever party or religion they were*, would in their judgment of *my con-* "*duct*, preserve the ballance of *equity and disinterestedness*. If ever re- "*ligion* admits of the assistance of *policy*, it ought to be of a policy *pure*, "*simple*, and *upright* as *itself;* any other may indeed *appear* to *serve* it, "but does not in *reality*, and sooner or later *never fails to ruin it.*"

" Having determin'd to be guided by *no other principle* in my transac-

any man will be long esteemed by a party, unless he is bound to it by PREJUDICES, *as well as by* PRINCIPLES.

To support the attrocious charge he has made against me, Mr. *Galloway* produces no kind of proof—except my differing in opinion from him, be proof. But if this be admitted, then Mr. *Norris*, Mr. *Richardson* and the two other gentlemen who differed from him, are villains also, influenced by the same views, attributed to me.

This would be too daring a charge, and more difficult perhaps for Mr. *Galloway* to support, than to crush by *calumnies* and *conspiracies*, a young man, who has excited more than one passion in more than one man's breast.

Had I intended to recommend myself to the government, I certainly might have given the sentiments I [36] delivered in the House a more courtier-like air than they now bear. Had I intended this, I should not have been one of the *first* and *warmest* to declare my *fixed resolution*, not to admit of the governor's construction of the stipulation he disputed with us; nor should I have steadily persisted in this opposition *to the last.*

Had I intended this, I should not have been the *only man* in the House who *constantly refused* to assent to the supply bill, *because* the money emitted by it, was made a legal tender in payment of all demands "except proprie-

"tions with the *assembly*, I thought I could not too carefully avoid all "appearances of affectation or disguise in my conduct; that those who "were influenced by an *imprudent zeal*, or actuated by a *spirit of cabal* "might have no hopes of *gaining* or *seducing* me: Therefore from the "beginning, I shewed myself solicitous to support on this occasion, THAT "CHARACTER by which the *public* was to know *how I would act on every* "*other;* that is, of a man sincerely attached to the *true principles and in-* "*terest of the protestant religion*, yet incapable of drawing the *false conse-* "*quences* which many of the protestants did, or of approving their *ir-* "*regular proceedings:* The *speech* I made at the opening of the *assembly*, "which lasted *half an hour*, was wholly *calculated* to produce *this effect*, "without troubling myself to consider, whether it would give pleasure or "offence to the greatest number."—SULLY's Memoirs, 4 Vol.

tary rents,"—when *that exception* might have been safely extended (as was granted by the most distinguished members) to the *rents of all other persons*—who would then have been *as well* secured as the proprietors, and a distinction in their favour alone avoided.

One thing more I beg leave to mention, since Mr. *Galloway* compels me to speak of myself. I was appointed to carry the bill to the governor the second time for his assent, after he had once refused it. This was long before the change of government was talked of. On my delivering it, some conversation arose between us on the subject, Mr. *Shippen*, the secretary, being present. As the passage of the bill was of the utmost importance to his majesty's service and the good of the public, I took the liberty, though my acquaintance with the governor was very slight, of mentioning several reasons to prove that the assembly's construction of the disputed stipulation was extremely equitable; consistent with the established rules of explaining a sentence capable of two meanings; and, therefore, ought to be admitted—and that his honour's conduct in passing the bill, as it then was framed, would not be disapproved of in *England.* I further added, that I was persuaded his refusal would throw everything into the greatest confusion [37].

Being soon after taken ill and confined to my room, so anxious was I to prevent any difference at that time between the governor and assembly that I sent for a gentleman, whom I knew to be intimately acquainted with the governor; and urging everything I could think of to convince him that our bill ought to be passed as we had formed it, I entreated him to go to the governor, and endeavour to prevail on him to give his assent.

I hope *this* cannot be called the conduct of a man influenced by "mischievous passions destructive of public liberty."

Another charge brought against me by Mr. *Galloway* is, that I neglected my duty of attending in the House, and never spoke my sentiments till it was too late.

Mr. *Galloway's* behaviour in making this charge, is a plain proof *to what lengths* he will proceed, in hopes of injuring *me*. The first time, since I have been a representative of this province, that a change of government was mentioned and debated in the assembly, was on Saturday the 24th day of March last, on the governor sending down to them his message absolutely refusing to pass the supply bill, unless the stipulation was literally complied with. *That day*, the assembly's answer was composed and sent—the frequent motions, with the "solemn debate" Mr. *Galloway* talks of, made—the resolves past—and the House adjourned to the 14th of May.

Mr. *Galloway must be conscious* that this day, and the day before, I was confined to my chamber, and mostly to my bed, by a sincere attack of the fever and ague. He knows, that on the *Thursday* before, I was so ill, that there not being a sufficient number of members [38] without *me*, those who were met, intended to come and sit at my house; and that to save the gentlemen this trouble, I determined to wait on *them*, and was carried up in the late speaker's chariot, which he was so kind as to send for me, it being a rainy day.

This state of my health at that time, being a fact well known to many persons, and particularly to Mr. *Galloway*, how *cruel* and *unjust* is it to blame me for not attending, when it was impossible—and when, if it had been possible, *I had not the least suspicion* that anything of such vast importance would come into consideration.

On the meeting of the House, the 14th day of last *May*, according to their adjournment, I constantly attended *every day*, untill this important matter was determined, except on *Monday*, the 21st—on which day there was no

House, only eighteen members meeting, Mr. *Galloway* and many others being absent. The following days the petition for a change came in—were read—as other petitions were —lay on the table—and not a word spoken on the subject.

Thus business went on till *Wednesday,* the 23d, when I was prevented *for the first time* from attending the House by a fever—which, as it was very injurious to my health, would also, if Mr. *Galloway's* charitable and humane wishes could prevail, prove destructive to my reputation. *This day* the matter was *started. In vain* did the speaker recommend the deferring to take any resolution till the House was more full—and the absent members, *then in town,* could attend.—He desired that the affair might be put off *to the next day—in vain*—the debate was begun— quickly determined—a committee appointed to prepare a draught of the petition—that draught made—brought in— presented—read— [39]

The next day, tho' still extremely indisposed, I attended —and was surprised to find so much business *of the utmost consequence* had been done in so short a time—and though I could have wished that *such a step* had not been taken, without allowing me, and every other member, *of whose attendance there was any probability,* an opportunity of of- fering our sentiments; yet I comforted myself with reflect- ing, that though it had been resolved, "that a petition "should be drawn," yet it was not resolved "that any peti- "tion should be presented," and that I should be at liberty to offer my opinion hereafter. I was determined therefore to attend diligently; and to take the *first opportunity,* which would be on the second reading of the petition, to oppose it. This I was induced to do, by considering, that if I did not say any thing, till the question was put for *transcribing,* or *signing* in order to be presented, it would look very odd for me to be silent so long, and that it would answer no purpose.

Accordingly, on the second reading of the petition, which was the *first opportunity I ever had*, since the change of government was attempted, I spoke against it.

The only objection *then* made by Mr. *Galloway* and every other member who spoke on the occasion, was—that I had offered my sentiments *too soon* to the House—and that I should have *staid* for the question to *transcribe* or *sign* the petition.

That I did not act with any stupid and useless reserve in lying by till this time, was never dreampt of by any member who knew, *why* I had been detained at home, whenever I *was* detained.

How vain is his attempt who strives to please *all men?* Or indeed to please one man *at all times?* Mr. *Galloway* [40] and *others* said, that I spoke *too soon.* He and some more *now* say, I spoke *too late.* Why too late? Were not my arguments as well understood *then*, and had they not the *same force*, as if they had been used before? And if they proved the measure to be *dangerous* and *improper*, ought they not *in a matter of such importance to the public*, to have been as much regarded, as if they were *one day older?*

If this affair had not been *so quickly decided*, I never should have been charged with omitting to speak in time. But I must not quit Mr. *Galloway.* What must the public think of a man who dares to abuse them by the grossest deceptions, with the pious intention of injuring another? He says "that during the time of the *several debates* respecting the change of government, I *seldom* attended, and was absent when the important one came on, which issued in the resolve, to adjourn and consult the people."

Yet the candid Mr. *Galloway* knows—that there never was any debate in the assembly, since I have been a member, respecting the change of government—until that which issued in the resolve to adjourn—and *that I was then ill.* Again he says, "at the next meeting, (meaning that in *May*) *several motions* were made to bring this resolution to an issue, and after *great deliberation*, it was resolved by a majority of 27 to 3, that a committee should be appointed to bring in the petition to his majesty to resume the powers of government.—But at none of these debates and resolutions was I present, tho' I well *knew*, or at least had great reason to *expect this business was in continual agitation.*"

Yet the correct Mr. *Galloway* knows, that there never was a motion—or debate—or resolution, concern-[41]ing this matter, upon the meeting of the house in *May*—untill *Wednesday* the 23d day of the month, when I was taken sick, as has been mentioned—and that *I attended as diligently as himself till that day.*

This account of the time when every transaction passed in the house—and of my attendance, is taken from the *minutes* of assembly, and the *book* for entring the attendance of the members—both which I have carefully looked over, in the presence of Dr. *Moore*, the clerk, who therefore is perfectly acquainted with the truth of every thing I have averred.

Another charge against me is, that "I formed my thoughts into order, and reduced what I had to say into writing, in an *unparliamentary* way."

I acknowledge myself guilty of taking some pains to put my thoughts into order, and that my notes were long and exact, that I might thereby be enabled to deliver my sentiments with clearness. I regarded this as a duty, upon an occasion where such an interesting subject was to be discussed—and I was *encouraged* to use *this mode* —because I once before had used it, and received such *public praises* from the present speaker, for introducing a method, highly commended, and the next day, imitated by him, as afforded me the sincerest pleasure—and I hope,

will* serve to console [42] me, ballancing the calumny
with which I am loaded, *because* I would not go THROUGH
with *measures*," which my conscience and reason commanded me to oppose.—A conduct! I am DETERMINED,
whatever "*moon*" shines on me or "*withdraws*" her
beams, upon all occasions, STEADILY TO PURSUE.—And
as its *own reward* is sufficient for *me*, I beg leave to
restore to the gentleman's "*brows*," from which it† *once
fell*, the "*laurel'd*" wreath, that *unenvied, unsought* and
unwished for by me, he has been pleased—*with what design* I will not presume to guess—to place upon *mine*.

Mr. *Galloway* also accuses me of having promised him a
copy of my speech, and of not performing my promise.
Here he is egregiously mistaken. I told him he should
have the copy that night it was delivered, *if I could get it
ready*. The house broke up late in the evening. He
soon after called upon me. It was not ready. He told me
it would be *too late*, if he had it not soon. I did not then
understand *his meaning*, as I did not in the least apprehend, the most important matter that ever came before the
house of assembly, was to be decided with less deliberation
than is generally bestowed on things of much slighter
moment. Next morning I took the copy to the House in

---

* Preface to pretended speech . . . pa. 25. "I would only advise him
"carefully to preserve the panegyricks with which the proprietary fac-
"tion have adorned him: In time, *they may serve to console him, by bal-
"ancing the calumny they shall load him with, when he does not go
"through with them in all their measures:* He will not probably do the
"one, and they will then assuredly do the other . . . There are mouths
"that can blow hot as well as cold, and blast on your *brows* the bays
"their hands have placed there . . . *Experto crede Roberto*. Let but
"the *moon* of proprietary favour *withdraw* its *shine* for a moment, and
"that great number of the principal gentlemen of *Philadelphia* who ap-
"plied to you for a copy of your speech, shall immediately despise and
"desert you" . . .

† Experto crete Roberto. Preface to pretended speech . . . pa. 25.

my pocket. No one called for it. I did the same in the afternoon. The like silence was observed. I did not chuse to shew any forwardness in forcing it on those who seemed willing to forget it. Had I acted otherwise, I should have been called impudent and conceited, by those who are fond of bestowing epithets.

Mr. *Galloway* says, "that I attempted to deliver my ob- jections against the measure *ore tenus;* but finding every thing I offered judiciously and sensibly refuted by several members, I was obliged to retreat [43] to my speech in writing, which after a short introductory apology, I read in a manner, not the most deliberate."

As to the last part of this whimsical charge, I shall not pretend to give any answer; because that would be in some measure allowing Mr. *Galloway* capable of judging, what is a "deliberate manner" of speaking.

As to the first part—any man but Mr. *Galloway* would have discovered *why* I began to speak, without recurring to my notes. The resolves were past—and the petition ordered to be drawn in my absence. I never had heard the change spoke of in the house—and did not know but by information of others, the reasons by which the mem- bers had been influenced. Before I offered my sentiments, it was therefore necessary for me to discover the arguments that would be used against me. On the information I had received, I had prepared my answer; but to make this answer appear with propriety, I thought it requisite to have the arguments of those who desired a change, repeated be- fore the house. I threw out general objections; and de- sired to know what reasons could be tho't sufficient to en- gage the house in so hazardous a measure? Then the "judicious and sensible members" Mr. *Galloway* men- tions, and he among them—for that phrase, I suppose, is his way of complimenting himself—discovered all the argu- ments on which they relied.—They proved to be the same

I expected; and I "retreated to my speech," which was prepared to answer them.

The last objection made by Mr. *Galloway*, of which I shall take notice, is, "that the speech, as printed, is different from that delivered—and that the preface sufficiently *demonstrates*, by whose hands it has been drest up, and with what views it has been published." [44]

Here he is again mistaken. The printed speech is exactly the same with that I pronounced, except the corrections and additions I made to compleat the sense, the evening before it was to be delivered to the Members, as is above mentioned—and except some slight alterations in a few places. *I futher declare*, that I have not received the least assistance from any person in composing and correcting it; not even so much as the addition of a single word; and that no man ever saw it, or knew that I had written it, except my clerk, who transcribed it—untill it was delivered in the House.

As to the preface, it makes no "*demonstration*" that can affect *me*. Finding that Mr. *Galloway* and his emissaries were traducing me in every company, and misrepresenting every thing I had said—I thought these aspersions might be removed, by laying before the public, the reasons by which I had been induced to act as I did. This consideration had the more weight with me, on receiving a letter from some gentlemen in this city, desiring a copy of the speech.

They being my constituents—and men of the clearest characters, I thought it my duty to comply with their request. I sent a copy to them—and they had it printed with such a title, and in such a manner, as they thought proper, *without even consulting me;* which could not conveniently be done as I was out of town.—For immediately after delivering the copy, I was obliged to go into the country for my health. I went to the *Jerseys*. While I was there, the preface was written, and printed. I never was made acquainted with its contents, till it was published. I do not even know at this time who wrote it, but by common report. [45]

Every thing I have said on these last heads, is known to be true, by my friends; whose virtue and good opinion I too much revere, to appeal to them as witnesses, if I was not conscious of the *sincerity* with which I speak.

Thus have I *faithfully* laid before the public, my whole conduct relating to the change of our government, and the reasons on which it was founded. If sensible and good men approve of my behaviour, I quit without regret the applauses of others, and all the attendant advantages, to those, who think proper to court them.

JOHN DICKINSON.

APPENDIX.

What sin of mine could merit such a fate?
That all the shot of dullness now must be
From this the BLUNDERBUSS discharg'd on me!
—*Pope.*

Weakness and ignorance when attended by modesty, are naturally entitled to pardon and to pity. But when they impudently pretend to the characters of wisdom and knowledge—when they aim at power, which they understand not how to exercise—and to honours, which they understand not how to deserve—when they make use of their *good fortune* in life to wound their country—insolently to *abuse* those, who *know* and *despise* them—and when with proud and solemn formality, they *demand* a respect by no means due to them—*then* they become the proper objects of *contempt* and *ridicule*, if not of *hatred.*

It is not my intention to trouble myself with observations, on Mr. *Galloway's* continual * breaches of the rules of grammar; his utter ignorance of the English [ii] language; the *pompous obscurity* and *sputtering prolixity* reigning through every part of his piece; and his innum-

---

* "But, Sir, let me ask, what public good, what service to our country can we do, when proprietary *instructions, and proprietary private interest* is to enslave our judgment, and to rule in our councils."
Pretended SPEECH, pa. 29, at the bottom.

"Besides, Sir, I have seen the opinions of some very great men, his majesty's servants, and often near his person, that the *powers* of government is an interest that cannot be transferred or aliened."
Pretended SPEECH, pa. 43.

erable and feeble * tautologies. *This labour would be too great.* I only intend to present to the public, stript of that *bundle of words* in which he has rolled them up, a small collection of his rhetorical flowers and figures. Sorry am I to say it—*flowers* without *fragrance*—and *figures* without *force*. Yet perhaps their *novelty* may recommend them.

Some authors have industriously endeavoured in their writings, to *surprize* their readers—and some readers have thought this a great merit in authors. With gentlemen of this taste, Mr. *Galloway* must be a darling writer—for no man ever possest so *surprizing* a way of *surprizing* his readers. A few instances will discover his excellence in this kind.

† "Let us but consider, says he, that the experience of ages, fully demonstrates *wealth* to be the parent of power, the *nurse* of influence : and that an increase of wealth, will as naturally *beget* an increase of power and influence, as an increase of velocity in the *falling stone* will produce more certain death."

In the third line of this simile, *wealth* is the *nurse* of influence—but in the fourth, this *nurse* is the *begetter* of influence—a transition somewhat sudden and odd—but it does not stop here—for ‡ three pages further, this *begetting nurse* is turned into a *weapon*, and put into the hands of its own child, INFLUENCE. What now, [iii] could a reader expect, that this wicked child, § "*improbus ille*

---

* "Pretended speech—passim—greatest wealth and most invaluable jewels—"bondage and thraldom"—"spending and wasting"—"fruitless and ineffectual"—"conduct and behaviour"—"such horrid guilt, such heinous offences"—"groundless fears and frightful apprehensions" —&c, &c, &c, &c.

† Pretended speech, pa. 10.

‡ Id., pa. 13, line 5 from the bottom.

§ Ovid.

puer," would do with the *nurse* that *begat* him, changed into a *weapon.*

Will he cut and destroy? No! With *that weapon*, he will—what will he do? * "En—crease our discredit, and the ministerial displeasure." What *vivacity* of invention? What *uncommonness* in the figure? What *strength* in the expression?

But this is not the only beauty of this curious simile. What *precision* is there in the expression of "*the falling stone?*" For what would an increase of velocity signify to any thing else but a "*stone?*" Or to any other stone but "*the fall—ing stone?*" Besides, how exactly has Mr. *Galloway* provided some unlucky *head* for this stone to fall upon, in order to produce "more certain death?"

Mr. *Galloway's* ingenuity, in forming the extraordinary *weapon* above-mentioned, out of the *nurse*, is nothing, when compared with his following feats. *Ovid* with his *Metamorphosis* was but a *type* of him.

In the forty-third and forty-fourth pages of his piece, he makes *Weapons*, (as has been hinted) out of the "*old contract*" between the crown, and the first proprietor; "out of an *opinion* of the king's servants;" and out of the "quit-rents in the lower counties." For having copiously mentioned these several matters, he concludes, † "THESE are the WEAPONS, which I am confident will be used for the restoration of our liberties."

If he can make *weapons* out of *such slight stuff*, it seems a probable opinion, that he can form them—*in his way I mean*—out of an "ideal shadow," or "a chimerical notion"—or what is still more extraordinary—even out of his own *courage.* [iv]

Mr. *Galloway*, ever *fruitful* in *useless* inventions, has

---

* Pretended speech, page 13, line 4 from the bottom.

† Pretended speech, page 44, line 1.

found another way of giving *surprise*—and that is, by
useing the same word in different senses in the same page
or sentence. Thus, speaking of our first impracticable
frame of government, and its change, he says— * "if it
(meaning the change) is *valid*, then the resolution of this
House for a change, assented to by nine tenths of the
members met, must be *valid also.*"

But the resolution of the assembly *alone* cannot make a
change of the government; and therefore he cannot mean,
that it is *valid*, in the *same manner* with the first change,
which was made with the consent of *every branch* of the
legislature. So that by these words, "*valid also*" must
be intended some *other* kind of *validity*, of which no man
but Mr. *Galloway* can form an idea—unless it be, that
this *valid resolution* binds those who made it, and no body
else.

Mr. *Galloway* seems to be very fond of these *abstruse
meanings*, which has inclined some people to think him
addicted to the study of the † "*occult sciences.*" What
else could induce him to talk of the king's *naming* our
governors with his hands—or of people's *reading* with
their *mouths*, and hearing with their *eyes*.

"We ask the king" says he, ‡ "to take the *nomination*
of the governor who is to rule his people into his [v] royal
hands"—and afterwards—"§ can we stop the MOUTHS,

* Pretended speech pa. 34.

† This supposition will not appear unreasonable, if it be considered,
that Mr. *Galloway* speaks in direct terms of "THE ROYAL MEDICINE,"
an expression used *only* by *adepts* in the occult sciences, with whom it
signifies some wonderful secret, by which dead persons may be restored
to life; and what renders the supposition more just, or indeed reduces
the matter to a certainty, is--that Mr. *Galloway* uses the expression, in
the very same sense.   Pretended Speech, pa. 44.

‡ Pretended speech, pa. 8 and 18.

§ Pretended speech, pa. 37. "But, Sir, should we waive these things,
and draw our petition in a different dress, can we annihilate the messages

and close the EYES of *all England* and *America*, or pre-vail on his majesty, or the ministers, to bury in oblivion what they have, e'er now, so often READ and HEARD?"

What a charming confusion, what a motley mixture is here—of "stopt mouths"—"closed eyes"—"reading and hearing"—"All *England* and *America*"—"majesty."

Who that meets with such expressions as these, and has read *Ecclesiasticus*, can forbear admiring the truth of that verse, which says—* "The *heart* of the *foolish* is like a "*cart-wheel;* and his *thoughts* are like a *rolling axle-tree.*"

Nothing less than a love of the "*occult sciences*," can give one a true relish of these *mystical lucubrations*, with which Mr. *Galloway's* piece abounds. Any person may observe, that *his meaning* always appears like an [vi] object in a *mist*, that renders it confused and indistinct; which kind of deception may cause persons of weak sight sometimes to a mistake a *lamb* for a *lion*, or Mr. *Galloway* for a *gentleman.*

between the governor and assembly? Can we withdraw the governor's proclamations? Can we hold the hands of his majesty's general, whose aid we were obliged to accept, from giving the intelligence? Can we stop the *mouths* and close the *eyes* of ALL *England* and *America*, or prevail on his *majesty*, or the *ministry*, to bury in oblivion what they have, e'er now, so often *read* and *heard*."

N. B. "*All England*" does not include *the king and ministry.*

Mr. *Galloway* may indeed say, that the expression of "*reading* with the *mouth*," is proper when a man reads *aloud.* I grant it under *that restriction*—and therefore let it be supposed, that ALL *England* AND *America*, AND his *majesty* AND the *ministry read aloud*, like boys in a country school.

Perhaps some persons may think *me* more obliged to Mr. *Galloway*, in this part of what he calls his speech, than I have yet acknowledged myself to be, since he seems to have aimed at an *imitation* of these my expressions.—Though *we* should keep the secret, can we seal up the lips of the proprietors? Can we recall our messages to the governor? Can we annihilate our own resolves? Will not *all*—will not *any* of these discover the *true cause* of the present attempt?"

* Ecclesiasticus xxxiii. 5.

How remote from the plain, common mode of speaking, is this sentence, * "We have often attempted to obtain relief from oppression from the proprietaries, but in vain."

The *reader* may guess at the meaning—but the writer leaves it doubtful whether application was made to oppression against the proprietors,—or to the proprietors against oppression.

What a beautiful obscurity is there in this sentence? "If, † Sir, a true representation of the uncommon mischiefs which attend the liberties of a free people,‡ arising from the very nature of proprietary government—If a true state of our present confusion, both in and out of our public councils—If a *just* account of our present insecurity of life and estate, given to the crown, be a *just* cause of terror, then the gentleman's pannick is *just*. But, Sir, *these things*, I conceive, are rather causes of *joy*, than fear. 'Tis from hence, we must hope to be relieved from our present unhappy circumstances."

Now what " *things* " can a reader find in this description, if he is a good man, that are " causes of *joy ?* " [vii] Not the public misfortunes to be sure.—What then? Not the " representation " " state " and " account " of calamities, because it is said " they are *true*." What then can be a " cause of joy ? " *Eureka ! Eureka !* This " representation " " state " and " account " may " relieve us from our present unhappy circumstances." May they so? But *until* we are so delivered, if we are the miserable people

---

* Pretended speech, pa. 5, line 2.   † Pretended speech, pa. 35.

‡ Quære—Whether the *mischiefs* or *liberties* arise " from the very nature of proprietary government?" The reader will no doubt take notice of the pretty repetition of that little word " if " which Mr. *Galloway* seems to have introduced with no other intention, but to rescue the poor monosyllable from the obscurity, in which hard hearted authors have suffered it to languish.—He has done the same justice in several places to the merit of that other diminitive word " OF " *In est sua gratia parvis.*

Virgil.

we have been described, a patriot in the midst of *present* misfortunes, would from an *uncertain* prospect of relief, hardly find "cause of joy" tho' he might entertain some *hope.* A man on the rack would scarcely feel *joy*, tho' he might have expectations that he would some time or other be released.

This may be called the true "twilight way of writing," which like the bat in the fable, keeps in the middle between *sense* and *nonsense*, to the exceeding edification and entertainment of those readers, who like paragraphs that are *mysterious* and *wordy*, because they show *depth* and *language.*

Another sentence in which Mr. *Galloway* gives the reader a very pretty *surprize*, is that, where he says—* "this colony has so remarkably flourished, and *now* takes off such vast quantities of *English* manufactures, *from no other cause but her extensive privileges.*"

How *new* and *striking* is this observation? Any other person would have said, that "the people took off such vast quantities by reason of their necessities or luxuries." But Mr. *Galloway* scorns such trite notions—He establishes a new dogma—" our extensive privileges take them off." † BROAD-SHOULDERED PRIVILEGES! *indeed.* [viii]

Perhaps if he should write a comment on his own text, he would say—that he meant, that the extensive privileges occasioned the *settlement* of this province—and the settlement occasioned the *demand* for the manufactures—and *so* the privileges were ‡ *Causa sine qua non.* But this argument will not extricate him—since, if he travels so far backwards, the same way of argument will oblige him to go still farther.—For those privileges would not have been granted by *William Penn*—unless *Charles* the second had

---

* Pretended speech, pa. 6.   † Pretended speech, page 15.

‡ That is "the cause without which the manufactures would not have been taken off."

first made a grant to *him*—which would not have been, *but for his father's services*—and so, *these services* of old admiral *Penn*, who died in the last century, "Now take off such vast quantities of *English* manufactures."

In this *extraordinary manner* does Mr. *Galloway* indulge himself in his *political reveries.* Even the most simple and common observations in life, utterly lose their force in his language.

The *mystical lucubrators*, among whom *he* may with justice claim the president's seat, seem to be *first-cousins* to the authors of the PROFUND style. Certain it is, that they are governed by the same laws, and that there is a wonderful resemblance in their productions. In order to prove this, I shall beg leave to mention the *rules* to be observ'd by that numerous and venerable society, as they are described by Mr. *Pope*, in his learned treatise ΠΕΡΙΒΑΘΟΥΣ.

* " I Will venture to lay it down, as the first maxim and corner-stone of this our art; that whoever would excell therein, must studiously avoid, detest, and *turn his head* from all the ideas, ways, and workings of that pestilent foe to wit, and destroyer of fine [ix] figures, which is known by the name of *common sense.* His business must be to contract the true *gout de travers*; and to acquire a most happy, *uncommon, unaccountable* way of thinking. His design ought to be like a *labyrinth*, out of which no body can get clear but himself."

Again—" † our authors of this style, should lay it down as a principle, *to say nothing in the usual way*, but (if possible) in the direct contrary; therefore the figures must be so turned, as to manifest that intricate and wonderful *cast of head*, which distinguishes all authors of this kind; or (as I may say) to represent exactly the *mold* in which

* Pope's works, vol. vi., page 172.
† Pope's works, vol. vi., pa. 190.

they were formed, in all its *inequalities, cavities, obliquities, odd crannies* and *distortions.*

"It may be observed, that the world has been long weary of *natural things.* How much the contrary are formed to please, is evident from the universal applause daily given to the admiral entertainments of Harlequins and Magicians on our stage. When an audience behold a coach turned into a wheel-barrow, a conjurer into an old woman, or a man's head where his heels should be; how are they struck with transport and delight?"

Yet what are *all these,* when compared with Mr. *Galloway's* changing in an instant a *nurse* into a *weapon,* and putting that *weapon* into the hand of *its* own child? Or what are they to his forging *weapons* out of an *old parchment,* an *opinion,* and *arrears of quit-rents?* What author of the *profund* can vie with this our Pennsylvanian patriot?

" *Ye little stars, hide your diminished heads.*" [x]

Not to dwell upon other instances, how exquisitely " *uncommon,*" " *unaccountable*" and " *unnatural*" is his making our privileges take off all the English beer and cloth imported into this province? And also his making the king strip us of liberties, of which we were stript before?

The great poet I have mentioned further observes, * "that the manner of these authors forming their thoughts is aided by familiarizing their minds to the *lowest objects;* and exercising them on the dregs of nature."

Numberless instances in our author's piece prove how much *his* thoughts have been formed on this plan. I will only mention one, where to revive and regale his reader's imagination he kindly puts him in mind of *a certain sweet-smelling place.*

These, "WITH MANY OTHER PARTS" of this our

---

* Mr. Pope's works, vi. vol., pa. 180, 181.

"political institutor" which must be remarked by any careful peruser, are "irrefragable proofs" with what diligence and success, he hath studied the aforesaid treatise.

I now proceed to that renowned page, where the whole powers of Mr. *Galloway's* genius are collected into one dreadful simile.

With great propriety, (says he,) a *political body* has often been compared to a *human constitution.* *Let us suppose* then, that a *human constitution* is attacked by a violent disease, the EFFECT whereof has *nearly destroyed* the *powers of life,* and *living motion,** and nature *is*† [xi] *no longer capable* of struggling for relief."—Surely this *human constitution,* whose *vital motion* as well as its *powers of life* are nearly destroyed," is now *sick enough* for any simile in the world.

"Is not this the time to apply the remedy? No! For it should have been applied before—and now nature is so much exhausted, may "entirely destroy" her—which frequently happens, when people will venture to take physick from "*quacks*;" who are a sort of gentry, never remarkable, before Mr. *Galloway* made the discovery, "for *waiting* in hopes of some lucky crisis"—Now NEVER, is a motto, that suits *all empirics.*

"The powers of legislature *truly resemble the soul,* which animates and directs" not only "the *conduct*" but "the *behaviour* of the *political institution.*" Yet these "powers of legislature *truly resembling the soul,*" nine lines afterwards, are so checked and controlled that they are "almost ANNIHILATED"—poor soul!

* This is a mistake – for it is "vital" in the original—however it is to be hoped this error will be excused, as the words "vital" and "living" have nearly the same meaning.

† It is to be remarked by the reader, that tho' nature is "*no longer* capable of struggling" at the *beginning* of this simile, yet this is only to heighten the description—a licence frequently taken by Mr. *Galloway*—for before the simile is finished, she "can and does struggle"—and the only danger is, that "death will put an end to them."

An *upright* administration of justice resembles "the *active blood,* which by its pure and uninterrupted course, preserves and supports ITS health and vigour." But *we* have no *upright* administration of justice in this province, according to our author, and therefore by his own simile, no *active blood* in our *political institution.* Yet immediately after, he says, "In these *two vital parts,*" to wit, the * passive soul and †active blood, "the fever of ambition and ‡arbitrary power is, and has been raging with unremitting violence."

Perhaps the author of this famous simile may say, that by the "vital parts" he means the power of legislature, and the administration of justice—But this will be a contradiction of himself, for he only allows "an *upright* administration of justice" to be a *vital part;* and as among us, "the stream of justice is become so *turbid* and *thick,* that it *can no longer discharge its duty,*" this "vital part" composed of "an upright administration" is wanting.

However, if both these *vital parts* should be *annihilated,* Mr. *Galloway* has allowed the *fever* room enough to exert itself. "It rages, says he, in these two vital parts, *with many others.*"—§ "Well chosen, *that expression,* and prudently guarded." It rages not only in the *soul* of the *legislature,* and the *active blood* of the *administration*—but in MANY OTHER VITAL PARTS. Unexampled energy of diction!

* This word "passive" is inserted here—it being suppos'd that it was omitted by a mistake in the original, as Mr. *Galloway* has given the epithet of "active" to the blood, in order to distinguish it from some opposite quality in the soul.

† Quære, if physicians, surgeons or anatomists reckon the "active blood" among the "vital parts?"

‡ Quære, what is the fever of *arbitrary power?*

§ Preface to pretended speech, page 24.

*When "active blood" shall flow in lifeless veins,
The wondring world shall praise thy "turbid" strains.

Perhaps some curious critics may be disgusted at the preference Mr. *Galloway* gives the *legislative powers* over an *upright administratian of justice*, in comparing the first to † "that particle of divine air" the *soul*; and the latter to mere matter—the *blood*.   But this seems to be too hasty a censure, by no means to be adopted—for *it is to be observed*, that soon after, in saying "these two vital parts" he places the *soul* and *blood* exactly *on a level*, making them both "vital parts" *without the least distinction.* Besides Mr. *Galloway*, when he uses the word "soul" or "spirit" does not annex the *same idea* to the term, that is always annex'd by others—for *he* talks of a "*spirit*" that may be "*worn out*," and "*dissolved*," and to which "*reviving medicines may be administered.*"   "And if such a medicine can be obtained, shall we not even attempt to obtain it, before the MIDNIGHT GLOOM approaches, and FATAL DEATH puts an end to our struggles?" Undoubtedly!   *Doctor*—and if it proves a *preventive* against these dreadful disorders—*midnight gloom* and *fatal death*—I shall hereafter entertain a better opinion than I do at present, of those bold pretenders, who undertake to cure all diseases "past, present and to come," by a ROYAL MEDICINE, or some other *nostrum*, with the like pompous title.

* Blansted.   † "*Divinæ particulam auræ.*"   Horace.

FINIS.

AN ANSWER

TO

JOSEPH GALLOWAY.

BY

JOHN DICKINSON

———

SEPTEMBER 29, 1764.

NOTE.

Dickinson's charge, that Galloway had not delivered the speech he printed, led to Galloway's preparing a reply, which he first (if we accept Dickinson's statement) offered to a newspaper, and on its refusal to print the reply, unless first shown to Dickinson, he printed it as a broadside, with the headlines:

To the / Public. / Philadelphia, September 29, 1764.

Before the printing, Dickinson heard of the piece, and prepared the following reply, which was published the same day as Galloway's squib, and before Dickinson had seen the latter. This evident foreknowledge caused criticism, and induced Dickinson to publish an explanation in the *Pennsylvania Gazette* of October 4, 1764:

Having heard that some Persons, on seeing a Paper that came out Yesterday in my Name, have supposed the Printer therein mentioned acted too busily, in giving me Intelligence of the Piece Mr. *Galloway* carried to him, in order to be published in his News-Paper; I think myself obliged, in Justice to the Printer, to declare, That having been informed by several Persons, without receiving the least Intelligence from the Printer, that Mr *Galloway* intended to publish something against me in the next Paper, I went to the Printer Yesterday was a Week, and, telling him what I had heard, desired that, if there was any Truth in the Report, he would be so just and impartial, as to print nothing that might affect my Reputation, without allowing me to see and answer it in the same News-Paper.

He said, that no such Writing was sent to him.—I called upon him again next morning, and made the same Request; but nothing was then come to his Hands.—I told him, that if he was desired to conceal the Paper from me, when sent, it could be with no other Intention than to injure me, by taking an unfair Advantage of me; and I entreated him to act in such a Manner on this Occasion, as he would wish me to do, was I the Printer, and he the Person attacked.

The Paper was soon after carried to him.—He desired to know

whether it might be shewn to me.—To this Mr. *Galloway* would not consent ;—and the Printer then acted as he thought right.

John Dickinson.

October 2, 1764.

The *Answer* was originally printed as a four paged, octavo pamphlet, without title or heading, the lining of the first three lines being :

Last Tuesday morning Mr. *Galloway* / carried a writing containing some reflec- / tions on me, to a printer in this city / and desired he would insert it in his / next News-Paper—

It was afterwards reprinted in the *Pennsylvania Journal* of May 2, 1765, with the following prefatory note :

Mr. BRADFORD. *By reprinting the following piece which was published by Mr.* DICKINSON, *on the day of the last election, you will oblige many of your readers, and particularly your humble servant. J. W.*

—EDITOR.

Last Tuesday morning Mr. *Galloway* carried a writing containing some reflections on me, to a printer in this city, and desired that he would insert it in his next News Paper. The printer told him he would print it, but that he thought it very *just* and *reasonable*, if his paper published anything against me, that I should see it first, and have an opportunity of defending myself in the same News Paper, and at the same moment that I was attacked. This Mr. *Galloway* utterly refused to consent to, and declared that he would not have it printed, unless it was kept a *secret* from me. The printer would not agree to this most *unjust* and *unchristian* proposal, and Mr. *Galloway* took away the writing, and said "*he would have it done somewhere else.*"

Thus am I exposed to the shafts which my ungenerous enemy shall please to shoot at me in the dark. I know not on which side the blow is to come—nor with what weapon it is to be given. Of this however I am assured, that it is to be a *poisoned weapon.*

I have been informed that Mr. *Galloway* has procured from some members of the assembly a certificate, "that he spoke the *substance* of his *pretended speech* in the House "—And thus he endeavours to shew, that I have told a falshood to the public by saying in my *Reply*, "that he never spoke a *sentence* of it in the House."

As I have not seen this certificate, I cannot speak of it with any certainty; and therefore if it is different from what I have heard it is, I hope every candid person will pardon any error I may commit in answering it.

I understand the certificate does not mention the day when Mr. *Galloway* delivered the *substance* of his pretended speech—Nor what the members mean by the "*substance* of it."

The public will please to take notice that there were *debates* (as Mr. *Galloway* says) on Saturday the twenty-fourth day of *March* last, when the resolves were past.— There were *debates* also on Wednesday the twenty-third day of *May* when the committee was appointed to draw up the petition to his Majesty—at both which times I was sick and absent from the House.

I have also informed the public in my *Reply*, that before I made my speech to the House, "I threw out general objections, in order to discover the arguments which induced the House to take so dangerous a step.—And that thereupon several members, among whom Mr. *Galloway* was one, assigned their reasons for the measure."

These reasons were—the injustice of the proprietors—the misery of this province—the danger from the rioters—the great advantage of our having a military force established among us—that able council, to wit, our agent had said we could have a change and preserve our privileges—that the proprietors had not so much interest as they used to have —and that if their interest was ever so great, our privileges would never be taken from us without an act, which the parliament would never pass.

All these things having been mentioned by several persons at different times, and part of them by Mr. *Galloway*, I cannot forbear thinking that the members who signed the certificate, having heard these things, and not carefully attending to the times when they were spoken, have confounded them all together, and bestowed them upon their friend, Mr. *Galloway*—as if spoken in answer to what I said.

But even *these Members* do not pretend (as I am informed) to say, that Mr. *Galloway* ever spoke in the House, one *Page*, or even *one Sentence*, as I said, of his *pretended* speech.

They say "he spoke the *substance*."—A loose expression! to which every one of them perhaps annexes a different idea. It is not improbable that these gentlemen might think themselves justifiable in giving *such a certificate* to half the members in the House.

One observation will sufficiently shew how greatly these certifying gentlemen must be mistaken. I delivered my sentiments to the House on *Wednesday*, the 24th of *May*. —The Petition to the King was signed by the Speaker on *Saturday*, the 27th of the same month. How incredible is it, that Mr. *Galloway* should *immediately* have delivered the "*substance*" of his pretended speech to the House— and yet should spend *eight weeks* in putting it into *form*. —If he could make the *body* in so short a time, it is most extraordinary, that he could not make the *cloaths* or *dress* for that body in eight weeks.

One thing more I beg leave to mention—it is this—that these certifying members must have the best memories in the world, to be able to say with certainty what was the "*substance*" of a Discourse they heard above three months before, of which they did not take a single note.

Having said thus much of this Certificate, I will now relate plainly what past in the House on my delivering my sentiments, and I appeal to every member of the House as witnesses of the truth with which I speak.

After I had spoken, Mr. *Galloway* rose up, and having spoke about four minutes, it was observed that the speaker was so ill, that it was proper to adjourn—The House agreed to an adjournment, and I was desired to leave my notes on the table. I excused myself from doing that, as they were imperfect; but I said I would get them ready for the members' perusal as soon as I could; and would let Mr. *Galloway* have them that evening, if I could get them ready.

Mr. *John Ross* declared, that I had thrown many new

lights on the affair, and he should be glad to have it more thoroughly considered.

The House adjourned—Mr. *Galloway* called on me for the notes—they were not ready. Next morning I took them to the House—no person asked for them. I did the same in the afternoon—no person asked for them.

The next time the Petition was mentioned, Mr. *Galloway* spoke—and said "it was IMPOSSIBLE to answer my speech, BECAUSE I had not given him my notes—and that it was quite UNNECESSARY to do it, BECAUSE the members who were for a change, intended to take those very precautions I had recommended.

Mr. *Ross* then rose and said, "that what I had said, had at first given him a great deal of uneasiness, as I had mentioned several difficulties and dangers that had not before occurred to him; but that upon considering the matter since, he was satisfied that my apprehensions were not so well grounded as he had thought them, because the House intended to act in the cautious manner I had recommended."

Thus IMPOSSIBLE and UNNECESSARY was it *at that time* to answer what I had said, or to take any more notice of it.

It was unworthy any further attention, till Mr. *Galloway* took it into his head to set up for the author of a speech.

Then his good friends furnished him with the best vouchers they could, to support his title as an author—and thus the certificate was produced. The contents of it have been basely concealed from me, to render the stab mortal —and why am I alone attacked with this malice and violence? BECAUSE I have endeavoured according to the best of my understanding, in obedience to the dictates of my conscience, and in discharge of my *duty* to my country, to preserve the rights and privileges of the good people of *Pennsylvania.*   JOHN DICKINSON.

September 29.

A RECEIPT

TO MAKE A

SPEECH.

BY

JOHN DICKINSON.

———————

OCTOBER, 1764.

NOTE.

This is a satire on the *Speech of Joseph Galloway, Esquire,* and shows what hot anger the whole controversy had occasioned. It was printed as a small quarto broadside, the headlines being.

A / Receipt / to make a / Speech. / By J . . . . . G . . . . . . Esquire.

Hildeburn (*Issues of the Press in Pennsylvania,* II, No. 2250) states that it was printed by William Bradford. A copy in the New York Historical Society has a manuscript poem, in Dickinson's handwriting, on the back.

EDITOR.

(143)

A RECEIPT TO MAKE A SPEECH.

BY J - - - - - G - - - - - - , ESQUIRE.

Take of the *Leaves* of *Law dry'd* in *Jacob's* * *Hortus Siccus*, as much as will lie on the Point of a Penknive; of History (*Bauers* if it can be got) a Scruple, *bruised* to a Pap; of the words "Liberty, Property, Proprietary, private Interest and Power, Injustice, Misery, Slavery, Thraldom, Bondage, Captivity, Magic Charm," *&c., &c., &c., &c., &c.,* two double handfuls; add to these "Midnight gloom," "Fatal Death" "Powers of Life" and "Vital Motion," strengthen the Composition with Independence, Malice, Envy, Hatred, Ill-Manners, and all kind of Uncharitableness, well moistened with two Bottles of *old Madeira*, that has been at *Havana;* put all these ingredients into an *Empty Head*, keep them covered warm (with a *large wig*, well powdered, for† *eight weeks*, shaking them together and stirring them about with an *electrified Rod* every twenty four Hours:—The Fermentation will at length grow very violent, and when it is highest, pour out the Mixture, which will by that time, become very "*Turbid and Thick*," on clean‡ *Pro Patria* Paper, that has been long kept in a damp foggy place.

This preparation has the greatest Success in giving a *flow of Spirits* to those who take it, of anything that was

* *Hortus Siccus*, is a term applied to a new Invented Method of drying Herbs in Sand, which preserves their Colour, but destroys their Virtue.

† So long a pretended Speech was breeding.

‡ In English a Term "for our own Country" from which Expression a particular kind of Paper takes its Name.

ever invented. A few pages will be a sufficient Doze for exhilerating a well grown *School Boy;* and such its Efficacy, that if it is only *opened* in a Room full of Company, it will immediately set them all a laughing. *Probatum est.*

A PROTEST

AGAINST THE APPOINTMENT

OF

BENJAMIN FRANKLIN

AS AGENT FOR THE

COLONY OF PENNSYLVANIA.

DRAFTED BY

JOHN DICKINSON.

———

OCTOBER 26, 1764.

NOTE.

In order to carry out the policy begun by the petition to the king to assume the government of Pennsylvania, the Assembly, on October 26, 1764, by a vote of 19 to 11, appointed Franklin an additional agent to act for the colony in London. The *Votes and Proceedings* record that :

It being moved by the Members on the Negative of the foregoing Question, that they be allowed to enter the Reasons of their Dissent on the Minutes of the House, a Debate arose, in which some Opposition being given to their Motion, the said members did not insist on the vote.

Eight of the protesting members, however, united in signing this protest, and it was printed in the *Pennsylvania Journal* for November 1, 1764, with a prefatory note as follows :

Mr. Bradford,

The Subscribers, at the Close of the late Debate in Assembly, concerning the sending Mr. Franklin to England as an Assistant to our Agent there, having offered a PROTEST against that Measure ; which was refused to be entered on the Minutes, it is now thought proper to take this Method, of laying before the Publick the Reasons on which their Dissent was founded.

The Protest was translated into German and printed as a pamphlet, with the title of:

Proteſtation / gegen die Beſtellung / Herrn Benjamin Franklin's zu einem Agenten für / dieſe Provinz, / [Followed by] Anmerkungen / üeber eine neuliche / Proteſtation / gegen die Beſtellung / Herrn Benjamin Franklin's zu einem Agenten für / dieſe Provinz / [Germantown : Christoph Saur. 1764.] Fol, pp. (4.)

It was also reprinted in Horace Smith's *Life and Correspondence of William Smith* (Philadelphia, 1878), from the types of which a small edition was separately printed with the title of:

The Reasons / on which were founded, / The Protest / offered by certain members of the / Assembly to that Body / Concerning the Sending of Mr. Franklin to England as Assistant / to our Agent there. / (From the Pennsylvania Journal of November 1st, 1764.) / Reprinted / Philadelphia, 1878. 8vo, pp. 4.

The authorship of the Protest was no secret at the time, and was re-

(149)

ferred to by Isaac Hunt, in his *Humble Attempt at Scurrility* (Philadelphia, 1765), in these terms :

> Is not the famous or rather *infamous*, Protest, considered as the *Protest* of Mr. A . . . n and the other Subscribers, tho' tis well known to be drawn up by the pitiful Mr. D . . . . . n, revised, corrected and amended by the Rev. *Sentiment-dresser-General* [William Smith] of the Pr . . . . ry Party ? "

See note to Dickinson's *Observations, post*, for more concerning this Protest.   EDITOR.

A PROTEST.

We whose Names are hereunto subscribed, do object and *protest* against the Appointment of the Person proposed as an Agent of this Province, for the following Reasons.

First, Because we believe him to be the Chief Author of the Measures pursued by the late Assembly, which have occasioned such Uneasiness and Distraction among the good People of this Province.

Secondly, Because we believe his fixed enmity to the Proprietors will preclude all Accommodation of our Disputes with them, even on just and reasonable Terms,—So that for these two Reasons, we are filled with the most affecting Apprehensions, that the Petitions lately transmitted to England, will be made use of to produce a Change of our Government, contrary to the Intention of the Petitioners; the greatest part of whom, we are persuaded, only designed thereby to obtain a Compliance with some equitable Demands—And thus, by such an Appointment, we, and a vast Number of our most worthy Constituents, are deprived of all hopes of ever seeing an End put to the fatal Dissensions of our Country; it being our firm Opinion, that any further Prosecution of the Measures for a Change of our Government at this Time, will lay the Foundations of unceasing Feuds, and all the Miseries of Confusion, among the People we represent, and their Posterity. This step gives us the more lively Affliction, as it is taken at the very Moment, when we are informed by a Member of this House, that the Governor has assured him of his having received Instructions from the Proprietors, on their hearing of our late

Dispute, to give his Assent to the Taxation of their Estates in the same manner that the Estates of other Persons are to be taxed, and also to confirm, for the Publick use, the several *Squares*, formerly claimed by the City;—On which Subjects, we make no doubt, the Governor would have sent a Message to the House, if this had been the usual Time of doing Business, and he had not been necessarily absent to meet the Assembly of the Lower Counties.—And therefore we cannot but anxiously regret that, at a Time when the Proprietors have shewn such a Disposition, this House should not endeavour to cultivate the same, and obtain from them every reasonable Demand that can be made on the part of the People; in vigorously insisting on which, we would most earnestly unite with the rest of this House.

Thirdly, Because the Gentleman proposed, as we are informed, is very unfavorably thought of by several of his Majesty's Ministers ; and we are humbly of Opinion, that it will be disrespectful to our most Gracious Sovereign, and disadvantageous to ourselves and our constituents, to employ such a person as our Agent.

Fourthly, Because the Proposal of the Person mentioned, is so extremely disagreeable to a very great Number of the most serious and reputable Inhabitants of this Province of all Denominations and Societies (one Proof of which is, his having been rejected, both by this City and County at the last Election, though he had represented the former in Assembly for 14 Years) that we are convinced no Measure this House can adopt, will tend so much to inflame the Resentments and imbitter the Divisions of the good People of this province, as his Appointment to be our Agent— And we cannot but sincerely lament, that the Peace and Happiness of Pennsylvania should be sacrificed for the Promotion of a Man, who cannot be advanced but by the Convulsions of his Country.

Fifthly, Because the unnecessary haste with which this

House has acted in proceeding to this Appointment (without making a small Adjournment, tho' requested by many Members, to consult our Constituents on the Matters to be decided, and) even before their Speaker has been presented to the King's Representative, tho' we are informed that the Governor will be in Town the Beginning of next Week;—may subject us to the Censures and very heavy Displeasure of our most gracious Sovereign and his Ministers.

Sixthly, Because the Gentleman propos'd, has heretofore ventured, contrary to an Act of Assembly, to place the* public Money in the Stocks, whereby this Province suffered a loss of £6000; and that sum added to £5000 granted for his Expences, makes the whole Cost of his former voyage to England, amount to ELEVEN THOUSAND POUNDS; which expensive kind of Agency we do not chuse to imitate, and burden the Public with unnecessary loads of Debt. For these and other Reasons we should think ourselves guilty of betraying the Rights of Pennsylvania, if we should presumptuously commit them to the Discretion of a Man, against whom so many and just obligations present themselves.

Lastly, We being extremely desirous to avert the Mischiefs apprehended from the intended Appointment, and as much as in us lies to promote Peace and Unanimity among us and our Constituents, do humbly propose to the House, that if they will agree regularly to appoint any †† Gentleman of Integrity, Abilities, and Knowledge in England, to assist Mr. Jackson as our Agent, under a Restriction not to present the Petitions for a Change of our Government, or any of them, to the King or his Ministers,

---

* The Money here meant was a Sum granted by Parliament as an Indemnification for part of our Expences in the late War, which by Act of Assembly was ordered for its better Security to be placed in the Bank.

†† Dr. Fothergill was mentioned by the Subscribers as a proper Person.

unless an express Order for that Purpose be hereafter given by the Assembly of this Province; we will not give it any Opposition; But if such an Appointment should be made, we must insist (as we cannot think it a necessary one) that our Constituents, already laboring under heavy Debts, be not burthened with fresh Impositions on that Account; and therefore, in Condescention to the Members, who think another Agent necessary, we will concur with them if they approve of this Proposal, in paying such Agent at our own Expence.

JOHN DICKINSON,   WILLIAM ALLEN,

DAVID MCCANAUGHY,   THOMAS WILLING,

JOHN MONTGOMERY,   GEORGE BRYAN,

ISAAC SANDERS,   AMOS STRETTELL,

GEORGE TAYLOR,   HENRY KEPPELE.

October 26, 1764.

OBSERVATIONS

ON

MR. FRANKLIN'S REMARKS

ON A LATE

PROTEST.

BY

JOHN DICKINSON.

———

NOVEMBER, 1764.

NOTE.

On the publication of the *Protest* (*ante*, page 149) Franklin, then on the point of sailing for England, wrote:

Remarks / on a late / Protest / Against the Appointment of / Mr. Franklin an Agent / for this Province / [Philadelphia: Printed by B. Franklin and D. Hall. 1764.] 8vo, pp. 7.

Which is also reprinted in Bigelow's edition of Franklin's *Writings* (III, 356). This was in turn replied to by the Rev. William Smith in:

An / Answer / to / Mr. Franklin's / Remarks / on a late / Protest. / Philadelphia: / Printed and Sold by William Bradford at his Book- / Store, in Market-street, adjoining the London Coffee-house. / M.DCC.- LXIV. 8vo, pp. 22.

Dickinson also wrote a reply to Franklin, which apparently was never published, and is now printed from the manuscript copy preserved in the Historical Society of Pennsylvania.

EDITOR.

(157)

OBSERVATIONS ON M.R FRANKLIN'S REMARKS.

As M.r Franklin's Remarks on the Protest against his Appointment as an additional Agent For this Province, were not publickly dispers'd till he had sett off from Philadelphia on his Voyage to England, I considered them as a parting Blow, and that the Publication of any observations thereon in his absence, might seem ungenerous; for which Reason, I took little Notice of the insulting Air wherewith some persons attributed the Neglect of his Remarks, to their being unanswerable: But on a Republication of them in the Pensilvania Journal a fortnight after the Author's Embarkation, all Considerations due to his absence appear'd at an End, and it became allowable if not necessary, at a Leisure Hour, to refute such vain opinions so industriously propagated; For which purpose, nothing may perhaps be more effectual, than to strip said Remarks of their artful Disguise, and consider them as consisting chiefly,

Of Misrepresentations.

Of Curious Anecdotes.

& Of Matters Foreign to the Protest.

These last shall be slightly pass'd over, the second briefly pointed out, and my Animadversions of course principally confin'd to the first Head.

Its observable that in the very Introduction, the Protest is contemptuously rank'd amongst such abusive pieces as M.r F. would insinuate he had generally treated with silent disregard; and in the next paragraph the bare mention of said Protest being offered for, and refused an Entry on the Minutes of the House, is called a *Complaint*, merely to

charge the Protestors with an *Absurdity*. But as no complaint was made, no such Absurdity can be consequently
chargeable on them, and thus the Force of that—Pompous
Paragraph falls to the Ground.

When the Remarker is obliged to own his Share in (or
his being the Chief Author of) the Measures pursued by
last Assembly, which the Protest justly represents productive of Uneasiness and Distraction amongst the good People of this Province, he attempts to evade the consequence,
by confounding the order of Time, and misleading his
Readers—into an opinion that the Publick Uneasiness and
Distraction pointed out in the protest, had preceded, not
follow'd said Measures; for which he gives what some may
esteem unanswerable proof, Viz., his own assertion, intirely unsupported, and unexplain'd:

he can as I conceive only mean the Confusion and Disorders produced by the Paxton Rioters,—which had subsided long before the extroadinary Resolves of last Assembly, and the subsequent measures, which (as set forth
in the Protest) confessedly occasioned a more serious Uneasiness, a more lasting Distraction, and finally rous'd a
Majority of the Electors of this Capital County, (who had
generally suffered the first of October to pass unregarded
by them for many preceding Years,) to chuse new Members in the place of Mr F. and some others, who had sig-
naliz'd themselves as the chief Authors and Supporters of
said Measures.

One *favourite* Step further back, falling under the third
General Head, there I leave it, being equally incapable of
understanding that the late Indian Ravages have been no
cause of *uneasiness*, or that any Act of the Proprietors *occasioned* those Ravages. Whether the Protesters Information that Mr F. is now very unfavourably thought of by
several of his Majestys Ministers, is essentially weakened by
his own sole unsupported apprehension that their Informer

is mistaken, can only be left to the impartial Judgment of
Well inform'd Readers:—I am too little acquainted with
the Black History of private Scandal to follow M.r F. further in that Paragraph, its falling under my third General
Head will likewise excuse me; I shall therefore only point
out an Anecdote or two which must carry weight, having
the Remarker himself for their Author, altho' his friends
might perhaps have clamour'd loudly, had any other person said, that "The great Patriot M.r F. ever since he had
"any Influence in the Province of Pensilvania, has con-
"stantly and uniformly promoted the Measures of the
"Crown." And that the same Patriot openly avows
"promoting the Change from a Proprietary to a Royal
"Government." What would have been thought of such
Principles two years ago? Could the Freemen of Pensilvania have swallow'd them contentedly? How happens it
now, that any Lovers of their Country can fondly wish to
risque their invaluable Charter Priviledges in this Man's
Hands? Are not such infatuated?

If sufficient objections against his appointment had not
been offered in the Protest, he has now himself given such
as are unanswerable; his Abilitys are notwithstanding confessedly great, and the Publick already experiences small
Specimen of the curious Schemes which may in time be
expected from so projecting an Head, to which we are not
a little indebted for that excellent Clause in the £55000
Act pass'd during the Session of last Assembly in May,
1764, obliging every Freeholder to make his or her Return
of Property, in Columns &c: should any one imagine that
inconvenient exposures of Private Property, hazard of incurring thro' inadvertence or neglect a double or fourfold
taxation, great disgust, and abundance of unnecessary
charge and trouble, may be occasioned by said Clause
throughout the whole Province—Is all this to be plac'd in
Competition with the Gratification of a few Patriots Re-

sentment against Mr T. P. & their Curiosity to pry into
the Proprietary Income? when such disinterested Patriot-
ick Ends were to be answered, did they attend to this
trifling Consideration, that the utmost possible addition
from Messrs Penn's Estate to the publick Tax, cannot
amount to one eighth part of the extra expence incurr'd
by pursuing this curious Plan?

In the protest it was alleg'd 4thly "Because the Proposal
"of the Person mentioned, is so extremely disagreable to
"a very great Number of the most serious and reputable
"Inhabitants of this Province of all Denominations and
"Societies, (one proof of which is, his having been re-
"jected, both by this City and County at the last Election,
"though he had represented the former in Assembly for
"14 years) that we are convinced no Measure this House
"can adopt, will tend so much to inflame the Resent-
"ments and imbitter the Divisions of the good People of
"this Province, as his Appointment to be our Agent"—
which Mr F. quotes thus, "Another of your Reasons is,
"that the Proposal of me for an Agent, is extremely dis-
"agreeable to a very great Number of the most serious
"and reputable Inhabitants of the Province; and the
"Proof is, my having been rejected at the last Election,
"tho' I had represented the City in Assembly for 14
Years."

By this artful variation what the Protesters call'd *one
proof*, and by including it in a Parenthesis evidently laid
small Stress thereon, Mr F. represents as the *Sole proof* of
their assertion—For what purpose—his triumphant insults and shocking Abuse in the two next Paragraphs
plainly shew.—It is sufficient however, that by a fair quotation from the Protest, and his remarks, I have remov'd
this fictitious Foundation, the whole Superstructure must
at once fall, and the protest be clear'd from that Ideal
Victory.—But the Rancour unguardedly thrown out by the

Remarker on that occasion—will remain on Record.—
Could a Majority of the Freemen of Philadelphia County
a few Years ago have expected that so great a Patriot
would in resentment for their only taking upon them to
reject him once in 14 years, have insulted them by the
opprobrious appellation of wretched Rabble brought to
swear themselves intituled to a Vote, and charg'd them
with the Guilt of numberless Falshoods and Perjuries?
Could it have been imagined that a Gentleman who had
long sat in the Honourable House of Assembly should be
so far lost to Decency as publickly to charge a Number of
the present Members of Assembly, with Artifices at the
Election, with double Tickets, and whole Boxes of Forged
Votes—when they are perfectly innocent of every part of
said Charge—if not, let those who republish'd Mr F's remarks, prove them guilty, and shew the World how
strictly their Patron related *the whole Truth* concerning
said Artifices, double Tickets, and whole Boxes of forged
Votes—a Transition might here be made from the *pre-*
tended Triumph wherewith Mr F. affects to ridicule the
Protesters, to that *vainglorious Triumph* actually puff'd
off at his Embarkation, for which silly Pageantry, ship
Guns were borrow'd in Philadelphia, and sent down to
Chester—the use there made of them, with other vain
Exultations are unworthy repetition.

Mr F. proceeds to censure the Protestors for reciting the
Governor's own expressions in Conversation with a Member of the House, and not making use of other words
which Mr F. thinks would have been more proper—and
on this also he exults immoderately, Let the impartial
Reader judge with how much reason, and determine
whether a Member of the House in repeating assurances
from the Governor, was at Liberty to change his words,
and put in others better suited either to his own Inclination, or that of the House:—if not, then all Mr F's. affected

Ridicule is without foundation, and must have been only calculated to amuse, or irritate.—Something further seems attempted in the Query & Insinuations which follow, and the introduction of an Extract from Messrs D. B. & Sons private Letter to Messrs J. & D.,* but with what Propriety all these are discharg'd upon the Protestors, Let me now examine: The Governor just before his setting out to meet the Assembly of the lower Countys, & at a time when he expected the Assembly of Pensilvania were on the point of adjourning to the usual Season of doing Business, had some conversation with a particular Member, which that Gentleman on finding such Measures likely to be pursued by the House as he concluded they would wave if appriz'd of the Substance of said Conversation, thereupon thought himself in Duty obliged to communicate it to the House, from a View to the Publick Good; the little regard shew to so seasonable and well design'd an Intimation, affected the Protesters in the manner they set forth. This is truly all their Concern in the matter, yet behold! how are they interrogated, censured, and abused! This I believe is the first time Members of Assembly were ever traduced for supposed Faults of a Governor, and I should have thought Mr F. the last Man upon Earth to have done so:—as to Messrs B's, their sincere regard and friendship for the Proprietors & people of this Province in general, and Mr A. in particular, is well known; common charity would therefore lead every humane candid person to conclude they must either have misunderstood the Proprietors concerning Mr A., or inadvertently express'd themselves in said Letter;—and in case such orders or Instructions as Mr F. supposes, were really sent by Mr A. to the Governor; as I have not discours'd his Honour on ye Subject, I can assign no sufficient reason why they were not laid be-

* From David Barclay & Sons to James & Drinker. *Cf.* Franklin's *Remarks on a late Protest.—Ed.*

fore the last Assembly in September, or the present immediately after the Speakers Presentment:—If there are
any Faults either in Governor, or Assembly, let them fall
were they ought, but I conceive nothing can justify M.ͬ
F's. Treatment of the Protesters in this and his next Paragraph when considered as Members of the present Assembly:—perhaps the affected Eminence from whence as
the Guard with assum'd Grandeur as a powerful Guardian of the Rights of Pensilvania he would seem to look
down, may not be found more proper or decent, than the
freedom he takes with the Proprietors and the Protester's
Characters.

Their 6.ᵗʰ Objection against his Appointment, he calls
an high Charge, and would insinuate being unfairly laid
before the Publick, by a concealment of some part of the
Truth which ought to have been told; whereto I answer, a
Concise Style is requisite in Protests, a Note however was
inserted to explain the Fact alluded to, and was sufficient
to direct any person to more Light in the matter than he
has thought proper to impart; the use made of it by the
Protesters, was only to shew that M.ͬ F. when formerly in
a publick Station in England, had shewn himself a very
venturesome and expensive Gentleman, which discourag'd
the Protesters from entrusting the invaluable priviledges
of the Freemen of Pensilvania into his Hands, and in-
duc'd them *rather* to think of employing some Gentleman
residing in England, who might transact the Business as
well, and afford to do it much cheaper. M.ͬ F. has established the Protesters account of his expence, amounting to
£5000 but would fain exculpate himself from the Loss of
£6000 to the Province, by throwing the Odium on the
Assembly of 175—who he says, not only adopted the
measure of placing that money in the Stocks, but even
passed a Bill directing the subsequent Sums granted
by Parliament to be plac'd with the former—whereupon

the Reader has probably absolv'd him from the high Charge of being a venturesome Man.—But I must now discover a part of the Truth, which directly after his formal Harrangue concerning the Truth, *the whole Truth*, and nothing but the Truth, it suited his purpose to conceal, viz: The Bill pass'd as above mentioned by the House *only*, was refus'd by the Governor, consequently never became a Law, but the former directing the Money to be lodg'd in the Bank continued an unrepealed Act of General Assembly notwithstanding which, a Majority of the Representatives in Assembly for the Year 175—who were Mr F's Friends, took upon them to give him directions to act contrary to said Law, and he was *venturesome* enough so to do; I therefore now repeat in the words of the Protest, "That Mr F. has heretofore *ventured* con-"trary to an Act of Assembly to place the Publick money "in the Stocks, whereby this Province suffered a loss of "£6000," and I say further, that in a Man of his Understanding, who well knew the Assembly had no Authority to dispense with Law, it was a *very venturesome* and unwarrantable act, and appears to many beside the Protesters, a sufficient Reason against entrusting to his *Discretion* the Rights of this Province.

The Remarker proceeds to triumph over and ridicule Mr A, because he joyns with the Protesters, altho' he had formerly been on the Committee who examin'd Mr F's acct. and reported it just, and afterwards propos'd for the Honour and Justice of the House, that the Compensation of £5000 should be made him :—these Instances would on the contrary reflect high Honour on Mr A if notwithstanding his dislike to Mr F. (and as the Remarker says being his Enemy of 7 years standing,) he did not suffer his Resentment to prevail against Justice, but of all others was the very Member that propos'd an handsome recompense to an Agent employ'd by the House, altho' by himself particularly dislik'd, and cheerfully joyn'd with the rest of the Comittee, in certifying his account of £714 10'' 7' expended in the Service of the Province to be just, when upon examination it was found so:—but all this neither demonstrates good Policy in sending Mr F. to England, nor removes the Plea that a Resident there, may afford to serve the Province cheaper, and in many respects transact Publick Business to better advantage.

I shall conclude with pointing out an Anecdote on Mr F's own Authority concerning the *judicious* Traffick in Stocks at the risque of this Province:—The Protesters have said, that by his *venturing* contrary to an Act of Assembly to place the Publick money in the Stocks, £6000. was lost to the Province.—

But it's really *pleasant* to observe, how Mr F. in his great zeal for once to discover *the whole Truth*, has not only attempted to shift this Game from himself upon the Assembly of 175 , but loaded a succeeding Assembly with a further Loss of £6000. by declaring 1st "that the Loss "arose not from *placing* the Money in the Stocks, but "from the imprudent and unnecessary Drawing it out at "the very time when they were lowest, on some slight un-"certain Rumours of a Peace concluded."

& 2d "That if the Assembly had let it remain another "Year, instead of losing they would have gained *Six* "*Thousand Pounds.*" Thus Mr F. by ingeniously accumulating *neglected Gain* with *actual Loss*, exaggerates what the Protesters modestly computed only £6000. to the prodigious Sum of £12,000. and fixes *that whole Loss* upon his good friends of the Assembly, at same time charging them with the Pursuit of *imprudent unnecessary Measures*, founded on *slight uncertain Rumours*. What may his Enemies expect, if he continues to use his Friends thus!

FINIS.

RESOLUTIONS

ADOPTED BY THE

ASSEMBLY OF PENNSYLVANIA

RELATIVE TO THE

STAMP ACT.

DRAFTED BY

JOHN DICKINSON.

———

SEPTEMBER 21, 1765.

NOTE.

On September 20, 1765, the Pennsylvania Assembly took action on the Stamp Act, reported in their *Votes and Proceedings* (v, 425), in these words:

The House taking into Consideration the Condition to which the Colonies are, and must be, reduced, in case the Stamp Act, with other late Acts of Parliament for restricting their Trade, should be carried into Execution, and continued upon them ; and being of Opinion, that it is incumbent on this Assembly, before they separate, to leave some Memorial on their Minutes, by which their Successors may be acquainted with the Sentiments they entertain of those unconstitutional Impositions ;

Ordered, That Mr. Strettell, Mr. Willing, Mr. Knight, Mr. Pearson, Mr. Wright, Mr. Allen and Mr. Ross be a Committee to prepare and bring in a Draught of such Resolves as may become the House to draw up, and enter in their Journals, upon this Occasion. . .

The Committee appointed to bring in Resolves upon the Stamp Act, and other late Acts of Parliament concerning the Colonies, reported they had essayed a Draught for that Purpose, which they presented to the Chair, where the same being read, and unanimously agreed to by the House, were ordered to be entered in the Journals, and follow in these words, viz. . .

Although Dickinson was not a member of this Committee, he prepared a draft, the similarity of which with the resolutions as adopted indicates that he was practically the scribe of the committee. This draft is printed from the original preserved among his own papers. The text as adopted is from the *Votes and Proceedings*, v, 426.

EDITOR.

STAMP ACT RESOLUTIONS.

DICKINSON'S DRAFT.

RESOLUTIONS AS ADOPTED.

The House taking into Consideration, that an Act of Parliament has lately passed in England, for imposing certain Stamp Duties on his Majesty's subjects in America, whereby they conceive some of their most essential and valuable Rights, as British Subjects, to be deeply affected, think it a Duty they owe to themselves and their Posterity, to come to the following Resolutions, viz.

Resolved, 1st. That the Constitution of Government in this Province, is founded on the natural Rights of Mankind, and the noble Principles of *English* Liberty, and is therefore perfectly free.

Resolved, 2ly. That in the opinion of this House, it is inseparably essential to a free Constitution of Government, that all internal Taxes

Resolved, N. C. D. 1. That the Assemblies of this Province have, from Time to Time, whenever requisitions have been made by his Majesty, for carrying on military Operations, for the Defence of America, most cheerfully and liberally contributed their full Proportion of Men and Money for those services.

Resolved, N. C. D. 2.

(173)

be levied upon the People *with their consent.*

Resolved, 3ly. That the sole Power and authority to levy Taxes upon the Inhabitants of this Province, is vested in the Crown or its Representative, and in the Assembly for the Time being, elected according to law.

Resolved, 4ly. That the People of this Province have constantly from its first settlement exercised and enjoyed, and *ought* to the latest Posterity to exercise & enjoy, this exclusive Right of levying Taxes upon themselves.

Resolved, 5ly. That the levying Taxes upon the Inhabitants of this Province *in any other Manner*, being manifestly subversive of public Liberty, must of necessary Consequence be utterly destructive of public Happiness.

Resolved, 6ly. That a *Trial by Jury* on every accusation in a Court of Justice, is the inherent and estimable Privilege of every Freeman of this Province,

That whenever his Majesty's Service shall, for the future, require the Aids of the Inhabitants of this Province, and they shall be called upon for that Purpose in a constitutional Way, it will be their indispensable Duty most chearfully and liberally to grant to his Majesty their Proportion of Men and Money for the Defence, Security, and other Public Services of the British American Colonies.

Resolved, N. C. D. 3. That the Inhabitants of this Province are entitled to all the Liberties, Rights and Privileges of his Majesty's Subjects in Great Britain, or elsewhere, and that the Constitution of Government in this Province is founded on the Natural Rights of Mankind, and the noble Principles of English Liberty, and therefore is, or ought to be, perfectly free.

Resolved, N. C. D. 4. That it is the inherent birthright and indubitable Privilege, of every British Subject, to be taxed only by his Consent, or that of his legal

which cannot be violated without breaking down the sacred Bulwark erected by the Virtue and Wisdom of our ancestors, for the Protection of Life, and of every Blessing that renders it valuable.

Resolved, 7ly. That it is the opinion of this House that the Restraints imposed by several late acts of Parliament on the Trade of this Province, at a Time when the People labour under an enormous Load of Debt, must of necessity be attended with the most fatal Consequences.

Resolved, 8ly. That it is the opinion of this House, that the Prosperity of this Province depends on the Preservation of its Rights, and the Continuance of an affectionate and advantageous Intercourse with *Great Britain* which must prove equally beneficial to that Kingdom.

Resolved, 9ly. That therefore it is the indispensable Duty of this House to the best of Sovereigns, whose truly paternal Tenderness Representatives, in Conjunction with His Majesty, or his Substitutes.

Resolved, N. C. D. 5. That the only legal Representatives of the Inhabitants of this Province are the persons they annually elect to serve as Members of the Assembly.

Resolved therefore, N. C. D. 6. That the Taxation of the People of this Province by any other Persons whatsoever than such their Representatives in Assembly, is unconstitutional, and is subversive to their most valuable Rights.

Resolved, N. C. D. 7. That the laying Taxes upon the Inhabitants of this Province in any other Manner, being manifestly subversive of public Liberty, must of necessary Consequence, be utterly destructive of public Happiness.

Resolved, N. C. D. 8. That the vesting an Authority in the Courts of Admiralty to decide in Suits relating to the Stamp Duty, and other Matters, foreign to their proper Jurisdiction, is

ever interests itself in the Welfare of his subjects, to the Mother Country and to this Province, with all Loyalty, Respect & Zeal, by every prudent Measure firmly to endeavor to procure a Repeal of the Stamp Act, & of the late Acts for the Restriction of *American* Commerce.

highly dangerous to the Liberties of his Majesty's American Subjects, contrary to Magna Charta, the great Charter and Fountain of English Liberty, and destructive of one of their most darling and acknowledged Rights, that of Trials by Juries.

Resolved, N. C. D. 9. That it is the Opinion of this House, that the Restraints imposed by several late Acts of Parliament on the Trade of this Province, at a Time when the People labour under an enormous Load of Debt, must of Necessity be attended with the most fatal Consequences, not only to this Province, but to the Trade of our Mother Country.

Resolved, N. C. D. 10. That this House think it their duty thus firmly to assert, with Modesty and Decency, their inherent Rights, that their Posterity may learn and know, that it was not with their Consent and and Acquiescence, that any Taxes should be levied on them by any persons but

their own Representatives;
and are desirous that these
their Resolves should Re-
main on their Minutes, as a
Testimony of their Zeal and
ardent Desire of the present
House of Assembly to pre-
serve their inestimable
Rights, which, as Englishmen, they have possessed
ever since this Province was
settled, and to transmit them
to their latest Posterity.

THE

DECLARATION OF RIGHTS

ADOPTED

BY THE

STAMP ACT CONGRESS.

DRAFTED BY

JOHN DICKINSON.

———

OCTOBER 19, 1765.

NOTE.

The action of Pennsylvania in regard to the Stamp Act Congress is best told in the *Votes and Proceedings of the House of Representatives of Pennsylvania*, (V, 419–421), where it is recorded :

Mr. Speaker laid before the House a Letter received in their Recess from the Honourable Samuel White, Esq ; Speaker of the Massachusetts Assembly . . .

The House resumed the Consideration of the Letter from the Speaker of the Massachusetts Assembly, which was again read by Order ; and after some Time spent in Debate thereon, the same was issued by the following Questions, viz.:

Whether it is the opinion of this House that, in Duty to their Constituents, they ought to remonstrate to the Crown against the Stamp Act, and other late Acts of Parliament, by which heavy Burdens have been laid on the Colonies? Resolved in the Affirmative, N. C. D.

Whether this House will appoint a Committee of three, or more, of their Members, to attend the Congress, proposed in the foregoing Letter to be held at New York on the first of next Month, for the Purposes mentioned in the said Letter? Resolved in the Affirmative.

Ordered, That Mr. Dickinson, Mr. Bryan, Mr. Morton, Mr. Knight, Mr. Sanders, Mr. M'Connaughy, Mr. Allen and Mr. Taylor be a Committee to prepare and bring in a Draught of Instructions for the Deputies to be sent from this House to the said Congress . . .

The House resumed the Consideration of their Resolution of Yesterday, to appoint a Committee of three, or more, of their Members to attend the general Congress of Committees from the several Assemblies on this Continent, to be held at New York on the first of October next, and, after some time spent therein,

Resolved, That Mr. Speaker, Mr. Dickinson, Mr. Bryan, and Mr. Morton, be, and they are, hereby nominated and appointed to attend that Service.

The Committee appointed to prepare the Instructions for the Delegates from this House to the proposed Congress at New York, on the first of next Month, reported they had made an Essay for that Purpose, which they presented to the Chair, and the same being read, and agreed to by the House, follows in these Words, viz.

Instructions to the Committee appointed to meet the Committees of the other British Continental Colonies at New York.

It is directed by the House that you shall, with the Committees that have been, or shall be, appointed by the several British Colonies on this Continent, to meet at New York, consult together on the present Circumstances of the Colonies, and the Difficulties they are and must be reduced to by the late Acts of Parliament for levying Duties and Taxes upon them, and join with the said Committees in loyal and dutiful Addresses to the King, and the two Houses of Parliament, humbly presenting the condition of these Colonies, and imploring Relief by the Repeal of the said Acts. And you are strictly required to take Care that such Addresses, in which you join, are drawn up in the most decent and respectful Terms, so as to avoid every Expression that can give the least occasion of Offence to his Majesty, or to either House of Parliament.

You are also directed to make a Report of your Proceedings herein to the succeeding Assembly.

The Speaker, Fox, did not go to the Congress, but the remaining three attended, and though Dickinson left before the Congress had completed its work, he was most prominent in its work, drafting for it the "Declaration of Rights" and the "Petition to the King," (see *post*). In the *Journal of the First Congress* (New York, 1845) the former, it is true, was claimed to have been drawn by John Cruger; but no authority is given, while a MS. in the Dickinson Papers distinctly states that "he [Dickinson] drew the resolves," and his rough draft was included in his *Political Writings*, I, 93. This draft, and the Declaration as finally adopted, are printed in parallel columns.

This "Declaration of Rights," or rather what was "said to be a copy," was first made public in the *Providence Gazette* in March, 1766, and from that was quickly republished in all the papers in the Colonies. It was first given with pseudo-authority in the *Authentic Account of the Proceedings of the Congress held at New York*. [*London :*] *MDCCLXVII.*

EDITOR.

RESOLUTIONS OF STAMP ACT CONGRESS.

DICKINSON'S DRAFT.

We, the Deputies from the colonies of Massachusetts Bay, Rhode Island, Connecticut, New York, New Jersey, Pennsylvania, the lower Counties on Delaware, Maryland, and South Carolina, in general congress assembled, Declare,

RESOLUTIONS AS ADOPTED.

The members of this congress, sincerely devoted, with the warmest sentiments of affection and duty to his majesty's person and government, inviolably attached to the present happy establishment of the protestant succession, and with minds deeply impressed by a sense of the present and impending misfortunes of the British colonies on this continent, having considered as maturely as time would permit, the circumstances of said colonies, esteem it our indispensable duty to make the following declarations, of our humble opinions, respecting the most essential rights and liberties of the colonists, and of the grievances under which they labor, by reason of several late acts of parliament.

1. That his majesty's subjects in these colonies, owe

I. Resolved, That his Majesty's Subjects in these col-

(183)

the same allegiance to the crown of *Great Britain*, that is due from his subjects born within the realm.

2. That all acts of parliament, not inconsistent with the principles of freedom, are obligatory on the colonists.

3. That his Majesty's liege subjects in these colonies, are as free as his subjects in *Great Britain.*

4. That it is inseparably essential to the freedom of a people, that no taxes be laid upon them, but with their own consent given personally, or by their representatives.

5. That the people of these colonies are not, and from local circumstances cannot be represented in the house of commons in *Great Britain.*

6. That the only representatives of the people of these colonies, are the persons chosen therein by themselves for that purpose.

7. That no taxes can be constitutionally imposed on the people of these colonies, but by their grants made in

onies owe the same Allegiance to the Crown of Great Britain, that is owing from his Subjects born within the Realm, and all due Subordination to that august Body the Parliament of Great Britain.

II. That his Majesty's liege Subjects in these Colonies, are intitled to all the inherent Rights and Liberties of his natural born subjects within the Kingdom of Great Britain.

III. That it is inseparably essential to the Freedom of a People, and the undoubted Right of Englishmen, that no Tax be imposed upon them, but with their own Consent, given personally, or by their Representatives.

IV. That the People of these Colonies are not, and from their local Circumstances, cannot be represented in the House of Commons in Great Britain.

V. That the only Representatives of the People of these Colonies, are the Persons chosen therein by themselves; and that no Taxes ever have been, or can be,

person or by their representatives.

8. That the power of
granting supplies to the
crown in *Great Britain* belonging solely to the commons, and consequently all
such grants being only *gifts*
of the people to the crown,
it therefore involves an inconsistency with the principle and spirit of the *British*
constitution, and with reason, for the commons of
Great Britain to undertake
to give to his majesty, according to the terms of the
late act of parliament, entituled, "An act for granting
certain duties in the *British*
colonies and plantations in
America," &c., the property
of the colonists.

9. That trial by jury is
the inherent and invaluable
right of every freeman in
these colonies.

10. That the late act of
parliament passed in the
fifth year of his majesty's
reign, entituled, "An act
for granting and applying
certain *stamp* duties and
other duties, in the *British*
colonies and plantations in

constitutionally imposed on
them but by their respective
Legislatures.

VI. That all Supplies to
the Crown being free Gifts
of the People, it is unreasonable, and inconsistent with
the Principles and Spirit of
the British Constitution, for
the People of Great Britain
to grant to his Majesty the
Property of the Colonies.

VII. That trials by jury
are the inherent and invaluable right of every British
Subject in these Colonies.

VIII. That the late Act
of Parliament, intitled, "An
Act for granting certain
Stamp Duties, and other
Duties, in the British Colonies and Plantations in
America," &c., by imposing
Taxes on the Inhabitants of
these Colonies, and the said
Act, and several other Acts,
by extending the Jurisdiction of the Courts of Ad-
miralty beyond its ancient
Limits, have a Tendency to
subvert the Rights and Liberties of the Colonists.

IX. That the Duties im-
posed by several Acts of
Parliament, from the pecu-

America," and by imposing taxes on the inhabitants of these colonies, and by extending the jurisdiction of the courts of admiralty, is subversive of their most sacred rights and liberties.

11. That the duties imposed by the said first mentioned act, will be, from the peculiar circumstances of these colonies, extremely grievous and burthensome.

12. That the restrictions imposed by several late acts of parliament on the trade of these colonies, must of necessity be attended by consequences very detrimental to the interests of *Great Britain* and *America.*

13. That the prosperity of these colonies depends on the reservation of their rights and liberties, and an intercourse with *Great Britain* mutually affectionate and advantageous.

14. That it is the indispensable duty of the colonies to the best of sovereigns, to the mother country, and to themselves, to endeavour by legal and dutiful addresses to his majesty, and both

liar Circumstances of these Colonies, will be extremely burthensome and grievous, and, from the Scarcity of Specie, the Payment of them absolutely impracticable.

X. That the Profits of the Trade of these Colonies, ultimately center in Great Britain, to pay for the Manufactures which they are obliged to take from thence, they eventually contribute very largely to all Supplies granted there to the Crown.

XI. That the Restrictions imposed by several late Acts of Parliament, on the Trade of these Colonies, will render them unable to purchase the Manufactures of Great Britain.

XII. That the Increase, Prosperity and Happiness of these Colonies depend on the full and free Enjoyment of their Rights and Liberties, and an Intercourse with Great Britain, mutually affectionate and advantageous.

XIII. That it is the Right of the British Subjects in these Colonies, to petition the King, or either House of Parliament.

houses of parliament, to procure the repeal of the "act for granting and applying certain stamp duties," of all clauses whereby the jurisdiction of the admiralty is extended as aforesaid, and of the other late acts for the restriction of American commerce.

15. That it is the right of the British subjects on this continent to petition the king, and lords and commons in parliament assembled, whenever they judge their liberties and interests to be so far affected, as to render such applications necessary.

Lastly. That it is the indespensable Duty of these Colonies to the best of Sovereigns, to the Mother-country and themselves, to endeavor, by a loyal and dutiful Address to his Majesty and humble Applications to both Houses of Parliament, to procure the Repeal of the Act for granting certain Stamp Duties, of all Clauses of any other Act of Parliament, whereby the Jurisdiction of the Admiralty is extended, as aforesaid, and of other Acts for the Restriction of American Commerce.

A PETITION

TO THE

KING

FROM THE

STAMP ACT CONGRESS

DRAFTED BY
JOHN DICKINSON.

––––––––

OCTOBER 19, 1765.

NOTE.

On October 19, the Stamp Act Congress "Upon motion, voted, That Robert R. Livingston, William Samuel Johnson, and William Murdock, Esqs., be a committee to prepare an address to his majesty and lay the same before the congress on Monday next." On that day a draft was reported, and "after sundry amendments, the same was approved by the congress, and ordered to be engrossed." According to the report of his fellow members (*Votes and Proceedings*, v, 437) "before the Addresses were finished, Mr. Dickinson was called Home on urgent Business," yet in spite of that and his not being on the Committee, he seems to have drafted this Petition to the King. Among the Dickinson MSS. is a printed copy of this petition, clipped from the *Pennsylvania Gazette*, with a MS. Note, which states that Dickinson "drew the resolves, and the petition to the Crown, which was altered, particularly in the title and middle of it, after he left the congress." And the petition so printed is corrected in Dickinson's handwriting, presumably to make it conform to his draft, and indicate the alterations made in it by the congress. As printed here, the text follows Dickinson's changes, the amendments of the congress being given in the foot notes.

EDITOR.

(191)

To the KING'S Most Excellent Majesty, The Petition of the Freeholders, and other Inhabitants of the Massachusetts Bay, Rhode Island, and Providence Plantations, New Jersey, Pennsylvania, the Government of the Counties New Castle, Kent and Sussex, upon Delaware, Province of Maryland, &c.

Most Humbly Sheweth,

That the Inhabitants of these Colonies, unanimously devoted with the warmest Sentiments of Duty and Affection to your Majesty's sacred Person and Government, inviolably attached to the present happy Establishment of the Protestant Succession in your illustrious House, and deeply sensible of your Royal Attention to their Prosperity and Happiness, humbly beg Leave to approach the Throne, and represent * to your Majesty, that these Colonies were originally planted by Subjects of the British Crown, who, animated with the Spirit of Liberty, encouraged by your Majesty's Royal Predecessors, and confiding in the public Faith for the Enjoyment of all the Rights and Liberties essential to Freedom, emigrated from their native Country to this Continent, and by their successful Perseverance in the Midst of innumerable Dangers and Difficulties,† with a Profusion of their Blood and Treasure, have happily added these vast and valuable Dominions to the Empire of Great Britain.

That for the Enjoyment of these Rights and Liberties, several Governments were early formed in the said Colonies, with full power of legislation, agreeable to the Principles of the English Constitution.

* Altered by the Congress to read "Throne, by representing."—*Ed.*
† The word "together" inserted by the Congress.—*Ed.*

(193)

That under those Governments these Rights and Liberties,* thus vested in their Ancestors, and transmitted to their Posterity, have been exercised and enjoyed, and by the inestimable Blessings thereof, under the Favour of Almighty God, the inhospitable Deserts of America have been converted into flourishing Countries; Science, Humanity, and the Knowledge of divine Truths, diffused through remote Regions of Ignorance, Infidelity and Barbarism; the Number of British Subjects wonderfully increased, and the Wealth and Power of Great-Britain proportionably augmented.

That by Means of these Settlements, and the unparallelled Success of your Majesty's Arms, a foundation is now laid for rendering the British Empire the most extensive and powerful of any recorded in History; our Connection with this Empire, we esteem our greatest Happiness and Security, and humbly conceive it may now be so established by your Royal Wisdom, as to endure to the latest Period of Time. This, with most humble Submission to your Majesty, we apprehend will be most effectually accomplished, by fixing the Pillars thereof on Liberty and Justice, and securing the inherent Rights and Liberties of your Subjects here, upon the principles of the English Constitution. To this Constitution these two Principles are essential, the Right of your faithful Subjects freely to grant to your Majesty such Aids as are required for the Support of your Government over them, and other public Exigencies, and Trials by their Peers. By the one, they are secured from unreasonable Impositions, and by the other, from arbitrary decisions of the executive Power. The Continuation of these Liberties to the Inhabitants of America, we ardently implore, as absolutely necessary to unite the several Parts of your widely extended Dominions

---

* "Rights and" struck out by the Congress.—*Ed.*

in that Harmony, so essential to the Preservation and Happiness of the whole. Protected in these Liberties, the Emoluments Great Britain receives from us, however great at present, are inconsiderable, compared with those she has the fairest Prospect of acquiring. By this Protection, she will forever secure to herself the Advantage of conveying to all Europe the Merchandizes which America furnishes, and of supplying thro' the same Channel whatever is wanted from thence. Here opens a boundless Source of Wealth, and Naval Strength; yet these immense Advantages, by the Abridgment of those invaluable Rights and Liberties, by which our Growth has been nourished, are in Danger of being forever lost, and our subordinate Legislatures in Effect rendered useless, by the late Acts of Parliament, imposing duties and taxes on these Colonies, and extending the jurisdiction of the Courts of Admiralty here, beyond its ancient Limits; Statutes by which your Majesty's Commons in Britain undertake absolutely to dispose of the Property of their Fellow Subjects in America, without their Consent, and for the Enforcing whereof, they are subjected to the Determination of a single Judge, in a Court unrestrained by the wise Rules of the Common Law, the Birthright of Englishmen, and the Safeguard of their Persons and Properties.

The invaluable Rights of taxing ourselves, and of Trial by our Peers, of which we implore your Majesty's Protection, are not, we most humbly conceive, unconstitutional, but confirmed by the great Charter of English Liberty. On the first of these Rights the Honourable the House of Commons found their Practice of originating Money Bills, a Right enjoyed by the Kingdom of Ireland, by the Clergy of England, until relinquished by themselves; a Right in fine, which all other your Majesty's Subjects, both within and without the Realm, have hitherto enjoyed.

With Hearts therefore impressed with the most indelible Characters of Gratitude to your Majesty, and to the Memory of the Kings of your illustrious House, whose Reigns have been signally distinguished by their auspicious Influence on the Prosperity of the British Dominions, and convinced by the most affecting proofs of your Majesty's Parental Love to all your People, however distant, and your incessant* and benevolent Desires to promote their Happiness; we most humbly beseech your Majesty, that you will be graciously pleased to take into your Royal Consideration, the Distresses of your faithful Subjects, on this Continent,† and to afford them such Relief as, in your Royal Wisdom, their unhappy Circumstances shall be judged to require.

* Changed to "unceasing" by the Congress.—*Ed.*

† The Congress here inserted: "and lay the same before your Majesty's Parliament."—*Ed.*

AN ADDRESS

TO

" FRIENDS AND COUNTRYMEN "

ON THE

STAMP ACT.

BY

JOHN DICKINSON.

———

NOVEMBER, 1765.

NOTE.

Original issued as a broadside, beginning :

   Friends and Countrymen, / The Critical time is now come, when you are reduced to the necessity of forming / a Resolution . . . / Fo. pp. 2.

The exact date of publication is in doubt. Mr. Hildeburn (*Issues of the Pennsylvania Press*, II, 35) relying on Du Simitiere, gives it Dec. 5, and concludes it to be from the press of Bradford. But a bill of Franklin and Hall to Dickinson, contains the item : " 1765. Decr. 10. To printing 200 Copies of an Address to the Inhabitants of Pennsylvania . . . . £3.5," which, unless we refer the charge to an absolutely unknown piece, must be this broadside. As it was reprinted in the New York Gazette on Dec. 5, it must clearly have been issued in November. These two bits of evidence are confirmed by the following statement from the *Pennsylvania Gazette* (Feb. 6, 1766), the printers of which (presuming them to have been the printers of the broadside as well) would have the most accurate knowledge as to the authorship and date of publication.

   A number of the SONS OF LIBERTY, in particular those of a neighboring Province, having expressed their Desire of knowing who is the Author of the Piece published and dispersed in this City in November last, and re-published in the New York Gazette of the 5th of December, in the New London Gazette of the 20th of the same Month, and so warmly recommended in the Connecticut Resolves, which are inserted in our Paper of the 23d of January ; in Compliance with their Desire, we inform them, that it is said, and believed, to be wrote by J—N D—CK—S—N, Esq., of this city.

The " Connecticut Resolves " referred to in this extract, were as follows:

   Resolutions of a great number of the respectable Inhabitants of the County of Windham and Parts adjacent, held at Pomfret, in the said County, on the 25th Day of December, 1765. . . . . . We recommend a

Piece wrote by a Master of Reason, and a true Friend to Liberty, in Pennsylvania, and inserted in the New London Gazette of the 20th instant.

EDITOR.

ADDRESS ON STAMP ACT.

Friends and Countrymen.

The critical Time has now come, when you are reduced to the Necessity of forming a Resolution, upon a Point of the most alarming Importance that can engage the Attention of Men. Your Conduct *at this Period* must decide the *future* Fortunes of yourselves, and of your Posterity— must decide, whether *Pennsylvanians*, from henceforward, shall be Freemen or Slaves. So vast is the Consequence, so extensive is the Influence of the Measure you shall *at present* pursue. May GOD grant that every one of you may consider your Situation with a Seriousness and Sensibility becoming the solemn Occasion; and that you may receive this Address with the same candid and tender Affection for the public Good by which it is dictated.

We have seen the Day on which an Act of Parliament, imposing Stamp Duties on the *British* Colonies in *America*, was appointed to take Effect ; and we have seen the Inhabitants of these Colonies, with an unexampled Unanimity, compelling the Stamp-Officers throughout the Provinces to resign their Employments. The virtuous Indignation with which they have thus acted, was inspired by the generous Love of Liberty, and guided by a perfect sense of Loyalty to the best of Kings, and of duty to the Mother Country. The Resignation of the Officers was judged the most effectual and the most decent Method of preventing the Execution of a Statute, that strikes the Axe into the Root of the Tree, and lays the hitherto flourishing Branches of *American* Freedom, with all its precious Fruits, low in the Dust.—

That this is the fatal Tendency of that Statute, appears from Propositions so evident, that he who runs may read and understand. To mention them is to convince. Men cannot be happy, without Freedom; nor free, without Security of Property; nor so secure, unless the sole Power to dispose of it be lodged in themselves; *therefore* no People can be *free*, but where Taxes are imposed on them *with their own Consent*, given personally, or by their Representatives. If then the Colonies are equally intitled to Happiness with the Inhabitants of *Great-Britain*, and Freedom is essential to Happiness, they are equally intitled to Freedom. If they are equally intitled to Freedom, and an exclusive Right of Taxation is essential to Freedom, they are equally intitled to such Taxation.

What further Steps you can now take, without Injury to this sacred Right, demands your maturest Deliberation.

If you comply with the Act, by using Stamped Papers, you fix, you rivet perpetual Chains upon your unhappy Country. You unnecessarily, voluntarily establish the detestable Precedent, which those who have forged your Fetters ardently wish for, to varnish the future Exercise of this new claimed Authority. You may judge of the Use that will be made of it, by the Eagerness with which the Pack of Ministerial Tools have hunted for Precedents to palliate the Horrors of this Attack upon *American* Freedom. After all their infamous Labour, they could find nothing that even *their* unlimited Audacity could dare to call *Precedents* in this Case, but the Statute for establishing a Post-Office in *America*, and the Laws for regulating the Force here, during the late War.

These Instances were greedily seized upon, and the Press groaned with Pamphlets to prove, that *they* would justify the Taxation of *America* by *Great-Britain.*—But no sooner were these boasted Examples produced to public View, and examined, than the Absurdity of applying them to the present Occasion, appeared so glaring, that they became more the Subject of Ridicule, than of Argument.—

Your Compliance with this Act, will save future Ministers the Trouble of reasoning on this Head, and your Tameness will free them from any Kind of Moderation, when they shall hereafter meditate any other Taxation upon you.

They will have a Precedent furnished by yourselves, and a Demonstration that the Spirit of *Americans*, after great Clamour and Bluster, is *a most submissive servile Spirit*—Ministers will rejoice in the Discovery, and as no Measure can be more popular at Home, than to lessen the Burthens of the People *there*, by laying Part of the Weight on you, they will of Course be tempted by that Motive, and emboldened by your Conduct, to make you "*Hewers of Wood*, and *Drawers of Water.*"

THE Stamp Act, therefore, is to be regarded only as an EXPERIMENT OF YOUR DISPOSITION. If you quietly bend your Necks to that Yoke, you prove yourselves ready to receive any Bondage to which your *Lords* and *Masters* shall please to subject you. Some Persons perhaps may fondly hope, it will be as easy to obtain a Repeal of the Stamp Act after it is put in Execution, as if the Execution of it is avoided. But be not deceived. The late Ministry publickly declared, "that it was *intended* to establish the Power of *Great-Britain* to tax the Colonies." Can we imagine then, that when so great a Point is carried, and *we have tamely submitted*, that any other Ministry will venture to propose, or that the Parliament will consent to pass, an Act to renounce this Advantage? No! Power is of a tenacious Nature: What it seizes it will retain.

ROUSE yourselves therefore, my dear Countrymen. Think, oh! think of the endless Miseries you *must* entail upon yourselves, and your Country, by touching the pestilential Cargoes that have been sent to you. Destruction lurks within them.——To receive them is Death—is worse than Death—it is SLAVERY!——If you do not, and I trust in Heaven you will not use the Stamped Papers, it will be necessary to consider how you are to act. Some Persons are of Opinion, that it is proper to stop all Business that requires written Instruments, subject to Duties.

AGAINST this Proposal there are many weighty Objections. In the first Place, it will be nearly the same Acknowledgment of the Validity of the Stamp Act, and of its legal Obligation upon you, as if you use the Papers. It will also be extremely injurious to Individuals, and I apprehend the Inconveniences arising from the Stoppage of Business will be so great, that many People, whose immediate Interest may have too much Influence on their Judgment, may be induced to believe, that this Obstruction will be more pernicious than the Execution of the Stamp Act; and thus I am afraid, that a mistaken Zeal to avoid the Execution, may really produce it. How long can this Stoppage be endured? Or how long must it be continued? Until we can obtain Relief, by a Repeal of the Law, perhaps some may say. If this *should* happen, you cannot expect to hear of the Repeal in less than three or four Months. But if you act in this Manner, in my Opinion, you will never hear of it. For as soon as the News of your stopping all Business arrives in *Great-Britain*, the Parliament, Ministry and People will be convinced of two Things; first, that you are intimidated to the utmost Degree; and secondly, that your Method of eluding the Act will at length compel you to comply with it.——They will therefore give themselves no further Trouble about you, unless it be to send over a few Regiments, to quicken the Execution.

FOR these Reasons, and many more, it appears to me the wisest and the safest Course for you to proceed in all Business as usual, without taking the least Notice of the

Stamp Act. If you behave in this spirited Manner, you may be assured, that every Colony on the Continent will follow the Example of a Province so justly celebrated for its Liberty. Your Conduct will convince *Great-Britain*, that the Stamp Act will never be carried into Execution, but by Force of Arms; and this one Moment's Reflection must demonstrate, that she will never attempt.

As to any Penalties that may be incurred, it will be vain to think of extorting them from the whole Continent, or from a whole Province. It may be objected, perhaps, that our Ships will be liable to Seizure, if their Clearances be not upon Stamped Papers; but I believe no Lawyer will say, that this would be a legal Reason for such Seizures. However, we need be under no Apprehension of this Kind; for proceeding in that Way, would be in Fact a Declaration of War against the Colonies, that at this Time would by no Means suit the Mother Country.—

THUS, my Friends and Countrymen, have I plainly laid before you my sentiments on your present affecting Situation; and may Divine Providence inspire you with Wisdom to act in such a Manner, as will most advance that Happiness I ardently wish you may enjoy.

THE

LATE REGULATIONS

RESPECTING THE

BRITISH COLONIES

CONSIDERED.

BY

JOHN DICKINSON.

DECEMBER 7, 1765.

NOTE.

The Pennsylvania Journal of December 5, 1765, announced that:
Next Saturday will be published, and to be sold by
W. BRADFORD, a piece intituled
THE
LATE REGULATIONS
RESPECTING THE
BRITISH COLONIES
ON THE CONTINENT OF
AMERICA
CONSIDERED,
In a letter from a gentleman in PHILADELPHIA to his
friend in LONDON.

The pamphlet was issued with the title of:

The / Late Regulations / respecting the / British Colonies / on the continent of / America / considered, / In a Letter from a Gentleman in Philadelphia / to his Friend in London / *Prosunt minus recte excogita; cum alios incitent saltem / ad veritatis investigationem.* Fulb. a. Bartol. / Philadelphia : / Printed and Sold by William Bradford, at the Corner of / Market and Front Streets. M.DCC.LXV. 8vo, pp. 38.

Two English editions, with some slight corrections, were also printed :

The / Late Regulations, / respecting the / British Colonies / on the continent of / America / considered : / In a Letter from a Gentleman in Philadel- / phia to his Friend in London. / . . . / . . . / Philadelphia Printed : / London Re-printed, for J. Almon, opposite Bur- / lington-House, in Piccadilly. M.DCC.LXV. 8vo, pp. 62, (1).

This edition was clearly not issued till February, 1766, (when the pamphlet was first advertised and noticed in the English press,) for the date of printing in Philadelphia, with the time necessary for transmission and reprinting, precludes the date given on the title from being correct. The title of the second English edition was :

The late / Regulations / respecting the / British Colonies / on the continent of / America / considered, / In a Letter from a Gentleman in

Philadelphia / to his Friend in London. / . . . / . . . / Philadelphia Printed : / London ; Re-printed for J. Almon, opposite / Burlington House, Piccadilly. / MDCCLXVI. 8vo, pp. (4), 39.

The pamphlet was briefly noticed in the *Monthly Review,* xxxiv, 238 ; and an " Extract from a Letter from a Gentleman in London, to his Friend in Philadelphia," dated Feb. 8, 1766, printed in the *Pennsylvania Gazette* for May 22, 1766, states :

> I have the Pleasure of your last with the Pamphlet, entituled, "The Late Regulations, respecting the British Colonies on the Continent of America, Considered." It is an excellent Performance, and its Author merits the Thanks of his Country,—mine he has most unfeignedly.—Its arrival, before the final Decision of the Cause, will, I flatter myself, have a happy Effect. It has been reprinted here, and the Bookseller advertised in the Papers, that it was written by Mr. Dickinson.—Though the Town has been, in a Manner, glutted with Pamphlets on American Affairs, yet its Sale has been very rapid. It is highly esteemed ; has gained the Author much Reputation, and most surely does him great Honour.

The present reprint is from the first edition, which is absolutely followed, except that the short "Errata" at the end is omitted, and the corrections embodied in the text. The numerals inserted in brackets indicate the paging of the original. The changes made by the author, in the text as printed in the *Political Writings of John Dickinson* (1, 47) are shown in foot notes.

EDITOR.

THE
LATE REGULATIONS

RESPECTING THE

BRITISH COLONIES

ON THE CONTINENT OF

AMERICA

CONSIDERED,

In a Letter from a Gentleman in PHILADELPHIA
to his Friend in L O N D O N.

---

*Prosunt minus reticë excogitata ; cum alios incitent saltem
ad veritatis investigationem.* FULB. A BARTOL.

P H I L A D E L P H I A:

Printed and Sold by WILLIAM BRADFORD, at the Corner of
Market and Front-Streets. M.DCC.LXV.

THE LATE REGULATIONS

Sir,

When I last wrote to you and said, "that the late measures respecting *America*, would not only be extremely injurious to the *Colonies*, but also to *Great-Britain*," I little thought I was entring into an engagement, which would oblige me to exceed the usual limits of a letter : but since you desire to have at large the reasons in support of this opinion, and I always think it my duty to comply with your requests, I will endeavour in the clearest manner I can, to lay my sentiments before you.

The *American* continental colonies are inhabited by persons of small fortunes, who *are* so closely employed in subduing a wild country, for their subsistence, and who *would* labour under such difficulties in contending with old and populous countries, which must exceed them in workmanship and cheapness, that they have not [4] time nor any temptation to apply themselves to manufactures.

Hence arises the *importance of the colonies to *Great-*

---

* It has been said in the House of Commons, when complaints have been made of the decay of trade to any part of *Europe*, "That such things were not worth regard, as *Great-Britain* was possest of colonies that could consume more of her manufactures than she was able to supply them with."

"As the case now stands, we shall shew that the *plantations* are a spring of *wealth* to this nation, that they *work* for us, that their treasure *centers all here*, and that the laws have tied them fast enough to us ; so that it must be through our own fault and mismanagement, if they become independent of *England*."

DAVENANT on the Plantation trade.

"It is better that the islands should be supplied from the Northern Colonies than from *England*, for this reason ; the provisions we might

Britain. Her prosperity depends on her commerce; her commerce on her manufactures; her [5] manufactures on the markets for them; and the most constant and advan-

send to *Barbados, Jamaica*, &c., would be *unimprov'd* product of the earth, as grain of all kinds, or such product where there is little got by the improvement, as malt, salt, beef and pork; indeed, the exportation of salt fish thither would be more advantageous, but the goods which we send to the *Northern Colonies* are such, whose *improvement* may be justly said one with another to be near *four-fifths* of the value of the *whole commodity*, as apparel, household-furniture, and many other things.

Idem.

"*New-England* is the most prejudicial plantation to the kingdom of *England;* and yet, to do right to that most industrious *English* colony, I must confess, that though we lose by their unlimited trade with other foreign plantations, yet we are very great gainers by their direct trade to and from *Old England*. Our yearly exportations of *English* manufactures, malt and other goods, from hence thither, amounting, in my opinion, to *ten times* the value of what is imported from thence; which calculation I do not make at random, but upon *mature consideration*, and, peradventure, upon *as much experience in this very trade*, as any other person will pretend to; and therefore, whenever reformation of our correspondency in trade with that people shall be thought on, it will, in my poor judgment, require GREAT TENDERNESS, and VERY SERIOUS CIRCUMSPECTION."

Sir JOSIAH CHILD'S discourse on trade.

"Our plantations spend mostly our *English* manufactures, and those *of all sorts almost imaginable,* in *egregious quantities,* and employ near *two-thirds of our* English *shipping;* so that we have *more people* in *England*, by reason of our plantations in *America*." 　　　*Idem.*

Sir JOSIAH CHILD says, in another part of his work, "That not more than fifty families are maintained in *England* by the refining of sugar." From whence, and from what *Davenant* says, it is plain, that the advantages here said to be derived from the plantations by *England*, must be meant chiefly of the continental colonies. *See notes to pages 12 & 13.*

"I shall sum up my whole remarks on our *American* colonies, with this observation, that as they are a certain annual revenue of several millions sterling to their Mother Country, they ought carefully to be protected, duly encouraged, and every opportunity that presents, improved for their increment and advantage, as every one they can possibly reap, must at last return to us with interest."

BEAWES's Lex merc. red.

"We may safely advance, that our trade and navigation are greatly en-

tageous markets are afforded by the colonies, as in all others the * rest of *Europe* interferes with her, and various accidents may interrupt them. The benefit from hence is at *present* immense ; but in *future* times when *America* shall be more fully peopled, must exceed with prudent management the warmest wishes of a *British* Patriot.

Our chief productions are provisions, naval stores, furs, iron and lumber. A few colonies yield tobacco and indigo. Some of these commodities are necessary to *Great-Britain;* but all that she requires are [6] vastly insufficient to pay for her manufactures which we want. The productions of some of the Southern Colonies may perhaps be equal to their demands, but the case is widely different with the Northern ; for in these, the importations from *Great-Britain* are computed to be generally more than double the value of their immediate exportations to that kingdom.

The only expedient left us for making our remittances, is to carry on some other trade, whereby we can obtain silver and gold, which our own country does not afford. Hence it is evident, that if our taking off and paying for

creased by our colonies, and that they really are a source of treasure and naval power to this kingdom, since *they work for us,* and *their treasure centers here.* Before their settlement, our manufactures were few, and those but indifferent ; the number of *English* merchants very small, and the whole shipping of the nation much inferior to what now belongs to the Northern Colonies only. *These are certain facts.* But since their establishment, our condition has altered for the better, almost to a degree beyond credibility.—Our MANUFACTURES are prodigiously increased, chiefly by the demand for them in the plantations, where they AT LEAST TAKE OFF ONE HALF, and supply us with many valuable commodities for exportation, which is as great an emolument to the Mother Kingdom, as to the plantations themselves.''

POSTLETHWAYT'S univ. dict. of trade and commerce.

* '' Most of the nations of *Europe* have interfered with us, more or less, in divers of our staple manufactures, within half a century, not only in our woolen, but in our lead and tin manufactures, as well as our fisheries.''

POSTLETHWAYT, *ibid.*

her manufactures, is beneficial to *Great-Britain*, the channels by which we acquire money for that purpose, ought to be industriously kept open and uninterrupted.

Our trade with *Spain*, *Portugal* and the foreign plantations in the *West-Indies* have chiefly answered this end, though with much difficulty, the mother country having long since drawn the *commercial cords with which the colonies are bound, extremely tight upon them. Every thing produced *here*, that *Great-Britain* chuses to take to herself, must be carried to that king- [7] dom† only—

* As far as regulations are requisite to confine the commerce of the colonies to *British* subjects and to *British* ships ; to give *Great Britain* the preference in being supplied with naval stores, so essential to her strength at sea ; with commodities necessary for carrying on her woollen manufactures, or such articles as can bear high duties upon them, and thereby make a considerable addition to the revenue ; or as far as they are requisite to prevent the colonies from being supplied with any thing in the place of *British* manufactures, they may be reasonable. These regulations, it is apprehended, establish the basis of the *British* power ; and form such a firm connection between the Mother Country and her Colonies, as will produce all the advantages she ought to wish for, or that they can afford her. Any further attempt to shackle *some* of the colonies in favour of *others*, or to advance the revenue in *America* by restraining her trade, is but regulating by a severe exercise of power, what wants no regulation, and losing by too much haste to gain. (*See Notes to page* 15.) *Unnecessary* and *irritating* restrictions, will at last cast *contempt* and *hatred* on those *substantial* ones, that length of time, and the natural reverence of Colonies for their Mother Country, would have consecrated ; for discontented minds are not apt to distinguish. "Narrow-limited notions in trade and planting, are only advanced by, and can only be of use to *particular* persons, but are always injurious to the *public* interests, in preventing the full employment of our own people, and giving our rivals and competitors in trade, the opportunity of employing greater numbers of theirs, producing greater quantities of merchandizes, and underselling us at foreign markets."

POSTLETHWAYT'S univ. dict. of trade and commerce.

† *Montesquieu*, speaking of the contract made by *Poland* for selling *all* her corn to *Dantzick* ONLY; and another of the like nature between some *Indian* princes and the *Dutch* for spices, says : "These agreements are proper for a poor nation, whose inhabitants are satisfied *to forego the hopes of enriching themselves* provided *they can be secure of a certain*

Every thing we chuse to import from *Europe*, must be shipped in * *Great-Britain*—Heavy duties have been laid on our importations from the foreign plantations.

However under all these restraints and some others that have been imposed on us, we have not till lately been unhappy. Our spirits were not depressed. We apprehended no design formed against our liberty. We for a long time enjoyed peace, and were quite free from any heavy debt, either internal or external. We had a paper currency which served as a medium of domestic commerce, and permitted us to employ all the gold and silver we could acquire, in trade abroad. We had a multitude of markets for our provisions, lumber and iron. These allowed liberties, with some others we assumed, enabled us to collect considerable sums of money for the joint benefit of ourselves and our mother country.[8]

But the modern regulations are in every circumstance afflicting. The remittances we have been able to make to *Great-Britain*, with all the licence hitherto granted or taken, and all the money brought among us in the course of the late war, have not been sufficient to pay her what we owe ; but there still remains due, according to a late calculation made by the *English* merchants, the sum of four millions sterling. Besides this, we are and have been for many years heavily taxed, for the payment of the debts contracted by our efforts against the common enemy. These seem to be difficulties severe enough for young colonies to contend with. The last † sinks our paper cur-

subsistence ; or for nations, whose SLAVERY consists either *in renouncing the use of those things which nature has given them ;* or in being OBLIGED TO SUBMIT TO A DISADVANTAGEOUS COMMERCE."

* Except Salt from any part of *Europe* for the fisheries of *Newfoundland, New England, New York* and *Pennsylvania ;* and a few things from *Ireland.*

† While the quantity of paper currency is proportioned to the uses for it, it must be beneficial ; and therefore to sink it below that quantity, must be prejudicial.

rency very fast. The former sweeps off our silver and gold in a torrent to *Great-Britain*, and leaves us continually toiling to supply from a number of distant springs the continually wasting stream.

Thus drained, we are prohibited by new and stricter restraints being laid on our trade, from procuring these coins as we used to do; and from instituting among ourselves bills of credit in the place of such portions of them as are required in our internal traffic; and in this exhausted condition, our languishing country is to strive to take up and to totter under the additional burthen of the STAMP ACT.

In defence of the prohibition to institute *bills of credit*, it may be said, "that some few colonies, by injurious emissions of paper currency, did great injury to indi- [9] viduals. It is true: But it is as true, that others * always supported the credit of their bills in such a manner, that their emissions were of vast benefit both to the provinces and to *Great-Britain*. The inconveniences under which the colonies laboured before these emissions are well remembered, and were produced by the same cause that distresses us at this time; that is, by *Great-Britain's* taking off all our gold and silver. There was then so little money among several of them, that a stop was put in a manner to buying and selling, and then shop-keepers were obliged to barter their goods for food. The effect produced by these emissions was surprizing—Trade revived; and the remarkable and immediate † increase of our importations shewed

* No attempt was ever made in this province and some others, to pay *English* debts any otherwise than according to the rate of exchange; and no complaint was ever made of injustice from the depreciation of the currency.

† Value of the exports from *England* to *Pennsylvania* at different periods.

In 1723 they were £15,992 19 4
1730 . . . . . 48,592 7 5
1737 . . . . . 56,690 6 7
1742 . . . . . 75,295 3 4

how advantageous they were to *Great-Britain*. If any
[10] inconveniences were feared from this kind of cur-

In the year 1723 the first bills of credit were emitted in *Pennsylvania*,
to the value of £45000. In 1728, part of the first emission being then
sunk, £30000 more were emitted. It appears from the account above,
that in seven years from 1723 to 1730, the exports increased £32 599 8 1
sterling.—In 1738, great part of the preceding emissions being then sunk,
there was an emission and re-emission amounting in the whole to £80000.
In five years afterwards it appears by the account above, the exports increased over £20000 sterling.

In later times when larger emissions have been made, the exports have
proportionately increased. In 1755 £55000 were emitted; and in 1756
£30000.—In 1757, the exports amounted to £268,426 6 6.—Afterwards
our emissions were still greater, and in one year of the war, the exports
rose to more than £700,000 sterling.

It is not pretended, that the increase of our importations is *solely* owing
to the emissions of paper money; but it is thought to be a very great
cause of that increase. It is undoubtedly owing in part to the increase
of people by propagation, and the influx of foreigners. But such *great*
and *sudden* increases as have been mentioned in the short space of seven
or five years, from 1723 to 1730, and from 1737 to 1742, could not in any
great degree proceed from the increase by propagation ; and at that time
I think foreigners did not flow in upon us in such numbers as they since
have done. In the war large sums were brought among us for the maintenance of the fleets and armies, it is true : but that our currency was
then of great utility is evident, because when the greatest quantity of it
was passing, bills of exchange were lower than they were for a long time
before, or have been since.

It may be objected, that the complaint of the scarcity of money in
America, particularly in this province, cannot be well founded, as we
have lately had such large emissions. I am very sensible how liable persons are to errors in questions of this nature, and therefore I think
myself obliged to speak with diffidence on the subject. Perhaps the following observations may in some measure answer the objection. 1st.
About one half of the emissions is sunk. 2dly. A very great part of the
bills now circulating, are passing in the neighbouring provinces. 3dly.
Our gold and silver are sent to *Great Britain*, so that but small quantities
thereof are now current among us—and therefore we must almost entirely rely on our paper for the medium of domestic commerce. Lastly,
it does not seem probable, that we should have heard such great complaints of the scarcity of money, if the extreme restrictions of our commerce had not so generally prevented our usual methods of acquiring it.

rency, means might have been found to prevent them, without utterly abolishing it: But now the apprehension of mischiefs that might have been more easily obviated, has deprived us of real benefits.

Perhaps no mode could be devis'd more advantageous to the public, or to individuals, than our method of emitting bills in this province for our own use. They are lent out upon good security, chiefly real, at the interest of *five per cent.* The borrowers are allowed a long term for payment, and the sums borrowed being divided into equal portions, they are obliged to pay one of these, with the interest of the whole, every year during the term. This renders the payments very easy; and as no person [11] is permitted to borrow a large sum, a great number are accommodated. The consequences of such regulations are obvious. These bills represent money in the same manner that money represents other things. As long therefore as the quantity is proportioned to the uses, these emissions have the same effects, that the gradual introduction of additional sums of money would have. People of very small fortunes are enabled to purchase and cultivate land, which is of so much consequence in settling new countries, or to carry on some business, that without such assistance they would be incapable of managing: For no private person would lend money on such favourable terms. From the borrowers the currency passes into other hands, encreases consumption, raises the prices of commodities, quickens circulation, and communicating a vigour to all kinds of industry, returns in its course into the possession of the borrowers, to repay them for that labour which it may properly be said to have produced. They deliver it, according to the original contracts, into the treasury, where the interest raises a fund without the imposition of taxes, for the public use.

While emissions are thus conducted with prudence, they may be compared to springs, whose water an industrious and knowing farmer spreads in many meandering rivulets through his gardens and meadows, and after it has refreshed all the vegetable tribes it meets with, and has set them a growing, leads it into a reservoir, where it answers some new purpose.

If it could be possible to establish a currency throughout the colonies, on some foundation of this kind, perhaps greater benefits might be derived from it, than would be generally believed without the trial. [12]

With respect to the restrictions laid on our trade in *foreign plantations*, it has been alleg'd, as a reason for them, "that our islands ought to be encouraged." They ought to be: But should the interest of one colony be preferred to that of another? Should the welfare of millions be sacrificed to the magnificence of a few? If the exorbitant profits of one colony must arise from the depression of another, should not such injustice be redressed?

There is a vast difference to be made in calculating the gains of any particular branch of business to the *public* and to *individuals*. The advantages to the last may be small, and yet great to the first, or the reverse. The statutes made to restrain the trade of the continent in *favour of

---

* " The agents for *New York*, in their contest with the sugar colonies, affirmed, That their winters being severe, obliged them to take off more of the woollen manufactures of this kingdom (*for which they remitted gold and silver*) than all the *islands* (*Jamaica* excepted) *put together;* and which I believe has remained uncontradicted."

BEAWES'S Lex merc. red.

If one province THEN exceeded all our *West Indies*, except *Jamaica*, in this particular, what proportion would that single island bear NOW, to *all the rest of the continental colonies ?*

The following account of the exports from ENGLAND to the *Northern Colonies*, and to the *West India Islands*, will shew they were nearly equal some time ago ; that those to the *Northern Colonies* now vastly exceed, and are prodigiously increasing, while those to the Islands have continued nearly the same.

the islands, seem to tend rather towards [13] promoting
partial than *general* interests, and it appears to me no

From 1744 to 1748, inclusive.

Northern Colonies.					*West India Islands.*			
1744 . .	£640 114	12	4	. . . .	£796 112	17	9
1745 . .	534 316	2	5	. . . .	503 669	19	9
1746 . .	754 945	4	3	. . . .	472 994	19	7
1747 . .	726 648	5	5	. . . .	856 463	18	6
1748 . .	830 243	16	9	. . . .	734 095	15	3

Total £3,486 268   1   2

Total £3,363 337   10 10
Difference   122 930   10   4

£3,486 268   1   2

From 1754 to 1758, inclusive.

Northern Colonies.					*West India Islands.*			
1754 . .	£1,246 615	1	11	. . . .	£685 675	3	0
1755 . .	1,177 848	6	10	. . . .	694 667	13	3
1756 . .	1,428 720	18	10	. . . .	733 458	16	3
1757 . .	1,727 924	2	10	. . . .	776 488	0	6
1758 . .	1,832 948	13	10	. . . .	877 571	19	11

Total £7,414 057   4   3

Total £3,767 841   12 11
Difference   3,646 215   11   4

£7,414 057   4   3

Total for the *Northern Colonies*, in the first Term .   £3,486,268   1   2
Ditto, in the second Term   7,414,057   4   3

Increase, £3,927,789   3   1

Total for the *West India Islands*, in the first Term .   £3,363,337   10 10
Ditto, in the second Term   3,767,841   12 11

Increase, only £0,404,504   2   1

The difference between the employment afforded to the manufacturers
of *England*, by the *Northern Colonies* and by the *West India Islands*, is
still greater than it may appear to be from the first view of the preceding
account : For a much greater quantity of *East India* goods is exported to
the last than to the first ; and the *English* manufactures consumed by
them generally derive their value from the richness of the materials,
many of which are brought from foreign countries, but those we consume, chiefly derive their value from the work bestowed upon them.
(Vide note to pages 4 and 5.)

* Vide Note to page 6.

paradox to say, that the public would be a great gainer, if estates there were so *moderate that not a tenth part of the *West-India* gentlemen that now sit in the House of Commons, could obtain that frequently expensive honor.

It is allowed by those well acquainted with the islands, that they cannot supply *Great-Britain* and these colonies [14] with sugar and other articles, and that they can by no means consume the productions of these colonies; yet in † favour to them, we are almost entirely prevented from sending these productions to any other markets. Hence it follows, that we are frequently obliged to sell our commodities to them at so low a price, as not to pay the first cost and freight; while we, being in a manner prohibited from getting the *West-India* productions, for which we

* "A great advantage which the *French* have over the *English* in their sugar colonies, is their *agrarian law,* whereby monopolists are prevented from engrossing too much land; so that the number of whites is greatly increased, the land improved, more commodities raised, the planters *obliged to a more frugal way of living,* and *all things rendered cheaper.* By these means *Martinico* can muster 16,000 fighting men; but *Jamaica,* which is near three times as large, only 4,000."

TUCKER on trade.

† It is recited in the 6th of Geo. 2d. ch. 13, now made perpetual, "that the Sugar colonies could not carry on their trade ON AN EQUAL FOOTING with the foreign Sugar Colonies, without some *advantage* and relief given to them by *Great Britain.*" That *advantage* GIVEN by *Great Britain*—was to compel the continental Colonies to take their productions at any price they please to ask.—In short, to grant them a MONOPOLY for Sugars. This was taking *from one* indeed to give *to another;* but goes not to the root of the evil; as the next preceding note evidently shews. For if *Great Britain* should sacrifice her own interests and those of her continental colonies still more, *if it be possible,* to the interest of these islanders, *they never will* "carry on their trade ON AN EQUAL FOOTING with the foreign sugar colonies," until there is the same moderation in their estates, and the same frugality in their living. By a very singular disposition of affairs, the colonies of an *absolute monarchy* are settled on a *republican principle;* while those of a kingdom in many respects *resembling a commonwealth,* are cantoned out among *a few lords,* vested with despotic power over *myriads of vassals,* and supported in the promp of *Bassa's* by *their* slavery.

have occasion, any where else but from them, must pay extravagantly for them.

Nor is this management attended, as it is presumed, with any benefit to the Mother Country, but with a disadvantage ; either where the productions of the foreign plantations are consumed among us, or re-exported to *Europe.* By the compulsion on us to take from our islands, the price of their productions is raised on the people of *Great-Britain.* The Revenue would be encreased by this restriction being taken off, as we should willingly pay a moderate duty upon importations from the *French* and *Spaniards,* without attempting to run them ; while a very considerable duty would be paid [15] on the *sugars of our islands, which, instead of coming to us, would then go to *Great-Britain.* Besides, whatever extraordinary price we pay for the productions of our own islands, must lessen our demand for *British* manufactures ; since it is an † undeniable

---

* The restriction on the trade of the colonies to foreign plantations for Molasses, is particularly grievous and impolitic, as the Molasses brought from thence was distilled for the *fisheries,* the *Indian* and *Guinea* trades, the profit of which centered in *Great-Britain.* It is said, our vessels now buy spirituous liquors on the coast of *Guinea* from the *Dutch.* [*In Dickinson's Political Writings this note is altered to read : "The restriction on the trade of the colonies to foreign plantations for molasses, is particularly hurtful and impolitic, as the molasses brought from thence was distilled for the fisheries, the Indian and other trades, the profit of which centered in Great Britain."—Ed.*]

† This cannot be disputed by any one who is acquainted with *America.* This increase of a man's wealth there shews itself in a great consumption of *British* manufactures of all kinds.—This reasoning in favour of the continental colonies trade with foreign plantations, is confirmed by what Sir *Josiah Child* mentions of *New-England.*—He says,—"*England* loses by the *unlimited trade* of this colony to other foreign plantations, but gains by her direct trade to Old *England,* from whence she exports manufactures to *ten times* the value of her imports." (See the note to page 4.) What was it then that enabled *New-England* to pay *ten times* the *value* of her *imports* to *England,* but the *profits of her trade to foreign plantations ?* This appears to be a direct authority in support of the ar-

truth, that what we [16] should save in that way, would
be chiefly spent in this. It may also justly be added, that
our commerce with the foreign plantations, carries to them
very considerable quantities of *British* manufactures, for
their consumption.*

If our importations from them should be re-exported to
Europe, the profits would center in *Great-Britain*, according to the usual course of our trade. The statute passed
in the twenty-fifth year of *Charles* the second, indeed mentions this practice as injurious. It might be so, if regarded
without its attendant circumstances; but if *they* are taken

guments hereafter used. It seems therefore that *Great-Britain* of late,
through too great eagerness to gather golden fruits, has shaken the tree
before they were full grown. With a little patience they would ripen
and then of themselves drop into her lap.

"The inhabitants of our colonies, by carrying on a trade with their
foreign neighbours, do not only occasion *a greater quantity of the goods
and merchandizes of Europe being sent from hence to them*, and a greater
quantity of the product of *America* to be sent from them hither, *which
would otherwise be carried from, and brought to Europe by foreigners*,
but an increase of the seamen and navigation in those parts, which is of
great strength and security, as well as of great advantage to our plantations in general. And though *some of our colonies* are not only for preventing the *importation of all goods of the same species they produce*, but
suffer particular planters to *keep great runs of land in their possession
uncultivated*, with design to prevent new settlements, whereby they
imagine the prices of their commodities may be affected ; yet if it be considered, that the Markets of *Great-Britain* depend on the markets of ALL
Europe in general, and that the *European* markets *in general* depend on
the proportion between the *annual consumption* and the *whole quantity*
of each species *annually produced* by ALL *nations ;* it must follow, that
whether we or foreigners are the producers, *carriers*, importers and exporters of *American* produce yet their respective prices in *each colony* (the
difference of freight, customs and importations considered) will always
bear proportion to the *general consumption* of the *whole quantity* of each
sort, *produced in all colonies*, and *in all parts*, allowing only for the usual
contingencies that trade and commerce, agriculture and manufactures are
liable to in all countries."

POSTLETHWAYT'S Univ. Dict. of Trade and Commerce.

* See the preceding note.

into view, and it be considered, that if *we* do not carry these productions to *Europe*, *foreigners* will, no mischief seems likely to ensue from our becoming the carriers.*

The restriction also with regard to our iron, is thought particularly severe. Whenever we can get a better price in *Great-Britain* than elsewhere, it is unnecessary; whenever we can get a better price in other places, it is †prejudicial. Cargoes composed of this metal, [17] provisions and lumber, have been found to answer very well at the *Portuguese* and some other markets; and as the last articles are frequently very low, and our foreign trade is reduced to so few commodities, the taking away any one of them must be hurtful to us. Indeed, to require us to send all our iron to *Great-Britain*, is, in the opinion of some of our most judicious merchants, to require an impossibility: For as this article is so heavy, and such small quantities can be sent in one vessel, they assert, that we cannot find freight directly home for one half of it.

Besides the circumstances already mentioned to prove the injurious consequences of the late restrictions, there is

* See the preceding note.

† If *Great-Britain* really takes off from *Sweden* iron to the value of £200,000, according to the calculation that has been made, yet she does not lose all that sum. Not to insist on the merely political advantage of having a commerce with that *protestant* kingdom, which by being beneficial to her, may more firmly attach her to our interest, it may be observed, that the trade of *Great-Britain* to *Sweden*, it is for iron in the gross, which is afterwards worked up, and large quantities of it re-exported : so that money may thereby be brought into the kingdom, and a great number of hands is employed. There is a vast difference between this trade, and that to *France*, from whence the importations into *Great-Britain* are merely for consumption, without affording any employment to her people, or any profit by re-exportation. Besides, if the colonies can get more by carrying their iron to foreign ports, than to *Great-Britain*, (and if they cannot, there is no occasion of a law to compel them to carry it to *Great-Britain*) they will be more able to make larger demands for *British* manufactures ; so that *Great-Britain* will gain the profits of our iron, to make up her loss by what she takes from *Sweden*.

another, which has great force in persuading me that our trade ought by all means to be more encouraged and extended at this time, than was formerly necessary. Our settlements then only comprehended a narrow strip along the shore of the ocean; they were less populous; and their distance from the sea ports being [18] small, they were supplied with every thing they wanted from thence, without any length of inland carriage. But now we have penetrated boundless forests, have passed over immense mountains, and are daily pushing further and further into the wilderness; the inhabitants of these remote regions, must of necessity hold very little intercourse with those which are near the sea, unless a very extensive commerce shall enable these to supply them with such quantities of *foreign commodities as they want, and at such prices as they can afford to pay. Every restriction on our trade, seems to be a restriction on this intercourse, and must gradually cut off the connection of the interior parts with the maritime and the mother country.

But it is unnecessary to endeavour to prove by reasoning on these things, that we *shall suffer*, for we *already suffer*. Trade is decaying,; and all credit is expiring. †Money is become so extremely scarce, that reputable freeholders find it impossible to pay debts which are trifling in comparison to their estates. If creditors sue, and take out executions, the lands and personal estate, as the sale must

---

* It is apprehended, that if the greatest part of the commodities demanded by the back country should not be *British* but *West-Indian*, yet it must be beneficial to *Great-Britain* to promote this trade by all means. For if the country nearer the sea grows rich by supplying them with the productions of the *West-Indies*, these will certainly consume greater quantities of *British* manufactures.

† It is said that in *Virginia*, the sheriffs, instead of raising the annual levies, have been obliged to make returns into the treasury, of effects which they have taken in execution, but could not sell, as there were no bidders for ready money. [*This note is struck out in Dickinson's Political Writings.—Ed.*]

be for ready money, are sold for a small part of what they were worth when the debts were contracted. The debtors are ruined. The creditors get but part of their debts, and that ruins them. Thus the consumers break the shop-keepers; they break the merchants; and the shock must be felt as far as *London*. Fortunate, indeed, is the man who can get satisfaction *in Money* for any part of his debt, in some countries; for in many instances, after lands and goods have been repeatedly advertised in the public gazettes, and exposed to sale, not a buyer appears.

By these means multitudes are already ruined, and the estates of others are melting away in the same manner. It must strike any one with great surprize and concern, to hear of the number of debtors discharged every court by our insolvent act. Though our courts are held every quarter, yet at the last term for the county of *Philadelphia* alone, no less than thirty-five persons applied for the bene-fit of that act. If it be considered, that this law extends only to those who do not owe any single debt above £.150, that many are daily released by the lenity of their cred-itors, and that many more remove, without their know-ledge, it will not be difficult to form a judgment of the con-dition to which the people are reduced.

If these effects are produced already, what can we ex-pect, when the same cause shall have operated longer? What can we expect, when the exhaused colonies shall feel the STAMP ACT drawing off, as it were, the last drops of their blood? From whence is the silver to come, with which the taxes imposed by this act, and the duties im-posed by other late acts, are to be paid? Or how will our *merchants* and the *lower ranks of people*, on whom the force of these regulations will fall first, and with the greatest violence, bear this additional load? [20]

These last are to be considered in a very different light from those of the same classes in *Great Britain*.

There the nature of their employments, and the plenty of money, gives them very little occasion to make contracts in writing; but *here* they are continually making them, and are obliged to do so. The STAMP ACT, therefore, will be severely felt by *these*, in whose welfare the prosperity of a state is always so much interested ; and* transfers of property, that ought, in new countries particularly, to be made as easy as possible, will be much discouraged. From the necessity they are under of making contracts *to be executed afterwards*, the lower ranks of people here are frequently engaged in law suits; and as the law is already a very heavy tax on the subject in all parts of the *British* dominions, this act will render it destructive here; for the necessaries, the follies and the passions of mankind, will not suffer them to cease from harassing one another in that way.

Neither are the merchants here by any means able to bear taxes, as they do at home. A very great number of them there put such stocks into trade, as would be thought large fortunes among us; and our merchants would think themselves very happy to leave off business with such estates as the others begin with. I speak of the merchants in general ; for we have on the continent individuals who are rich, but their number [21] is too inconsiderable to deserve any notice on this occasion. Besides, the interest of money being lower at home than it is here, those who trade on borrowed stocks, can do it to much greater advan-

---

* In the present scarcity of money, the sellers of lands, negroes, &c., &c., always insist on having part of the purchase-money in hand.—The buyers, unless they happen to be rich men, find it impossible to comply with this term, unless they borrow money, which cannot now be done but in very small parcels from different persons.—Each of these must have a bond ; and each of those bonds must pay a stamp-duty of one shilling sterling, if the sum be above ten pounds and under twenty—and if above twenty pounds and under forty, one shilling and six pence sterling—besides a duty on the original contract.

tage there than we can.   Indeed, among us it is almost impossible to get money to trade upon at any rate.   How unequal, under the present disadvantages, a merchant's commerce will be to the payment of all the taxes imposed by the STAMP ACT on his policies, fees with clerks, charter parties, protests, his other notarial acts, his letters, and even his advertisements, experience, I am afraid will unhappily prove.

Thus, I apprehend, that this Act will be extremely heavy on those who are least able to bear it ; and if our merchants and people of little substance languish under it, all others must be affected.   Our mode of taxation, hath always been by making as exact an estimate as could be formed of each man's estate ; by which means, our taxes have been proportioned to the abilities of those who were to pay them.   Few persons are employed in the collection of them ; their allowance is very moderate ; and therefore the expence is small.   No excessive penalties, no tribes of informers, no dreadful and detestable courts are necessary. This I imagine, is the mode of taxation, which in young colonies, will be found to be least oppressive and destructive, and certainly the most equal : But by the STAMP ACT, the * wealthy who have money to let out at interest, or to make purchases, and undoubtedly ought to pay the most towards the public charges, will escape these taxes, while the whole [22] weight of them will fall on the necessitous and industrious, who most of all require relief and encouragement.

But it may be said, "That the merchants will not be affected by these taxes, because they will raise the prices of their goods in proportion, and that at length *all taxes must arise from lands.*"

* If a rich man buys land, it is generally from the distressed, and therefore the seller's situation will oblige him to pay for the deed, when the other insists on it ; and when a man borrows money, everybody knows who pays for the bonds and mortgages.

This rule seems more applicable to very populous and rich countries, where the manufacturers and land-holders through necessity or the force of fashions, have pressing demands upon the merchants, than to such a country as this, where a great majority of the people live on their lands in a very plain way. For by practising a strict frugality and industry, *we* may render ourselves more independent of the merchants, than the circumstances of more populous and wealthy states will permit the other classes of their people to be. The high prices therefore which our merchants impose upon their goods, will discourage the sale of them, and consequently they must "be affected by the taxes," which oblige them to raise the prices in this manner.

However, granting that all taxes must arise from lands; it follows, that where the profits of the lands are small, they can bear but small taxes. The more labour is bestowed on them, the greater the profits *will* be, and the taxes *may be.* In old populous countries there is an opportunity of bestowing this labour, and the manner of doing it is well understood. Thus in *England*, the profits of land are so great, as to support a very large number of nobility and gentry in splendor, and to afford means of raising taxes to an amazing amount. Nor are the workers of the land unrewarded ; for the farmers have such long leases, and other encouragements, that they thrive and live comfortably, and many of them are very wealthy. [23]

How different is the case in *America?* The inhabitants being scattered thin through the country, and labourers being very scarce, they think themselves fortunate, if they can clear their land, fence it, and any how put their grain into the ground in season. Manuring or *

* " Further, it may be observed, that our lands are not sufficiently cultivated, even where they are capable of great improvement. Hence large tracts serve only to maintain a small number of people. If we ask, why

improving soils is not known, except in some small closes
near cities ; but every one must be content with what his
land will yield of itself.   With this it must be considered,
that at least four fifths of the people in *America*, live upon
farms either of their own, or rented, and spend their small
profits in maintaining their families ; and it frequently
happens from the length and severity of our winters, that
the whole produce of a man's farm is not sufficient to
maintain his family and stock. *

    We are informed, that an opinion has been industriously
propagated in *Great-Britain*, that the colonies are † wal-

our lands (meaning in *Scotland*) are so ill cultivated, besides the OBVIOUS
CAUSES arising from the POVERTY and UNSKILLFULNESS of many of our
farmers, the SHORTNESS OF THEIR LEASES, and other things which will
occur upon the least reflection, it is not a little owing to a want of inclination for agriculture, etc."

                    DISSERTATION on the numbers of mankind.

    * Small as the value of our land is, it is still daily decreasing, by the
number of markets for their produce being lessened ; which must in
time give the people an inclination to try what they can make by manufactures.

    The *riches* of a people are always in proportion to the number of hands
employed in works of SKILL and LABOUR.   Where these are few, there
can be but little wealth ; and where there is little wealth, but very small
taxes can be borne.   [*This note is struck out in Dickinson's Political
Writings.—Ed.*]

    † "It is certain, that from the very time Sir *Walter Raleigh*, the father
of our *English* colonies, and his associates, first projected these estab-
lishments, there have been persons who have found an interest in *misrepresenting*, or lessening the value of them.—The attempts were called
chimerical, and dangerous.   Afterwards many malignant suggestions
were made about sacrificing so many *Englishmen* to the obstinate desire
of settling colonies in countries which then produced very little advantage.   But as these difficulties were gradually surmounted, those complaints vanished.   No sooner were *these lamentations* over but *others*
arose in their stead ; when it could no longer be said, that the colonies
were useless, it was alleged that they were not *useful enough* to their
mother country ; that while we were loaded with taxes, they were absolutely free ; that the *planters* lived like *princes*, while the inhabitants of
England laboured hard for a tolerable subsistence.   This produced cus-

lowing in wealth and luxury, while she is la- [24] bouring under an enormous load of debt. Never was there a greater mistake. This opinion has arisen from slight observations made in our cities during the late war, when large sums of money were spent here in support of fleets and armies. Our productions were then in great demand, and trade flourished. Having a number of strangers among us, the people naturally not ungenerous or inhospitable, indulged themselves in many uncommon expenses. But the cause of this gaiety has ceased, and all the effect remaining, is, that we are to be treated as a rich people, when we are really poor. *Tully* mentions a man who lost an honorable office, by the homely entertainment he gave the people of *Rome*, when he could have afforded a better; but we have lost vastly more by the imprudent excess of kindness, with which we have [25] treated the people of *Great-Britain* who have come among us, at an expence that did not suit our fortunes.

To all the disadvantages that have been mentioned, it must be added, that our markets are much more precarious than those at home. It is computed, that one half of the people there live in cities, and consequently there must be a perpetual domestic demand for the productions of the

toms and impositions, which, if grievous to the plantations, must turn to our disadvantage, as well as theirs, and consequently become detrimental to both."

POSTLETHWAYT'S univ. dict. of trade and commerce.

In pursuance of this design to bring down the pride of these PRINCELY PLANTERS, such heavy impositions were laid in *Great-Britain* on tobacco, that the inhabitants of *Maryland* and *Virginia* were discouraged from raising it. Then the mother country FELT her error, and these PRINCES were found to be very poor people. The same *unhappy spirit* is now producing the same mistake There wants but a very little more weight upon *Maryland* and *Virginia*, to prevent their raising tobacco, and to make them and all their sister colonies sink under their multiplied burthens. [*This note is struck out in Dickinson's Political Writings.* —*Ed.*]

earth ; and foreign markets are not far distant for the over-plus.   Here the quantity sold for consumption among us is small, and most of the foreign markets are very remote.

These reasons induce me to think, that the colonies, unless some fortunate event, not to be expected, should happen, cannot bear the restrictions and taxations laid upon them by the mother country, without suffering very severely.   What then can we do?   Which way shall we turn ourselves?   How may we mitigate the miseries of our country?   *Great-Britain* gives us an example to guide us.   SHE TEACHES US TO MAKE A DISTINCTION BETWEEN HER INTERESTS AND OUR OWN.   Teaches !   She requires—commands—insists upon it—threatens—compels—and even distresses us into it.

We have our choice of these two things—to continue our present limited and disadvantageous commerce—or to promote manufactures among ourselves, with a habit of œconomy, and thereby remove the necessity we are now under of being supplied by *Great-Britain.*

It is not difficult to determine which of these things is most eligible.   Could the last of them be only so far [26] executed, as to bring our demand for *British* manufactures below the profits of our foreign trade, and the amount of our commodities immediately remitted home, these colonies might revive and flourish.   States and families are enriched by the same means ; that is, by being so industrious and frugal, as to spend less than what they raise can pay for.

We have examples in this province, which if imitated by others, must unavoidably produce the most happy effects for us : I mean the examples of the industrious, frugal, honest *Germans.*   Their lands are as well cultivated as they can be in this new country, and they have the good sense to require very little provisions and cloaths more than they can get from their own farms, and make with their own hands. If we only consider for a moment the consequences of such a conduct, should it be general, we must be convinced it must produce commerce, since all superfluities would be exported, and the Owners having few demands in return, *that commerce* would of course produce wealth.

Indeed we shall be compelled, I apprehend, generally to imitate these examples. The late regulations, and our constant remittances to *Great-Britain,* have extremely lessened the quantity of money among us, and yet these remittances are not sufficient to pay for those things we want from home. Necessity will teach us two ways to relieve ourselves. The one is, to keep the *British* manufactures we purchase longer in use for wear than we have been accustomed to do. The other is, to supply their place by manufactures of our own. I don't suppose our difficulties will *immediately* produce expert artists among us; but as the inhabitants here generally [27] reside on their lands, and live in a plain rustic way, they will be able to supply themselves with many articles. Some author, and I think *Keysler,* says, that in *Switzerland,* every family has all the trades in it that are necessary for its use. Their work is not, it may be presumed, at all in the taste of *London* or *Paris,* but it serves their purpose; and their coarse cloaths and simple furniture enable them to live in plenty, and to defend their liberty. Something of this kind will be, nay, already is, practiced by us. It is surprising to see the linen and cloth that have been lately made among us. Many gentlemen in this city dress now in suits produced, manufactured, and made up in this province. The cloth is not equal in fineness to the best broad-cloth, but it is warm, strong, and not very homely; and when the *British* workmen understand that they may meet with better encouragement here than they do at home, I believe in a few years we shall have very different kinds of cloth among us from these we now make. Instances are not wanting to justify the most sanguine expectations on this head. *Spain* used formerly to be entirely supplied with cloths from *England;* but in the reigns only of their two last kings, *Philip* the Vth, and *Ferdinand* the Vth, their manufactures have been improved to such a degree, even by that proud and indolent people, that this commerce has entirely ceased in most parts of that kingdom. The same thing has happened in *France*, notwithstanding the destructive wars in which she has been continually involved. *Switzerland* some time ago spent large sums of money in foreign commodities; but now they make excellent cloths, and good silks, though the scheme at first laboured under very great difficulties. That country used also to be supplied by *Savoy* with [28] wine; but the Duke laying a duty upon it, the *Switzers* remonstrated; but in vain. At last some of the principal men promoted the cultivation of vines, though their precedessors had never planted any. The result exceeded their hopes. * "The demand for the *Savoyard* wine daily decreased, and instead of the precarious advantage arising from this *impolitic duty*, the certain revenue was *irretrieveably lost*, and the industrious subject deprived of the benefit of his labour."

"Before the settlement of these colonies," says *Postlethwayt*, "our manufactures were few, and those but indifferent. In those days we had not only our naval stores, but our ships from our neighbours. *Germany* furnished us with all things made of metal, even to nails. Wine, paper, linens, and a thousand other things, came from *France*. *Portugal* supplied us with sugar; all the products of *America* were poured into us from *Spain;* and the *Venetians* and *Genoese* retailed to us the commodities of the *East-Indies*, at their own price."

* *Keysler.*

The astonishing alterations in all these particulars, are too well known to need enumeration.

These instances, and many others that might be mentioned, may convince us, that nothing is too difficult for men to effect, whose hearts are filled with a generous love of their country ; and they may convince the world of the dangers that attend provoking innovations in commerce. A branch of trade once lost, is lost for ever. In short, so strong a spirit is raised in these colonies by late measures, and such success- [29] ful efforts are already made among us, that it cannot be doubted, that before the end of this century, the modern regulations will teach *America*, that she has resources within herself, of which she never otherwise would have thought. Individuals, perhaps, may find their benefit in opposing her use of these resources ; but I hope very, very few, will wish to receive benefits by such means. The man who would promote his own interests by injuring his country, is unworthy of the blessings of society.

It has hitherto been thought, by the people of *Great-Britain*, and I hope it will still be thought, that sufficient advantages are derived by her from the colonies, without laying taxes upon them. To represent them as an "expensive appendage of the *British* empire, that can no other way repay the trouble and treasure they cost her," is certainly one of the greatest errors ; and to spend much time in refuting this notion, would be unnecessary. Every advantage accruing to the colonies by their connection with the mother country, is *amply—dearly*—paid for, by the benefits derived to her from them, and by the restrictions of their commerce. These benefits have been allowed by the best writers to be immense, and * consist in the various employment and the support they afford her people.

---

* Chiefly ; even the supplying her with naval stores, &c., being inconsiderable, when compared with the other advantages.

If the colonies enable *her* to pay taxes, is it not as useful to her, as if *they* paid them? Or, indeed, may not the colonies with the strictest propriety be said to pay a great part of those taxes, when they consume the *British* manufactures * loaded with the advanced prices occasioned by such taxes? Or, further, as the colonies are compelled to take those manufactures thus [30] loaded, when they might furnish themselves so much cheaper from other countries, may not the difference between these prices be called an *enormous tax* paid by them to *Great-Britain?* May they not also be said to pay *an enormous tax* to her, by being compelled to carry their most valuable productions *to her alone*, and to receive what she pleases to give for them, when they might sell them at other markets to much greater advantage? Lastly, may they not be said to pay a heavy tax to her, in being prohibited from carrying on such manufactures as they could have employed themselves in with advantage, and thus being obliged to resort to her for those things with which they might supply themselves? If these things are true, and can they be denied! may not

---

* "If it be asked, whether foreigners, for what goods they take of us, do not pay on *that consumption* a great portion of our taxes? It is admitted they do."

POSTLETHWAYT'S *Great Britain's* true system.

By the consumption of *British* manufactures in *America*, we pay a heavier tax to *Great Britain*, than if they were consumed at home. For in the bringing them here, a vast number of merchants, factors, brokers and seamen are employed, every one of which must have such a profit, as will enable him to support himself and his family, if he has any, in a country where everything is dear by reason of the high taxes.

So far was the parliament from thinking in the last war, that any further taxes should be laid on the colonies, so convinced indeed were they that we had exceeded our abilities in the supplies we gave to the crown, that several sums of money were granted to us as indemnifications for the too heavy expences in which we had involved ourselves.

The sums thus given, paid part of our debts, but we are still labouring under the remainder.

the mother country more justly be called *expensive* to her colonies, than they can be called *expensive* to her?

What would *France* give for such *extensive* dominions? Would she refuse the empire of *North America*, unless the inhabitants would submit to any taxes she should please to impose? Or would she not rather afford them her utmost protection, if ever they should [31] be wretched enough to require it, for one half of the emoluments *Great-Britain* receives from them? In short, the amazing increase of the wealth and strength of this kingdom, since the reign of queen *Elizabeth*, in whose time the colonies began to be settled, appears to be a sufficient proof of their importance: And therefore I think it may justly be said, that THE FOUNDATIONS OF THE POWER AND GLORY OF GREAT BRITAIN ARE LAID IN AMERICA.

When the advantages derived by the mother country from her colonies are so * important* and *evident*, it is amazing, that any persons should venture to assert, "that she poured out her wealth and blood in the late war, *only for their defence and benefit;* and that she cannot be recompensed for this expence and loss, *but by taxing them.*"

If any man who does not chuse to spend much time in considering this subject, would only read the speeches from the throne during that period, with the addresses in answer to them, he will soon be convinced *for whose benefit Great-Britain* thought she was exerting herself. For my part, I should not now be surprized, if those who maintain the abovementioned assertions, should contend, that *Great-Britain* ought to tax *Portugal*. For was not that kingdom "defended by the troops and treasure of *Great-Britain?*" And how can she be "otherwise recompensed for this expence and loss?" If the protection of *Portugal*, though no taxes are received from thence, was beneficial

* Vide notes to page 4.

to *Great-Britain*, infinitely more so was the protection of the colonies.

So far I must beg leave to dissent from these gentlemen, that if the colonies, by an increase of industry [32] and frugality, should become able to bear this taxation, it will, in my apprehension, notwithstanding be injurious to *Great-Britain.* If the sum be trifling, it cannot be worth the discontent and unhappiness the taking it will produce among so many faithful subjects of his Majesty. If it be considerable, it must also be hurtful in another respect.

It must be granted, that it is not merely the bringing money into a nation that makes it wealthy, but the bringing money into it by the general industry of its inhabitants. A country may perpetually receive vast sums, and· yet be perpetually poor. It must also be granted, that almost all the money acquired by the colonies in their other branches of trade, is spent by them in *Great-Britain*, and finds employment for her people. Whatever then lessens the sum so spent, must lessen that employment. This I think will be one consequence of the STAMP ACT: For our demand will be as much less for *British* manufactures, as the amount of the sums raised by the taxes. So much the fewer *British* merchants, artists, seamen and ships will be employed by us, and so much the more distressed at first, and afterwards so much the more frugal, * ingenious, laborious and independent will the colonists become.

It is evident from the concurrent testimony of her own most noted authors on this subject, that *Great-Britain* is sure of having our money at † last; and it appears no difficult matter to determine, whether it is better to take it in

---

* *Great Britain* will not only lose in such case, the annual amount of the taxes, but the people of *America* establishing manufactures through discontent, will in time entirely withdraw their intercourse with her.— And therefore her loss of the whole *American* trade, may be justly attributed to this inauspicious beginning.

† See notes to page 4.

taxes or trade.—Suppose the [33] STAMP ACT, enforced by uncommon penalties and unheard of jurisdictions, should pick up every piece of gold and silver that shall wander into the plantations, what would *Great-Britain* gain by this measure? Or rather what would she not lose, by attempting to advance her revenue by means so distressing to commerce?

But if the late restrictions shall not prove *profitable;* perhaps they may by some be called *prudent* for another reason. We are informed that many persons at home affect to speak of the *colonists*, as of a people designing and endeavoring to render themselves independent, and therefore it may be said to be proper as much as possible to depress them. This method for securing obedience, has been tried by many powerful nations, and seen to be the constant policy of commonwealths: But the attempt in almost every instance from *Athens* down to *Genoa*, has been unsuccessful. Many states and kingdoms have lost their dominions by severity and an unjust jealousy. I remember none that have been lost by kindness and a generous confidence. Evils are frequently precipitated, by imprudent attempts to prevent them. In short, we never can be made an independent people, except it be by * *Great-Brit-*

---

* "If we are afraid that one day or other the colonies will revolt, and set up for themselves, as some seem to apprehend, let us not *drive* them to a *necessity* to *feel* themselves independent of us; as they *will* do, the moment they perceive that *they can be supplied with all things from within themselves*, and do not need our assistance. If we would keep them still dependent upon their mother country, and in some respects *subservient* to their *views* and welfare ; let us make it their INTEREST always to be so."

TUCKER on trade.

"Our colonies, while they have *English* blood in their veins, and have relations in *England*, and WHILE THEY CAN GET BY TRADING WITH US, the *stronger* and *greater they* grow, the *more* this *crown* and *kingdom* will *get* by them ; and nothing but such an arbitrary power as shall make them desperate can bring them to rebel."

DAVENANT on the plantation trade.

ain herself; [34] and the only way for her to do it, is to make us frugal, ingenious,* united and discontented.

"The Northern colonies are not upon the same footing as those of the South; and having a worse soil to improve, they must find the recompence some other way, which only can be in property and dominion. Upon which score, any innovations in the form of government there, should be cautiously examined, for fear of entering upon measures, by which the industry of the inhabitants be quite discouraged. 'Tis ALWAYS UNFORTUNATE for a people, either by CONSENT or upon COMPULSION, to depart from their PRIMITIVE INSTITUTIONS, and THOSE FUNDAMENTALS, by which they were FIRST UNITED TOGETHER."   *Idem.*

* The most effectual way of *uniting* the colonies, is to make it their common interest to oppose the designs and attempts of *Great Britain.*

"All wise states will well consider how to preserve the advantages arising from colonies, and avoid the evils. And I conceive that there can be but TWO ways in nature to hinder them from throwing off their dependence; *one*, to keep it out of their *power*, and the *other*, out of their *will*. The *first* must be by *force;* and the *latter*, by *using them well*, and keeping them employed in such productions, and making such manufactures, as will support themselves and families comfortably, *and procure them wealth too*, and at least not prejudice their mother country.

Force can never be used effectually to answer the end, *without destroying the colonies themselves.* Liberty and encouragement are necessary to carry people thither, and to keep them together when they are there; and violence will hinder both. Any body of troops considerable enough to awe them, and keep them in subjection under the direction too of a needy governor, often sent thither to make his fortune, and at such a distance from any application for redress, will soon put an end to all planting, and leave the country to the soldiers alone, and if it did not, *would eat up all the profit of the colony.* For this reason, arbitrary countries have not been equally successful in planting colonies with free ones; and what they have done in that kind, has either been by force at a vast expence, or *by departing from the nature of their government*, and *giving such privileges to planters* as were *denied to their other subjects.* And I dare say, that a few prudent laws, and a little prudent conduct, would soon give us far the greatest share of the riches of all *America*, perhaps drive many of other nations out of it, or into our colonies for shelter.

There are *so many exigencies* in all states, *so many foreign wars*, and *domestic disturbances*, that these colonies CAN NEVER WANT OPPORTUNITIES, if they watch for them, *to do what they shall find their interest to do;* and therefore we ought to take all the precautions in our power,

But if this event shall ever happen, which Providence I hope will never permit, it must when the present generation and the present set of sentiments are extinct. Late measures have indeed excited an universal and unexampled grief and indignation throughout the colonies. What man who wishes the welfare of *America*, can view without pity, without passion, her restricted and almost stagnated trade, with its numerous train of evils—taxes [35] torn from her without her consent—Her legislative assemblies, the principal pillars of her liberty, crushed into insignificance—A formidable force established in the midst of peace, to bleed her into obedience—The sacred right of trial by jury, violated by the erection of arbitrary and unconstitutional jurisdictions—and general poverty, discontent and despondence stretching themselves over his unoffending country?

The reflections of the colonists on these melancholy subjects are not a little embittered by a firm persuasion, that they never would have been treated as they are, if *Canada* still continued in the hands of the *French*. Thus, their hearts glowing with every sentiment of duty and affection towards their mother country, and expecting, not unreasonably perhaps, some mark of tenderness in return, are pierced by a fatal discovery, that the vigo-[36] rous assistance which they faithfully afforded her in extending her domains, has only proved the glorious but destructive cause of the calamities they now deplore and resent.

that it shall never be *their interest* to act against that of their native country; an evil which can no otherwise be averted, than by keeping them *fully employed* in such trades *as will increase their own*, as well as our wealth; for it is much to be feared, if we do not find employment for *them*, they might find it for *us*. The interest of the mother country, is always to keep them dependent, and so employed; and it requires all her address to do it; and it is certainly more *easily* and *effectually* done by *gentle* and *insensible* methods, than by *power* alone."

CATO'S letters.

Yet still their resentment is but the resentment of dutiful children, who have received unmerited blows from a beloved parent. Their obedience to *Great-Britain* is secured by the best and strongest ties, *those of affection;* which alone *can*, and I hope *will* form an everlasting union between her and her colonies. May no successes or suspicions ever tempt *her*, to deviate from the natural generosity of her spirit—And may no dreadful revolution of sentiments, ever teach *them*, to fear her victories or to repine at her glories. [37]

I am, &c.

POSTSCRIPT.

I have omitted mentioning one thing that seems to be connected with the foregoing subject.

With a vast expence of blood and wealth, we fought our way in the late war up the doors of the *Spanish* treasuries, and by the possession of *Florida*, might obtain some recompence for that expence. *Pensacola* and the other ports in that country, are convenient places, where the *Spaniards* might meet us, and exchange their silver for the manufactures of *Great-Britain*, and the provisions of these colonies. By this means, a commerce inconceivably beneficial to the *British* subjects, might be carried on. This commerce the *Spaniards* wish and have endeavoured to carry on. Many hundred thousand dollars have been brought by them to *Pensacola* to lay out there; but the men of war at that station have compelled them to take back their cargoes, *the receipt of which*, it may from thence be presumed, *would be destructive to the interests of Great Britain.*—Thus we receive less advantage from *Florida*, now it belongs to us, than we did when in was possessed by our enemies ; for then by permission from the *Spanish* governors, to trade there, we deprived considerable emoluments from our intercourse with them.

Upon what reasons this conduct is founded, is not easy to determine. Sure no one considers *Florida* in the same light with *these colonies*, and thinks that no vessels should be permitted to trade there, but *British* shipping. This would be to apply the acts of navi- [38] gation to purposes directly opposite to the spirit of them. They were intended to preserve an intercourse between the *mother country* and her *colonies*, and thus to cultivate a *mutual affection;* to promote the interests of *both*, by an exchange of *their* most valuable productions for *her* manufactures; thereby to increase the shipping of both; and thus render them capable of affording aid to each other. Which of these purposes is answered by prohibiting a commerce, that can be no other way carried on? That is, by forbidding the *Spaniards* to bring their wealth *for us* to *Florida*, which is an unhealthy sandbank, held by a garrison, at a great expence of money, and a greater of lives, that cannot for ages, if ever it will, yield a single advantage to *Great-Britain*, but *that* she refuses to enjoy.

FINIS.

AN ADDRESS

TO THE

COMMITTEE OF CORRESPONDENCE

IN

BARBADOS.

BY

JOHN DICKINSON.

———

1766.

NOTE.

The letter of the Committee of Correspondence, appointed by the Assembly of Barbados, to the agent of the colony in London, in relation to the Stamp Act, was printed "by authority" in the *Barbados Mercury* of April 19, 1766. In its republication from that or some other source, it was altered, so as to charge the American provinces with "rebellious opposition," the true text merely having styled it "present opposition." After careful search, I have not been able to trace this garbling to its origin, but it was the version generally printed in the American newspapers, and was the one on which Dickinson based the attack contained in the following pamphlet, which was printed with the title of:

An / Address / to / The Committee of Correspondence / in / Barbados. / Occasioned by a late letter from them / to / Their Agent in London. / By a North-American. / This word Rebellion hath froze them up / Like Fish in a pond. Shakespeare. / Philadelphia. / Printed and Sold by William Bradford, at / his Book-Store in Market-Street, adjoining the / London Coffee-House. M,DCC,LXVI. 8vo, pp. 18.

The fact that the text printed and answered by Dickinson was not the correct one, stirred up the writers in Barbados, and three replies were published as follows:

A / Letter / to the / North-American, / On Occasion of his / Address / to the / Committee of Correspondence / in / Barbados. / By a Native of the Island. / All your attempts / Shall fall on me, like brittle Shafts on Armour / That break themselves; or like Waves against a Rock, / That leave no Sign of their o'erboiling Fury / But Foam and Splinters: My Innocence, like these, / Shall stand triumphant.—Massinger. / Barbados: / Printed by George Esmand and Comp. / M.DCC.LXVI. / Sm. 8vo, pp. 47.

An / Essay / Towards the Vindication / of the / Committee of Correspondence / in / Barbados, / from the Aspersions and Calumnies thrown upon / them in an anonymous Piece, printed in Phi- / ladelphia, under the Title of an Address to / them. occasioned by their Letter to their

(249)

Agent / in London. / In a letter to a Friend. / By a Barbadian. / Though Loyalty, well held, to Fools does make / Our Faith mere Folly ; — Shakespear. / Barbados : / Printed by George Esmand and Comp. / M,DCC / LXVI. / Sm. 8vo, pp. 24+.

Candid / Observations / on / Two Pamphlets lately published, / viz. / *"An Address to the Committee of Correspondence / in Barbados."* By a North-American. / and / *"An Essay towards the Vindication of the Com- / mittee of Correspondence."* By a Barbadian. / By a Native of Barbados. / Amicus Plato, Amicus Socrates, sed magis Amica Veritas. / Barbadoes : / Printed by George Esmand and Comp. / M.DCC.LXVI. / 8vo, pp. 37.

A series of extracts from the second of these replies, was republished in *The Pennsylvania Chronicle* of August 1 and 8, 1768 ; and the former issue also contains a reply to Dickinson's *Address*, by "a Countryman."

EDITOR.

A N

ADDRESS

T O

The Committee of Correspondence

I N

BARBADOS.

Occasioned by a late letter from them

T O

Their Agent in London.

By a NORTH-AMERICAN.

This word REBELLION hath froze them up
Like Fiſh in a pond.   Shakespeare.

PHILADELPHIA.
Printed and Sold by WILLIAM BRADFORD, at
his *Book-Store* in Market-Street, adjoining the
London Coffee-House. M,DCC,LXVI.

PREFACE.

Had the charge of REBELLION *been made by a private person against the colonies on this continent, for their opposition to the* Stamp Act, *I should not have thought it worth answering.—But when it was made by men vested with a public character, by a committee of correspondence, representing two branches of legislature in a considerable government, and the charge was not only approved, as it is said, by those branches, but was actually published to the world in newspapers, it seemed to me to deserve notice. I waited some time, in hopes of seeing the cause espoused by an abler advocate ; but being disappointed, I resolved, "favente Deo," to snatch a little time from the hurry of business, and to place, if I could, the letter of those gentlemen to their agent in a proper light.*

It is very evident from the generality *of their accusation against their "fellow subjects on the northern continent"; of the expressions they use in the latter part of their letter, when they speak of the "violent spirit raised in the North American colonies," and from what follows, that they do not apply the opprobrious term they use, only to those few of the lower rank, who disturbed us with two or three mobs in some of the provinces, nor to any other particular class of people ; but that the censure is designed for* ALL the inhabitants of these colonies *who were* any way *concerned in the* opposition that has been given, *and consequently that the* modes of that opposition *are thereby condemned. Two considerations therefore have induced me to undertake their* [ii] *defence. First, to vindicate the honour of my country, which I think grossly and wantonly insulted. Secondly, to refute opinions, that in unfortunate times, may, if adopted, be injurious to liberty.*

Many good pieces have been published in these colonies to shew their title to the rights claimed by them ; the invasion of those rights by the Stamp Act ; the other hardships imposed on them, and the bad consequences that probably would follow these meas-

ures ; but nothing has appeared, at least I have seen nothing that I recollect, in defence of the principle *on which the opposition has been made, and of the* manner *in which it has been conducted. These are points entirely new ; and the consideration of them is now rendered necessary, by the public reproach that has been thrown on the people of this continent.*

A LETTER from the COMMITTEE *of* CORRESPONDENCE *in* BARBADOS, *to their* AGENT *in* LONDON.
 Sir,

 ' In compliance with the united resolution of the two branches
' of our legislature, of which we have severally the honor to be
' members, and to compose their committee of correspondence,
' We are now to desire you to lay our complaints before his
' Majesty and the Parliament, on the hardships which this com-
' munity labours under by the imposition of the Stamp Duties,
' lately put in force amongst us. We have, indeed, submitted,
' with all obedience, to the act of Parliament ; yet our *submis-*
' *sion* has, by no means, arisen from any consciousness of our
' ability to bear the burden of these taxes, or from the want of
' a due sense of the *oppressive weight of them in all its parts*, but
[iii] ' from a *principle of loyalty* to our King and Mother Coun-
' try, which has carried us above every consideration of our
' own distresses : yet, if we have suffered without resistance, we
' have learnt by it to complain with reason ; and, since we have
' raised no clamours from our own fears, we must surely have
' the better title to *remonstrate from our feelings*. But, with re-
' spect to the manner in which our grievances in this case,
' along with so good a proof of our *obedience to the laws of our*
' *mother country*, are to be reported to his Majesty and the par-
' liament, we must *refer ourselves to your good judgment and dis-*
' *cretion ;* so much better circumstanced as you are on that side
' of the water to judge for us, than we can do at this distance
' for ourselves ; and so perfectly assured as we are also of your
' ability and zeal, in the conduct of every matter of importance
' that can be intrusted to your agency for this country's service.
' To you, Sir, therefore we give the power, in the name of our
' council and assembly, to present such a *memorial*, or *memor-*

'*ials*, to his Majesty, and the two houses of parliament (if to
'all be necessary) as to yourself shall seem most proper and
'adviseable ; setting forth the anxiety and distresses of our
'country, under this new and extraordinary burden of taxation,
'by which we not only find ourselves *loaded with a charge more*
'*than is proportioned to our circumstances, but deprived also of a*
'*privilege, which renders the oppression beyond measure grievous.*
'We *see two of the most important objects* to such a colony as
'ours, *trade and justice crouching under the load of these new*
'*duties ; and by the manner in which the duties have been im-*
'*posed, we find too the most valuable of all our civil rights and*
'*liberties sinking along with them.* The design of this new and
'extraordinary charge upon our country is, towards defraying
'the expences of defending, protecting and securing, the col-
'onies of AMERICA. But what new and extraordinary ex- [iv]
'pence has this colony put the nation to, for the expence of
'maintaining of troops quartered in the several provinces of
'NORTH AMERICA, for the protection and security of those
'parts of the British dominions? This is just as reasonable,
'and just as merciful too, as it would be to impose a heavy
'mulct on the inhabitants of this place, by way of a punishment
'for the present *REBELLIOUS opposition given to authority,*
'*by our fellow subjects on the Northern continent.* But if we are
'to be *subject to the power of the parliament of Great Britain in*
'*our internal taxes, we must be always liable to impositions, that*
'*have nothing but the will of the imposers to direct them in the*
'*measure*, since we have there no representatives to inform them
'of the true state of our circumstances, and of the degree of our
'strength to bear the burdens that are imposed. How far,
'indeed, we are intitled, by the constitution of ENGLAND, or
'our own peculiar *charter*, to an *exemption* from every other in-
'ternal tax, than such as may be laid upon us by the represen-
'tatives of our own people, in conjunction with the two other
'branches of our legislative body, *we cannot positively say ;* but
'this is certain, that we have enjoyed that privilege, that *seem-*
'*ing birthright* of every BRITON, ever since the first establish-
'ment of a civil government in this island to the present time.
'And why we should at this period be condemned to the loss

'of so *inestimable a blessing of society*, we can see no cause ; since
'the present period has afforded some instances of loyalty and
'affection to our King and mother country, which might rather
'have intitled us to new favours from the crown and nation,
'than have left us exposed to any deprivation of our *old and*
'*valuable rights.* Yet, how far it may be prudent and necessary
'to press this last consideration in your *memorial* to our super-
'iors, *must be referred to your good judgment;* for as we mean to
'obtain a redress of our grievances by a dutiful representation
[v] 'only of our case, so would we have any thing avoided in the
'*stile and substance of that representation* as might give offence
'to those from whom only our redress can come, our appeal
'being to the very powers by whom we think ourselves op-
'pressed ; tho' we may remonstrate to them with justice, *we*
'*cannot reproach them without danger;* and the most effectual
'means of giving ourselves all the merit we hope for, and
'intend, both with our sovereign and the parliament, will
'be, we think, by giving our complaint on this matter the
'*complexion of our conduct*, shewing an *humble submission to*
'*authority*, even under the most painful *heartburnings* of our
'community, at its *severe decrees.* But, great as our distresses
'are, upon account of this new Taxation in its general course,
'we are yet fortunate enough not to have suffered so much
'greater, as by the particular calamity you seem to have appre-
'hended for us, on the supposed seizure of the North American
'traders ; for the masters of those vessels, producing certificates
'at our custom-house, that no stamp papers were to be had at
'the ports they came from, have been admitted to an entry of
'their several ships and cargoes, being supposed only liable to
'the penalties inflicted by the Stamp Act, and of these no notice
'have been taken ; so that our danger from the circumstances
'you suggested to the ministers is over. But we see another
'arising from the violent spirit raised in the North American
'colonies against this act, which threatens us with the same ill
'consequences ; we mean, from their avowed resentment at the
'people of this island, for having so tamely submitted to the
'act, which they had been pleased so resolutely to oppose.
'This having led them to some extraordinary attempts (as we

'have been informed) to prevent any vessels coming hither
'with provisions for our support, how far a combination of this
'kind, which has to struggle with the private interests of so
'many indivi-[vi] duals, can be formed amongst them, we may at
'first be led to doubt; yet, on a second review of things, how
'far the excesses of *popular fury*, which has no bounds, may
'hurry away all those individuals, to their own, as well as our
'immediate prejudice, we may reasonably fear; and we think
'it, at least, necessary to make mention of it to you, that you
'may take this, amongst all the other unhappy consequences
'we may feel from that injurious act, into your proper consid-
'eration.'

N. B. The words in *italics*, are those animadverted upon in
the following address; and are printed in that manner, to be
more easily distinguished and referred to by the reader.

AN ADDRESS, &c.

Gentlemen,

I am a *North-American*, and my intention is, in addressing you at present, to answer so much of a late letter from
you to your agent in *London*, as casts unmerited censure
on my countrymen. After this declaration, as you entertain such unfavorable sentiments of the "popular fury"
on this continent, I presume you expect to be treated with
all the excess of passion natural to a rude people. You
are mistaken. I am of their opinion, who think it almost
as infamous to disgrace a good cause by illiberal language, as *to betray it by unmanly timidity.* Complaints
may be made with dignity, insults retorted with decency;
and violated rights vindicated without violence of words.

You have nothing therefore to apprehend from me, *gentlemen*, but such reflections on your conduct, as may tend
to rouse that remorse in you, which always arises in the
minds of ingenuous persons, when they find that they have
wounded by their rash calumnies the honor of those, who
merit their highest esteem,—their warmest praises. [2]

I know there are in the island of *Barbados*, many men
of sense, spirit, and virtue; and therefore I chuse to
consider you rather in the character of such, whose understanding, resolution, and integrity, have been drugg'd by
some pernicious draught into a slumber, than of those who
with irretrievable depravity, want all the qualities requisite to make them serviceable to their countrymen, or just
to others.

Had I only heard, *gentlemen*, that you had called the

behavior of these colonies, a "REBELLIOUS OPPOSITION given to authority," I should have thought it a vain attempt, to aim at convincing you, how unjustifiable an assertion that expression contained; because I should immediately have concluded, that you were so ignorant of the rights of *British* subjects, and so insensible of all concern on the invasion of those rights, that any man who should endeavour to shew you your error, would engage in as unpromising a project, as if he should think to communicate an idea of sound to the deaf, or of colour to the blind.

When I read your letter, however, with an agreeable surprise I observed that *you*, at the same time you have made the attack, have laid the foundation of a defence for my countrymen. Permit me to erect the superstructure, though I had much rather see it built by more skilful hands.

You acknowledge, the "burthen of the taxes imposed by the stamp act, to be OPPRESSIVE IN ALL ITS PARTS;" that you are thereby not only "loaded with a charge more than is proportioned to your circumstances, but DEPRIVED ALSO OF A PRIVILEGE, which renders the OPPRESSION BEYOND MEASURE GRIEVOUS:" that you "see two of the most important objects, TRADE and JUSTICE CROUCHING under the load of the [3] new duties; and by the manner in which these duties have been imposed, find too the MOST VALUABLE OF ALL YOUR CIVIL RIGHTS AND LIBERTIES SINKING ALONG WITH THEM."

You say that if you "are to be subject to the power of the parliament of *Great-Britain*, in your internal taxes, you must always be liable to impositions, that have nothing but the WILL OF THE IMPOSERS to direct them in the measure." With what consistency you afterwards hesitate, and "cannot say," whether the privilege of taxing yourselves, exclusively belongs to you, or talk of a "SEEMING *birthright*," I will leave to be determined by yourselves, or the agent to whose "good judgment and discretion," you with such strange, I had almost said "humble submission" "refer" your most important affairs. However, your sentiments soon veer about again, and you speak of "AN INESTIMABLE BLESSING OF SOCIETY;" of "OLD AND VALUABLE RIGHTS;" and even hazard the hardy appellation of "SEVERE DECREES."

When it is so evident, that all these assertions are equally true with regard to yourselves, and "your fellow-subjects on the northern continent," it affords no slight cause of amazement, to see in the same letter that contains these assertions, the opposition of those confessedly destructive measures, branded as "REBELLIOUS." Wherefore this needless stroke against your "fellow-subjects?" Could not your "principle of loyalty" sink you to a satisfactory depth of humiliation, unless you flung yourselves down with such a rage of prostration as to spatter all around you? Was not your surrender of "*the most valuable of all rights and liberties*" sufficiently completed by your declaration, that you "COULD NOT POSITIVELY SAY *you were intitled to them*," without reproaching those who have the mis-[4]fortune of differing so widely from you in their sentiments, that they had rather die than make such a declaration?

To talk of your "charter" *gentlemen*, on this occasion, is but weakening the cause by relying on false aids. Your opinion on this head seems to be borrowed from the doctrine of the unhappy *Stuarts*. They thought, or pretended to think, all the liberties of the subject were mere favours granted by charters from the crown. Of consequence, all claims of liberties not expressly mentioned in those charters, were regarded as invasions of the prerogative, which according to them, was a power vested in the prince, *they could not tell how*, for no better purpose than to do as he pleased. But what said the nation? They asserted, that

the royal charters were *declarations* but not *gifts* of liberties, made as occasions required, on those points in which
they were most necessary, without enumerating the rest;
and that the prerogative was a power vested in *one* for the
benefit of *all.*

Kings or parliaments could not *give* the *rights essential
to happiness*, as you confess those invaded by the Stamp
Act to be. We claim them from a higher source—from
the King of kings, and Lord of all the earth. They are
not annexed to us by parchments and seals. They are
created in us by the decrees of Providence, which establish
the laws of our nature. They are born with us; exist with
us; and cannot be taken from us by any human power,
without taking our lives. In short, they are founded on
the immutable maxims of reason and justice. It would be
an insult on the divine Majesty to say, that he has given
or allowed any man or body of men *a right to make me
miserable.* If no man or body of men has *such a right*, I
have a *right to be happy.* If there can be no hap-[5]piness
without freedom, I have a *right to be free.* If I cannot
enjoy freedom without security of property, I have a *right
to be thus secured.* If my property cannot be secure, in
case others over whom I have no kind of influence may
take it from me by taxes, under pretence of the public
good, and for enforcing their demands, may subject me to
arbitrary, expensive, and remote jurisdictions, I have an
exclusive right to lay taxes on my own property, either by
myself or those I can trust; of necessity to judge in such
instances of the public good; and to be exempt from such
jurisdictions.—But no man can be secure in his property,
who is "liable to *impositions*, that have NOTHING BUT THE
WILL OF THE IMPOSERS to direct them in the measure;"
and that make "JUSTICE TO CROUCH UNDER THEIR
LOAD."

Thus you prove, *gentlemen*, that the fatal act you allude

to in these expressions, is destructive of our property, our freedom, our happiness: that it is inconsistent with reason and justice; and subversive of those sacred rights which GOD himself from the infinity of his benevolence has bestowed upon mankind.

Yet after these expressed or implied concessions, you term the opposition made by my countrymen to the execution of this—imagination cannot supply me with an epithet equal to my meaning—act, "REBELLIOUS."

Pray, *gentlemen*, let me not mistake your notion of "humble submission to authority." Do you maintain, that because the parliament may legally make *some* laws to bind us, it therefore may legally make *any* laws to bind us? Do you assert, that where power is constitutionally vested in particular persons for certain purposes, the same obedience is due to the commands [6] of those persons, when they exceed the limits of that power, as when they are restrained within them? Do you say, that all acts of authority are sanctified by the mere pleasure of their authors, and that "humble submission" is due to them, however injurious they may be to those over whom they are exercised—or that the oppressed ought to content themselves with "giving the COMPLEXION of your CONDUCT" to PALE petitions—and that *all other* opposition is "rebellious?"

Greatly I am afraid, that you have published to the world too convincing proofs, that you hold these sentiments: sentiments, which I solemnly profess are so horrible to me, that I cannot wish the infection of them even to the bitterest enemies of my country.

Have you considered, *gentlemen*, the importance of the points to which your political creed may be applied? What is your opinion of the *revolution*, that made the *British* liberty and *British* glory blaze out with their brightest lustre? Had you lived in those days of ignorance, with what lucky assistance might you have propp'd up the tottering tyrant, by maxims of law to prove, *that kings can do no wrong;* and texts of scripture to shew, *that submission is due to the powers that be!*

It is as manifest, that the great and good men who then placed the throne in the temple of liberty, disdained your sentiments, as it is, that if they had approved them, you would not at present enjoy the satisfaction of being ruled by a prince whose virtues do honour to his rank. All the happiness you possess, you owe to the force of the principle, which you now reproach; and your professing your resolution to persist in an "humble submission" to acts that you expressly say, "make your oppression beyond measure grievous," and destroy "the most valuable of your [7] civil rights and liberties," is deserting and betraying as much as you can, that principle, on which the constitution of *Great-Britain* is established—A principle, that has operated differently among these colonies, as became them, from what it did in that kingdom at the memorable period above mentioned—not in *action*, but negatively, in a *refusal to act*, in a manner destructive to them.

Let me speak plainly. In such a cause to prevaricate or fear, is worse, if possible, than falsehood or cowardice. Good breeding in private life, or good behavior in public life, can never require a deviation from truth or virtue. Our obligation to these, is co-existent with us, and unchangeable. No other relation therefore can dissolve or diminish the primary, unalterable duty.

Do you believe, *gentlemen*, that parliaments never did, or never will do wrong? Do you profess an infallibility in politics, which you ridicule in religion? If any man should tell the present parliament, they are all-wise and all-perfect, I am persuaded, it would be esteemed a wretched insult both on their understanding and piety. Say they are the wisest and justest assembly on earth; and you say right. But human wisdom and human justice partake of human frailties. Such is the lot of our nature—and to bestow the attributes of heaven on mortals, who to day are, and to-morrow are not, is the wildness of adulation.

Surely, you cannot persevere in your error. If the *stamp act*, DETESTABLE *as you have described it*, cannot wake you from dreams of submission, yet is there no idea of danger or distress which your fancy can represent to you, that you think would justify you in something else than petitioning? Have you no "feelings" by which you might be tortured a little beyond [8] "remonstrating?" *I do not know what is dreadful to* YOU, nor can I form the least guess what would be so: but suppose to yourselves an act of parliament commanding you to do or suffer something the most dreadful in the world—to YOU: something ten thousand times more dreadful—to YOU I mean—than "oppression beyond measure grievous;" "crushing justice under insupportable burthens;" or "sinking the most valuable of all civil rights and liberties." Whatever that *would be* to *you*, the stamp act *is* to *my countrymen*.

Here permit me, *gentlemen*, to ask, whether *in such a case* you would "humbly submit," tho it should be in your power effectually to refuse? To make your conduct consistent with the sentiments avowed in your letter, you must. Would you? Then, if what we are told of the antient *Cappadocians* be true, you would exhibit the second instance since the creation of mankind, of a people *chusing* to be *slaves*. Would you refuse? What then becomes of your "principle of loyalty," and your "obedience to the laws of your mother country?" If so, they are only fine words, with which you intend to purchase some sort of reputation with some sort of people; you are then *loyal* and *obedient*, as you call yourselves, *because you apprehend you can't safely be otherwise;* and the pretended virtues you claim, like forced fruits, partake too strongly of the manure that gave them growth, to afford any agreeable relish. Thus you reduce yourselves to the miserable dilemma of making a choice between two of the meanest characters—of those who *would be slaves* from *inclination*, tho they pretend to love liberty—and of those who *are dutiful* from fear, tho they pretend to love submission.

Pardon me, *gentlemen*, if I attribute to you the virtue, which your excessive modesty disclaims. Since [9] you were deterred from reproaching, by the cautious consideration, that you could not "*reproach* WITHOUT DANGER;" I am *almost* persuaded, that you would prefer refusal to slavery, if you were assured, that you could "*refuse* WITHOUT DANGER."

You greatly injure me, *gentlemen*, if you imagine from what I have said, that I am not a hearty friend to my king, his illustrious family, to *Great-Britain*, or to the connexion between her and these colonies. In what I am now to say, I shall speak not only my own, but the universal sentiments of my countrymen. I am devoted to my gracious sovereign, and his truly royal house, by principle and affection. They appear to me to have been called by providence to the throne; not to have gained it by the least share of the guilt, or even of the art, that has so often exalted the most unworthy to the most splendid stations. They have risen with brightness upon the world, in due course, to shed blessings over mankind; and all history cannot furnish an instance of a family, whose virtues have had a more auspicious influence on the happiness of men, particularly of their subjects. Their government does not afford only gleams of joy, but cheers with a flowing uniformity, except when some evil spirit interrupts our felicity—But these interruptions have never lasted : can never last, while princes of the line of *Brunswick*

"chara deo soboles "*

* Struck out in Dickinson's *Political Writings.—Ed.*

preside over us. Their amiable qualities are hereditary ; these render, if I may be allowed the expression, our happiness hereditary ; and I might therefore be justly deemed very deficient in sense or integrity, if it was not among my most ardent prayers, that the scepter of his dominions may be held by our present monarch and his family, till time shall be no more. [10]

As to *Great-Britain,* I glory in my relation to her. Every drop of blood in my heart is *British;* and that heart is animated with as warm wishes for her prosperity, as her truest sons can form. As long as this globe continues moving, may she reign over its navigable part ; and may she resemble the ocean she commands, which recruits without wasting, and receives without exhausting, its kindred streams in every climate. Are these the sentiments of disloyalty or disaffection? Do these sentiments point at independency? Can you believe it? Will you assert it? I detest the thought with inexpressible abhorrence, for these reasons ; first, because it would be undutiful to our sovereign ; secondly, because it would be unjust to our mother-country ; and thirdly, because it would be destructive both to her and to us.

The *British* nation is *wise* and *generous.* They can distinguish between a disgust to government and to the administration of it ; a distinction, which bad ministers are continually striving to confound. *They* set up *their passions* for the interests of their king and country ; and then, whoever is offended with their conduct, is convicted by a very plain deduction of ministerial logic, of being an enemy to his king and country. No farmer dislikes the sun ; but if it collects such thick clouds as too much intercept its beams, surely the poor man who sees all his hopes sickening and withering, may very innocently dislike the gloom, and wish the reviving rays may be felt again. The *British* nation aims not at empire over vassals. And must,

I am convinced, be better pleased to hear their children speaking the plain language of freemen, than muttering the timid murmurs of slaves. Can you believe, *gentlemen*, that they will be better pleased with the "stile and sub-stance" of "your representation," than with the honest transports of *North-American* breasts, so exactly like what *they* [11] feel, when they think themselves injured? If there is any people whose character it is, to submit to wrongs, basely pretending to prefer the pleasure of those who offer them, to their own welfare or honor, while cowardly hatred and malice lurk rankling and "heart-burning" in their bosoms, watching, wishing opportunities of dire revenge, it belongs not to *Britons*, or their true sons. *They* can neither dissemble injuries, nor unreasonably resent them. These are vices of little, cruel minds. Much better, much safer is it for all parties, particularly when we contend with noble spirits, manfully to speak what we think, and thereby put it in their power—such will always have it in their inclination—to give us ample satisfaction. They know that those who are most sensible of injuries, are most sensible of benefits. There can be no friendship between freemen and slaves ; and I have the strongest hopes that our mutual affection will henceforward be more cemented than it hitherto has been—on their part, because we have *proved* ourselves worthy of their esteem ; and on our part, because their generosity will excuse the manner in which we *have proved it*.

Suppose all this continent had imitated your example, and had repeated your doleful, doubtful notes, from one end of it to the other: had acknowledged upon their knees, "that they COULD NOT POSITIVELY SAY whether they were intitled to the exemption" they required, was there the least probability of their obtaining it? I do not object to the probability, for want of justice or of affection towards us in our mother country; but for want of proper attention, which the artifices of our enemies in support of their own darling measures, would always have prevented.

Every man must remember, how immediately after the tempest of the late war was laid, another storm began to gather over *North-America.* Every wind [12] that blew across the *Atlantic,* brought with it additional darkness. Every act of the administration seemed calculated to produce distress, and to excite terror. We were alarmed—we were afflicted. Many of our colonies sent home petitions; others ordered their agents to make proper applications on their behalf. What was the effect? They were rejected without reading. They could not be presented, "without breaking through a rule of the house." They insisted upon a right, that, it "was *previously* determined, should not be admitted." The language of the ministry was, "that *they* would teach the insolent *North-Americans,* the respect due to the laws of their mother country." They moved for a resolution "that the parliament could legally tax us." 'Twas made. For a bill—'Twas framed. For a dispatch—'Twas past. The badges of our shame were prepared—too gross—too odious—even in the opinion of that administration, to be fastened upon us by any but *Americans.* Strange delusion! to imagine that treachery could reconcile us to slavery. They looked around : they found *Americans*—O Virtue ! they found *Americans,* to whom the confidence of their country had committed the guardianship of her rights, on whom her bounty had bestowed all—the wreck of her fortunes could afford, ready to rivet on their native land, the nurse of their infancy, the protectrix of their youth, the honorer of their manhood, the fatal fetters which *their information* had helped to forge. *They* were to be gratifyed with part of the plunder in oppressive offices for themselves and their creatures. By *these,* that *they* might reap the rewards of their corruption, were we advised—by *these,* that *they* might

return *masters* who went out *servants*, were we desired—
to put on the chains, and then with shackled hands *to
drudge in the dark*, as well as we could, forgetting the
light we had lost. "IF I FORGET THEE, LET MY RIGHT
HAND FORGET HER CUNNING—IF I DO NOT REMEMBER
THEE, MAY MY TONGUE CLEAVE TO THE ROOF OF MY
MOUTH." [13]

When the intelligence of these astonishing things reached
America,
"then flam'd her spirit high."
What could she do? send home petitions again? The
first had been treated with contempt. What could be expected from a second trial? We knew, that the humble
petition of meek, pious, venerable bishops, supplicating
for the laws and religion of their country, had been called
a false and seditious libel by a daring administration, who
were resolved to have no law but their own pleasure. We
knew, that the liberty of our fellow subjects had been
lately so boldly invaded even in our mother country, in
that spot where the dignity of the empire may be said
more peculiarly to reside, that their oppressors were hardly
stopp'd in their career, by the united voice of an injured
and offended people. We knew, that the men who designed to oppress us, held up to those whose assistance
they were obliged to use, specious pretences of immediate
advantage, while every remoter mischief, every disagreeable truth, was artfully concealed from them. They were
persuaded, that they were to promote their own interests,
the public interests, by adopting the new-invented policy
proposed to them. In short we knew, in what line every
thought and act relating to us, ran. All was arbitrary,
rigid, threatening, dreadful. What resource had we? We
wondered and wept—At last, imploring the divine protection, and appealing to the *British* goodness, we were
driven by apprehension and affliction into a conduct, that

might justly have rendered us to the humane rather objects of pity, than resentment; but which you *gentlemen*,
are pleased to call a "REBELLIOUS opposition to authority."

How much farther these colonies might have gone; how
much farther it would have been proper for them to go, I
will not pretend to say. I confine myself en-[14] tirely to
your state of the case, and to *their* behavior in that case.
My soul sickens at the scenes that obtrude themselves on
my imagination, while I reflect on what *might* have happened. My attention turns with unspeakable pleasure to
those brighter prospects now * opening on my country,
and the approaching times, when thro the mercy of AL-
MIGHTY GOD, to whom be ascribed everlasting glory, the
inhabitants of these colonies, animated with sentiments of
the most perfect gratitude, confidence, affection, and veneration, justly heightened by the engaging clemency of
our amiable sovereign, and the endearing tenderness of
our mother country,† shall be diligently and delight-
fully employed in demonstrating, that they are not unworthy of the blessings bestowed upon them. *Great-
Britain* has long been distinguished—she must be now
perpetually celebrated, for her *moderation*. This is her
peculiar praise. Other states have been as great in arms;
as learned in arts; but none ever equalled her in moderation—a virtue, and the parent of virtues.

I am very sorry that these colonies had any reason given
them to think they were right in going so far as they
lately did: yet tho many things have been done, *that* I
sincerely wish had not been done, I should be glad to
know what particular part of their conduct has provoked
you to issue, if I may use one of your expressions, so "severe a decree" against them.

* The news of the STAMP ACT being repealed, arrived while this piece
was in the press.

† Changed to "excellent mother country" in Dickinson's *Political
Writings.—Ed.*

Did the resolutions made by their several assemblies in vindication of their rights, deserve such a censure? You grant they were founded on truth and justice. Can it be criminal to maintain these? Perhaps you think they were guilty, in forming and persisting in their universal determination not to use stamped papers, as they were commanded to do. No man can be blamed for doing any thing, which if he had not done, he [15] must have committed a worse action. Remember the opinion you have expressed of the liberties for which these colonies were struggling. Had they accepted the stamped papers, they would not only have betrayed themselves, and you, whose prosperity they wish from a generosity of temper, of which they hope you will hereafter give them more agreeable proofs than you have yet done, but they would also have basely betrayed ages yet unborn, to a condition that would have rendered their birth a curse. You think "a memorial or memorials" would have relieved them, "if they had humbly submitted;" that is, that injuries *that* could not be prevented by a regard to justice, liberty, and the happiness of millions, might be redressed by well-penned petitions. No! The right would have been surrendered by our act —a precedent would have been established by our acquiescence, for perpetual *servility*. Where would the demands of ministers, where would the miseries of *America* have stopped?

I believe your island and its neighbours have been more fortunate in "memorialising" than this continent. Had we any reason to expect relief from the conduct proposed? Has anything happened since, to shew that we should have succeeded by it? Let any person consider the speeches lately made in parliament, and the resolutions said to be made there, notwithstanding the convulsions occasioned through the *British empire* by the *opposition* of these colonies to the stamp-act, and he may easily judge what would have been their situation, in case they had bent down and humbly taken up the burden prepared for them. What would have been their fate, since they have opposed, if one man the victor of his country's foreign and domestic foes, had not by his wisdom and virtue checked the rage that deception might artfully have kindled in the most honest and humane people upon earth, heaven alone can tell. [16]

When the *exclusion* bill was depending in the house of commons, Col. *Titus* made this short speech—"Mr. speaker, I hear a lion roaring in the lobby. Shall we secure the door, and keep him there: or shall we let him in, *to try* if we can turn him out again."

Can it be possible, gentlemen, that our stopping on this continent the importation of goods from *Great-Britain*, has brought your resentment upon us? If it has, it is the first time that industry and frugality have met with such hard judges.

The only thing I can think of besides, which might induce you to treat my countrymen as you have done, is the behavior of the mobs composed of the lower ranks of people in some *few* of the colonies, to those who were favorers of the stamp-act—But surely that could not produce so *general* in accusation of "your fellow-subjects on the northern continent." It was indeed a very improper way of acting; but may not these agonies of minds *not quite so polished as your own*, be in some measure excused? if as the absolute monarch of *Judea* said "oppression maketh a wise man mad;" and if as the loyal committee of correspondence in *Barbados* says, "the subversion of justice" and "the most valuable of all civil rights and liberties" is "oppression beyond measure grievous." It is needless to dwell longer on this head; but if you chuse to enquire into the circumstances of every mob that has happened here, taking for granted that the stamp-act is constitutional, I believe even you, on cool consideration, would not term any of them a rebellion.

Upon the whole, I acknowledge, that a regard to *themselves*, has influenced the inhabitants of these colonies; but it was not a regard void of the truest loyalty to *their* king, the warmest affection, the profoundest [17] veneration, for *their* parent country. If my father, deceived and urged on by bad or weak men, should offer me a draught of poison, and tell me it would be of service to me, should I be undutiful, if, knowing what it is I refuse to drink it? or if inflamed by passion, he should aim a dagger at my heart, should I be undutiful, if I refuse to bare my breast for the blow? Should he complain, would it not be the complaint of *Catiline*, that the senator he attempted to assassinate, *was so disrespectful to him, he* WOULD NOT *receive the sword in his body?* * Or should I act like a man in his senses, if I swallow the dose or receive the stroke, in expectation that those who prompted or provoked my father to the action, would afterwards give me a certain antidote or balsam—especially, if they would probably get a large part of my estate? I will beg leave to trouble you, *gentlemen*, with one more comparison. If a fortune of immense value comes into my possession by being settled on me, as the lawful son of my father, which till then had been held solely by him, and my enemies should persuade my excellent parent to attempt to bastardize me, and take the whole into his hands again, I not having the least prospect of happiness without it, and he not having the least occasion for it—should I be undutiful, if after endeavoring by intreaties to prevent his proceedings, I care-

* This sentence is struck out in Dickinson's *Political Writings*. In a copy of the original pamphlet, Dickinson has written in *MS:* "It was Nimbria, the Rival of *Catiline* in wickedness, who made this audacious complaint," but has run his pen through it, as well as through the original passage.—*Ed.*

fully record all the proofs of my being legitimate, stop the circulation of all false vouchers to the contrary, decline the correspondence of those who join with him, and even break the head of a man, who slanders my honour and my title, by spreading an opinion that I am basely born? With how much less reason will the charge of undutifulness be made against me, if I have regularly advanced for my father all such sums as he has from time to time required, and have assured him by my possessions and behavior, that he shall have all the profits of the estate, allowing me a comfortable [18] maintenance, if he will suffer it to continue in my possession—and all the world knows, that by a condition annexed to this estate, I cannot part with it, without acknowledging myself to be a bastard.

To conclude—*gentlemen*—I know none of you; not even one of your names. I mean no personal reflections in this address. I detest them. If you should take anything I have said, so much in that way, as to feel uneasiness from it, I shall be very sorry. Neither do I intend any reflections on your country, tho you represented *her* when you attacked *mine*. I always detested these loose aspersions, that ever give most pain to bosoms that honour and delicacy have rendered most sensible; and this detestation has been greatly encreased, since, within these few years, we have seen such loads of obloquy thrown upon a * nation, whose magnanimity in bearing them will be sufficient I hope, to procure them the esteem of those, who have been so much blinded by passion, as to deny it to their other numerous virtues and accomplishments. Your island is respectable. Your private characters may be amiable; but in a public capacity, you have cast a most high and unprovoked censure on a gallant, generous, loyal people. You have propagated a set of sentiments, and have pro-

* The Scots.

moted a tenor of conduct, that may be hurtful to the cause of freedom. I have engaged with too unequal arms perhaps, to oppose you; but to *fail* in such a contest, will afford me some kind of pleasure. I wish you every blessing that men can enjoy; and as a foundation and security of all the rest, I wish you a true love of liberty.

A NORTH-AMERICAN.

FINIS.

LETTERS

OF

A FARMER

IN

PENNSYLVANIA.

BY

JOHN DICKINSON.

———

1768.

NOTE.

No American political argument, at the date of the appearance of the "Farmer's Letters," had achieved such a marvelous popularity and success, and few writings of the same character have since then equalled it. It ran through the Colonies like wild fire, causing an enthusiasm which led Town Meetings, Societies, and Grand Juries to vote thanks to the author; which made him a toast at public dinners, and the subject of laudatory articles and poems in the press. In the earlier arguments against the taxation of the colonies, the plea of the injustice of "taxation without representation," if a popular cry, was only too easily answered by the frequent acquiescence of the colonies in such taxation, before the Stamp Act. All claims based on "natural rights" therefore were discredited by precedent, and the grounds taken by each writer varied according to the influences these opposing forces had with him personally. In this confusion of ideas, the Pennsylvania Farmer advanced his distinction, between taxation for the regulation of trade, and taxation for the purpose of revenue, and supplied common ground for all the Whigs to fight upon. At this day the distinction seems inadequate and fine spun, but to the men of the time, determined not to be taxed by any but themselves, yet loyal to England to a degree now almost incomprehensible, it was hailed with acclamation, as the one escape between taxation without representation, and independence.

The American Whig view of the "Letters" is practically presented in the preface of the Virginia edition, and the English Whig view is well given in the notice in the *Monthly Review*, (LIX, p. 18), which says:

"We have, in the Letters now before us. a calm yet full inquiry into the right of the British parliament, lately assumed, to tax the American colonies; the unconstitutional nature of which attempt is maintained in a well-connected chain of close and manly reasoning. . . . When we review a performance well written, and founded upon laudable principles, if we do not restrain ourselves to a general approbation, which may be given in few words, the article will unavoidably contain more from the author of it, than from ourselves ; this, if any excuse is needful for enabling our Readers, in some measure, to judge for themselves, is pleaded as an apology for our copious extracts from these excellent letters.—To conclude ; if reason is to decide between us and our colonies, in the affairs here controverted, our Author, whose name the Advertisements inform us is Dickinson, will not perhaps easily meet with a satisfactory refutation."

There was, however, another side to the question, and the " Farmer's Letters " was not without its critics. A single answer by "A Citizen," was published in the *Pennsylvania Journal* for December 17, 1767, and a number of scurrilous little paragraphs dealt more with the Farmer than with his arguments. A series in rebuttal did appear in the *Boston Gazette.* Private criticism was able to speak plainer, and Samuel Rhoads, one of the leading Quakers of Pennsylvania, alluded in a letter to his regret at the letters, "as calculated to excite the passions of the unthinking, and produce again the unfortunate heats that can do nought but render a just and friendly union with the parent state more difficult." The attitude of the conservatives in Pennsylvania is indicated by William Goddard, who wrote in *The Partnership* (Philadelphia, 1770) :

"The *Farmer's* Letters appeared in the *Chronicle, supposed* to be written by the ingenious Mr. *Dickinson,* a gentleman, whom, at that time, I had never seen. Here the ignorance of Mr. *Wharton,* and the envy of Mr. *Galloway,* and the wickedness of both united were clearly manifested. They were angry, they fretted, they *swore* and *affirmed,* that they were too inflammatory for this latitude. While Mr. *Galloway* exclaimed, with a countenance expressive of the deepest envy, that they were '*damned ridiculous ! mere stuff ! fustian ! altogether stupid, inconsistent ! only a compilation by* Dickinson *and* Thomson !' the very *sagacious* and *deep-read* Mr. *Wharton,* with a great deal of solemn dump and grimace in his look, signified that 'Friend *Goddard* was very *imprudent* in introducing such pieces into OUR *Chronicle* at such a time—that he had observed, with no small concern, that I published pieces that were inconsistent with *their* views in establishing a press, and that I should not go on headlong against the interest of my BENE-FACTORS.' I *presumed* to reason with them, and assured them that the letters were extremely agreeable to the people, and for my part I thought they deserved the serious attention of all *North America.* Mr.

Galloway ridiculed my notions about liberty and the rights of mankind, and he observed that 'the people in *America* were mad—they
knew not what they wanted—and indeed were incapable of judging on
such matters—that such factious pieces would answer for the selectmen
of *Boston*, and the mob meetings of *Rhode-Island*, but he was sure they
would soon be despised here, *Pennsylvanians* (a few hot-headed people
excepted) being of a different make, of more solidity, none of *your*
damned republican breed—but loyal to the king, and friends to monarchy—that they had great expectations from the favour of the ministry, and that such performances would injure the province at the *British* court, and shew that they were as refractory as the other colonies,
and that they might thereby destroy *their best hopes centered in their
agent.*' I formed my own opinions of the men, waved conversing
upon such subjects, and still continued, with my usual '*obstinacy*,' as
they express themselves, to publish the letters, and every other patriotic
piece which I judged had the least tendency to promote the common
cause of this much injured country. The *Farmer's* Letters grew more
and more admired, and these *gentlemen* then judged it dangerous
openly to declaim against them, or vilify their supposed author. They
therefore would call together a select number of malcontents, to whom
they would disgorge their malignity of heart, and who would, without
remorse, circulate their calumnies abroad. I could here call forth a
series of letters dated *Virginia*, but wrote in *Philadelphia*, now deposited in a certain desk, designed for a competent answer to the *Farmer's*
letters; but I suppress them at present."

Franklin too, though causing the letters to be reprinted, spoke of them
most cautiously in his preface, and in private seemed neither to understand nor approve of the doctrines advanced. He wrote his son :

"My Lord Hillsborough mentioned the "Farmer's Letters" to me,
said he had read them, that they were well written, and he believed he
could guess who was the author, looking in my face at the same time
as if he thought it was me. He censured the doctrines as extremely
wild. I have read them as far as No. 8. I know not if any more have
been published. . . . I am not yet master of the idea these and the
New England writers have of the relation between Britain and her
colonies. I know not what the Boston people mean by the 'subordination' they acknowledge in their Assembly to Parliament, while they
deny its powers to make laws for them, nor what bounds the Farmer
sets to the power he acknowledges in Parliament to 'regulate the trade
of the colonies,' it being difficult to draw lines between duties for regulation and those for revenue; and if the Parliament is to be the
judge, it seems to me that establishing such principles of distinction
will amount to little."

The English Tory view is indicated by the notice in the *Critical Review* (XXVI, 62):

"The author of these Letters, which are generally ascribed to one Mr. Dickinson, tells us, that he has had a liberal education, and has been engaged in the busy scenes of life ; that his affairs are easy ; that he has money at interest ; that he has a library, with some friends who are gentlemen of abilities and learning ; and that he believes he has acquired a greater knowledge in history, the laws and constitutions of his country than is generally obtained by men of his class.

"Thus much Mr. Dickinson says for himself ; but without impeaching his veracity, we cannot help thinking that he would have proved a much better member of society had he never learned either to read or write. The work before us is seditious in its principles, superficial in its execution, and tending to the perdition of the country for which the author is so furious an advocate. . . . The remaining letters of the publication tend to prove the wisdom and necessity of the Americans taking arms, rather than subject themselves to the operation of any British act of parliament. We shall not be at all surprized, if this author and his fellow labourers in the vineyard of sedition, should insist upon the repeal of the navigation act ; for if any one of Mr. Dickinson's arguments are valid, it will hold perhaps more strongly against that act than any which has been made since : for when analyzed, it will be found to lay the severest tax that ever was imposed upon the produce and commerce of our American colonies. But tho' the inhabitants of that continent refuse to be good subjects, we hope they do not disdain being honest men. Let the mother-country draw out her account since their first settlement in America, and let us see whether the fee simple of all their possessions in America can repay her.

The first letter appeared in *The Pennsylvania Chronicle and Universal Advertiser*, Volume I, Number 46, December 2, 1767, with the following notice :

"Having received a Series of Papers entitled, 'Letters from a Farmer,' &c., with several other pieces from our Correspondents, all which we are importuned to publish as speedily as possible ; and as we find there will not be Room in our Monday's Chronicle, to insert the Whole—from a Desire to oblige, we are induced to give this Half-Sheet, containing such of the Pieces as we could get ready, beginning with the Farmer's first Letter, being as he observes, on a Subject of the utmost Importance to the Welfare of our common Country."

These famous letters were therefore begun in a special issue. They appeared in *The Pennsylvania Chronicle* in the following dates :

Letter I. Dec. 2, 1767. Letter VII. Jan. 11, 1768.
" II. " 7, " " VIII. " 18, "
" III. " 14, " " IX. " 25, "
" IV. " 21, " " X. Feb. 1, "
" V. " 28, " " XI. " 8, "
" VI. Jan. 4, 1768. " XII. " 15, "

They were headed "For the Pennsylvania Chronicle," but each was reprinted in the issues of the *Pennsylvania Journal* and *Pennsylvania Gazette*, immediately following their appearance in the *Chronicle*. Such was their instant success, that they were republished in every newspaper then printed in the thirteen colonies, with but four known exceptions. Nor did this begin to satisfy the public demand. Less than a month after the appearance of the last letter, they were published in pamphlet form, the advertisement of it appearing in the *Pennsylvania Gazette* of March 10. The title page of this edition was:

Letters / From a / Farmer / In / Pennsylvania, / To the / Inhabitants / of the / British Colonies. / Philadelphia : / Printed by David Hall, and William Sellers. / MDCCLXVIII. / 8vo, pp. 71.

The reason for Goddard's not printing this edition are given by him in *The Partnership*, as follows:

"The *Farmer's* Letters having been published with universal applause, throughout the continent, the worthy author began to receive the generous acknowledgments of his grateful countrymen. These were very offensive to my partners, who were apprehensive that the inhabitants of this city and county would, at the next election, give him their suffrages as a representative, and make him a guardian of those rights, which he had so ably and so zealously defended, in which case they imagined he would, as he had done before, '*marr all their plans*.' A signal from them was sufficient to raise up a host of angry scribblers, who were ever ready to draw their servile pens, in the most of causes, against the best. It became at length a very serious matter with a certain cabal, and the word went forth—'*No* Farmer *in the assembly*.' There then was *crouded* upon me a number of libels against the Farmer, &c. under the signatures of *A Countryman, A Miller, Frank Meanwell, Jack White-Oak, A Barbadian, A Country Farmer, Son of Liberty*, &c. &c. I found myself obliged to publish them, tho' I was very averse to it, and was confident it would terminate in the loss of many good customers, which was really the case. These publications gave my partners much pleasure; they complimented me, declared that I was 'now in the right way,' that they would make my fortune, if I would but attend to the advice of my real friends, meaning themselves, and gave out everywhere that I printed the best paper in the King's dominions. But all this could not compensate for the uneasiness I gave my friends, and the concern I felt in being reduced to such a cruel alternative—either to abuse a man I highly esteem, or to fall an immediate sacrifice to party fury and resentment. My friends in *New-England*, and a number of gentlemen in this province, on the first appearance of the *Farmer's* Letters, engaged to take several hundred of them in a handsome pamphlet. I mentioned this to my partners; but they objected to my doing it in such a manner as discouraged me; so that their ill-will to the author, and their enmity to the liberties and good of mankind, deprived me of a job that would have produced a handsome sum, which fell into other hands."

A second edition was issued in June:

Letters / From a / Farmer / in / Pennsylvania, / To the / Inhabitants / of the / British Colonies. / The second Edition / Philadelphia : / Printed by David Hall, and William Sellers. / MDCCLXVIII. / 8vo, pp. 71.

Another Philadelphia edition, with a different printer, was issued with the title page of:

Letters / From a / Farmer / in / Pennsylvania, / To the / Inhabitants / of the / British Colonies. / The Third Edition. / Philadelphia : / Printed by William and Thomas Bradford, at the / London Coffee-House. M,DCC,LXIX. / 8vo. (2), 104.

Besides these Philadelphia issues, other editions were printed in the colonies, as follows:

Letters / from a / Farmer / in / Pennsylvania / to the / Inhabitants / / of the / British Colonies. / New-York : re-printed by John / Holt, near the Exchange, 1768. / 12mo, pp. 118.

Letters / from / a Farmer in *Pennsylvania*, / To the Inhabitants / of the / British Colonies. / Boston : / Printed by Mein and Fleeming, and to / be sold by John Mein, at the / London Book-store, North- / side of King-street. / MDCCLXVIII. / 12mo., pp. 146.

Letters / from A / Farmer / in / Pennsylvania, / to the / Inhabitants / of the / British Colonies. / Boston : / Printed and Sold by Edes & Gill, in Queen-Street. / MDCCLXVIII. / 12mo, pp. 146.

Both these Boston editions reprint the resolutions of the Boston Town Meeting to "The Farmer" and Dickinson's reply, which is also given in the reprint of the "Farmer's Letters" in Dickinson's *Political Writings* (I, 138). The following edition has added to it a preface, written by Richard Henry Lee :—

The / Farmer's and Monitor's / Letters, / to the / Inhabitants / of the / British Colonies. / Williamsburg : / Printed by William Rind, M DCC LXIX. / Sm. 4to, pp. iii, 97, (1).

They were reprinted in London, at the instance of Franklin, who wrote a brief preface to the edition :—

Letters / from a / Farmer in Pennsylvania, / to the / Inhabitants / of the / British Colonies. / London. / Printed for J. Almon, opposite Burlington-house, Piccadilly. / M DCC LXVIII. / 8vo, pp. (4), iii, 118.

Franklin's preface was again reprinted in the following edition, as well as an additional preface by the "Dublin Editor" :

Letters / From a / Farmer in Pennsylvania, / To the Inhabitants of the / British Colonies ; / Regarding, / The Right of Taxation, and several / other Important Points. / To which are Added, as an / Appendix, / The Speeches of / Lord Chatham, and Lord Camden, / The one upon the Stamp Act, the other / on the Declaratory Bill, / with a / Preface by the Dublin Editor. / Printed for J. Sheppard in Skinner-Row. / M,DCC,LXVIII. / 8vo, pp. viii, 9–119, (1), 29.

Franklin was also probably instrumental in getting it translated, and republished in France, for the translator and editor, Jean Barbeu Dubourg, was his personal friend, and he included two pieces by Franklin, as well as Franklin's preface.

Lettres / d'un / Fermier de Pensylvanie, / aux Habitans. / de l'Amérique Septentrionale, / Traduites de l'Anglois. / A Amsterdam, / Aux dépens de la Compagnie. / M.DCC.LXIX. / 12mo, pp. xxviij, 258.

This edition was really printed in France. The last to be issued, which is a mere reprint of the letters, is the following edition :

Letters / from a / Farmer, / in / Pennsylvania, / To the Inhabitants / of the / British Colonies. / Philadelphia / Printed ; and London reprinted for J. Almon / opposite Burlington-House in Piccadilly. / M DCCLXXIV. / 8vo, pp. 136.

The present reprint is made from the first pamphlet edition. The text of this differs in quite a degree from that of the original newspaper text, but as the larger part of the changes are merely verbal, only those which seemed worth indicating are noted. The same rule has also been applied to the revised text of the "Letters" given in Dickinson's *Political Writings*, only essential changes being given here. The prefaces, written by Richard Henry Lee, Benjamin Franklin, the "Dublin Editor" and Jean Barbeu Dubourg, precede the reprint as necessary and interesting additions.

EDITOR.

PREFACE TO ENGLISH EDITION.

THE BRITISH EDITOR TO THE READER.*

When I consider our fellow subjects in *America* as *rational creatures*, I cannot but wonder, that during the present wide difference of sentiments in the two countries, concerning the power of parliament in laying taxes and duties on *America*, no application has been made to their *understandings*, no able and learned pen among us has been employed in *convincing* them that they are in the wrong; proving clearly, that by the established law of nations, or by the terms of their original constitution, they are taxable by our parliament, *though they have no representative in it.*

On the contrary, whenever there is any news of discontent in *America*, the cry is, "Send over an army or a fleet, and reduce the dogs to *reason.*"

It is said of choleric people, that with them there is *but a word, and a blow.*

I hope *Britain* is not so choleric, and will never be so angry with her colonies as to *strike* them; but that if she should ever think it *may be* necessary, she will at least let the *word* go before the *blow*, and reason with them.

To do this clearly, and with the most probability of success, by removing their *prejudices*, and rectifying their *misapprehensions* (if they are such) it will be necessary to learn what those prejudices and misapprehensions are; and before we can either refute or admit their reasons or arguments, we should certainly know them.

It is to that end I have handed the following letters (lately published in *America*) to the press here. They were occasioned

* Written by Benjamin Franklin.

(287)

by the act made (since the repeal of the Stamp-act) for raising a revenue in *America* by duties on glass, paper, *&c.*

The Author is a gentleman of repute in that country for his knowledge of its affairs, and, it is said, speaks the *general sentiments* of the inhabitants. How far those sentiments are right or wrong, I do not pretend at present to judge. I wish to see first, what can be said on the other side of the question. I hope this publication will produce a *full answer*, if we can make one. If it does, this publication will have had its use. No offence to government is intended by it; and it is hoped none will be taken.

N. N.

London, May 8, 1768.

PREFACE TO WILLIAMSBURG EDITION.

THE PREFACE.*

It may perhaps seem strange to slight consideration, that these LETTERS which have already passed through all *America*, should now a second time be produced before the Public in their present form. But a little further reflection will shew the UTILITY of this WORK. The sacred cause of liberty is of too great consequence, and the necessity of freedom for the security of human happiness too obvious, not to render every precaution wise, that tends to prevent the introduction of slavery. Notwithstanding therefore, these letters have been already published, yet here, they have been seen only in the Gazettes, which, from the uncertainty of their dispersion, and the length of time passing between the reception of newspapers in the country, may probably have prevented much benefit to be derived from a collective, uninterrupted view of the manly reasoning, the timely information, and the true constitutional principles of liberty with which these letters every where abound. Whoever considers again that the nature of men in authority is inclined rather to commit two errors than retract one,† will not be surprised to see the *Stamp-Act* followed by a Bill of Rights, declaring the power of Parliament to bind us in all cases whatsoever; and this act again followed by another, imposing a duty on paper, paint, glass, *&c.*, imported into these colonies. But however unbounded may be the wish of power to extend itself, however unwilling it may be to acknowledge mistakes, tis surely the duty of every wise and worthy *American*, who at once wishes the prosperity of the mother country and the colonies, to point out all invasions of

* By Richard Henry Lee.—*Ed.*
† Clarendon's History of the Rebellion.

(289)

the public liberty, and to shew the proper methods of obtaining redress. This has been done by the Authors of the following LETTERS with a force and spirit becoming freemen, *English* freemen, contending for our just and legal possession of property and freedom. A possession that has its foundation on the clearest principle of the law of nature, the most evident declarations of the *English* constitution, the plainest contract made between Crown and our forefathers, and all these sealed and sanctified by the usage of near two hundred years. *American* rights thus resting on the best and strongest ground, it behooves all her inhabitants with united heads, hearts, and hands, to guard the sacred deposit committed by their fathers to their care, as well to bless posterity as to secure the happiness of the present generation. In vain 'tis for some few (and very few I hope they are) who, governed either by base principles of fear, or led by vile hopes of gain, the reward of prostituted virtue, to say, "your rights are indeed invaded, *but Great-Britain* is too strong. What can we do against superior strength?" Let these evil designing men remember what the highest authority has told us, "that the race is not always to the swift, nor the battle to the strong." And if inspiration needed to receive assistance from genius, Shakespeare says, "thrice is he armed that has his quarrel just, and he but naked, tho' locked up in steel, whose conscience with injustice is oppressed." History also informs us, that Xerxes with his armed millions could not accomplish his purpose of reducing to slavery the much weaker but free States of *Greece.* Three hundred brave men at Thermophylæ, contending for liberty, destroyed twenty thousand who attempted its ruin. In later times we see the States of *Holland* free, and the generous Corsicans likely to be so, although the far greater powers of *Spain, Germany*, and *France*, have at different periods combined to enslave these noble nations.

The truth is, that the great Author of nature has created nothing in vain, and having with the life of man joined liberty, the virtuous enjoyment and free possession of property honestly gained, has undoubtedly furnished all nations with the means of defending their natural rights, if they have the wisdom and fortitude to make the proper use of such means. In this instance we find ourselves three thousand miles removed from *great*-Britain, we possess a country abounding with woods in all parts, and in many with mountains of difficult and dangerous access. The ease with which the staple colonies could put an entire stop to the exportation of their commodities, and the peaceable but vital injury that this would convey to those who might insist on oppressing them, are truths so plain as to require no further animadversion. *Verbum sapienti sat est.* The nature of the climate, the soil, and its various produce, point out the ease and extent with which manufactories may be conducted here. These things are mentioned as proof of what is above asserted, that the bountiful Author of nature has furnished his creatures with the means of securing their proper rights, and that the event depends on their own wise and brave determinations. A benevolent mind, indeed, cannot but lament that either ambition, avarice, or ill-placed resentment, should ever be so exercised as to force men into the investigation of those methods by which they may be secure from the operation of those bad passions. For certain it is, that there is nothing more becoming to human nature than well-ordered government, or more valuable than liberty. How ignominious then must his conduct be who turns the first into confusion, and the latter into slavery! But whatever may be the opinion, or the design of a rapacious ill-advised Minister, the *Americans* have in their view this happy prospect; that the people of *Great*-Britain are generous and brave, they know the value of liberty, because they have purchased that knowledge with much of their blood, and therefore they cannot but esteem us their children for venerating the good old cause which they themselves have contended for in many a well-fought field. It is really wonderful that this unhappy dispute between *Great*-Britain and her colonies should ever have existed, when a moment's retrospection shews the Mother country for near two centuries exercising legislative authority here without complaint, while she abstained from that single destructive clause of taking our money from us without consent of our representatives. The exercise of which claim, would indeed reduce *America*, to a state of slavery more deplorable and more ignominious than has ever yet been known in the world.   But to what purpose this should be desired is still more amazing, when *Britain* from her exclusive trade to these colonies, and from the manner in which she tied up our manufacturing hands, not only received the entire produce of the lands and labour of these colonies, but has besides involved the people here in a heavy debt, which agriculture, without arts, and a trade so confined, will probably never pay.   Mr. *Grenville* it seems had the honor of devising this new system of *American* policy.

PREFACE TO DUBLIN EDITION.

THE EDITOR'S PREFACE.

The Farmer of *Pennsylvania* has (in our Opinion) treated his Subject with that Loyalty and becoming Spirit, which distinguishes the Cause of Liberty from that of Licentiousness. In our happy Constitution, no man can be properly said to be just to his prince, without being just to the Rights of his Fellow-subjects; as on the other hand, he cannot be true to his Country, without being true to his King.

A very unfavorable Opinion of the People of *America* has, I know not how, crept abroad: And there are those in these Kingdoms, who rashly brand their Cause with the name of Rebellion; but methinks we, who are united under the same Head should be very cautious how we entertain illiberal Prejudices against our Fellow-subjects; and ought, before we pass our Censure upon them, to examine what their Rights are, and with what justice they can complain that these Rights are invaded. This End will be best answered by a careful Perusal of the following Sheets; where the *Irish* Reader cannot fail to find many useful and very interesting Reflections. In short, if we are generally tender of the Reputation of an Individual, let us now be tender of the Reputation of a People: By neglecting the former, we may injure the Happiness of one, by neglecting the latter, we may *heedlessly conspire with an artful Minister to destroy the Hopes of* * *Millions.*

The Right of *Great-Britain* to tax *America*, is thoroughly examined in the following Letters. It has been already generously and, I might perhaps say, unanswerably opposed in the grand Council of that Nation. Two noble Lords, the one distinguished for his Abilities as a Statesman, the other for his

* The Inhabitants of the *British* Colonies are estimated at 3,000,000.

Knowledge in the Laws, and both for their powerful Eloquence, have bravely contended for the Liberty of *America*. Such exalted Characters, who possess so much feeling for the Rights of others, are a Blessing to a Nation: They preserve her from committing Injustice. He who supports the Rights of his own Country is an useful Citizen; but he who will go further and generously defend the Rights of others, is a virtuous one. By the Counsel and Conduct of *Themistocles*, *Athens* flourished. He raised her to a greater Height of Glory and Reputation than any of his Predecessors: But his Ambition to augment her Power, drove him to Designs of the blackest Treachery against her Friends and Fellow-conquerors. The Probity and Prudence of *Aristides* were a necessary Check upon him.

But Justice, indeed, has ever been the peculiar Attribute of *Great-Britain*. Always watchful and jealous of her own Liberty, she regards, as sacred, the Liberty of others. That Freedom which she enjoys, in the most reasonable Extent, she has imparted to the remotest Corners of her Empire: Wisely judging, that nothing will render her Children so attentive to her Interest, and so affectionate to her Person, as the free Enjoyment of their Liberty and Property; which Rights, once confounded and destroyed, it might be pretty equal to them *who exercised the Despotism*.

"It is," says an *Author on trade, "the Interest, and ought to "be the Care, of such as are entrusted with the Administration "of Government, to see that every Part of the *British* Empire "*amply* enjoys the Advantages derived from the Laws, and "*that glorious Freedom*, which is the Result of maintaining "them in full Vigour.—"And as Obedience," says he a little farther, "is expected from the remotest Quarters as well as "from those bordering upon the Center of Government, so they "are intitled to the *same Protection and Encouragement;* which, "*while they receive*, there is no Doubt but Affairs will continue "in a flourishing Condition, and the Fears which may have "entertained, that some of the distant Colonies may throw off

* *Rolt*, in his Dictionary of Trade and Commerce, under the Head of *Great-Britain*.

"their Obedience to their Mother Country, will disappear as "visionary Shadows: For it is in the Body Politic as in the "Natural Body; while the vital Parts are strong and sound, "the Constitution will be every where brisk and lively, and the "Effects of it perfectly felt to its very Extremities." These Words are remarkably strong and pertinent to the present Posture of Affairs; and I protest, when I add them to what has been said by other Authors on the same Subject, I am much startled at the present adopted Policy.

"*We have hitherto," says *Postlethwayt* speaking of the *Americans*, "supplied them with a great Quantity of their Ma- "terials for wearing Apparel, Household Furniture, &c, but if "they should establish these Manufactures among themselves, "and encourage every Species of Artificers to settle among "them, our Plantations may at length prove detrimental, in- "stead of beneficial to these Kingdoms."

Whether a more ingenious Way than has lately been taken, could possibly be devised, to bring about all that this Author so justly apprehends, I will leave to every body to determine.

We have already seen the spirited Colonists unanimously resolve to put a stop to *British* Importations. An armed Force, perhaps, may awe them to comply with strange Taxes; but we can hardly be persuaded that it will ever be able to dictate to them how they shall dispose of that Fund, which *Great Britain may think proper to leave them for their private Necessities.*

In fine, it were much to be wished by every true Lover of his King and Country, that if any rash Measures have been projected, that they may be wisely and seasonably relinquished: That *America*, on her Part, may ever adhere to that dutiful Dependence, which, to do her Justice, she continues respectfully to acknowledge; and that *Great Britain*, on her's, may re-assume her wonted Generosity and Good-nature, that, being united firmly with her *own Kindred*, she may have none to oppose, but *Foreign Enemies.*

---

* Postlethwayt's Dissertations on Commerce, Volume the 1st. Page the 104th.

PREFACE TO FRENCH EDITION.

PRÉFACE DU TRADUCTEUR.*

L'Amérique Septentrionale est aujourd'hui dans un état fort différent de ce qu'elle étoit il y a deux cens ans; ce n'est plus cette Terre sauvage & presque déserte, dont on seroit tenté de dire que les Habitans les plus distingués, tant par leur nombre que par leur industrie, étoient des Castors. Peu-à-peu les Côtes maritimes & les Provinces adjacentes se sont couvertes d'hommes, & les progrès de la population y ont été si rapides, que l'on compte déjà dans les seules Colonies Angloises du Continent, trois millions d'ames, qui connoissent peu de super-fluités, mais à qui il ne manque rien, ni pour les besoins, ni même pour les commodités de la vie.

Comment ces Colonies agricoles sont-elles devenues en si peu de tems si considérables, tandis que les Colonies, tant Militaires que Mercantiles, des autres Nations de l'Europe, à peu-près dans les mêmes climats, n'ont pas fait à beaucoup près les mêmes progrès? Cette question, quoique de l'Histoire le plus moderne, est aussi intéressante qu'aucune de l'Histoire Romaine, Greque ou Egyptienne.

Il n'en faut, à mon avis, cher cher la solution que dans la simplicité de leurs moeurs & de leurs loix, Toit doit constamment prospérer là où l'Agriculture est en honneur, où l'industrie se développe sans contrainte, où l'émulation anime tout, & où l'intrigue ne peut rien; en un mot, je regarde comme un théorême fondamental de toute saine politique, que la prospérité d'un peuple est en proportion de son exactitude à se conformer à l'ordre que la Nature nous a elle-même prescrit.

L'intolérance Européenne a fait les principaux frais de la population de l'Amérique Angloise. La haute Commission des

---

* Jacques Barbeu Dubourg.—*Ed.*

Episcopaux, sous Charles Premier, donna la chasse à une multitude de non-Conformistes Anglois & Ecossois de différentes Sectes, qui allerent fonder la Nouvelle-Angleterre vers l'an 1628.

La même espece d'inquisition Protestante occasionna peu après une semblable émigration de Catholiques, qui, sous la conduite du Lord Baltimore, fonderent le Maryland en 1631.

La Pensylvanie, aujourd'hui si florissante, ne fut fondée qu'en 1681, par Guillaume Pen, à la tête de cinq cens Quakers persécutés dans leur Patrie, & qui furent bientôt suivis d'environ deux mille autres.

Vers le même tems, un grand nombre de Protestans réfugiés d'Allemagne, & sur-tout du Palatinat, trouverent un asyle à la Nouvelle-Yorck. Et la Virginie, la plus ancienne de toutes ces Colonies, fut pareillement recrutée de quantité de François réfugiés, après la révocation de l'Edit de Nantes, en 1685.

La Caroline, la Géorgie, &c. ont tour-à-tour puisé plus ou moins dans les mêmes sources. Toutes, enfin, ont tendu les bras à ces malheureux Herrenhutters, ou Freres Moraves, à qui, depuis trois cens ans, la Bohême, la Hongrie, la Pologne, la Russie, la Prusse, & le Dannemarck avoient successivement interdit le feu & l'eau.

Il est à remarquer que les non-Conformistes qui ont fondé la Nouvelle Angleterre, porterent dans les forêts du nouveau Monde cet esprit d'intolérance, dont ils avoient eu tant à souffrir dans leur pays natal ; que le Lord Baltimore, avec ses Catholiques, donna à l'Amérique le premier exemple de cette tolérance chrétienne, qui a fait la base de sa félicité ; mais que c'est sur-tout aux Quakers que l'on doit l'établissement de la pleine liberté de conscience & de la paix fraternelle, son incomparable compagne, qui de leur Colonie de Pensylvanie, s'est répandue successivement dans toutes les autres Colonies Angloises.

Est-il surprenant que son example ait fait impression ? Quoique sa fondation ne remonte pas encore à un siécle, on l'estime déja quatre fois plus riche elle seule, que ces trois fameuses conquêtes des Anglois, le Canada, l'Acadie & la Floride, toutes ensemble.

Les premiers Quakers étoient des enthousiastes, des convulsionaires, des trembleurs, comme leur nom le porte; mais leur nom est tout ce qui leur en reste, & ne doit pas nous en imposer. Ce qu'ils ont de plus singulier aujourd'hui, c'est plus de modestie, plus de frugalité, plus de modération en toutes choses, & conséquemment plus d'union entr'eux, qu'on n'en trouveroit peut-être chez aucun autre Peuple de l'Univers. S'ils ont démenti le nom de leur Secte, il paroît qu'ils soutiennent à merveille celui de leur Ville capitale (Philadelphia, c'est-à-dire, amour fraternel). Eh! qui ne seroit touché de cette franchise honnête avec laquelle on va voir qu'ils défendent leur Liberté; de ces sentimens inaltérables de respect & de bienveillance qu'ils ne cessent de témoigner envers ceux qui les maltraitent; enfin, de cette heureuse sérénité avec laquelle ils attendent, sans armes, une armée destinée à les subjuguer?

Indépendamment de l'affluence des nouveaux Colons, que la douceur du Gouvernement de la Pensylvanie y attire de jour en jour, ses plus grandes ressources sont & seront toujours en elle-même. Comme le Pays est grand, le sol fertile, l'air sain, la Liberté assurée, tous les hommes s'y marient & tous se marient jeunes, n'ayant aucune inquiétude sur l'établissement de leur famille, si nombreuse qu'elle puisse être; de forte que que chaque mariage produisant aisément 4 à 5 nouveaux sujets, le nombre des hommes y double au moins de vingt ans en vingt ans.

La plûpart des autres Colonies Angloises, soit pour être moins heureusement, situées ou moins sagement régies, ne prosperent pas autant; mais il passe pour constant que, le fort compensant le foible, le somme totale des habitans de ces Colonies double tous les vingt-cinq ans.

Le Continent de l'Amérique Septentrionale est si vaste, qu'avant que la terre & manque à ses habitans, il faudra qu'elle soit beaucoup plus peuplée que n'est aujourd'hui l'Europe. Mais quand verra-t-on cela? Si l'instablité des choses humaines pouvoit être soumise au calcul, des Politiques spéculatifs ont supputé que cet événement ne se feroit attendre gueres plus d'un siecle.

On pourra crier au paradoxe; mais daignons faire attention

au cours que les choses ont pris. Deux causes sensibles con-
courent à peupler très promptement ces Régions ; l'une ex-
terne, dépendante de la déraison & de la mauvaise politique de
notre Europe ; l'autre interne, dépendante de la saggesse & de
la bonne conduite de ces Colonistes. Quant à la premiere, il
est vrai que nous avons commercé à reconnoître nos torts, mais
nous ne paroissons pas encore tellement disposés à nous corri-
ger, que l'Amérique ne puisse encore se promettre de nos vexa-
tions politiques, ou religieuses, un assez non nombre d'emigrans.
Quant à la cause interne, pour savoir ce que l'on en peut attendre, suivons un peu la progression cidessus établie. On ne
compte encore que trois millions d'habitants dans ces Colonies,
tandis qu'on évalue constamment ceux de l'Europe à cent millions ; mais si le nombre de ceux-là continue à doubler tous les
25 ans, ils auront au bout d'un siecle seize hommes pour un, &
16 fois 16 à la sin du siecle suivant. Multipliez donc trois millions par 16, & le produit encore par 16, vous verrez ce qui en
résultera, & de combien l'Amérique l'emporteroit sur l'Europe
avant deux siecles, si ces Peuples pouvoient conserver leur
régime autant de tems.

La progression réguliere d'une population si peu commune,
aura sans doute des bornes ; mais d'où viendront-elles ? peut-
être d'où on les attend le moins. Tout ce que je puis entrevoir
au travers des ténèbres d'un futur contingent, c'est que 1° le
Pays, tout immense qu'il paroît, ne fournira certainement pas
toujours de nouvelles terres à défricher. 2° N'est-il pas à pré-
sumer que le luxe s'y introduisant tôt ou tard, amollira & aba-
tardira ce Peuple simple & généreux. 3° Il est très probable
qu'au défaut de voisins à redouter pour eux, la jalousie de
l'Angleterre même leur suscitera des embarras, qui ralentiront
au moins leurs progrès, s'ils ne les arrêtent pas tout-à-fait : cette
jalousie a même déja éclaté, & de petites menaces paroissent
avoir de grandes suites.

Il ne faut pas confondre les Colonies en question, avec quelques autres Etablissemens formés aussi par les Anglois, sur le
même Continent de l'Amérique Septentrionale. Des Comptoirs
établis pour le seul intérêt des Marchands de l'ancienne Angleterre, & des Forts construits pour la sûreté de ces Comptoirs,

n'ont rien de commun avec les Colonies purement agricoles, dont ils bordent la frontiere.

Cependant le Parlement de la Grande-Bretagne, sur lequel les Marchands Pelletiers de Londres ont plus d'influence que tout les Colons & Planteurs de l'Amérique, a enterpris depuis quelques années de faire supporter aux Colonies la dépense qu' exige l'entretien de ces Forts, & de leur imposer à cet effet des taxes, non-seulement inusitées, mais encore sous une forme qui leur paroît illégale. Les Assemblées de toutes les Colonies se montrent fermement résolues a soutenir leurs droits; on les soupçonne d'aspirer à l'indépendance. La Prospérité les a t-elle enivrées? ou le Parlement en a-t-il pris ombrage mal-é-propos? c'est sur quoi je n'oserois prononcer.

Quoi qu'il en soit, quiconque aime à voir une grande cause bien discutée aura de quoi se satisfaire en cette occasion; ces Lettres d'un Fermier de ·Pensylvanie suffisent au moins pour remontrer qu'en ce Pays-là (& il en pourroit être ainsi de tout autre) la culture des terres n'a point nui à celle des esprits.

M. Dickinson, de Philadelphie, est l'Auteur de ces Lettres, dont la première est datée avec affectation du 5 Novembre, jour anniversaire du débarquement du Prince d'Orange en Angleterre. D'ailleurs, elles, sont écrites avec autant de sagesse que de vigueur. Aussi ont-elles fait un effet prodigieux, en excitant le Peuple de toutes les Colonies à s'opposer aux nouvelles impositions avec la plus grande unanimité. Si l'éloquence, dont on n'a communément qu'une très fausse ou très frivole idée, n'est autre chose (comme je le crois fermement) que ce grand art de gouverner les hommes par la parole, l'Orateur Romain fut moins éloquent que ce bon Fermier.

Il y a eu trente Editions de ses Lettres en Amérique dans l'espace de six mois; & elles ont été réimprimées à Londres par les soins de M. Franklin. Quel honneur pour l'Ouvrage, d'avoir métité in tel Editeur!

J'aurois dû sentir qu'il ne m'appartenoit point de traduire un tel Ouvrage, & moins encore de le traduire à la hâte; mais je m'étois passionné à le lecture, & la passion ne réfléchit gueres. Heureux donc si le peu de tems que j'ai eu à donner à cette Traduction ne m'attire d'autres reproches que celui d'y laisser trop sentir un certain goût de terroir, que je n'aurois pû lui enlever, qu'en la remaniant beaucoup & long-tems !

Pour moi, ce que je regrette le plus, c'est de n'être pas assez instruit des affaires de l'Amérique, pour mettre le Lectuer parfaitement au fait de la matiere de ces Lettres ; cependant comme bien des gens sont peut-être encore moins avancés que moi à cet égard, j'ai cru devoir exposer succinctement ici le peu que j'en sais.

Tout Anglois tient pour principe qu'il doit contribuer à proportion de ses moyens aux charges de l'Etat, dont la protection fait sa sûreté ; mais que cette contribution ne doit être levée que de son consentment, accordé par lui-même, ou par ses représentans ; que c'est un droit essentiel à sa condition de sujet libre, n'y ayant point de liberté, lé où il n'y a point de propriété assurée.

Les Anglois établis dans les Colonies ont été formellement assurés, par les Chartes mêmes de leurs fondations respectives, qu'ils seroient toujours traités comme vrais Anglois, & jouiroient de tous les droits inhérens à ce titre.   Il ont été maintenus en cette possession depuis peur premier établissement.   Ils demandent ce qu'ils ont fait pour mériter d'en étre dépouillés ? en quoi ont-ils manqué à leur Mere-Patrie ?

Pendant 150 ans, le Couronne (c'est-à-dire le Roi, ou le Ministre en son nom) leur a fait de tems-en-tems des demandes pour contribuer aux besoins de l'Etat & leur Assemblées respectives lui ont octroyé de bonne grace ce qu'elles ont cru que les besoins publics requeroient, & que leur propre situation comportoit. Leur zele les avout même tellement aiguillonnés, qu'ayant contribué pendant quelques années de la dernier guerre, non-seulement en raison de leurs moyens, mais même beaucoup audelà, le Parlement de la Grande-Bretagne, qui tient par sa constitution la balance générale des devoirs & des droits respectifs de toutes les parties intégrantes de l'Empire Britannique, jugea à propos de leur faire remettre des sommes considérables par forme de restitutions ou d'indemnités.

Il paroît singulier que ce foit à-peu près dans ce même tems qu'un Acte émané de ce même Parlement a exigé de ces mêmes Colonies une chose qui n'étoit pas d'usage, & qu'elles ne croyoient

pas qu'il fût en droit d'exiger : c'étoit de fournir différentes provisions pour la subsistance des troupes réparties sur leur terri-
toire, ou dans leur voisinage. Les Assemblées de ces diverses
Colonies ne voulant ni lutter contre le Parlement, ni abandonner
leurs privileges, prirent presque universellement le parti d'ac-
corder, comme de leur propre mouvement, ces provisions aux
troupes, sans faire aucune mention de l'Acte par lequel on avoit
prétendu leur en faire un devoir. La seule Assemblée de la
Nouvelle-Yorck, pour marquer un peu mieux son indépendance,
accorda toutes les mêmes provisions, à l'exception de trois articles : du sel, du poivre & du viniagre.

La majesté du Peuple Anglois* se trouvant blessée par cette
restriction, on résolut d'en faire repentir les Colonistes de la
Nouvelle-Yorck, & d'en imposer aux autres par leur exemple.
Pour cet effet, le Parlement suspendit, par un Acte exprés,
l'Autorité législative de l'Assemblée de cette Colonie.

M. Dickinson s'attache dans sa premiere Lettre, à faire sentir
les conséquences de cette entreprise Parlementaire, & la néces-
sité de la concorde entre toutes les Colonies de l'Amérique, qui
ressentiroient tôt ou tard le contre-coup d'une telle innovation,
mais dont l'attention avoit été détournée de cet objet par un
autre, auquel elles étoient toutes plus directement intéressées.

Cet autre objet étoit le fameux Acte du Timbre par lequel le
Parlement établissoit des droits sur le papier marqué, & défendoit
d'en employer d'autre dans toutes les écritures publiques, tant
judiciaires, qu'extra judiciaires : cet Acte est de l'année 1764.

L'opposition des Colonies à son exécution fut si universelle,
si vive & si constante, & parut si légitime à quelques personnes
du premier ordre, même en Angleterre, que le Parlement l'a
enfin révoqué au bout de deux ans.

Rien n'a tant contribué à le faire revenir ainsi sur ses pas, que
la conspiration patriotique des Colonies à se priver absolument
de toutes marchandises des Fabriques de la Grande-Bretagne,
jusqu'à ce qu'on leur eût donné satisfaction sur tous les objets
de leurs Remontrances. Cette généreuse résolution, enlevant

---

* Voyez par rapport a cette expression les Lettres Philosophiques de M.
Voltaire.—*Note of French Editor.*

trés pacifiquement à l'Angleterre un bénéfice annuel de 50 millions de notre monnoie, fit jetter les plus hauts cris à tout les Marchands de la Nation, & força, en quelque sorte, la main au Gouvernement: circonstance qui mérite la plus grande attention de notre part, & qui, en supposant même qu'elle n'affectât le reste de l'Europe que par simple curiosité, peut intéresser la France d'une maniere trés particuliere.

Le Parlement n'ayant pû se dispenser de révoquer l'Acte du Timbre, a bientôt cherché une autre teurnure pour y suppléer; il a passé un nouvel Acte, par lequel il octroie quelques petits droits sur le Verre, le Papier, &c. exportés de la Grande-Bretagne pour les Colonies, qui ne sont pas expressément obligées d'en acheter, mais qui ne sauroient s'en passer, & à qui il est défendu d'en tirer d'ailleurs.

C'est contre cet Acte, dont il est aisé de pressentir les consequences, que M. Dickinsons' éleve dans le reste de ces Lettres (c'est-à-dire, depuis la deuxieme jusqu'à lé douzieme); mais il me tarde de le faire entendre lui même, & que l'on voie avec quelle douceur la persuasion coule de ses levres.

P. S. Cette Traduction étoit presque achevée d'imprimer, lorsqu'un Jeune Pensylvain (le Dr. Benjamin Rush) m'a appris que M. Dikinson, Auteur de ces Lettres, est à peine âgé de 32 à 33 ans, qu'il est Avocat à Philadelphie, qu'on l'a surnommé le de la Virginie lui a fait présent de dix mille livres sterlings; que ce généreux Virginien est un Ecclesiastique; qu'il ne s'en rappelle pas le nom, mais qu'il me le mandera de's qu' il sera de retour dans sa chere Patrie.

LETTERS

FROM A

FARMER

IN

PENNSYLVANIA,

TO THE

INHABITANTS

OF THE

BRITISH COLONIES.

PHILADELPHIA:

Printed by DAVID HALL, and WILLIAM SELLERS.
MDCCLXVIII.

LETTERS FROM A FARMER.

LETTER I.

My dear Countrymen,*

I am a *Farmer*, settled, after a variety of fortunes, near the banks of the river *Delaware*, in the province of *Pennsylvania*. I received a liberal education, and have been engaged in the busy scenes of life; but am now convinced, that a man may be as happy without bustle, as with it. My farm is small; my servants are few, and good; I have a little money at interest; I wish for no more; my employment in my own affairs is easy; and with a contented grateful mind, (undisturbed by worldly hopes or fears, relating to myself,) I am completing the number of days allotted to me by divine goodness.

Being generally master of my time, I spend a good deal of it in a library, which I think the most valuable part of my small estate; and being acquainted with two or three gentlemen of abilities and learning, who honour me with their friendship, I have acquired, I believe, a greater knowledge in history, and the laws and constitution of my country, than is generally attained by men of my class, many of them not being so fortunate as I have been in the opportunities of getting information.

From my infancy I was taught to love *humanity* and *liberty*. Enquiry and experience have since confirmed my reverence for the lessons then given me, by convincing me more fully of their truth and excellence. Benevolence

---

*In the newspaper text the first letters began "My beloved Countrymen."—*Ed.*

(307)

towards mankind, excites wishes for their welfare, and such wishes endear the means of fulfilling them. *These* can be found in liberty only, and therefore her sacred cause ought to be espoused by every man, on every occasion, to the utmost of his power. As a charitable, but poor person does not withhold his *mite*, because he cannot relieve *all* the distresses of the miserable, [4] so should not any honest man suppress his sentiments concerning freedom, however small their influence is likely to be. Perhaps he "may touch some wheel,*" that will have an effect greater than he could reasonably expect.

These being my sentiments, I am encouraged to offer to you, my countrymen, my thoughts on some late transactions, that appear to me to be of the utmost importance to you. Conscious of my own defects, I have waited some time, in expectation of seeing the subject treated by persons much better qualified for the task; but being therein disappointed, and apprehensive that longer delays will be injurious, I venture at length to request the attention of the public, praying, that these lines may be *read* with the same zeal for the happiness of *British America*, with which they were *wrote.*

With a good deal of surprize I have observed, that little notice has been taken of an act of parliament, as injurious in its principle to the liberties of these colonies, as the *Stamp-Act* was: I mean the act for suspending the legislation of *New-York.*

The assembly of that government complied with a former act of parliament, requiring certain provisions to be made for the troops in *America*, in every particular, I think, except the articles of salt, pepper and vinegar. In my opinion they acted imprudently, considering all circumstances, in not complying so far as would have given satisfaction, as several colonies did: But my dislike of their

* Pope.

conduct in that instance, has not blinded me so much, that I cannot plainly perceive, that they have been punished in a manner pernicious to *American* freedom, and justly alarming to all the colonies.

If the *British* parliament has a legal authority to issue an order, that we shall furnish a single article for the troops here, and to compel obedience to *that* order, they have the same right to issue an order for us to supply those troops with arms, cloths, and every necessary ; and to compel obedience to *that* order also; in short, to lay *any burthens* they please upon us. What is this but *taxing* us at a *certain sum*, and leaving to us only the *manner* of raising it? How is this mode more tolerable than the *Stamp Act ?* Would that act have appeared more pleasing to *Americans*, if being ordered thereby to raise the sum total of the taxes, the mighty privilege had been left to them, of saying how much should be paid for an instrument of writing on paper, and how much for another on parchment?

An act of parliament, commanding us to do a certain thing, if it has any validity, is a *tax* upon us for the expence that accrues in complying with it ; and for this reason, I believe, every colony on the continent, that chose to give a mark of their respect for *Great-Britain*, in complying with the act relating to the troops, cautiously [5] avoided the mention of that act, lest their conduct should be attributed to its supposed obligation.

The matter being thus stated, the assembly of *New-York* either had, or had not, a right to refuse submission to that act. If they had, and I imagine no *American* will say they had not, then the parliament had *no right* to compel them to execute it. If they had not *that right*, they had *no right* to punish them for not executing it ; and therefore *no right* to suspend their legislation, which is a punishment. In fact, if the people of *New-York* cannot be legally taxed but by their own representatives, they cannot be legally deprived of the privilege of legislation, only for insisting on that exclusive privilege of taxation. If they may be legally deprived in such a case, of the privilege of legislation, why may they not, with equal reason, be deprived of every other privilege? Or why may not every colony be treated in the same manner, when any of them shall dare to deny their assent to any impositions, that shall be directed? Or what signifies the repeal of the *Stamp-Act*, if these colonies are to lose their *other* privileges, by not tamely surrendering *that* of taxation?

There is one consideration arising from this suspension, which is not generally attended to, but shews its importance very clearly. It was not *necessary* that this suspension should be caused by an act of parliament. The crown might have restrained the governor of *New-York*, even from calling the assembly together, by its prerogative in the royal governments. This step, I suppose, would have been taken, if the conduct of the assembly of *New-York* had been regarded as an act of disobedience *to the crown alone;* but it is regarded as an act of * "disobedience to the authority "of the BRITISH LEGISLATURE." This gives the suspension a consequence vastly more affecting. It is a parliamentary assertion of the *supreme authority* of the *British* legislature over these colonies, in *the point of taxation*, and is intended to COMPEL *New-York* into a submission to that authority. It seems therefore to me as much a violation of the liberty of the people of that province, and consequently of all these colonies, as if the parliament had sent a number of regiments to be quartered upon them till they should comply. For it is evident, that the suspension is meant as a *compulsion;* and the *method* of compelling is totally indifferent. It is indeed probable, that the sight of red coats, and the hearing of drums, would have been most alarming; because people

* See the act of suspension.

are generally more influenced by their eyes and ears, than by their reason. But whoever seriously considers the matter, must perceive that a dreadful stroke is aimed at the liberty of these colonies. I say, of these colonies; for the cause of *one* is the cause of *all.* If the parliament may lawfully deprive *New-York* of any of *her* rights, it may deprive any, or all the other colonies of *their* rights; and nothing can [6] possibly so much encourage such attempts, as a mutual inattention to the interests of each other. *To divide, and thus to destroy,* is the first political maxim in attacking those, who are powerful by their union. He certainly is not a wise man, who folds his arms, and reposes himself at home, viewing, with unconcern, the flames that have invaded his neighbour's house, without using any endeavours to extinguish them. When Mr. *Hampden's* ship money cause, for *Three Shillings* and *Four-pence,* was tried, all the people of *England,* with anxious expectations, interested themselves in the important decision; and when the slightest point, touching the freedom of *one* colony, is agitated, I earnestly wish, that *all the rest* may, with equal ardour, support their sister. Very much may be said on this subject; but I hope, more at present is unnecessary.

With concern I have observed, that *two* assemblies of this province have sat and adjourned, without taking any notice of this act. It may perhaps be asked, what would have been proper for them to do? I am by no means fond of inflammatory measures; I detest them. I should be sorry that any thing should be done, which might justly displease our sovereign, or our mother country: But a firm, modest exertion of a free spirit, should never be wanting on public occasions. It appears to me, that it would have been sufficient for the assembly, to have ordered our agents to represent to the King's ministers, their sense of the suspending act, and to pray for its repeal.

Thus we should have borne our testimony against it; and might therefore reasonably expect that, on a like occasion, we might receive the same assistance from the other colonies.

Concordia res parvæ crescunt.
Small things grow great by concord.

A FARMER.

Nov. 5. [7]

LETTER II.

My dear Countrymen,

There is another late act of parliament, which appears to me to be unconstitutional, and as destructive to the liberty of these colonies, as that mentioned in my last letter; that is, the act for granting the duties on paper, glass, etc.

The parliament unquestionably possesses a legal authority to *regulate* the trade of *Great-Britain*, and all her colonies. Such an authority is essential to the relation between a mother country and her colonies; and necessary for the common good of all. He, who considers these provinces as states distinct from the *British Empire*, has very slender notions of *justice*, or of their *interests*. We are but parts of a *whole;* and therefore there must exist a power somewhere to preside, and preserve the connection in due order. This power is lodged in the parliament; and we are as much dependent on *Great-Britain*, as a perfectly free people can be on another.

I have looked over *every statute* relating to these colonies, from their first settlement to this time; and I find every one of them founded on this principle, till the *Stamp-Act* administration.† *All before,* [8] are calculated to reg-

* The day of King WILLIAM the Third's landing.

† For the satisfaction of the reader, recitals from the former acts of parliament relating to these colonies are added. By comparing these with

ulate trade, and preserve or promote a mutually beneficial intercourse between the several constituent parts of the empire; and though many of them imposed duties on trade, yet those duties were always imposed *with design* to restrain the commerce of one part, that was injurious to another, and thus to promote [9] the general welfare. The raising a revenue thereby was never intended. Thus the King, by his judges in his courts of justice, imposes fines which all together amount to a very considerable sum, and contribute to the support of government: But this is merely

the modern acts, he will perceive their great difference in *expression* and *intention.*

The 12th *Cha.,* Chap. 18, which forms the foundation of the laws relating to *our* trade, by enacting that certain productions of the colonies should be carried to *England* only, and that no goods shall be imported from the plantations but in ships belonging to *England, Ireland, Wales, Berwick,* or the *Plantations,* etc., begins thus: *For the increase of shipping, and encouragement of the navigation of this nation,* wherein, under the good providence and protection of *GOD,* the wealth, *safety,* and strength of this kingdom is so much concerned," *&c.*

The 15th *Cha.* II., Chap. 7, enforcing the same regulation, assigns these reasons for it. "In regard his Majesty's plantations, beyond the seas, are inhabited and peopled by his subjects of this his kingdom of *England, for the maintaining a greater correspondence and kindness between them,* and keeping them in a firmer dependence upon it, and rendering them yet more beneficial and advantageous unto it, *in the further employment and increase of* English *shipping and seamen,* vent of *English* woollen, and other manufactures and commodities, *rendering the navigation to and from the same more safe and cheap,* and making this kingdom a *staple,* not only of the commodities of those plantations, but also of the commodities of other countries and places *for the supplying of them;* and it being the *usage* of other nations to keep their plantations trade to themselves," *&c.*

The 25th *Cha.* II., Chap. 7, made expressly *"for the better securing the plantation trade,"* which imposes duties on certain commodities exported from one colony to another, mentions this cause for imposing them: "Whereas by one act, passed in the 12th year of your Majesty's reign, intituled, An act for *encouragement of shipping and navigation,* and by several other laws, passed since that time, it is permitted to ship, *&c.* sugars, tobacco, *&c.* of the growth, *&c.* of any of your Majesty's plantations in *America, &c.* from the places of their growth, *&c.* to any other

a consequence arising from restrictions, that only meant to keep peace, and prevent confusion; and surely a man would argue very loosely, who should conclude from hence, that the King has a right to levy money in general upon his subjects.   Never did the *British* parliament, till the period above mentioned, think of imposing duties in *America*, FOR THE PURPOSE OF RAISING A REVENUE. Mr. *Grenville* first introduced this language, in the preamble to the 4th of *Geo.* III., Chap. 15, which has these words "And whereas it is just and necessary that A REVE-

of your Majesty's plantations in those parts, *&c.* and that *without paying custom for the same*, either at the lading or unlading the said commodities, by means whereof the trade and navigation in those commodities, from one plantation to another, is greatly increased, and the inhabitants of divers of those colonies, *not contenting themselves with being supplied with those commodities for their own use, free from all customs* (while the subjects of this your kingdom of *England* have paid great customs and impositions for what of them hath been spent here) *but, contrary to the express letter of the aforesaid laws, have brought into divers parts of* Europe great quantities thereof, and do also vend great quantities thereof to the shipping of other nations, who bring them into divers parts of *Europe*, to the great hurt and diminution of your Majesty's customs, and of the *trade* and *navigation* of this your kingdom ; FOR THE PREVENTION THEREOF, *&c.*

The 7th and 8th *Will.* III., Chap. 22, intituled, "An act for preventing frauds, and regulating abuses in the plantation trade," recites that, "notwithstanding divers acts, *&c.* great abuses are daily committed *to the prejudice of the* English *navigation, and the loss of a great part of the plantation trade* to this kingdom, by the *artifice* and *cunning* of ill disposed persons ; FOR REMEDY WHEREOF, *&c.* And whereas in some of his Majesty's *American* plantations, a doubt or misconstruction has arisen upon the before mentioned act, made in the 25th year of the reign of King *Charles* II. whereby certain duties are laid upon the commodities therein enumerated (which by law may be transported from one plantation to another, for the supply of each others wants) *as if* the same were, by the payment of those duties in one plantation, discharged from giving the securities intended by the aforesaid acts, made in the 12th, 22d and 23d years of the reign of King *Charles* the II. and consequently be at liberty to go to any foreign market in *Europe*," *&c.*

The 6th *Anne*, Chap. 37, reciting the advancement of trade, and encouragement of ships of war, *&c.* grants to the captors the property of

NUE BE RAISED IN YOUR MAJESTY'S SAID DOMINIONS IN AMERICA, *for defraying the expences of defending, protecting, and securing the same:* We your Majesty's most dutiful and loyal subjects, THE COMMONS OF GREAT-BRITAIN, in parliament assembled, being desirous to make some provision in this present session of parliament, TOWARDS RAISING THE SAID REVENUE IN AMERICA, have resolved to GIVE and GRANT unto your Majesty the several rates and duties herein after mentioned," *&c.*

A few months after came the *Stamp-Act,* which reciting

all prizes carried into *America,* subject to such customs and duties, as if the same had been first imported into any part of *Great-Britain,* and from thence exported, *&c.*

This was a *gift to persons acting under commissions from the crown,* and therefore it was reasonable that the *terms* prescribed in that gift, should be complied with—more especially as the payment of such duties was intended to give a preference to the productions of *British* colonies, over those of other colonies. However, being found inconvenient to the colonies, about four years afterwards, this act was, for that reason, so far repealed, that by another act "all prize goods, imported into any part of *Great-Britain,* from any of the plantations, were made liable to such duties only in *Great-Britain,* as in case they had been of the growth and produce of the plantations."

The 6th *Geo.* II. Chap. 13, which imposes duties on foreign rum, sugar and molasses, imported into the colonies, shews the reasons thus—"Whereas, the welfare and prosperity of your Majesty's sugar colonies in *America,* are of the greatest consequence and importance to the *trade, navigation* and *strength* of this kingdom ; and whereas the planters of the said sugar colonies, have of late years *fallen into such great discouragements,* that they are unable to improve or carry on the sugar trade, *upon an equal footing* with the foreign sugar colonies, *without some advantage and relief be given to them from* Great-Britain : FOR REMEDY WHEREOF, AND FOR THE GOOD AND WELFARE OF YOUR MAJESTY'S SUBJECTS," *&c.*

The 29th *Geo.* II. Chap. 26, and the 1st *Geo.* III. Chap. 9, which continue the 6th *Geo.* II. Chap. 13, declare, that the said act hath, by experience, been found *useful* and *beneficial, &c.* These are all the most considerable statutes relating to the commerce of the colonies ; and it is thought to be utterly unnecessary to add any observations to these extracts, to prove that they were all intended *solely as regulations of trade.*

this, proceeds in the same strange mode of expression, thus—"And whereas it is just and necessary, that provision be made FOR RAISING A FURTHER REVENUE WITHIN YOUR MAJESTY'S DOMINIONS IN AMERICA, *towards defraying the said expences*, we your Majesty's most dutiful and loyal subjects, the COMMONS OF GREAT-BRITAIN, *&c.* GIVE and GRANT, *&c.* as before.

The last act, granting duties upon paper, *&c.* carefully pursues these modern precedents. The preamble is, "Whereas it is expedient THAT A REVENUE SHOULD BE RAISED IN YOUR MAJESTY'S DOMINIONS IN AMERICA, *for making a more certain and adequate provision for defraying the charge of the administration of justice, and the support of civil government in such provinces, where it shall be found necessary; and towards the further defraying the expences of defending, protecting and securing the said dominions*, we your Majesty's most dutiful and loyal subjects, the COMMONS OF GREAT-BRITAIN, *&c.* GIVE and GRANT," *&c.* as before.

Here we may observe an authority *expressly* claimed and exerted to impose duties on these colonies ; not for the regulation of trade; not [10] for the preservation or promotion of a mutually beneficial intercourse between the several constituent parts of the empire, heretofore the *sole objects* of parliamentary institutions; *but for the single purpose of levying money upon us.*

This I call an *innovation; and a most dangerous innovation. It may perhaps be objected, that *Great-Britain* has a right to lay what duties she pleases upon her † ex-

---

* "It is worthy observation how quietly subsidies, granted in forms *usual* and *accustomable* (though heavy) are borne ; such a power hath use and custom. On the other side, what discontentments and disturbances subsidies *framed in a new mould* do raise (SUCH AN INBRED HATRED NOVELTY DOTH HATCH) is evident by examples of former times."

Lord *Coke's* 2d Institute, p. 33.

† Some people ["whose minds seem incapable of uniting two ideas,"

ports, and it makes no difference to us, whether they are paid here or there.

To this I answer. These colonies require many things for their use, which the laws of *Great-Britain* prohibit them from getting any where but from her. Such are paper and glass.

That we may legally be bound to pay any *general* duties on these commodities relative to the regulation of trade, is granted ; but we being *obliged by the laws* to take from *Great-Britain*, any *special* duties imposed on their exportation *to us only, with intention to raise a revenue from us only*, are as much *taxes*, upon us, as those imposed by the *Stamp-Act.*

What is the difference in *substance* and *right* whether the same sum is raised upon us by the rates mentioned in the *Stamp-Act*, on the *use* of paper, or by these duties, on the *importation* of it. It is only the edition of a former book, shifting a sentence from the *end* to the *beginning*.*

Suppose the duties were made payable in *Great-Britain.*

It signifies nothing to us, whether they are to be paid here or there. Had the *Stamp-Act* directed, that all the paper should be landed at *Florida*, and the duties paid there, before it was brought to the *British* colonies, would the act have raised less money upon us, or have been less

follows in newspaper text.—Ed.] think that *Great-Britain* has the same right to impose duties on the exports to these colonies, as on the exports to *Spain* and *Portugal*, &c. Such persons attend so much to the idea of exportation, that they entirely drop *that of the connection between the mother country and her colonies.* If *Great-Britain* had always claimed, and exercised an authority to compel *Spain* and *Portugal* to import manufactures from her only, the cases would be parallel : But as she never pretended to such a right, they are at liberty to get them where they please ; and if they chuse to take them from her, rather than from other nations, they voluntarily consent to pay the duties imposed on them.

* The original newspaper text reads: "It is nothing but the edition of a former book, with a new title page."—*Ed.*

destructive of our rights? By no means : For as we were under a necessity of using the paper, we should have been under the necessity of paying the duties. Thus, in the present case, a like *necessity* will subject us, if this act continues in force, to the payment of the duties now imposed.

Why was the *Stamp-Act* then so pernicious to freedom? It did not enact, that every man in the colonies *should* buy a certain quantity [11] of paper—No: It only directed, that no instrument of writing should be valid in law, if not made on stamped paper, *&c.*

The makers of that act knew full well,* that the confusions that would arise from the disuse of writings, would COMPEL the colonies to use the stamped paper, and therefore to pay the taxes imposed. For this reason the *Stamp-Act* was said to be a law THAT WOULD EXECUTE ITSELF. For the very same reason, the last act of parliament, if it is granted to have any force here, WILL EXECUTE ITSELF, and will be attended with the very same consequences to *American* liberty.

Some persons perhaps may say, that this act lays us under no necessity to pay the duties imposed, because we may ourselves manufacture the articles on which they are laid; whereas by the *Stamp-Act* no instrument of writing could be good, unless made on *British* paper, and that too stamped.

Such an objection amounts to no more than this, that the injury resulting to these colonies, from the total disuse of *British* paper and glass, will not be *so afflicting* as that which would have resulted from the total disuse of writing among them; for by that means even the *Stamp-Act* might have been eluded. Why then was it universally detested by them as slavery itself? Because it presented to these devoted provinces nothing but a † choice of calamities,

* Changed to "expected" in *Political Writings.—Ed.*

† Either the *disuse* of writing, or the payment of *taxes* imposed by others *without our consent.*

imbittered by indignities, each of which it was unworthy of freemen to bear. But is no injury a violation of right but the *greatest* injury? If the eluding the payment of the taxes imposed by the *Stamp-Act*, would have subjected us to a more dreadful inconvenience, than the eluding the payment of those imposed by the late act; does it therefore follow, that the last is *no violation* of our rights, tho' it is calculated for the same purpose the other was, that is, *to raise money upon us*, WITHOUT OUR CONSENT.

This would be making *right* to consist, not in an exemption from *injury*, but from a certain *degree of injury*.

But the objectors may further say, that we shall suffer no injury at all by the disuse of *British* paper and glass. We might not, if we could make as much as we want. But can any man, acquainted with *America*, believe this possible? I am told there are but two or three *Glass-Houses* on this continent, and but very few *Paper-Mills;* and suppose more should be erected, a long course of years must elapse, before they can be brought to perfection. This continent is a country of planters, farmers, and fishermen; not of manufacturers. The difficulty of establishing particular manufactures in such a country, is almost insuperable. For one manufacture is connected with others in such a manner, that it may be said to be impossible to establish one or two, without establishing several [12] others. The experience of many nations may convince us of this truth.

Inexpressible therefore must be our distresses in evading the late acts, by the disuse of *British* paper and glass. Nor will this be the extent of our misfortune, if we admit the legality of that act.

Great-Britain has prohibited the manufacturing *iron* and *steel* in these colonies, without any objection being made to her *right* of doing it. The *like* right she must have to prohibit any other manufacture among us. Thus

she is possessed of an undisputed *precedent* on that point.
This authority, she will say, is founded on the *original intention* of settling these colonies; that is, that we should
manufacture for them, and that they should supply her
with materials.   The *equity* of this policy, she will also
say, has been universally acknowledged by the colonies,
who never have made the least objections to statutes for
that purpose; and will further appear by the *mutual benefits* flowing from this usage ever since the settlement of
these colonies.

Our great advocate, Mr. *Pitt*, in his speeches on the debate concerning the repeal of the *Stamp-Act*, acknowledged,
that *Great-Britain* could restrain our manufactures.   His
words are these—"This kingdom, as the supreme governing and legislative power, has ALWAYS bound the colonies
by her regulations and RESTRICTIONS in trade, in navigation, in MANUFACTURES—in every thing, *except that
of taking their money out of their pockets*, WITHOUT THEIR
CONSENT."   Again he says, "We may bind their trade,
CONFINE THEIR MANUFACTURES, and exercise every power
whatever, *except that of taking their money out of their
pockets*, WITHOUT THEIR CONSENT.

Here then, my dear countrymen, ROUSE yourselves, and
behold the ruin hanging over your heads.   If you ONCE
admit, that *Great-Britain* may lay duties upon her exportations to us, *for the purpose of levying money on us only*,
she then will have nothing to do, but to lay those duties
on the articles which she prohibits us to manufacture—
and the tragedy of *American* liberty is finished.   We have
been prohibited from procuring manufactures, in all cases,
any where but from *Great-Britain* (excepting linens,
which we are permitted to import directly from *Ireland*).
We have been prohibited, in some cases, from manufacturing for ourselves; and may be prohibited in others.   We
are therefore exactly in the situation of a city besieged,

which is surrounded by the works of the besiegers in every part *but one.* If *that* is closed up, no step can be taken, *but to surrender at discretion.* If *Great-Britain* can order us to come to her for necessaries we want, and can order us to pay what taxes she pleases before we take them away, or when we land them here, we are as abject slaves as *France* and *Poland* can shew in wooden shoes, and with uncombed hair*. [13]

Perhaps the nature of the *necessities* of dependent states, caused by the policy of a governing one, for her own benefit, may be elucidated by a fact mentioned in history. When the Carthaginians were possessed of the island of *Sardinia,* they made a decree, that the *Sardinians* should not raise *corn,* nor get it any other way than from the *Carthaginians.* Then, by imposing any duties they would upon it, they drained from the miserable *Sardinians* any sums they pleased; and whenever that oppressed people made the least movement to assert their liberty, their tyrants starved them to death or submission. This may be called the most perfect kind of political necessity.

From what has been said, I think this uncontrovertible conclusion may be deduced, that when a ruling state obliges a dependent state to take certain commodities from her alone, it is implied in the nature of that obligation; is essentially requisite to give it the least degree of justice ; and is inseparably united with it, in order to preserve any share of freedom to the dependent state; *that those commodities should never be loaded with duties,* FOR THE SOLE PURPOSE OF LEVYING MONEY ON THE DEPENDENT STATE.

Upon the whole,† the single question is, whether the par-

---

* The peasants of *France* wear wooden shoes; and the vassals of *Poland* are remarkable for matted hair, which never can be combed. [The words "France and Poland" in the text, and this footnote, are struck out in the *Political Writings.—Ed.*]

† "The plan of paying the duties, imposed by the late act, appears to me therefore to be totally immaterial," takes the place of these three words in the newspaper text, the remaining words forming a new sentence.—*Ed.*

liament can legally impose duties to be paid *by the people of these colonies only*, FOR THE SOLE PURPOSE OF RAISING A REVENUE, *on commodities which she obliges us to take from her alone*, or, in other words, whether the parliament can legally take money out of our pockets, without our consent. If they can, our boasted liberty is but

> *Vox et præterea nihil.*
> A sound and nothing else.

A FARMER. [14]

LETTER III.

My dear Countrymen,

I rejoice to find that my two former letters to you, have been generally received with so much favour by such of you, whose sentiments I have had an opportunity of knowing. Could you look into my heart, you would instantly perceive a zealous attachment to your interests, and a lively resentment of every insult and injury offered to you, to be the motives that have engaged me to address you.

I am no further concerned in any thing affecting *America*, than any one of you; and when liberty leaves it, I can quit it much more conveniently than most of you: But while Divine Providence, that gave me existence in a land of freedom, permits my head to think, my lips to speak, and my hand to move, I shall so highly and gratefully value the blessing received, as to take care, that my silence and inactivity shall not give my implied assent to any act, degrading my brethren and myself from the birthright, wherewith heaven itself "*hath made us free.*" *

Sorry I am to learn, that there are some few persons, who shake their heads with solemn motion, and pretend to wonder, what can be the meaning of these letters. "*Great-Britain*," they say, " is too powerful to contend with; she

* GAL. V. I.

is determined to oppress us; it is in vain to speak of right on one side, when there is power on the other; when we are strong enough to resist, we shall attempt it; but now we are not strong enough, and therefore we had better be quiet; it signifies nothing to convince us that our rights are invaded, when we cannot defend them; and if we should get into riots and tumults about the late act, it will only draw down heavier displeasure upon us.''

What can such men design? What do their grave observations amount to, but this—''that these colonies, totally regardless of their liberties, should commit them, with humble resignation, to *chance, time,* and the tender mercies of *ministers.*''

Are these men ignorant, that usurpations, which might have been successfully opposed at first, acquire strength by continuance, and thus become irresistable? Do they condemn the conduct of these colonies, concerning the *Stamp-Act?* Or have they forgot its successful issue? Ought the colonies at that time, instead of acting as they did, to have trusted for relief to the fortuitous events of futurity? If it is needless ''to speak of rights '' now, it was as needless then. If the behavior of the colonies was prudent and glorious then, and successful too; it will be equally prudent and glorious [15] to act in the same manner now, if our rights are equally invaded, and may be as successful. Therefore it becomes necessary to enquire, whether ''our rights *are* invaded.'' To talk of ''defending'' them, as if they could be no otherwise ''defended'' than by arms, is as much out of the way, as if a man having a choice of several roads to reach his journey's end, should prefer the worst, for no other reason, but because it *is* the worst.

As to ''riots and tumults,'' the gentlemen who are so apprehensive of them, are much mistaken, if they think that grievances cannot be redressed without such assistance.

I will now tell the gentlemen, what is, "the meaning of these letters." The meaning of them is, to convince the people of these colonies, that they are at this moment exposed to the most imminent dangers; and to persuade them immediately, vigorously, and unanimously, to exert themselves, in the most firm, but most peaceable manner, for obtaining relief.

The cause of *liberty* is a cause of too much dignity to be sullied by turbulence and tumult. It ought to be maintained in a manner suitable to her nature. Those who engage in it, should breathe a sedate, yet fervent spirit, animating them to actions of prudence, justice, modesty, bravery, humanity and magnanimity.

To such a wonderful degree were the ancient *Spartans*, as brave and free a people as ever existed, inspired by this happy temperature of soul, that rejecting even in their battles the use of trumpets, and other instruments for exciting heat and rage, they marched up to scenes of havoc, and horror,* with the sound of flutes, to the tunes of which their steps kept pace—"exhibiting," as *Plutarch* says, "at once a terrible and delightful sight, and proceeding with a deliberate valor, full of hope and good assurance, as if some divinity had sensibly assisted them."

I hope, my dear countrymen, that you will, in every colony, be upon your guard against those, who may at any time endeavour to stir you up, under pretences of patriotism, to any measures disrespectful to our Sovereign and our mother country. Hot, rash, disorderly proceedings, injure the reputation of a people, as to wisdom, valor and virtue, without procuring them the least benefit. I pray GOD, that he may be pleased to inspire you and your posterity, to the latest ages, with a spirit of which I have an idea, that I find a difficulty to express. To express it in

* *Plutarch* in the life of *Lycurgus.* Archbishop *Potter's* Archæologia Græca.

the best manner I can, I mean a spirit, that shall so guide you, that it will be impossible to determine whether an *American's* character is most distinguishable, for his loyalty to his Sovereign, his duty to his mother country, his love of freedom, or his affection for his native soil.

Every government at some time or other falls into wrong measures. [16] These may proceed from mistake or passion. But every such measure does not dissolve the obligation between the governors and the governed. The mistake may be corrected; the passion may subside. It is the duty of the governed to endeavour to rectify the mistake, and to appease the passion. They have not at first any other right, than to represent their grievances, and to pray for redress, unless an emergence is so pressing, as not to allow time for receiving an answer to their applications, which rarely happens. If their applications are disregarded, then that kind of *opposition* becomes justifiable, which can be made without breaking the laws, or disturbing the public peace.

This consists in the *prevention of the oppressors reaping advantage from their oppressions*, and not in their punishment. For experience may teach them, what reason did not; and harsh methods cannot be proper, till milder ones have failed.

If at length it become UNDOUBTED, that an inveterate resolution is formed to annihilate the liberties of the governed, the *English* history affords frequent examples of resistance by force. What particular circumstances will in any future case justify such resistance, can never be ascertained, till they happen. Perhaps it may be allowable to say generally, that it never can be justifiable, until the people are FULLY CONVINCED, that any further submission will be destructive to their happiness.

When the appeal is made to the sword, highly probable is it, that the punishment will exceed the offence; and the

calamities attending on war out-weigh those preceding it.
These considerations of justice and prudence, will always
have great influence with good and wise men.

To these reflections on this subject, it remains to be
added, and ought for ever to be remembered, that resistance, in the case of colonies against their mother country,
is extremely different from the resistance of a people
against their prince.   A nation may change their king, or
race of kings, and, retaining their antient form of government, be gainers by changing.   Thus *Great-Britain*, under the illustrious house of *Brunswick*, a house that seems
to flourish for the happiness of mankind, has found a
felicity, unknown in the reigns of the *Stewarts*.   But if
once *we* are separated from our mother country, what new
form of government shall we adopt,* or where shall we find
another *Britain*, to supply our loss?   Torn from the body,
to which we are united by religion, liberty, laws, affections, relation, language and commerce, we must bleed at
every vein.

In truth—the prosperity of these provinces is founded in
their dependence on *Great-Britain;* and when she returns
to her "old good humour, and her old good nature," as
Lord *Clarendon* expresses it, I hope they will always think
it their duty and interest, as [17] it most certainly will be,
to promote her welfare by all the means in their power.

We cannot act with too much caution in our disputes.
Anger produces anger ; and differences, that might be accommodated by kind and respectful behavior, may, by imprudence, be enlarged to an incurable rage.   In quarrels
between countries, as well as in those between individuals, when they have risen to a certain height, the
first cause of dissension is no longer remembered, the
minds of the parties being wholly engaged in recollecting
and resenting the mutual expressions of their dislike.

* In the newspaper text this is "accept."—*Ed.*

When feuds have reached that fatal point, all considerations of reason and equity vanish; and a blind fury governs, or rather confounds all things. A people no longer regards their interest, but the gratification of their wrath. The sway of the *Cleons and *Clodius's*, the designing and detestable flatterers of the *prevailing passion*, becomes confirmed. Wise and good men in vain oppose the storm, and may think themselves fortunate, if, in attempting to preserve their ungrateful fellow citizens, they do not ruin themselves. Their *prudence* will be called *baseness;* their *moderation* will be called *guilt;* and if their virtue does not lead them to destruction, as that of many other great and excellent persons has done, they may survive to receive from their expiring country the mournful glory of her acknowledgment, that their counsels, if regarded, would have saved her.

The constitutional modes of obtaining relief, are those which I wish to see pursued on the present occasion; that is, by petitions of our assemblies, or where they are not permitted to meet, of the people, to the powers that can afford us relief.

We have an excellent prince, in whose good dispositions towards us we may confide. We have a generous, sensible and humane nation, to whom we may apply. They may be deceived. They may, by artful men, be provoked to anger against us. I cannot believe they will be cruel or unjust; or that their anger will be implacable. Let us behave like dutiful children, who have received unmerited blows from a beloved parent. Let us complain to our parent; but let our complaints speak at the same time the language of affliction and veneration.

If, however, it shall happen, by an unfortunate course of affairs, that our applications to his Majesty and the par-

---

* *Cleon* was a popular firebrand of *Athens*, and *Clodius* of *Rome;* each of whom plunged his country into the deepest calamities.

liament for redress, prove ineffectual, let us THEN take *another step*, by withholding from *Great-Britain* all the advantages she has been used to receive from us. THEN let us try, if our ingenuity, industry, and frugality, will not give weight to our remonstrances. Let us all be united with one spirit, in one cause. Let us invent—let us work [18]—let us save—let us, continually, keep up our claim, and incessantly repeat our complaints—But, above all, let us implore the protection of that infinitely good and gracious being, * "by whom kings reign, and princes decree justice."

Nil desperandum.
Nothing is to be despaired of.

A FARMER.

LETTER IV.

My dear Countrymen,

An objection, I hear, has been made against my second letter, which I would willingly clear up before I proceed. "There is," say these objectors, "a material difference between the *Stamp-Act* and the *late Act* for laying a duty on paper, *&c.* that justifies the conduct of those who opposed the former, and yet are willing to submit to the latter. The duties imposed by the *Stamp-Act* were *internal* taxes; but the present are *external*, and therefore the parliament may have a right to impose them."

To this I answer, with a total denial of the power of parliament to lay upon these colonies any "tax" whatever.

This point, being so important to this, and to succeeding generations, I wish to be clearly understood.

To the word "*tax*," I annex that meaning which the constitution and history of *England* require to be annexed

* PRO. viii. 15.

to it; that is—that it is *an imposition on the subject, for the sole purpose of levying money.*

In the early ages of our monarchy, certain * services were rendered to the crown *for the general good.* These were personal: † But in [19] process of time, such institutions being found inconvenient, *gifts* and *grants* of their own property were made by the people, under the several names of aids, tallages, tasks, taxes and subsidies, *&c.* These were made, as may be collected even from the names, *for public service* upon "need and necessity."‡ All these sums were levied upon the people by virtue of their voluntary gift.§ Their design was to support the

---

* In the newspaper text in place of "certain" the word "the" is used. —*Ed.*

† It is very worthy of remark, how watchful our wise ancestors were, lest their *services* should be encreased beyond what the law allowed. No man was bound to go out of the realm to serve the King. Therefore, even in the conquering reign of *Henry* the *Fifth,* when the martial spirit of the nation was highly enflamed by the heroic courage of their Prince, and by his great success, they still carefully guarded against the establishment of illegal services. "When this point (says Lord Chief Justice *Coke*) concerning maintenance of wars out of *England,* came in question, the COMMONS did make their *continual claim* of their *ancient freedom* and *birthright,* as in the first of *Henry the Fifth,* and in the seventh of *Henry the Fifth,* &c. the COMMONS made a PROTEST, that they were not bound to the maintenance of war in *Scotland, Ireland, Calice, France, Normandy,* or other *foreign* parts, and caused their PROTESTS to be entered into the parliament rolls, where they yet remain ; which, in effect, agreeth with that which, upon like occasion, was made in the parliament of 25th *Edward* I." 2d Inst. p. 528.

‡ 4th Inst. p. 28.

§ *Reges* Angliæ, *nihil tale, nisi convocatis primis ordinibus, et assentiente populo suscipiunt.* Phil. Comines, 2d *Inst.*

These gifts entirely depending on the pleasure of the donors, were proportioned to the abilities of the several ranks of people who gave, and were regulated by *their* opinion of the public necessities. Thus *Edward* I. had in his 11th year a *thirtieth* from the *laity,* a *twentieth* from the *clergy ;* in his 22d year, a *tenth* from the *laity,* a *sixth* from *London,* and other corporate towns, *half of their benefices* from the

national honor and interest. Some of those grants comprehended duties arising from trade; being imposts on merchandizes. These Lord Chief Justice *Coke* classes under "subsidies," and "parliamentary aids." They are also called "customs." But whatever the *name* was, they were always considered as *gifts of the people to the crown, to be employed for public uses.*

Commerce was at a low ebb, and surprizing instances might be produced how little it was attended to for a succession of ages. The terms that have been mentioned, and, among the rest, that of "*tax,*" had obtained a national, parliamentary meaning, drawn from the principles of the constitution, long before any *Englishman* thought of *imposition of duties, for the regulation of trade.*

Whenever we speak of "taxes" among *Englishmen,* let us therefore speak of them with reference to the *principles* on which, and the *intentions* with which they have been established. This will [20] give certainty to our expres-

---

clergy; in his 23d year an *eleventh* from the *barons* and others, a *tenth* from the *clergy,* a *seventh* from the *burgesses, &c. Hume's Hist. of England.*

The same difference in the grants of the several ranks is observable in other reigns.

In the famous statute *de tallagio non concedendo,* the king enumerates the several *classes,* without whose consent, he and his heirs never should set or levy any tax . . . "*nullum tallagium, vel auxilium per nos, vel hæredes nostros in regno nostro ponatur seu levetur, sine voluntate et assensu archiepiscoporum, episcoporum, comitum, baronum, militum, burgensium, et alienum liberorum com. de regno nostro.*" 34th *Edward* I.

Lord Chief Justice *Coke,* in his comment on these words, says . . . "for the quieting of the *commons,* and for a *perpetual and constant law for ever after,* both in this AND OTHER LIKE CASES, this act was made. These words are *plain,* WITHOUT ANY SCRUPLE, *absolute,* WITHOUT ANY SAVING." 2d *Coke's* Inst. p. 532, 533. Little did the venerable judge imagine, that "*other* LIKE *cases*" would happen, in which the spirit of this law would be despised by *Englishmen,* the posterity of those who made it.

sion, and safety to our conduct: But if, when we have in view the liberty of these colonies, we proceed in any other course, we pursue a *Juno* * indeed, but shall only catch a cloud.

In the national, parliamentary sense insisted on, the word "tax" †was certainly understood by the congress at *New-York*, whose resolves may be said to form the *American* "bill of rights." ‡

The third, fourth, fifth, and sixth resolves, are thus expressed.

III. "That it is *inseparably essential to the freedom of a people*, and the *undoubted right* of *Englishmen*, that § NO TAX be imposed on them, *but with their own consent*, given personally, or by their representatives."

IV. "That the people of the colonies are not, and from their local circumstances, cannot be represented in the house of commons in *Great-Britain*."

V. "That the only representatives of the people of the colonies, are the persons chosen therein by themselves; and that NO TAXES ever have been, or can be constitutionally imposed on them, but by their respective legislatures."

VI. "That all *supplies to the crown*, being free gifts of the people, it is *unreasonable, and inconsistent with the*

* The Goddess of *Empire*, in the Heathen Mythology; according to an antient fable, *Ixion* pursued her, but she escaped in a cloud.

† In this sense *Montisquieu* uses the word "tax," in his 13th book of *Spirit of Laws.*

‡ In the newspaper text this reads: "I am satisfied that the congress was of opinion, that no impositions could be legally laid on the people of these colonies, for the purpose of levying money, but by themselves or their representatives."—*Ed*

§ The rough draught of the resolves of the congress at *New-York* are now in my hands, and from some notes on that draught, and other particular reasons, I am satisfied that the congress understood the word "tax" in the sense here contended for. [This note is not in the newspaper publication.—*Ed.*]

principles and spirit of the British *constitution*, for the people of *Great-Britain to* grant to his Majesty *the property of the colonies.*"

Here is no distinction made between *internal* and *external* taxes. It is evident from the short reasoning thrown into these resolves, that every imposition "to grant to his Majesty *the property of the colonies*," was thought a "tax;" and that every such imposition, if laid any other way than "with their consent, given personally, or by their representatives," was not only "unreasonable, and inconsistent with the principles and spirit of the *British* constitution," but destructive "to the freedom of a people."

This language is clear and important. A "TAX" means an imposition to raise money. Such persons therefore as speak of *internal* and *external* "TAXES," I pray may pardon me, if I object to that expression, as applied to the privileges and interests of these colonies. There may be *internal* and *exter-* [21] *nal* IMPOSITIONS, founded on *different principles*, and having *different tendencies*, every "tax" being an imposition, tho' every imposition is not a "tax." But *all taxes* are founded on the *same principles;* and have the *same tendency*.

External impositions, for the regulation of our trade, do not "grant to his Majesty *the property of the colonies*." They only *prevent the colonies acquiring property*, in things not necessary, in a manner judged to be injurious to the welfare of the whole empire. But the last statute respecting us, "grants to his Majesty *the property of the colonies*," by laying duties on the manufactures of *Great-Britain* which they MUST take, and which she settled on them, on purpose that they SHOULD take.

What * *tax* can be more *internal* than this? Here is

---

* It seems to be evident, that Mr. *Pitt* in his defence of *America*, during the debate concerning the repeal of the *Stamp Act*, by "*internal* taxes," meant any duties "for the purpose of raising a revenue;" and

money drawn, *without their consent,* from a society, who
have constantly enjoyed [22] a constitutional mode of
raising all money among themselves. The payment of
their *tax* they have no possible method of avoiding; as they
cannot do without the commodities on which it is laid,
and they cannot manufacture these commodities themselves. Besides, if this unhappy country should be so
lucky as to elude this act, by getting parchment enough,
in the place of paper, or by reviving the antient method
of writing on wax and bark, and by inventing something
to serve instead of glass, her ingenuity would stand her in

by "*external* taxes," meant duties imposed "for the regulation of
trade." His expressions are these . . . "If the gentleman does not understand the difference between *internal* and *external* taxes, I cannot
help it; but there is a plain distinction between taxes levied FOR THE
PURPOSES OF RAISING A REVENUE, and duties imposed FOR THE REGU-
LATION OF TRADE, for the accommodation of the subject; although, in
the consequences, some revenue might incidentally arise from the latter."

These words were in Mr. *Pitt's* reply to Mr. *Grenville,* who said he
could not understand the difference between external and internal taxes.

In every other part of his speeches on that occasion, his words confirm
this construction of his expressions. The following extracts will shew
how positive and general were his assertions of our right.

"It is my opinion that this kingdom has NO RIGHT to lay A TAX upon
the colonies." . . . "The *Americans* are the SONS, not the BASTARDS of
England. TAXATION is NO PART of the *governing* and *legislative*
power." . . . "The *taxes* are a voluntary *gift* and *grant* of the *com-
mons* ALONE. In LEGISLATION the THREE estates of the realm are
ALIKE concerned, but the concurrence of the PEERS and the CROWN to a
TAX, is only necessary to close with the FORM of a law. The GIFT *and*
GRANT is of the COMMONS ALONE." . . . "*The distinction between* LEG-
ISLATION *and* TAXATION *is essentially necessary to liberty.*" . . . "THE
COMMONS of *America,* represented in their several assemblies, have ever
been in possession of the exercise of this their constitutional right, of
GIVING and GRANTING their own MONEY. *They would have been
SLAVES, if they had not enjoyed it.*" "The idea of a *virtual* repre-
sentation of *America* in this house, is the most contemptible idea that
ever entered into the head of man . . . It does not deserve a serious
refutation."

He afterwards shews the unreasonableness of *Great-Britain* taxing

little stead; for then the parliament would have nothing to do but to prohibit such manufactures, or to lay a tax on *hats* and *woollen cloths*, which they have already prohibited the colonies *from supplying each other with;* or on instruments, and tools of *steel* and *iron*, which they have prohibited the provincials *from manufacturing at all:* * And then, what little gold and silver they have, must be torn from their hands, or they will not be able, in a short time, to get an ax,† for cutting their firewood, nor a plough, for raising their food.   In what respect, therefore, I beg leave to ask, is the late act preferable to the *Stamp-*

America, thus . . . "When I had the honor of serving his Majesty, I availed myself of the means of information, which I derived from my office. I SPEAK THEREFORE FROM KNOWLEDGE. My materials were good.   I was at pains to *collect,* to *digest,* to *consider* them: and *I will be bold to affirm,* that the profit to *Great-Britain* from the trade of the colonies, through all its branches, is TWO MILLIONS A YEAR. *This* is the fund that carried you triumphantly through the last war.   The estates that were rented at two thousand pounds a year, threescore years ago, are three thousand pounds at present. Those estates sold then from fifteen to eighteen years purchase ; the same may now be sold for thirty. YOU OWE THIS TO AMERICA.   THIS IS THE PRICE THAT AMERICA PAYS YOU FOR HER PROTECTION." . .   "I dare not say how much higher these profits may be augmented." . . . "Upon the whole, I will beg leave to tell the house what is really my opinion : it is, that the *Stamp Act* be repealed absolutely, totally, and immediately. That the reason for the repeal be assigned, because it was founded on an ERRONEOUS PRINCIPLE."

* "And that *pig* and *bar iron,* made in his Majesty's colonies in *America,* may be FURTHER MANUFACTURED IN THIS KINGDOM, be it further enacted by the authority aforesaid, that from and after the twenty-fourth day of *June,* 1750, no *mill,* or *other engine,* for *fitting* or *rolling* of *iron,* or any *plating forge,* to work with a *tilt hammer,* or any *furnace* for *making steel,* shall be erected; or, after such erection, continued IN ANY OF HIS MAJESTY'S COLONIES IN AMERICA." 23d *George* II., Chap. 29, Sect. 9.

† Tho' these particulars are mentioned as being absolutely necessary, yet perhaps they are not more so than glass in our severe winters, to keep out the cold from our houses; or than paper, without which such inexpressible confusions must ensue.

Act, or more consistent with the liberties of the colonies? For my own part, I regard them both with equal apprehensions; and think they ought to be in the same manner opposed.

> *Habemus quidem senatus consultum,—tanquam gladium in vagina reposilum.*
> We have a statute, laid up for future use, like a sword in the scabbard.

A FARMER. [23]

LETTER V.

My dear Countrymen,

Perhaps the objection to the late act, imposing duties upon paper, *&c.* might have been safely rested on the argument drawn from the universal conduct of parliaments and ministers, from the first existence of these colonies, to the administration of Mr. *Greenville.*

What but the indisputable, the acknowledged exclusive right of the colonies to tax themselves, could be the reason, that in this long period of more than one hundred and fifty years, no statute was ever passed for the sole purpose of raising a revenue on the colonies? And how clear, how cogent must that reason be, to which every parliament, and every minister, for so long a time submitted, without a single attempt to innovate?

England, in part of that course of years, and *Great-Britain*, in other parts, was engaged in several fierce expensive wars; troubled with some tumultuous and bold parliaments; governed by many daring and wicked ministers; yet none of them ever ventured to touch the *Palladium* of *American* liberty. Ambition, avarice, faction, tyranny, all revered it. Whenever it was necessary to raise money on the colonies, the requisitions of the crown were made, and dutifully complied with. The parliament, from time to time, regulated their trade, and that of the rest of the empire, to preserve their dependence, and the connection of the whole in good order.

The people of *Great-Britain,* in support of their privileges, boast much of their antiquity. It is true they are antient ; yet it may well be questioned, if there is a single privilege of a *British* subject, supported by longer, more solemn, or more uninterrupted testimony, than the exclusive right of taxation in these colonies. The people of *Great-Britain* consider that kingdom as the sovereign of these colonies, and would now annex to that sovereignty a prerogative never heard of before. How would they bear this, was the case their own? What would they think of a *new* prerogative claimed by the crown? We may guess what their conduct would be from the transports of passion into which they fell about the late embargo, tho' laid to relieve the most emergent necessities of state, admitting of no delay; and for which there were numerous precedents. Let our liberties be treated with the same tenderness, and it is all we desire.

Explicit as the conduct of parliaments, for so many ages, is, to prove that no money can be levied on these colonies by parliament, for the purpose of raising a revenue, yet it is not the only evidence in our favour. [24]

Every one of the most material arguments against the legality of the *Stamp-Act,* operates with equal force against the act now objected to; but as they are well known, it seems unnecessary to repeat them here.

This general one only shall be considered at present: That tho' these colonies are dependent on *Great-Britain ;* and tho' she has a legal power * to make laws for preserving that dependence; yet it is not necessary for this purpose, nor essential to the relation between a mother country and her colonies, as was eagerly contended by the advocates

* In the newspaper text this is "right."—*Ed.*

for the *Stamp-Act*, that she should raise money on them without their consent.

Colonies were formerly planted by warlike nations to keep their enemies in awe; to relieve their country, over-burthened with inhabitants ; or to discharge a number of discontented and troublesome citizens. But in more modern ages, the spirit of violence being in some measure, if the expression may be allowed, sheathed in commerce, colonies have been settled by the nations of *Europe* for the purposes of trade. These purposes were to be attained, by the colonies raising for their mother country those things which she did not produce herself; and by supplying themselves from her with things they wanted. These were the *national objects*, in the commencement of our colonies, and have been uniformly so in their promotion.

To answer these grand purposes, perfect liberty was known to be necessary; all history proving, that trade and freedom are nearly related to each other. By a due regard to this wise and just plan, the infant colonies, exposed in the unknown climates and unexplored wildernesses of this new world, lived, grew and flourished.

The parent country, with undeviating prudence and virtue, attentive to the first principles of colonization, drew to herself the benefits she might reasonably expect, and preserved to her children the blessings, on which those benefits were founded. She made laws, obliging her colonies to carry to her all those products which she wanted for her own use ; and all those raw materials which she chose herself to work up. Besides this restriction, she forbad them to procure *manufactures* from any other part of the globe, or even the *products* of *European* countries, which alone could rival her, without being first brought to her. In short, by a variety of laws, she regulated their trade in such a manner as she thought most conducive to their mutual advantage, and her own welfare. A power

was reserved to the crown of *repealing* any laws that
should be enacted: The *executive* authority of government
was also lodged in the crown, and its representatives; and
an *appeal* was secured to the crown from all judgments
in the administration of justice.

For all these powers, established by the mother country
over the colonies; for all these immense emoluments derived by her from [25] them; for all their difficulties and
distresses in fixing themselves, what was the recompence
made them? A communication of her rights in general,
and particularly of that great one, the foundation of all the
rest—that their property, acquired with so much pain and
hazard, should be disposed of by none but *themselves—
or to use the beautiful and emphatic language of the sacred
scriptures,† "that they should sit *every man* under his
vine, and under his fig-tree, and NONE SHOULD MAKE
THEM AFRAID."

Can any man of candor and knowledge deny, that these
institutions form an affinity between *Great-Britain* and
her colonies, that sufficiently secures their dependence
upon her? Or that for her to levy taxes upon them, is to
reverse the nature of things? Or that she can pursue such
a measure, without reducing them to a state of vassallage?

If any person cannot conceive the supremacy of *Great-
Britain* to exist, without the power of laying taxes to levy
money upon us, the history of the colonies, and of *Great-
Britain*, since their settlement, will prove the contrary.
He will there find the amazing advantages arising to her
from them—the constant exercise of her supremacy—and
their filial submission to it, without a single rebellion, or
even the thought of one, from their first emigration to this

---

* "The power of *taxing themselves*, was the privilege of which the
English were, WITH REASON, *particularly jealous.*" *Hume's Hist. of
England.*

† MIC. iv. 4.

moment—And all these things have happened, without one instance of *Great-Britain's* laying taxes to levy money upon them.

How many* *British authors* have demonstrated, that

* It has been said in the House of Commons, when complaints have been made of the decay of trade to any part of *Europe,* "That such things were not worth regard, as *Great-Britain* was possessed of colonies that could consume more of her manufactures than she was able to supply them with."

"As the case now stands, we shall shew that the *plantations* are a spring of *wealth* to this nation, that they *work* for us, that their TREASURE CENTERS ALL HERE, and that the laws have tied them fast enough to us ; so that it must be through our own fault and mismanagement, if they become independent of *England.*"

DAVENANT *on the Plantation Trade.*

"It is better that the islands should be supplied from the Northern Colonies than from *England ;* for this reason, the provisions we might send to *Barbados, Jamaica,* &c. would be *unimproved* product of the earth, as grain of all kinds, or such product where there is little got by the improvement, as malt, salt beef and pork ; indeed the exportation of salt fish thither would be more advantageous; but the goods whichwe send to the *Northern Colonies,* are such whose *improvement* may be justly laid, one with another, to be near *four-fifths* of the value of the *whole commodity,* as apparel, houshold furniture, and many other things." *Idem.*

"*New-England* is the most prejudicial plantation to the kingdom of *England ;* and yet to do right to that most industrious *English* colony, I must confess, that though we lose by their unlimited trade with other foreign plantations, yet we are very great gainers by their direct trade from *Old England.* Our yearly exportation of *English* manufactures, malt and other goods, from hence thither, amounting in my opinion, to *ten times* the value of what is imported from thence; which calculation I do not make at random, but upon *mature consideration,* and, peradventure, upon *as much experience in this very trade,* as any other person will pretend to ; and therefore, whenever reformation of our correspondency in trade with that people shall be thought on, it will, in my poor judgment, require GREAT TENDERNESS, and VERY SERIOUS CIRCUMSPECTION."   *Sir* JOSIAH CHILD'*s Discourse on Trade.*

"Our plantations spend mostly our *English* manufactures, and those *of all sorts almost imaginable,* in *egregious quantities,* and employ near *two thirds of all our* English *shipping ;* so that we have *more people* in *England,* by reason of our plantations in *America.*"   *Idem.*

Sir JOSIAH CHILD says, in another part of his work, "That not more

the present wealth, power and glory of their country, are
founded upon these [26] colonies? As constantly as streams
tend to the ocean, have they been pouring the fruits of all
their labors into their mother's lap.   Good heaven! and
shall a total oblivion of former tenderness and blessings,
be spread over the minds of a good and wise nation, by

than fifty families are maintained in *England* by the refining of sugar."
From whence, and from what *Davenant* says, it is plain, that the advantages here said to be derived from the plantations by *England* must
be meant chiefly of the continental colonies.

"I shall sum up my whole remarks on our *American* colonies, with
this observation, that as they are a certain annual revenue of SEVERAL
MILLIONS STERLING to their mother country, they ought carefully to
be protected, duly encouraged, and every opportunity that presents,
improved for their increment and advantage, as every one they can possibly reap, must at last return to us with interest."
                                                BEAWES'S *Lex Merc. Red.*

"We may safely advance, that our trade and navigation are greatly
increased by our colonies, and that they really are a source of treasure
and naval power to this kingdom, since THEY WORK FOR US, & THEIR
TREASURE CENTERS HERE. Before their settlement, our manufactures
were few, and those but indifferent; the number of *English* merchants
very small, and the whole shipping of the nation much inferior to what
now belongs to the Northern Colonies only. *These are certain facts.*
But since their establishment, our condition has altered for the better,
almost of a degree beyond credibility. . . . Our MANUFACTURES are prodigiously increased, chiefly by the demand for them in the plantations,
where they AT LEAST TAKE OFF ONE HALF, and supply us with many
valuable commodities for exportation, which is as great an emolument
to the mother kingdom, as to the plantations themselves."
                       POSTLETHWAYT'S *Univ. Dict. of Trade and Commerce.*

" Most of the nations of *Europe* have interfered with us, more or less,
in divers of our staple manufactures, within half a century, not only in
our woollen, but in our lead and tin manufactures, as well as our fisheries."   POSTLETHWAYT, *ibid.*

"The inhabitants of our colonies, by carrying on a trade with their
foreign neighbours, do not only occasion *a greater quantity of the goods
and merchandize of* Europe *being sent from hence to them,* and a greater
quantity of the product of *America* to be sent from them hither, *which
would otherwise be carried from and brought to* Europe *by foreigners,* but
an increase of the seamen and navigation in those parts, which is of
great strength and security, as well as of great advantage to our plan-

the sordid arts of intriguing men, who, covering their
selfish projects under pretences of public good, first enrage
their countrymen into a frenzy of passion, and then advance their own influence and interest, by gratifying the
passion, which they themselves have basely excited. [27]
Hitherto *Great-Britain* has been contented with her

tations in general. And though *some of our colonies* are not only for preventing the *importation of all goods of the same species they produce*, but
suffer particular planters to *keep great runs of land in their possession
uncultivated*, with design to prevent new settlements, whereby they imagine the prices of their commodities may be affected ; yet if it be considered, that the markets of *Great-Britain* depend on the markets of
ALL *Europe in general*, and that the *European* markets *in general* depend on the proportion between the *annual consumption* and the *whole
quantity* of each species *annually produced* by ALL *nations ;* it must follow, that whether we or foreigners are the producers, *carriers*, importers
and exporters of *American* produce, yet their respective prices in *each
colony* (the difference of freight, customs and importations considered)
will always bear proportion to the *general consumption* of the *whole
quantity* of each sort, *produced in all colonies*, and *in all parts*, allowing
only for the usual contingencies that trade and commerce, agriculture
and manufactures, are liable to in all countries."

POSTLETHWAYT, *ibid.*

"It is certain, that from the very time Sir *William Raleigh*, the father
of our *English* colonies, and his associates, first projected these estab-
lishments, there have been persons who have found an interest, in *misrepresenting*, or lessening the value of them. . . . The attempts were
called chimerical and dangerous. Afterwards many malignant suggestions were made about sacrificing so many *Englishmen* to the obstinate
desire of settling colonies in countries which then produced very little
advantage. But as these difficulties were gradually surmounted, those
complaints vanished. No sooner were *these lamentations* over, but *others*
arose in their stead ; when it could be no longer said, that the colonies
were *useless*, it was alledged that they were not *useful enough* to their
mother country ; that while we were loaded with taxes, they were absolutely free ; that the *planters* lived like *princes*, while the inhabitants of
England laboured hard for a tolerable subsistence."

POSTLETHWAYT, *ibid.*

"Before the settlement of these colonies," says *Postlethwayt*, "our
manufactures were few, and those but indifferent. In those days we had
not only our naval stores, but our ships from our neighbours. *Germany*
furnished us with all things made of metal, even to nails. Wine, paper,

prosperity. Moderation has been the rule of her conduct. But now, a generous humane people, that so often
has protected the liberty of *strangers*, is enflamed into an
attempt to tear a privilege from her own children, which,
if executed, must, in their opinion, sink them into slaves:
AND FOR WHAT? For a pernicious power, not necessary

linens, and a thousand other things, came from *France. Portugal* supplied us with sugar; all the products of *America* were poured into us
from *Spain;* and the *Venetians* and *Genoese* retailed to us the commodities of the *East-Indies*, at their own price.''

"If it be asked, whether foreigners, for what goods they take of us,
do not pay on *that consumption* a great portion of our taxes? It is admitted they do.'' POSTLETHWAYT'S *Great-Britain's True System*.

"If we are afraid that one day or other the colonies will revolt, and
set up for themselves, as some seem to apprehend, let us not *drive* them
to a *necessity* to *feel* themselves independent of us; as they *will* do, the
moment they perceive that *THEY CAN BE SUPPLIED WITH
ALL THINGS FROM WITHIN THEMSELVES*, and do not need
our assistance. If we would keep them still dependent upon their
mother country, and in some respects, *subservient* to her *views* and
welfare; let us make it their INTEREST always to be so.''
TUCKER *on Trade*.

"Our colonies, while they have *English* blood in their veins, and have
relations in *England*, and WHILE THEY CAN GET BY TRADING WITH US,
the *stronger* and *greater they* grow, the *more* this *crown* and *kingdom*
will *get* by them: and nothing but such an arbitrary power as shall
make them desperate, can bring them to rebel.''
DAVENANT *on the Plantation Trade*.

"The Northern colonies are not upon the same footing as those of the
South; and having a worse soil to improve, they must find the recompence some other way, which only can be in property and dominion:
Upon which score, any INNOVATIONS in the form of government there,
should be cautiously examined, for fear of entering upon measures, by
which the industry of the inhabitants be quite discouraged. 'TIS ALWAYS
UNFORTUNATE for a people, either by CONSENT, or upon COMPULSION,
to depart from their PRIMITIVE INSTITUTIONS, and THOSE FUNDAMENTALS,
by which they were FIRST UNITED TOGETHER.'' *Idem.*

"The most effectual way of *uniting* the colonies, is to make it their common interest to oppose the designs and attempts of *Great-Britain*. [*This
paragraph is not in newspaper text.—Ed.*]

"All wise states will well consider how to preserve the advantages
arising from colonies, and avoid the evils. And I conceive that there can

to her, as her own experience may convince her; but horribly dreadful and detestable to them. [28]

It seems extremely probable, that when cool, dispassionate posterity, shall consider the affectionate intercourse, the reciprocal benefits, and the unsuspecting confidence, that have subsisted between these colonies and

be but TWO ways in nature to hinder them from throwing off their dependence; *one* to keep it out of their *power*, and the *other*, out of their *will.* The first must be by *force*, and the *latter* by *using them well*, and keeping them employed in such productions, and making such manufactures, as will support themselves and families comfortably, *and procure them wealth too*, and at least not prejudice their mother country.

"*Force* can never be used effectually to answer the end, *without destroying the colonies themselves.* Liberty and encouragement are necessary to carry people thither, and to keep them together when they are there; and violence will hinder both. Any body of troops, considerable enough to awe them, and keep them in subjection, under the direction too of a needy governor, often sent thither to make his fortune, and at such a distance from any application for redress, will soon put an end to all planting, and leave the country to the soldiers alone, and if it did not, *would eat up all the profit of the colony.* For this reason, arbitrary countries have not been equally successful in planting colonies with free ones; and what they have done in that kind, has either been by force, or at a vast expence, or *by departing from the nature of their government*, and *giving such privileges to planters* as were *denied to their other subjects.* And I dare say, that a few prudent laws, and a little prudent conduct, would soon give us far the greatest share of the riches of all *America*, perhaps drive many of other nations out of it, or into other colonies for shelter.

"There are *so many exigencies* in all states, *so many foreign wars*, and *domestic disturbances*, that these colonies CAN NEVER WANT OPPORTUNITIES, if they watch for them, *to do what they shall find their interest to do;* and therefore we ought to take all the precautions in our power, that it shall never be *their interests* to act against that of their native country; an evil which can no otherwise be averted, than by keeping them *fully employed* in such trades *as will increase their own*, as well as our wealth; for it is much to be feared, if we do not find employment for *them*, they may find it for *us;* the interest of the mother country, is always to keep them dependent, and so employed; and it requires all her address to do it; and it is certainly more *easily* and *effectually* done by *gentle* and *insensible* methods, than by *power* alone." CATO'S *Letters.*

their parent country, for such a length of time, [29] they will execrate, with the bitterest curses the infamous memory of those men, whose pestilential ambition unnecessarily, wantonly, cruelly, first opened the sources of civil discord between them; first turned their love into jealousy; and first taught these provinces, filled with grief and anxiety, to enquire—

Mens ubi materna est?
Where is maternal affection?

A FARMER.

LETTER VI.

My dear COUNTRYMEN,

It may perhaps be objected against the arguments that have been offered to the public, concerning the legal power of the parliament, "that it has always exercised the power of imposing duties, for the purposes of raising a revenue on the productions of these colonies carried to *Great-Britain*, which may be called a tax on them." To this objection I answer, that this is no violation of the rights of the colonies, it being implied in the relation between them and *Great-Britain*, that they should not carry such commodities to other nations, as should enable them to interfere with the mother country. The imposition of duties on these commodities, when brought to her, is only a consequence of her parental right; and if the point is thoroughly examined, the duties will be found to be laid on the people of the mother country. Whatever they are, they must proportionably raise the price of the goods, and consequently must be paid by the consumers. In this light they were considered by the parliament in the 25th *Charles* II. Chap. 7, Sect. 2, which says, that the productions of the plantations were carried from one to another free from all customs, "while the subjects of this your

kingdom of *England* have paid *great customs and impositions for what of them have been* SPENT HERE," *&c.*

Besides, if *Great-Britain* exports these commodities
again, the duties will injure her own trade, so that she
cannot hurt us, without plainly and immediately hurting
herself; and this is our check against her acting arbitrarily in this respect.

* It may be perhaps further objected, "that it being
granted that statutes made for regulating trade, are binding upon us, it will [30] be difficult for any person, but

* If any one should observe that no opposition has been made to the
legality of the 4th *Geo.* III. Chap. 15, which is the FIRST act of parliament that ever imposed duties on the importations into *America*, for the
expressed purpose of raising a revenue there; I answer, First, That tho'
the act expressly mentions the raising a revenue in *America*, yet it
seems that it had as much in view the "improving and securing the
trade between the same and *Great-Britain*," which words are part of its
title: And the preamble says, "Whereas it is expedient that new provisions and regulations should be established for improving the revenue
of this kingdom, and *for extending and securing the navigation and commerce between* Great-Britain, *and your Majesty's dominions in* America,
which by the peace have been so happily extended and enlarged," *&c.*
Secondly, *All* the duties mentioned in that act are imposed solely on the
productions and manufactures of foreign countries, and not a single
duty laid on any production or manufacture of our mother country.
Thirdly, the authority of the provincial assemblies is not therein so
plainly *attacked* as by the last act, which makes provision for defraying
the charges of the "administration of justice," and "the support of
civil government." Fourthly, That it being *doubtful*, whether the intention of the 4th *Geo.* III. Chap. 15, was not as much *to regulate trade*,
as *to raise a revenue*, the minds of the people here were wholly engrossed
by the terror of the *Stamp-Act*, then impending over them, about the
intention of which there could be no *doubt*.

These reasons so far distinguish the 4th *Geo.* III. Chap. 15, from the
last act, that it is not to be wondered at, that the first should have been
submitted to, tho' the *last* should excite the most universal and spirited
opposition. For *this* will be found, on the strictest examination, to be,
in the *principle* on which it is founded, and in the *consequences* that
must attend it, if possible, more destructive than the *Stamp-Act*. It is,
to speak plainly, a *prodigy* in our laws; not having one *British* feature.

the makers of the laws, to determine, which of them are made for the regulating of trade, and which for raising a revenue; and that from hence may arise confusion."

To this I answer, that the objection is of no force in the present case, or such as resemble it; because the act now in question, is formed *expressly* FOR THE SOLE PURPOSE OF RAISING A REVENUE.

However, supposing the design of parliament had not been *expressed*, the objection seems to me of no weight, with regard to the influence which those who may make it, might expect it ought to have on the conduct of these colonies.

It is true, that *impositions for raising a revenue*, may be hereafter called *regulations of trade:* But names will not change the nature of things. Indeed we ought firmly to believe, what is an undoubted truth, confirmed by the unhappy experience of many states heretofore free, that UNLESS THE MOST WATCHFUL ATTENTION BE EXERTED, A NEW SERVITUDE MAY BE SLIPPED UPON US, UNDER THE SANCTION OF USUAL AND RESPECTABLE TERMS.

Thus the *Cæsars* ruined the *Roman* liberty, under the titles of *tribunical* and *dictatorial* authorities, old and venerable dignities, known in the most flourishing times of freedom. In imitation of the same policy, *James* II. when he *meant* to establish popery, *talked* of liberty of conscience, the most sacred of all liberties; and had thereby almost deceived the Dissenters into destruction.

All artful rulers, who strive to extend their power beyond its just limits, endeavor to give to their attempts as much semblance of [31] legality as possible. Those who succeed them may venture to go a little further; for each new encroachment will be strengthened by a former. "* That which is now supported by examples, growing old, will become an example itself," and thus support fresh usurpations.

* TACITUS.

A free people therefore can never be too quick in observing, nor too firm in opposing the beginnings of *alteration* either in *form* or *reality*, respecting institutions formed for their security. The first kind of alteration leads to the last : Yet, on the other hand, nothing is more certain, than that the *forms* of liberty may be retained, when the *substance* is gone. In government, as well as in religion, "The *letter* killeth, but the *spirit* giveth life." *

I will beg leave to enforce this remark by a few instances. The crown, by the constitution, has the prerogative of creating peers. The existence of that order, in due number and dignity, is essential to the constitution; and if the crown did not exercise that prerogative, the peerage must have long since decreased so much as to have lost its proper influence. Suppose a prince, for some unjust purposes, should, from time to time, advance so many needy, profligate wretches to that rank, that all the independence of the house of lords should be destroyed; there would then be a manifest violation of the constitution, *under the appearance of using legal prerogative.*

The house of commons claim the privilege of forming all money bills, and will not suffer either of the other branches of the legislature to add to, or alter them ; contending that their power simply extends to an acceptance or rejection of them. This privilege appears to be just : but under pretence of this just privilege, the house of commons has claimed a licence of tacking to money bills, clauses relating to things of a totally different kind, and thus forcing them in a manner on the king and lords. This seems to be an abuse of that privilege, and it may be vastly more abused. Suppose a future house, influenced by some displaced, discontented demagogues—in a time of danger, should tack to a money bill, something so injurious to the king and peers, that they would not assent

* 2 COR. iii. 6.

to it, and yet the commons should obstinately insist on it; the whole kingdom would be exposed to ruin by them, *under the appearance of maintaining a valuable privilege.*

In these cases it might be difficult for a while to determine, whether the king intended to exercise his prerogative in a constitutional manner or not; or whether the commons insisted on their demand factiously, or for the public good : But surely the conduct of the crown or of the house, would in time sufficiently explain itself.

Ought not the PEOPLE therefore to watch? to observe facts? to search into causes? to investigate designs? And have they not a right [32] of JUDGING from the evidence before them, on no slighter points than their *liberty* and *happiness?* It would be less than trifling, wherever a *British* government is established, to make use of any arguments to prove such a right. It is sufficient to remind the reader of the day, on the anniversary of which the first of these letters is dated.*

I will now apply what has been said to the present question.

The *nature* of any impositions laid by parliament on these colonies, must determine the *design* in laying them. It may not be easy in every instance to discover that design. Wherever it is doubtful, I think submission cannot be dangerous; nay, it must be right; for, in my opinion, there is no privilege these colonies claim, which they ought in *duty* and *prudence* more earnestly to maintain and defend, than the authority of the *British* parliament to regulate the trade of all her dominions. Without this authority, the benefits she enjoys from our commerce, must be lost to her: The blessings we enjoy from our dependence upon her, must be lost to us. Her strength must decay; her glory vanish ; and she cannot suffer

---

* In the newspaper text this read "It is sufficient to remind the reader of the day on which King William landed at *Torbay.*" — *Ed.*

without our partaking in her misfortune. *Let us there-fore cherish her interests as our own, and give her every thing, that it becomes* FREEMEN *to give or to receive.*

The *nature* of any impositions she may lay upon us may, in general, be known, by considering how far they relate to the preserving, in due order, the connection between the several parts of the *British* empire. One thing we may be assured of, which is this—Whenever she imposes duties on commodities, to be paid only upon their exportation from *Great-Britain* to these colonies, it is not a regulation of trade, but a design to raise a revenue upon us. Other instances may happen, which it may not be necessary at present to dwell on. I hope these colonies will never, to their latest existence, want understanding sufficient to discover the intentions of those who rule over them, nor the resolution necessary for asserting their interests. They will always have the same rights, that all free states have, of judging when their privileges are invaded, and of using all prudent measures for preserving them.

> *Quocirca vivite fortes,*
> *Fortiaque adversis opponite pectora rebus.*
> Wherefore keep up your spirits, and gallantly oppose this
> adverse course of affairs.

A FARMER. [33]

LETTER VII.

My dear COUNTRYMEN,

This letter is intended more particularly for such of you, whose employments in life may have prevented your attending to the consideration of some points that are of great and public importance : For many such persons there must be even in these colonies, where the inhabitants in general are more intelligent than any other people whatever, as has been remarked by strangers, and it seems with reason.

Some of you, perhaps, filled, as I know your breasts are, with loyalty to our most excellent Prince, and with love to our dear mother country, may feel yourselves inclined, by the affections of your hearts, to approve every action of those whom you so much venerate and esteem. A prejudice thus flowing from goodness of disposition, is amiable indeed. I wish it could be indulged without danger. Did I think this possible, the error should have been adopted, and not opposed by me. But in truth, all men are subject to the frailties of nature; and therefore whatever regard we entertain for the *persons* of those who govern us, we should always remember that their conduct, as *rulers*, may be influenced by human infirmities.

When any laws, injurious to these colonies, are passed, we cannot suppose, that any injury was intended us by his Majesty, or the Lords. For the assent of the crown and peers to laws, seems, as far as I am able to judge, to have been vested in them, more for their own security, than for any other purpose. On the other hand, it is the particular business of the people, to enquire and discover what regulations are useful for themselves, and to digest and present them in the form of bills, to the other orders, to have them enacted into laws. Where these laws are to bind *themselves*, it may be expected, that the house of commons will very carefully consider them: But when they are making laws that are not designed to bind *themselves*, we cannot imagine that their deliberations will be as * cautious and scrupulous, as in their own case. [34]

* Many remarkable instances might be produced of the extraordinary inattention with which bills of great importance, concerning these colonies, have passed in parliament; which is owing, as it is supposed, to the bills being brought in by the persons who have points to carry, so artfully framed, that it is not easy for the members in general, in the haste of business, to discover their tendency.

The following instances shew the truth of this remark. When Mr.

I am told, that there is a wonderful address frequently used in carrying points in the house of commons, by persons experienced in these affairs.—That opportunities are watched—and sometimes votes are passed, that if all the members had been present, would have been rejected by a great majority. Certain it is, that when a

Greenville, in the violence of reformation, formed the 4th *Geo.* III. Chap. 15th, for regulating the *American* trade, the word *"Ireland"* was dropt in the clause relating to our iron and lumber, so that we could send these articles to no part of *Europe,* but to *Great-Britain.* This was so unreasonable a restriction, and so contrary to the sentiments of the legislature for many years before, that it is surprizing it should not have been taken notice of in the house. However the bill passed into a law. But when the matter was explained, this restriction was taken off by a subsequent act. I cannot positively say how long after the taking off this restriction, as I have not the act, but I think, in less than 18 months, another act of parliament passed, in which the word *"Ireland"* was left out, just as it had been before. The matter being a second time explained, was a second time regulated.

Now if it be considered, that the omission mentioned struck off with ONE word SO VERY GREAT A PART OF OUR TRADE, it must appear *remarkable ;* and equally so is the method by which *Rice* became an enumerated commodity.

"The enumeration was obtained (says Mr. [*a*] *Gee*) by one *Cole,* a Captain of a ship, employed by a company then trading to *Carolina,* for several ships going from *England* thither, and purchasing rice for *Portugal* prevented *the aforesaid Captain* of a loading. Upon his coming home, he possessed one Mr. *Lowndes,* a member of parliament (*who was very frequently employed to prepare bills*) with an opinion, that carrying rice directly to *Portugal,* was a prejudice to the trade of *England,* and PRIVATELY got a clause into an act, to make it an enumerated commodity; *by which means he secured a freight to himself.* BUT THE CONSEQUENCE PROVED A VAST LOSS TO THE NATION."

I find that this clause, "PRIVATELY got into an act," FOR THE BENEFIT OF CAPTAIN COLE, to the "VAST LOSS OF THE NATION," is foisted into the 3d and 4th *Ann,* Chap. 5th, intituled, "An act for granting to her Majesty a further subsidy on wines and merchandizes imported," with which it has no more connection, than with 34th *Edward* I. the 34th and 35th of *Henry* VIII. and the 25th of *Charles* II. WHICH PROVIDE, THAT NO PERSON SHALL BE TAXED BUT BY HIMSELF OR HIS REPRESENTATIVE.

[*a*] *Gee* on Trade, page 32.

powerful and artful man has determined on any measure against these colonies, he has always succeeded in his attempt. Perhaps therefore it will be proper for us, whenever any oppressive act affecting us is passed, to attribute it to the inattention of the members of the house of commons, and to the malevolence or ambition of some factious great man, rather than to any other cause.

Now I do verily believe, that the late act of parliament, imposing duties on paper, *&c.* was formed by Mr. *Greenville*, and his party, because it is evidently a part of that plan, by which he endeavoured to render himself POPULAR at home; and I do also believe, that not one half of the members of the house of commons, even of those who heard it read, did perceive how destructive it was to *American* freedom. For this reason, as it is usual in *Great-Britain*, to consider the King's speech as the speech of the ministry, it may be right here to consider this act as the act of a *party*—perhaps I should speak more properly, if I was to use another term. [35]

There are two ways of laying taxes. One is, by imposing a certain sum on particular kinds of property, to be paid by the *user* or *consumer*, or by rating the *person* at a certain sum. The other is, by imposing a certain sum on particular kinds of property, to be paid by the *seller*.

When a man pays the first sort of tax, he *knows with certainty* that he pays so much money *for a tax*. The *consideration* for which he pays it, is remote, and, it may be, does not occur to him. He is sensible too, that he is *commanded and obliged* to pay it *as a tax;* and therefore people are apt to be displeased with this sort of tax.

The other sort of tax is submitted to in a very different manner. The purchaser of an article, very seldom reflects that the seller raises his price, so as to indemnify himself for the tax *he* has paid. He knows that the prices of things are continually fluctuating, and if he thinks about the tax, he thinks at the same time, in all probability, that he *might* have paid as much, if the article he buys had not been taxed. He gets something *visible* and *agreeable* for his money; and tax and price are so confounded together, that he cannot separate, or does not chuse to take the trouble of separating them.

This mode of taxation therefore is the mode suited to arbitrary and oppressive governments. The love of liberty is so natural to the human heart, that unfeeling tyrants think themselves obliged to accommodate their schemes as much as they can to the appearance of justice and reason, and to deceive those whom they resolve to destroy, or oppress, by presenting to them a miserable picture of freedom, when the inestimable original is lost.

This policy did not escape the cruel and rapacious *NERO.* That monster, apprehensive that his crimes might endanger his authority and life, thought proper to do some popular acts, to secure the obedience of his subjects. Among other things, says *Tacitus,* "he remitted the twenty-fifth part of the price on the sale of slaves, but rather in *shew* than *reality;* for the *seller* being ordered to pay it, it became part of the price to the *buyer.*" *

This is the reflection of the judicious *Historian;* but the deluded *people* gave their infamous Emperor full credit for his false generosity. Other nations have been treated in the same manner the *Romans* were. The honest, industrious *Germans,* who are settled in different parts of this continent, can inform us, that it was this sort of tax that drove them from their native land to our woods, at that time the seats of perfect and undisturbed freedom.

Their Princes, enflamed by the lust of power, and the lust of avarice, two furies that the more they are gorged, the more hungry they grow, transgressed the bounds they

* *Tacitus's Ann.,* Book 13, § 31.

ought, in regard to themselves, to have observed. To keep up the deception in the minds of [36] subjects, "there must be," says* a very learned author, "some proportion between the impost and the value of the commodity; wherefore there ought not to be an excessive duty upon merchandizes of little value. There are countries in which the duty exceeds seventeen or eighteen times the value of the commodity. In this case the Prince removes the illusion. His subjects plainly see they are dealt with in an unreasonable manner, which renders them most exquisitely sensible of their slavish situation." From hence it appears, that subjects may be ground down into misery by this sort of taxation, as well as by the former. They will be as much impoverished, if their money is taken from them in this way as in the other; and that it will be taken, may be more evident, by attending to a few more considerations.

The merchant or importer, who pays the duty at first, will not consent to be so much money out of pocket. He therefore proportionably raises the price of his goods. It may then be said to be a contest between him and the person offering to buy, who shall lose the duty. This must be decided by the nature of the commodities, and the purchaser's demand for them. If they are mere luxuries, he is at liberty to do as he pleases, and if he buys, he does it voluntarily: But if they are absolute *necessaries* or *conveniences*, which use and custom have made requisite for the comfort of life, and which he is not permitted, by the power imposing the duty, *to get elsewhere*, there the seller has a plain advantage, and the buyer *must* pay the duty. In fact, the seller is nothing less than a collector of the tax for the power that imposed it. If these duties then are extended to the necessaries and conveniences of life in general, and enormously encreased, the people must

* *Montesquieu's Spirit of Laws*, Book 13, Chap. 8.

at length become indeed "most exquisitely sensible of their slavish situation." Their happiness therefore entirely depends on the moderation of those who have authority to impose the duties.

I shall now apply these observations to the late act of parliament. Certain duties are thereby imposed on paper and glass,* imported into these colonies. By the laws of *Great-Britain* we are prohibited to get these articles from any other part of the world. We cannot at present, nor for many years to come, tho' we should apply ourselves to these manufactures with the utmost industry, make enough ourselves for our own use. That paper and glass are not only convenient, but absolutely necessary for us, I imagine very few will contend. Some perhaps, who think mankind grew wicked and luxurious, as soon as they found out another way of communicating their sentiments than by speech, and another way of dwelling than in caves, may advance so whimsical an opinion. But I presume no body will take the unnecessary trouble of refuting them. [37]

From these remarks I think it evident, that we *must* use paper and glass; that what we use *must* be *British;* and that we *must* pay the duties imposed, unless those who sell these articles, are so generous as to make us presents of the duties they pay.

Some persons may think this act of no consequence, because the duties are so *small.* A fatal error. *That* is the very circumstance most alarming to me. For I am convinced, that the authors of this law would never have obtained an act to raise so trifling a sum as it must do, had they not intended by *it* to establish a *precedent* for future use. To console ourselves with the *smallness* of the duties, is to walk deliberately into the snare that is set for us, praising the *neatness* of the workmanship. Sup-

---

* In the newspaper text "etc" is here added.—*Ed.*

pose the duties imposed by the late act could be paid by these distressed colonies with the utmost ease, and that the purposes to which they are to be applied, were the most reasonable and equitable that can be conceived, the contrary of which I hope to demonstrate before these letters are concluded; yet even in such a supposed case, these colonies ought to regard the act with abhorrence. For WHO ARE A FREE PEOPLE? Not *those*, over whom government is reasonably and equitably exercised, but *those*, who live under a government so *constitutionally checked* and *controuled*, that proper provision is made against its being otherwise exercised.

The late act is founded on the destruction of this constitutional security. If the parliament have a right to lay a duty of Four Shillings and Eight-pence on a hundred weight of glass, or a ream of paper, they have a right to lay a duty of any other sum on either. They may raise the duty, as the author before quoted says has been done in some countries, till it "exceeds seventeen or eighteen times the value of the commodity." In short, if they have a right *to* levy a tax of *one penny* upon us, they have a right to levy a *million* upon us: For where does their right stop? At any given number of Pence, Shillings or Pounds? To attempt to limit their right, after granting it to exist at all, is as contrary to reason—as granting it to exist at all, is contrary to justice. If *they* have any right to tax *us*—then, whether *our own money* shall continue in *our own pockets* or not, depends no longer on *us*, but on *them*. * "There is nothing which" we can call our own; or, to use the words of Mr. *Locke*—"WHAT PROPERTY HAVE WE IN THAT, WHICH ANOTHER MAY, BY RIGHT, TAKE, WHEN HE PLEASES, TO HIMSELF?"

These duties, which will inevitably be levied upon us—

---

* Lord *Cambden's* speech. [*In the newspaper text this note is*]: "The speech of a noble Lord lately published."—*Ed.*

which are now levying upon us—are *expressly* laid FOR THE SOLE PURPOSES OF TAKING MONEY. This is the true definition of "*taxes.*" They are therefore *taxes.* This money is to be taken from *us. We* [38] are therefore *taxed. Those* who are *taxed* without their own consent, expressed * by themselves or their representatives, are *slaves. We are taxed* without our own consent, expressed by ourselves or our representatives. *We* are therefore†— ‡ SLAVES.

Miserable vulgus
A miserable tribe.

A FARMER. [39]

* In the newspaper text "given" is used instead of "expressed."—*Ed.*

† In the newspaper text this is: "We are therefore—I speak it with grief—I speak it with indignation—We are SLAVES."—*Ed.*

‡ "It is my opinion, that this kingdom has no right to lay a TAX upon the colonies."—"The *Americans* are the SONS, not the BASTARDS of *England.*"—"The distinction between LEGISLATION and TAXATION is essentially necessary to liberty."—"The COMMONS of *America*, repre- sented in their several assemblies, have ever been in possession of this their constitutional right, of GIVING AND GRANTING THEIR OWN MONEY. They would have been *SLAVES*, if they had not enjoyed it." "The idea of a *virtual representation* of *America* in this house, is the most contemptible idea, that ever entered into the head of man.—It does not deserve a serious refutation." *Mr.* Pitt's *speech on the* Stamp-Act.

That great and excellent man Lord *Cambden*, maintains the same opinion. His speech in the house of peers, on the declaratory bill of the sovereignty of *Great-Britain* over the colonies, has lately appeared in our papers. The following extracts so perfectly agree with, and confirm the sentiments avowed in these letters, that it is hoped the inserting them in this note will be excused.

"As the Affair is of the *utmost importance*, and in its consequences may involve the *fate of kingdoms*, I took the strictest review of my arguments; I re-examined all my authorities; fully determined if I found myself mistaken, publickly to own my mistake, and give up my opinion; But my searches have more and more convinced me, that the *British* parliament have *NO RIGHT TO TAX* the *Americans.*"— "Nor is the doctrine new; it is as old as the the constitution; it grew up with it; indeed it is its support."—"TAXATION and REPRESENTATION

LETTER VIII.

My dear COUNTRYMEN,

IN my opinion, a dangerous example is set in the last act relating to these colonies. The power of parliament to levy money upon us for raising a revenue, is therein *avowed* and *exerted.* Regarding the act on this single

are inseparably united. *GOD* hath joined them: No *British* parliament can separate them: To endeavour to do it, is to stab our vitals."

"My position is this—I repeat it—I will maintain it to my last hour— TAXATION and REPRESENTATION are inseperable—this position is founded on the laws of nature; it is more, it is itself AN ETERNAL LAW OF NATURE; for whatever is a man's own, is absolutely his own; NO MAN HATH A RIGHT TO TAKE IT FROM HIM WITHOUT HIS CONSENT, either expressed by himself or representative; *whoever attempts to do it, attempts an injury;* WHOEVER DOES IT, *COMMITS A ROBBERY;* HE THROWS DOWN THE DISTINCTION BETWEEN LIBERTY AND SLAVERY." —"There is not a *blade of grass,* in the most obscure corner of the kingdom, which is not, which was not ever *represented,* since the constitution began: There is not a *blade of grass,* which, when taxed, *was not taxed by the consent of the proprietor.*" "The forefathers of the *Americans* did not leave their native country, and subject themselves to every danger and distress, TO BE REDUCED TO A STATE OF SLAVERY. They did not give up their rights: They looked for protection, and *not for* CHAINS, from their mother country. By her they expected to be defended in the possession of their property, and not to be deprived of it: For should the present power continue, THERE IS NOTHING WHICH THEY CAN CALL THEIR OWN; or, to use the words of Mr. *Locke,* *"WHAT PROPERTY HAVE THEY IN THAT, WHICH ANOTHER MAY, BY RIGHT, TAKE, WHEN HE PLEASES, TO HIMSELF?"*

It is impossible to read this speech, and Mr. *Pitt's,* and not be charmed with the generous zeal for the rights of mankind that glows in every sentence. These great and good men, animated by the subject they speak upon, seem to rise above all the former glorious exertions of their abilities. A foreigner might be tempted to think they are *Americans,* asserting with all the ardor of patriotism, and all the anxiety of apprehension, the cause of their native land—and not *Britons,* striving to stop their mistaken countrymen from oppressing others. Their reasoning is not only just—it is, as Mr. *Hume* says of the eloquence of *Demosthenes,* "vehement." It is disdain, anger, boldness, freedom, involved in a continual stream of argument.

principle, I must again repeat, and I think it my duty to repeat, that to me it appears to be *unconstitutional.*

No man, who considers the conduct of the parliament since the repeal of the *Stamp-Act,* and the disposition of many people at home, can doubt, that the chief object of attention there, is, to use Mr. *Greenville's* expression, "providing that the DEPENDENCE and OBEDIENCE of the colonies be asserted and maintained."

Under the influence of this notion, instantly on repealing the *Stamp-Act,* an act passed, declaring the power of parliament to bind these colonies *in all cases whatever.* This however was only planting a barren tree, that cast a *shade* indeed over the colonies, but yield no *fruit.* It being determined to enforce the authority on which the *Stamp-Act* was founded, the parliament having never renounced the right, as Mr. *Pitt* advised them to do; and it being thought proper to disguise that authority in such a manner, as not again to alarm the colonies: some little time was required to find a method, by which both these points should be united. At last the ingenuity of Mr. *Greenville* and his party accomplished the matter, as it was thought, in "an act for granting certain duties in the *British* colonies and plantations in *America,* for allowing drawbacks," *&c.* which is the title of the act laying duties on paper, *&c.*

The parliament having several times before imposed duties to be paid in *America,* IT WAS EXPECTED, NO DOUBT, THAT THE REPETITION OF SUCH A MEASURE WOULD BE PASSED OVER, AS AN USUAL THING. But to have done this, without expressly "asserting and maintaining" the power of parliament to take our money without our consent, and to apply it as they please, would not [40] have been, in Mr. *Greenville's* opinion,* sufficiently declar-

---

* In the newspaper text the words "in Mr. Greenville's opinion" are not printed.—*Ed.*

ative of its supremacy, nor sufficiently depressive of *American* freedom.

Therefore it is, that in this memorable act we find it *expressly* "provided," that money shall be levied upon us without our consent, for PURPOSES, that render it *if possible*, more dreadful than the *Stamp-Act.*

That act, alarming as it was, declared, the money thereby to be raised, should be applied "towards defraying the expences of defending, protecting and securing the *British* colonies and plantations in *America.*" And it is evident from the whole act, that by the word "*British*," were intended colonies and plantations *settled by* British *people*, and not generally, *those subject to the* British *crown.* That act therefore seemed to have something gentle and kind in its intention, and to aim only at *our own welfare*: But the act now objected to, impose duties upon *British* colonies, "to defray the expences of defending, protecting and securing *his Majesty's* DOMINIONS *in* America."

What a *change* of words! What an *incomputable addition* to the expences intended by the *Stamp-Act!* "*His Majesty's* DOMINIONS" comprehended not only *the* British *colonies*, but also *the conquered provinces of* Canada *and* Florida, *and the* British *garrisons of* Novia Scotia; for *these* do not deserve the name of *colonies.*

What justice is there in making US pay for "defending, protecting and securing" THESE PLACES? What benefit *can* WE, or have WE ever derived *from them?* None of them was conquered *for* US; nor will "be defended, protected or secured" *for* US.

In fact, however advantageous the subduing or keeping any of these countries may be to *Great Britian*, the acquisition is greatly injurious to these colonies. Our chief property consists in *lands*. These would have been of much greater value, if such prodigious additions had not been made to the *British* territories on this continent.

The natural increase of our own people, if confined within the colonies, would have raised the value still higher and higher every fifteen or twenty years : Besides we should have lived more compactly together, and have been there- fore more able to resist any enemy. But now the in- habitants will be thinly scattered over an immense region, as those who want settlements, will chuse to make new ones, rather than pay great prices for old ones.

These are the consequences to the colonies, of the hearty assistance they gave to *Great-Britain* in the late war—a war *undertaken solely for her own benefit.* The objects of it were, the securing to herself the rich tracts of land on the back of these colonies, with the *Indian* trade; and *Nova-Scotia,* with the fishery. *These and much more, has that kingdom gained*; but the *inferior animals,* that hunted with the *lion,* have been amply re- warded for all the sweat and blood their loyalty cost them, by the honor of having sweated and bled in such com- pany.

I will [41] not go so far as to say, that *Canada* and *Nova-Scotia* are curbs on *New-England*; the *chain of forts* through the back woods, on the *Middle Provinces*; and *Florida,* on the *rest:* But I will venture to say, that if the products of *Canada, Nova-Scotia,* and *Florida,* deserve any consideration, the two first of them are only rivals of our Northern Colonies, and the other of our Southern.

It has been said, that without the conquest of these countries, the colonies could not have been "protected, defended, and secured." If that is true, it may with as much propriety be said, that *Great-Britain* could not have been "defended, protected, and secured," without that conquest : For the colonies are parts of her empire, which it *as much* concerns *her* as *them* to keep out of the hands of any other power.

But these colonies, when they were much weaker, defended themselves, before this Conquest was made ; and could again do it, against any that might properly be called *their* Enemies.   If *France* and *Spain* indeed should attack them, *as members of the* British *empire*, perhaps they might be distressed ; but it would be in a *British* quarrel.

The largest account I have seen of the number of people in *Canada*, does not make them exceed 90,000. *Florida* can hardly be said to have any inhabitants.   It is computed that there are in our colonies 3,000,000. *Our* force therefore must increase with a disproportion to the growth of *their* strength, that would render us very safe.

This being the state of the case, I cannot think it just that these colonies, labouring under so many misfortunes, should be loaded with *taxes*, to maintain countries, not only not useful, but hurtful to them.   The support of *Canada* and *Florida* cost yearly, it is said, half a million sterling.   From hence, we may make some guess of the load that is to be laid *upon* us; for we are not only to "defend, protect and secure" *them*, but also to make "an adequate provision for defraying the charge of the administration of justice, and the support of civil government, in such provinces where it shall be found necessary."

Not one of the provinces of *Canada*, *Nova-Scotia*, or *Florida*, has ever defrayed *these expences within itself:* And if the duties imposed by the last statute are collected, *all of them together*, according to the best information I can get, will not pay *one quarter as much as* Pennsylvania *alone*.   So that the *British colonies* are to be drained of the rewards of their labor, to cherish the scorching sands* of *Florida*, and the icy rocks of *Canada* and *Nova-Scotia*, which never will return to us one farthing that we send to them.

*"Lands" in newspaper text.—*Ed*.

Great-Britain—I mean the ministry in *Great-Britain*, has cantoned *Canada* and *Florida* out into *five* or *six* governments, and may form *as many more.* There now are *fourteen* or *fifteen* regiments on this continent; and there soon may be as *many more.* To make [42] "an adequate provision" FOR ALL THESE EXPENCES, is, no doubt, to be the *inheritance* of the colonies.

Can any man believe that the duties upon paper, *&c.,* are the *last* that will be laid for these purposes? It is in vain to hope, that because it is imprudent to lay duties on the exportation of manufactures from a mother country to colonies, as it may promote manufactures among them, that this consideration will prevent such a measure.

Ambitious, artful men have made it popular, and whatever injustice or destruction will attend it in the opinion of the colonists, at home it will be thought just and salutary.*

The people of *Great-Britain* will be told, and have been told, that *they* are sinking under an immense debt—that great part of this debt has been contracted in defending the colonies—that *these* are so ungrateful and undutiful, that they will not contribute one mite to its payment— nor even to the support of the army now kept up for their "defence and security,"—that they are rolling in wealth, and are of so bold and republican a spirit, that they are aiming at independence—that the only way to retain them in "obedience," is to keep a strict watch over them, and to draw off part of their riches in *taxes*—and that every burden laid upon *them*, is taking off so much from *Great-Britain*—These assertions will be generally believed, and the people will be persuaded that they cannot be too angry with their colonies, as that anger will be profitable to themselves.

---

* So *credulous*, as well as *obstinate*, are the people in believing *every thing*, which flatters their *prevailing passion.*
                                   Hume's Hist. of England.

In truth, *Great-Britain* alone receives any benefit from *Canada*, *Nova-Scotia* and *Florida;* and therefore she alone ought to maintain them. The old maxim of the law is drawn from reason and justice, and never could be more properly applied, than in this case.*

> *Qui sentit commodum, sentire debet et onus.*
> They who feel the benefit, ought to feel the burden.

A FARMER.

[43].

LETTER IX.

My dear COUNTRYMEN,

I have made some observations on the PURPOSES for which money is to be levied upon us by the late act of parliament. I shall now offer to your consideration some further reflections on that subject: And, unless I am greatly mistaken, if these purposes are accomplished according to the *expressed* intention of the act, they will be found effectually to *supersede* that authority in our respective assemblies, which is essential to liberty. The question is not, whether some branches shall be lopt off—The ax is laid to the root of the tree; and the whole body must infallibly perish, if we remain idle spectators of the work.

No free people ever existed, or can ever exist, without keeping, to use a common, but strong expression, "the purse strings," in their own hands. Where this is the case, *they* have a *constitutional check* upon the administration, which may thereby be brought into order *without violence:* But where such a power is not lodged in the *people*, oppression proceeds uncontrouled in its career, till the governed, transported into rage, seek redress in the midst of blood and confusion.

The elegant and ingenious Mr. *Hume*, speaking of the *Anglo Norman* government, says—" Princes and Ministers

*This concluding paragraph is not in the newspaper text.—*Ed.*

were too ignorant, to be themselves sensible of the advantage attending an equitable administration, and there was no established council or *assembly*, WHICH COULD PROTECT THE PEOPLE, and BY WITHDRAWING SUPPLIES, regularly and PEACEABLY admonish the king of his duty, and ENSURE THE EXECUTION OF THE LAWS.''

Thus this great man, whose political reflections are so much admired, makes *this power* one of the foundations of liberty.

The *English* history abounds with instances, proving that *this* is the proper and successful way to obtain redress of grievances. How often have kings and ministers endeavoured to throw off this legal curb upon them, by attempting to raise money by a variety of inventions, under pretence of law, without having recourse to parliament? And how often have they been brought to reason, and peaceably obliged to do justice, by the exertion of this constitutional authority of the people, vested in their representatives?

The inhabitants of these colonies have, on numberless occasions, reaped the benefit of this authority lodged *in their assemblies.*

It has been for a long time, and now is, a constant instruction to all governors, *to obtain a* PERMANENT *support for the offices of government.* But as the author of ''the administration of the colonies'' says, ''this order of the crown is generally, if not universally, rejected by the legislatures of the colonies.''

They [44] perfectly know *how much* their grievances would be regarded, if they had *no other* method of engaging attention, than by *complaining.* Those who rule, are extremely apt to think well of the constructions made by themselves in support of their own power. *These* are frequently erroneous, and pernicious to those they govern. Dry remonstrances, to shew that such constructions are wrong and oppressive, carry very little weight with them, in the opinions of persons who gratify their own inclinations in making these constructions. *They* CANNOT understand the reasoning that opposes *their* power and desires. But let it be made *their interest* to understand such reasoning—and a *wonderful light* is instantly thrown upon the matter; and then, rejected remonstrances become as clear as* "proofs of holy writ."

The three most important articles that our assemblies, or any legislatures can provide for, are, First—the defence of the society: Secondly—the administration of justice: And Thirdly—the support of civil government.

Nothing can properly regulate the expence of making provision for these occasions, but the *necessities* of the society; its *abilities ;* the *conveniency* of the modes of levying money in it; the *manner* in which the laws have been executed: and the conduct of the officers of governments. *All which* are circumstances, that *cannot* possibly be properly *known*, but by the society itself ; or if they should be known, *will not* probably be properly *considered* but by that society.

If money be raised upon us by *others*, without our consent, for our "defence," those who are the judges in *levying* it, must also be the judges in *applying* it. Of consequence the money *said* to be taken from us for our defence, *may be employed* to our injury. We may be chained in by a line of fortifications—obliged to pay for the building and maintaining them—and be told, that they are for our defence. With what face can we dispute the fact, after having granted that those who *apply* the money, had a right to *levy* it? For surely, it is much easier for their wisdom to understand how to apply it in the best manner, than how to levy it in the best manner. Besides, the *right of levying* is of infinitely more consequence, that *that of applying.*

*SHAKESPEARE.

The people of *England*, who would burst out into fury, if the crown should attempt to *levy* money by its own authority, have always assigned to the crown the *application* of money.

As to "the administration of justice"—the judges ought, in a well regulated state, to be equally independent of the executive and* legislative powers. Thus in *England*, judges hold their commissions from the crown "*during good behaviour*," and have salaries, suitable to their dignity, *settled* on them by parliament. The purity [45] of the courts of law since this establishment, is a proof of the wisdom with which it was made.

But in these colonies, how fruitless has been every attempt to have judges appointed "*during good behaviour?*" Yet whoever considers the matter will soon perceive, that *such commissions* are beyond all comparison more necessary in these colonies, than they were in *England*.

The chief danger to the subject *there*, arose from the arbitrary *designs of the crown;* but *here*, the time may come, when we may have to contend with the *designs of the crown, and of a mighty kingdom*. What then must be our chance, when the laws of life and death are to be spoken by judges totally dependent on *that crown*, and *that kingdom*—sent over perhaps *from thence*—filled with *British prejudices*—and *backed by a* STANDING *army*—supported out of OUR OWN pockets, to "assert and maintain" OUR OWN "dependence and obedience."

But supposing that through the extreme lenity that will prevail in the government *through all future ages*, these colonies will never behold any thing like the campaign of chief justice *Jeffereys*, yet what innumerable acts of injustice may be committed, and how fatally may the principles of liberty be sapped, by a succession of judges *utterly independent of the people?* Before such judges the supple

* "Executive and " not in newspaper text.—*Ed.*

wretches, who cheerfully join in avowing sentiments inconsistent with freedom, will always meet with smiles; while the honest and brave men, who disdain to sacrifice their native land to their own advantage, but on every occasion boldly vindicate her cause, will constantly be regarded with frowns.

There are two other considerations relating to this head, that deserve the most serious attention.

By the late act, the officers of the customs are "impowered to enter into any HOUSE, warehouse, shop, cellar, or other place, in the *British* colonies or plantations in *America*, to search for or seize prohibited or unaccustomed goods," *&c.*, on "writs granted by the superior * or supreme court of justice, having jurisdiction within such colony or plantation respectively."

If we only reflect that the judges of these courts are to be *during pleasure*—that they are to have "*adequate provision*" made for them, which is to continue *during their complaisant behaviour*—that they may be *strangers* to these colonies—what an engine of oppression may this authority be in such hands?

I am well aware, that writs of this kind may be granted at home, under the seal of the court of exchequer: But I know also, that the greatest asserters of the rights of *Englishmen* have always strenuously contended, that *such a power* was dangerous to freedom, and expressly contrary to the common law, which ever regarded a man's *house* as his castle, or a place of perfect security.

If [46] such power was in the least degree dangerous *there*, it must be utterly destructive to liberty *here*. For the people there have two securities against the undue exercise of this power by the crown, which are wanting with us, if the late act takes place. In the first place, if any injustice is done *there*, the person injured may bring his ac-

---

* "Inferior" in newspaper text.—*Ed.*

tion against the offender, and have it tried before INDE-PENDENT JUDGES, who are* NO PARTIES IN COMMITTING THE INJURY. *Here* he must have it tried before DEPEND-ENT JUDGES, being the men WHO GRANTED THE WRIT.

To say, that the cause is to be tried by a jury, can never reconcile men who have any idea of freedom, to *such a power.* For we know that sheriffs in almost every colony on this continent, are totally dependent on the crown; and packing of the juries has been frequently practised even in the capital of the *British* empire. Even if juries are well inclined, we have too many instances of the influence of over-bearing unjust judges upon them. The brave and wise men who accomplished the revolution, thought the *independency of judges* essential to freedom.

The other security which the people have at home, but which we shall want here, is this.

If this power is abused *there*, the parliament, the grand resource of the oppressed people, is ready to afford relief. Redress of grievances must precede grants of money. But what regard can *we* expect to have paid to our assemblies, when they will not hold even the puny privilege of *French* parliaments—that of registering, before they are put in ex-ecution, edicts that take away our money.

The second consideration above hinted at, is this. There is a *confusion* in our laws, that is quite unknown in *Great-Britain.* As this cannot be described in a more clear or exact manner, than has been done by the in-genious author of the history of *New-York*, I beg leave to use his words. "The state of our laws opens a door to much controversy. The *uncertainty*, with respect to them, RENDERS PROPERTY PRECARIOUS, and GREATLY EXPOSES

---

*The writs for searching houses in *England*, are to be granted "under the seal of the court of exchequer," according to the statute—and that seal is kept by the chancellor of the exchequer.

4th Inst., p. 104.

US TO THE ARBITRARY DECISION OF BAD JUDGES. The common law of *England* is generally received, together with such statutes as were enacted before we had a legislature of our own, but our courts EXERCISE A SOVEREIGN AUTHORITY, in determining *what parts of the common and statute law* ought to be extended : For it must be admitted that the *difference of circumstances* necessarily requires us, in some cases *to* REJECT *the determination of both.* In many instances, they have also extended even acts of parliament, passed since we had a distinct legislature, *which is greatly adding* [47] *to our confusion.* The practice of our courts is no less *uncertain* than the law. Some of the *English* rules are adopted, others rejected. Two things therefore seem to be ABSOLUTELY NECESSARY for the PUBLIC SECURITY. First, the passing an act for settling the extent of the *English* laws. Secondly, that the courts ordain a general sett of rules for the regulation of the practice.''

How easy it will be, under this '' state of our laws,'' for an artful judge, to act in the most arbitrary manner, and yet cover his conduct under specious pretences ; and how difficult it will be for the injured people to obtain relief, may be readily perceived. We may take a voyage of 3000 miles to complain ; and after the trouble and hazard we have undergone, we may be told, that the collection of the revenue, and maintenance of the prerogative, must not be discouraged—and if the misbehavior is so gross as to admit of no justification, it may be said, that it was an error in judgment only, arising from the confusion of our laws, and the zeal of the King's servants to do their duty.

If the commissions of judges are *during the pleasure of the crown*, yet if their salaries are *during the pleasure of the people*, there will be *some check* upon their conduct. Few men will consent to draw on themselves the hatred and contempt of those among whom they live, for the empty honor of being judges. It is sordid love of gain, that tempts men to turn their backs on virtue, and pay their homage where they ought not.

As to the third particular, "the support of civil government,"—few words will be sufficient. Every man of the least understanding must know, that the *executive* power may be exercised in a manner so disagreeable and harassing to the people, that it is absolutely requisite, that *they* should be enabled by the gentlest method which human policy has yet been ingenious enough to invent, that is, *by shutting their hands*, to "ADMONISH" (as Mr. *Hume* says) certain persons "OF THEIR DUTY."

What shall we now think when, upon looking into the late act, we find the assemblies of these provinces thereby stript of their authority *on these several heads?* The *declared* intention of the act is, "that a revenue should be raised IN HIS MAJESTY'S DOMINIONS IN AMERICA, for making a more certain and adequate provision *for defraying the charge of* THE ADMINISTRATION OF JUSTICE, and *the support of* CIVIL GOVERNMENT in such provinces where it shall be found necessary, and *towards further defraying the expences of* DEFENDING, PROTECTING AND SECURING THE SAID DOMINIONS."

Let the reader pause here one moment—and reflect—whether the colony in which *he* lives, has not made such "certain and adequate provision" *for these purposes*, as is *by the colony judged suitable to its abilities, and all other circumstances.* Then let him reflect—whether if this act takes place, money is not to be raised on *that* colony [48] *without its consent*, to make "provision" *for these purposes*, which *it does not judge to be suitable to its abilities, and all other circumstances.* Lastly, let him reflect—whether the people of that country are not in a state of the most abject slavery, *whose property may be taken from them* under the notion of right, *when they have refused to give it.*

For my part, I think I have good reason for vindicating the honor of the assemblies on this continent, by publicly asserting, that THEY *have made as "certain and adequate provision" for the purposes abovementioned, as they ought to have made*, and that it should not be presumed, that they will not do it hereafter. Why then should *these most important trusts* be wrested out of their hands? Why should they not now be permitted to enjoy that authority, which they have exercised from the first settlement of these colonies? Why should they be scandalized by this innovation, when their respective provinces are now, and will be, for several years, labouring under loads of debt, imposed on them for the very purpose now spoken of? Why should all the inhabitants of these colonies be, with the utmost indignity, treated as a herd of despicable stupid wretches, so utterly void of common sense, that they will not even make "adequate provision" for "the administration of justice, and the support of civil government" among them, or for their own "defence"—though without such "provision" every people must inevitably be overwhelmed with anarchy and destruction? Is it possible to form an idea of a slavery more *compleat*, more *miserable*, more *disgraceful*, than that of a people, where *justice is administered, government exercised*, and a *standing army maintained*, AT THE EXPENCE OF THE PEOPLE, and yet WITHOUT THE LEAST DEPENDENCE UPON THEM? If we can find no relief from this infamous situation,* it will be fortunate for us, if Mr. *Greenville*, setting his fertile fancy again at work, can, as by one exertion of it he has stript us of our *property* and *liberty*, by another deprive us of so much of our *understanding;* that, unconscious of what we *have been* or *are*, and ungoaded by tormenting reflections,

---

*From this point the newspaper text reads: "let Mr. *Grenville* set his fertile fancy again at work, and as by one exertion of it, he has stript us of our *property* and *liberty*, let him by another," etc.—*Ed.*

we may bow down our necks, with all the stupid serenity of servitude, to any drudgery, which our lords and masters shall please to command.

When the charges of the "administration of justice," the "support of civil government," and the expences of "defending, protecting and securing" us, are provided for, I should be glad to know, upon *what occasions* the crown will ever call our assemblies together. Some few of them may meet of their own accord, by virtue of their charters. But what will they have to do, when they are met? To what shadows will they be reduced? The men, whose deliberations heretofore had an influence on every matter relating to the *liberty* and *happiness* of themselves and their constituents, and whose authority in domestic affairs at least, might well [49] be compared to that of *Roman* senators, will *now* find their deliberations of no more consequence, than those of *constables.* They may *perhaps* be allowed to make laws *for the yoking of hogs,* or *the pounding of stray cattle.* Their influence will hardly be permitted to extend *so high,* as the *keeping roads in repair,* as *that business* may more properly be executed by those who receive the public cash.

One most memorable example in history is so applicable to the point now insisted on, that it will form a just conclusion of the observations that have been made.

Spain was once *free.* Their *Cortes* resembled our parliaments. No *money* could be raised on the subject, *without their consent.* One of their Kings having received a grant from them, to maintain a war against the *Moors,* desired, that if the sum which they had given, should not be sufficient, he might be allowed, *for that emergency only,* to raise more money *without assembling the Cortes.* The request was violently opposed by the best and wisest men in the assembly. It was, however, complied with by the votes of a majority ; and this single concession was a PRE-

CEDENT for other concessions of the like kind, until at last
the crown obtained a general power of raising money, in
cases of necessity. From that period the *Cortes* ceased to
be *useful*,—the *people* ceased to be *free*.

> *Venienti occurite morbo.*
> Oppose a disease at its beginning.

A FARMER.

LETTER X.

My dear COUNTRYMEN,

The consequences, mentioned in the last letter, will not
be the utmost limits of our *misery* and *infamy*,* if the late
act is acknowledged to be binding upon us. We feel too
sensibly, that *any ministerial measures*† relating to these
colonies, are soon carried successfully through the parliament. Certain prejudices [50] operate there so strong
against us, that it may be justly questioned, whether *all*
the provinces united, will ever be able effectually to call
to an account before the parliament, any minister who
shall abuse the power by the late act given to the crown in
America. He may divide the spoils torn from us in what
manner he pleases, *and we shall have no way of making
him responsible.* If he should order, that every *governor*
shall have a yearly salary of 5000 l. sterling ; every *chief
justice* of 3000 l.; every inferior officer in proportion ; and
should then reward the most profligate, ignorant, or needy

* From this point, to the end of the sentence, is not in the newspaper
text.—*Ed.*

† "The gentleman must not wonder he was not contradicted, when, as
minister, he asserted the right of parliament to tax *America.* I know
not how it is, but there is a MODESTY in this house, *which does not chuse
to contradict a minister.* I wish gentlemen would get the better of this
modesty. IF THEY DO NOT, PERHAPS THE COLLECTIVE BODY MAY BE-
GIN TO ABATE OF ITS RESPECT FOR THE REPRESENTATIVE."

Mr. Pitt's *Speech.*

dependents on himself or his friends, with places of the greatest trust, because they were of the greatest profit, this would be called an arrangement in consequence of the "adequate provision for defraying the charge of the administration of justice, and the support of the civil government:" And if the taxes should prove at any time insufficient to answer all the expences of the numberless offices, which ministers may please to create, surely the members of the house of commons will be so "*modest,*" as not to "contradict a minister" who shall tell them, it is become necessary to lay a new tax upon the colonies, for the laudable purposes of defraying the charges of the "administration of justice, and support of civil government," among them. Thus, in fact, we shall be* taxed by ministers. In short, it will be in their power to settle upon us any CIVIL, ECCLESIASTICAL, or MILITARY establishment, which they choose.†

We may perceive, by the example of *Ireland*, how eager ministers are to seize upon any settled revenue, and apply it in supporting their own power. Happy are the men, and *happy the people, who grow wise by the misfortunes of others.* Earnestly, my dear countrymen, do I beseech the author of all good gifts, that you may grow wise in this manner; and if I may be allowed to take such a liberty, I beg leave to recommend to you in general, as the best method of attaining this wisdom, diligently to study the

* "Within this act (*statute de tallagio non concedendo*) are all *new* offices erected, with *new* fees, or *old* offices, with *new* fees, for that is a tallage put upon the subject, which cannot be done without common assent by act of parliament. And this doth notably appear by a petition to parliament in anno 13 *H.* IV. where the commons complain, that an office was erected for measurage of cloths and canvas, with a new fee for the same, by colour of the king's letter patents, and pray that these letters patents may be revoked, for that the king could erect no offices with new fees to be taken of the people, who may not so be charged but by parliament." *2d. Inst. p. 533.*

† This sentence is not in the newspaper text.—*Ed.*

histories of other countries. You will there find all the arts, that can possibly be practiced by cunning rulers, or false patriots among yourselves, so fully delineated, that, changing names, the account would serve for your own times.

It is pretty well known on this continent, that *Ireland* has, with a regular consistency of injustice, been cruelly treated by ministers in the article of *pensions;* but there are some alarming circumstances [51] relating to that subject, which I wish to have better known among us.

* The revenue of the crown there arises principally from

* An enquiry into the legality of pensions on the *Irish* establishment, by *Alexander M'Aulay*, Esq; one of the King's council, *&c.*

Mr. *M'Aulay* concludes his piece in the following beautiful manner. "If any *pensions* have been obtained on that establishment, to SERVE THE CORRUPT PURPOSES OF AMBITIOUS MEN.—If his Majesty's revenues of *Ireland* have been employed in pensions, TO DEBAUCH HIS MAJESTY'S SUBJECTS of both kingdoms.—If the treasure of *Ireland* has been expended in pensions, FOR CORRUPTING MEN OF THAT KINGDOM TO BETRAY THEIR COUNTRY ; and men of the neighboring kingdom to betray both.—If *Irish* pensions have been procured, TO SUPPORT GAMESTERS AND GAMING-HOUSES ; promoting a vice which threatens national ruin. —If pensions have been purloined out of the national treasure of *Ireland*, under the MASK OF SALARIES ANNEXED TO PUBLIC OFFICES, USELESS TO THE NATION ; newly invented, FOR THE PURPOSES OF CORRUPTION.—If *Ireland*, just beginning to recover from the devastations of massacre and rebellion, be obstructed in the progress of her cure, BY SWARMS OF PENSIONARY VULTURES PREYING ON HER VITALS.—If, by squandering the national substance of *Ireland*, in a LICENTIOUS, UNBOUNDED PROFUSION OF PENSIONS, instead of employing it in nourishing and improving her infant *agriculture, trade* and *manufactures*, or in *enlightening* and *reforming* her *poor, ignorant, deluded, miserable natives* (by nature most amiable, most valuable, most worthy of public attention)—If *by such abuse of the national substance, sloth* and *nastiness, cold* and *hunger, nakedness* and *wretchedness, popery, depopulation* and *barbarism*, still maintain their ground ; *still deform a country abounding with all the riches of nature*, yet hitherto destined to beggary.—If SUCH PENSIONS be found on the *Irish* establishment ; let such be cut off : And let the perfidious advisers be branded with indelible characters of public infamy ; adequate, if possible, to the dishonor of their crime."*

* This extract is not in the newspaper text.—*Ed.*

the Excise granted "*for pay of the army and defraying other* PUBLIC *charges, in defence and preservation of the kingdom*"—from the tonnage and additional poundage granted "*for protecting the trade of the kingdom at sea, and augmenting the* PUBLIC *revenue* "—from the hearth money granted—as a " PUBLIC *revenue, for a* PUBLIC *charge and expences.*" There are some other branches of the revenue, concerning which there is not any *express* appropriation of them for PUBLIC *service*, but which were plainly *so intended.*

Of *these* branches of the revenue the crown is only *trustee* for the public. They are unalienable. They are inapplicable to any other purposes, but those for which they were established ; and therefore are not *legally* chargeable with pensions.

There is another kind of revenue, which is a private revenue. This is not limited to any public uses ; but the crown has the same property in it, that any person has in his estate. This does not amount, at the most, to *Fifteen Thousand Pounds* a year, probably not to *Seven*, and is the only revenue, that can be *legally* charged with pensions.

If ministers were accustomed to regard the rights or happiness of the people, the pensions in *Ireland* would not exceed the sum just mentioned : But long since have they exceeded that limit; and in *December* 1765, a motion was made in the house of commons in [52] that kingdom, to address his Majesty on the great increase of pensions on the *Irish* establishment, amounting to the sum of 158,685 l. —in the last two years.

Attempts have been made made to gloss over these gross encroachments, by this specious argument—"That expending a competent part of the PUBLIC REVENUE in pensions, from a principle of charity or generosity, adds to the dignity of the crown ; and is *therefore* useful to the PUBLIC." To give this argument any weight, it must appear, that the pensions proceed from *charity* or *generosity* only"—and that it "adds to the dignity of the crown," *to act directly contrary to law.*—

From this conduct towards *Ireland* in open violation of law, we may easily foresee what *we* may expect, when a minister will have the *whole revenue* of *America* in his own hands, to be disposed of at his own pleasure : For *all* the monies raised by the late act are to be "*applied* by virtue of warrants under the sign manual, countersigned by the high treasurer, or any three of the commissioners of the treasury." The "RESIDUE" indeed is to be "paid into the receipt of the exchequer, and to be disposed of by parliament." So that a minister will have nothing to do, but to take care, that there shall be no "residue," and he is superior to all controul.

Besides the burden of *pensions* in *Ireland*, which have enormously encreased within these few years, almost all the *offices* in that poor kingdom, have been, since the commencement of the present century, and now are bestowed upon *strangers*. For tho' the merit of persons born there, justly raises them to places of high trust when they go abroad, as all *Europe* can witness, yet he is an uncommonly lucky *Irishman*, who can get a good post *in his* NATIVE *country*.

When I consider the* manner in which that island

*In *Charles* the Second's time, the house of commons, influenced by some factious demagogues, were resolved to prohibit the importation of *Irish* cattle into *England*. Among other arguments in favour of *Ireland* it was insisted . . . "That by cutting off almost entirely the trade between the kingdoms, ALL THE NATURAL BANDS OF UNION WERE DISSOLVED, and nothing remained to keep the *Irish* in their duty, but *force* and *violence*."

" The king (says Mr. *Hume*, in his history of *England*) was so convinced of the justness of these reasons, that he used all his interest to oppose the bill, and he openly declared, that he could not give his assent to it with a safe conscience. But the commons were resolute in their purpose." . . . "And the spirit of *TYRANNY*, *of which* NATIONS *are*

has been uniformly depressed for so many years past, with this pernicious particularity [53] *of their* † *parliament con-*

as *susceptible as* INDIVIDUALS, had animated the *English* extremely TO EXERT THEIR SUPERIORITY *over their dependent state.* No affair could be conducted with greater violence, than this by the commons. They even went so far in the preamble of the bill, as to declare the importation of *Irish* cattle to be a NUISANCE. By this expression they gave scope to their *passion,* and at the same time *barred the king's prerogative,* by which he might think himself intituled to dispense with a law, SO FULL OF INJUSTICE AND BAD POLICY. The lords expunged the word, but as the king was sensible that no supply would be given by the commons, unless they were gratified in all their PREJUDICES, he was obliged both to employ his interest with the peers, to make the bill pass, and to give the royal assent to it. He could not however, forbear expressing his displeasure, at the jealousy entertained against him, and at the intention which the commons discovered, of retrenching his prerogative.

THIS LAW BROUGHT GREAT DISTRESS FOR SOME TIME UPON IRELAND, BUT IT HAS OCCASIONED THEIR APPLYING WITH GREATER INDUSTRY TO MANUFACTURES, AND HAS PROVED IN THE ISSUE BENEFICIAL TO THAT KINGDOM.''

Perhaps the *same reason* occasioned the "barring the king's prerogative " in the late act suspending the legislation of *New York.*

This we may be assured of, that WE are as dear to his *Majesty,* as the people of *Great-Britain* are. WE are his *subjects* as well as they, and *as faithful subjects;* and his Majesty has given too many, too constant proofs of his piety and virtue, for any man to think it possible, that *such a prince* can make any unjust distinction between *such subjects.* It makes no difference to his Majesty, whether supplies are raised in *Great-Britain,* or *America ;* but it makes *some* difference to the commons of that kingdom.

To speak plainly as becomes an honest man on such important occasions, all our misfortunes are owing to a LUST OF POWER in men of *abilities* and *influence.* This prompts them to seek POPULARITY by *expedients* profitable to themselves, though ever so destructive to their country.

Such is the accursed nature of lawless ambition, and yet . . . What heart but melts at the thought! . . . Such false, detestable PATRIOTS, in *every state,* have led their blind, confiding country, shouting their applauses, into the jaws of *shame* and *ruin.* May the wisdom and goodness of the people of *Great-Britain,* save them from the usual fate of nations.

" . . . . MENTUM MORTALIA TANGUNT.''

† The last *Irish* parliament continued 33 years, during all the late King's

tinuing as long as the crown pleases, I am astonished to observe *such a love of liberty* still animating that LOYAL and GENEROUS nation; and nothing can rise higher my idea of the INTEGRITY and * PUBLIC SPIRIT of a people, [54] who have preserved the sacred fire of freedom from being extinguished, tho' the altar on which it burnt, has been overturned.

In the same manner shall we unquestionably be treated, as soon as the late taxes laid upon us, shall make posts in the "government," and the "administration of justice" *here*, worth the attention of persons of influence in *Great-Britain*. We know enough already to satisfy us of this truth. But this will not be the worst part of our case.

The *principals*, in all great offices, will reside in *England*, making some paltry allowance to deputies for doing the business *here*. Let any man consider what an ex-

reign. The present parliament there has continued from the beginning of this reign; and probably will continue till this reign ends.

* I am informed, that within these few years, a petition was presented to the house of commons, setting forth, "that herrings were imported into *Ireland* from some foreign parts of the north so cheap, as to discourage the *British* herring fishery, and therefore praying that some remedy might be applied in that behalf by parliament."

That upon this petition, the house came to a resolution, to impose a duty of Two Shillings sterling on every barrel of foreign herrings imported into *Ireland*; but afterwards dropt the affair, FOR FEAR OF ENGAGING IN A DISPUTE WITH IRELAND ABOUT THE RIGHT OF TAXING HER.

So much higher was the opinion, which the house entertained of the spirit of *Ireland*; than of that of these colonies.

I find, in the last *English* papers, that the resolution and firmness with which the people of *Ireland* have lately asserted their freedom, have been so alarming in *Great-Britain*, that the Lord Lieutenant, in his speech on the 20th of last *October*, "recommended to that parliament, that such provision may be made for securing the judges in the enjoyment of their *offices* and *appointments*, DURING THEIR GOOD BEHAVIOR, as shall be thought most expedient."

What an important concession is thus obtained, by making demands becoming freemen, with a courage and perseverance becoming Freemen!

hausting drain this must be upon us, when ministers are possessed of the power of creating what posts they please, and of affixing to such posts what salaries they please, and he must be convinced how destructive the late act will be. The injured kingdom lately mentioned, can tell us the mischiefs of ABSENTEES ; and we may perceive already the same disposition taking place with us. The government of *New-York* has been exercised by a deputy. That of *Virginia* is now held so ; and we know of a number of secretary-ships, collector-ships, and other offices, held in the same manner.

True it is, that if the people of *Great-Britain* were not too much blinded by the passions, that have been artfully excited in their breasts, against their dutiful children the colonists, these considerations would be nearly as alarming to them as to us. The influence of the crown was thought by wise men, many years ago, too great by reason of the multitude of pensions and places bestowed by it. These have been vastly encreased since,* and perhaps [55] it

---

*One of the reasons urged by that great and honest statesman, Sir *William Temple* to *Charles* the Second, in his famous remonstrance, to dissuade him from aiming at arbitary power, was, that the King "had few offices to bestow."

Hume's Hist. of *England.*

"Tho' the wings of perogative have been clipt, the influence of the crown is greater than ever it was in any period of our history. For when we consider in how many boroughs the government has the votes at command ; when we consider the vast body of persons employed in the collection of the revenue, in every part of the kingdom, the inconceivable number of placemen, and candidates for places in the customs, in the excise, in the post-office, in the dock-yards, in the ordinance, in the salt-office, in the stamps, in the navy and victualling offices, and in a variety of other departments; when we consider again the extensive influence of the money corporations, subscription jobbers and contractors, the endless dependencies created by the obligations conferred on the bulk of the gentlemen's families throughout the kingdom, who have relations preferred in our navy and numerous standing army ; when I say, we consider how wide, how binding a dependence on the crown is created by

would be no difficult matter to prove that the people have decreased.

Surely therefore, those who wish the welfare of their country, ought seriously to reflect, what may be the consequence of such a new creation of offices, in the disposal of the crown. The *army*, the *administration of justice*, and the *civil government* here, with such salaries as the crown shall please to annex, will extend *ministerial influence* as much beyond its former bounds, as the late war did the *British* dominions.

But whatever the people of *Great-Britain* may think on this occasion, I hope the people of these colonies will unanimously join in this sentiment, that the late act of parliament is injurious to their liberty, and that this sentiment will unite them in a firm opposition to it, in the same manner as the dread of the *Stamp-Act* did.

Some persons may imagine the sums to be raised by it, are but small, and therefore may be inclined to acquiesce under it. A conduct more dangerous to freedom, as before has been observed, can never be adopted. Nothing is wanted at home but a* PRECEDENT, the force of which shall be established, by the tacit submission of the colonies. With what zeal was the statute erecting the post-

the above enumerated particulars, and the great, the enormous weight and influence which the crown derives from this extensive dependence upon its favor and power, any lord in waiting, any lord of the bed-chamber, any man may be appointed minister."

A doctrine to this effect is said to have been the device of L—— H——.
Late News Paper.

* "Here may be observed, that when any ancient law or custom of parliament is broken, and the crown *possessed* of a *precedent*, how *difficult a thing it is to restore the subject again to his* FORMER FREEDOM *and* SAFETY."   2*d. Coke's Inst. p.* 529.

"It is not almost credible to *foresee,* when any maxim or *fundamental law* of this realm is altered (as elsewhere hath been observed) what *dangerous inconvenience* do follow."   4*th Coke's Inst. p.* 41.

These two footnotes are not in the newspaper text.—*Ed.*

office, and another relating to the recovery of debts in
America, urged and tortured, as *precedents* in support of
the *Stamp-Act*, tho' wholly inapplicable. If the parliament succeeds in this attempt, other statutes will impose
other duties. Instead of taxing ourselves, as we have
been accustomed to do, from the first settlement of these
provinces, all our usual taxes will be converted into par-
liamentry taxes on our importations ; and thus the parliament will levy upon us such sums of money as they chuse
to take, *without any other* LIMITATION, *than their* PLEA-
SURE.

We know how much labor and care have been bestowed
by these colonies, in laying taxes in such a manner, that
they should be most *easy* to the people, by being laid on
the proper articles ; most *equal*, by being proportioned to
every man's circumstances ; and *cheapest*, by the method
directed for collecting them.

But *parliamentary taxes* will be laid on us, without any
consideration, whether there is any *easier* mode. The
only point regarded will be, the *certainty of levying the
taxes*, and not the *convenience* of the people on whom they
are to be levied ; and therefore all statutes on this head
will be such as will be most likely, according to the favorite phrase, "*to execute themselves.*"

Taxes [56] in every free state have been, and ought to
be, as exactly *proportioned as is possible to the abilities of
those who are to pay them.* They cannot otherwise be *just.*
Even a *Hottentot* would comprehend the *unreasonableness*
of making a poor man pay as much for "defending" the
property of a rich man, as the rich man pays himself.

Let any person look into the late act of parliament, and
he will immediately perceive, that the immense estates of
Lord *Fairfax*, Lord * *Baltimore*, and our *Proprietaries*,

* *Maryland* and *Pennsylvania* have been engaged in the warmest disputes, in order to obtain an equal and just taxation of their Proprietors'

which are amongst his Majesty's other "Dominions" to
be "defended, protected and secured" by the act, will not
pay a *single farthing* for the duties thereby imposed, except Lord *Fairfax* wants some of his windows glazed; Lord
Baltimore and our *Proprietaries* are quite secure, as they
live in *England.*

I mention these particular cases, as striking instances
how far the late act is a deviation from *that principle of
justice,* which has so constantly distinguished our own
laws on this continent, and ought to be regarded in all
laws.*

The third consideration with our continental assemblies
in laying taxes, has been the *method* of collecting them.
This has been done by a few officers, with moderate allowances, under the inspection of the respective assemblies. *No more was raised from the subject,* than was used
for the intended purposes. But by the late act, a minister
may appoint *as many officers as he pleases* for collecting
the taxes ; may assign them *what salaries he thinks* "adequate ;" and they are subject to *no inspection but his own.*

In short, if the late act of parliament takes effect these
colonies must dwindle down into "common corporations," as their enemies, in the debates concerning the repeal of the *Stamp-Act, strenuously insisted they were;* and
it seems not improbable that some future historian may
thus record our fall.

"The eighth year of this reign was distinguished by *a
very memorable event,* the *American* colonies then submit-
ting, for the *FIRST* time, to be *taxed* by the *British* par-

estates : But this late act of parliament does more for those Proprietors,
than they themselves would venture to demand. It *totally exempts* them
from taxation—tho' their vast estates are to be "secured" by the taxes
of other people.

In this note, all after the dash was not included in the newspaper text.
—*Ed.*

* "And ought to be regarded in all laws" not in newspaper text.—*Ed.*

liament. An attempt of this kind had been made about
two years before, but was defeated by the vigorous exertions of the several provinces, in defence of their liberty.
Their behavior on that occasion rendered their name very
celebrated *for a short time* all over *Europe;* all states
being extremely attentive to a dispute between *Great-Britain*, and so considerable a part of her dominions. For as
she was thought to be grown too powerful, by the successful conclusion of the late war she had been engaged in, it
was hoped by many, that as it had happened before to
other kingdoms, civil discords would afford [57] opportunities of revenging all the injuries supposed to be received from her. However, the cause of dissention was removed, by a repeal of the statute that had given offence.
This affair rendered the SUBMISSIVE CONDUCT of the colonies so soon after, the more extraordinary; there being *no
difference* between the mode of taxation which they opposed, and that to which they submitted, but this, that by
the first, they were to be continually *reminded* that they
were taxed, by certain marks *stamped* on every piece of
paper or parchment they used. The authors of *that statute*
triumphed greatly on this conduct of the colonies, and insisted, that if the people of *Great-Britain* had persisted in
enforcing it, the *Americans* would have been, in a few
months, *so fatigued with the efforts of patriotism*, that they
would have yielded obedience.

"Certain it is, that tho' they had before their eyes *so
many illustrious examples* in their mother country, of *the
constant success* attending *firmness* and *perseverance*, in
opposition to dangerous encroachments on liberty, yet
they quietly gave up a point of the LAST IMPORTANCE.
From thence the decline of their freedom began, and its
decay was extremely rapid ; for as *money* was always raised
upon them by the parliament, their *assemblies* grew immediately *useless*, and in a short time *contemptible :* And

in less than one hundred years, the people sunk down into that *tameness* and *supineness* of spirit, by which they still continue to be distinguished."

> *Et majores vestros & posteros cogitate.*
> Remember your ancestors and your posterity.

A FARMER.

LETTER XI.

My dear COUNTRYMEN,

I have several times, in the course of these letters, mentioned the late act of parliament, as being the *foundation* of future measures injurious to these colonies; and the belief of this truth I wish to prevail, because I think it necessary to our safety.

A perpetual *jealousy*, respecting liberty, is absolutely requisite in all free-states. The very texture of their constitution, in *mixt* governments, demands it. For the *cautions* with which power is *distributed* among the several orders, *imply*, that *each* has that share which is proper for the general welfare, and therefore that any further [58] acquisition must be pernicious. * *Machiavel* employs a whole chapter in his discourses, to prove that a state, to be long lived, must be frequently corrected, and reduced to its first principles. But of all states that have existed, there never was any, in which this jealousy could be more proper than in these colonies. For the government here is not only *mixt*, but *dependent*, which circumstance occasions *a peculiarity in its form*, of a very delicate nature.

Two reasons induce me to desire, that this spirit of apprehension may be always kept up among us, in its utmost vigilance. The first is this—that as the happiness of these provinces indubitably consists in their connection

* *Machiavel's Discources—Book* 3. *Cap.* 1.

with *Great-Britain*, any separation between them is less likely to be occasioned by civil discords, if every disgusting measure is opposed *singly*, and *while it is new:* For in this manner of proceeding, every such measure is most likely to be rectified. On the other hand, oppressions and dissatisfactions being permitted to accumulate—*if ever* the governed throw off the load, *they will do more.* A people does not reform with moderation. The rights of the subject therefore cannot be *too often* considered, explained or asserted: And whoever attempts to do this, shews himself, whatever may be the rash and peevish reflections of pretended wisdom, and pretended duty, a friend to *those* who injudiciously exercise their power, as well as *them* over whom it is so exercised.

Had all the points of prerogative claimed by *Charles* the First, been separately contested and settled in preceding reigns, his fate would in all probability have been very different ; and the people would have been content with that liberty which is compatible with regal authority. But * he thought, it would be as dangerous for him to give up the powers which at any time had been by usurpation exercised by the crown, as those that were legally vested in it. This produced an equal excess on the part of the people. For when their passions were excited by *multiplied* grievances, they thought it would be as dangerous for them to allow the powers that were legally vested in the crown, as those which at any time had been by usurpation exercised by it. Acts, that might *by themselves*

---

* The author is sensible, that this is putting the gentlest construction on *Charles's* conduct ; and that is one reason why he chooses it. Allowances ought to be made for the errors of those men, who are acknowledged to have been possessed of many virtues. The education of this unhappy prince, and his confidence in men not so good or wise as himself had probably *filled* him with mistaken notions of his own authority, and of the consequences that would attend concessions of any kind to a people, who were represented to him, as aiming at too much power.

have been upon many considerations excused or extenu-
ated, derived a contagious malignancy and odium from
other acts, with which they were connected.   They were
not regarded according to [59] the simple force of each,
but as parts of a system of oppression.   Every one therefore, however small in itself, became alarming, as an
additional evidence of tyrannical designs.   It was in vain
for prudent and moderate men to insist, that there was no
necessity to abolish royalty.· Nothing less than the utter
destruction of monarchy, could satisfy those who *had* suffered, and thought they had reason to believe, they always
should suffer under it.

The consequences of these mutual distrusts are well
known :   But there is no other people mentioned in
history, that I recollect, who have been so constantly
watchful of their liberty, and so successful in their struggles for it, as the *English.*   This consideration leads me
to the second reason, why I " desire that the spirit of apprehension may be always kept up among us in its utmost
vigilance."

The first principles of government are to be looked for
in human nature.   Some of the best writers have asserted,
and it seems with good reason, that " government is
founded on* *opinion.*"

* "Opinion is of two kinds, *viz. opinion* of INTEREST, and *opinion* of
RIGHT.   By *opinion* of *interest*, I chiefly understand, *the sense of the
public advantage which is reaped from government;* together with the
persuasion, that the particular government which is established, is
equally advantageous with any other, *that could be easily settled.*"

"*Right* is of two kinds, *right* to *power*, and *right* to *property.*   What
prevalence *opinion* of the first kind has over mankind, may easily be
understood, by observing the attachment which all nations have to their
ancient government, and even to those names which have had the sanction of antiquity.   *Antiquity always begets the opinion of right.*" . . .
"It is sufficiently understood, that the *opinion* of *right* to *property*, is of
the greatest moment in all matters of government."   *Hume's Essays.*
This footnote is not printed in the newspaper text.—*Ed.*

Custom undoubtedly has a mighty force in producing *opinion*, and reigns in nothing more arbitrarily than in public affairs. It gradually reconciles us to objects even of dread and detestation; and I cannot but think these lines of Mr. *Pope* as applicable to vice in *politics*, as to vice in *ethics*—

> "Vice is a monster of so horrid mien,
> "As to be hated, needs but to be seen;
> "Yet *seen too oft*, familiar with her face,
> "We first *endure*, then *pity*, then *embrace*."

When an act injurious to freedom has been *once* done, and the people *bear* it, the *repetition* of it is most likely to meet with *submission*. For as the *mischief* of the one was found to be tolerable, they will hope that of the second will prove so too ; and they will not regard the *infamy* of the last, because they are stained with that of the first.

Indeed nations, in general, are not apt to *think* until they *feel**; and therefore nations in general have lost their liberty : For as violations of the rights of the *governed*, are commonly not only † *specious*, [60] but *small* at the beginning, they spread over the multitude in such a manner, as to touch individuals but slightly. ‡ Thus they are disre-

---

*In the newspaper text this reads: "are more apt to feel than to think;"—*Ed.*

† Omnia mala exampla ex bonis initiis orta sunt.

SALLUST. Bell. Cat. S. 50.

‡ "The *republic* is always *attacked* with greater vigor, than it is *defended ?* For the *audacious* and *profligate*, prompted by their natural enmity to it, are *easily impelled* to act by the *least nod* of their *leaders :* Whereas the honest, I know not why, are generally *slow* and *unwilling* to stir ; and •*neglecting* always the *BEGINNINGS of things*, are *never roused* to exert themselves, but by the *last necessity :* So that through IRRESOLU-TION and DELAY, when they would be glad to compound at last for their QUIET, at the expence even of their HONOR, they *commonly lose them* BOTH." CICERO'S *Orat. for* SEXTIUS.

Such were the sentiments of this great and excellent man, whose vast abilities, and calamities of his country during his time, enabled him, by

regarded. The power or profit that arises from these violations, *centering in few persons*, is to them considerable.
For this reason the *governors* having in view their particular purposes, successively preserve an uniformity of
conduct for attaining them. They regularly encrease the
first injuries, till at length the inattentive people are compelled to perceive the heaviness of their burthens.—They
begin to complain and enquire—but too late. They find
their oppressors so strengthened by success, and themselves
so entangled in examples of express authority on the part
of their rulers, and tacit recognition on their own part, that
they are quite confounded: For millions entertain no other
idea of the *legality* of power, than that it is founded on the
exercise of power. They voluntarily fasten their chains,
by adopting a pusillanimous *opinion*, "that there will be
too much *danger* in attempting a remedy,"—or another
opinion no less fatal,—" that the government has a *right* to
treat them as it does." They then seek a wretched relief
for their minds, by persuading themselves, that to yield
their *obedience*, is to discharge their *duty*. The deplorable
poverty of spirit, that prostrates all the dignity bestowed
by Divine Providence on our nature—*of course succeeds.*

From these reflections I conclude, that every free state
should incessantly watch, and instantly take alarm on any
addition being made to the power exercised over them.
Innumerable instances might be produced to shew, from
what slight beginnings the most extensive consequences
have flowed : But I shall select two only from the history
of *England.*

Henry the Seventh was the *first* monarch of that kingdom, who established A STANDING BODY OF ARMED MEN.
This was a band of *fifty* archers, called yeomen of the

mournful experience, to form a just judgment on the conduct of the
friends and enemies of liberty.
This footnote is not in the newspaper text.—*Ed.*

guard : And this institution, notwithstanding the smallness of the number, was, to *prevent discontent,† "disguised under pretence of majesty and grandeur." In 1684 the standing forces were so much augmented, that [61] *Rapin* says—"The king, in order to make his people *fully sensible of their new slavery*, affected to muster his troops, which amounted to 4000 well armed and disciplined men." I think our army, at this time, consists of more than *seventy* regiments.

The method of taxing by EXCISE was first introduced amidst the convulsions of civil wars. Extreme necessity was pretended for it, and its short continuance promised. After the restoration, an excise upon *beer, ale* and *other liquors*, was granted to the ‡ king, one half in fee, the other for life, as an equivalent for the *court of wards.* Upon *James* the Second's accession, the parliament § gave him the first *excise*, with an additional duty on *wine, tobacco*, and some *other* things. Since the revolution it has been extended to salt, candles, leather, hides, hops, soap, paper, paste-boards, mill-boards, scale-boards, vellum, parchment, starch, silks, calicoes, linens, stuffs, printed, stained, *&c.* wire, wrought plate, coffee, tea, chocolate, *&c.*

Thus a *standing army* and *excise* have, from their first slender origins, tho' always *hated*, always *feared*, always *opposed*, at length swelled up to their vast present bulk.

These facts are sufficient to support what I have said. 'Tis true, that all the mischiefs apprehended by our ancestors from a *standing army* and *excise*, have not *yet happened:* But it does not follow from thence, that they *will*

* In the newspaper text, "occasional discontent" is used in place of "was to prevent discontent," and the rest of the sentence is omitted.—*Ed.*

† *Rapin's* History of *England.*

‡ 12 *Char.* II. Chap. 23 and 24.

§ 1 *James* II. Chap. 1 and 4.

not happen. The inside of a house may catch fire, and the most valuable apartments be ruined, before the flames burst out. The question in these cases is not, what evil *has actually attended* particular measures—but, what evil, in the nature of things, *is likely to attend* them. Certain circumstances may for some time delay effects, that *were reasonably expected*, and that *must ensue.* There was a long period, after the *Romans* had prorogued his command to * *Q Publilius Philo*, before *that example* destroyed their liberty. All our kings, from the revolution to the present reign, have been *foreigners.* Their *ministers* generally continued but a short time in authority ;† and they themselves were *mild* and *virtuous* princes.

A bold, [62] *ambitious* prince, possessed of *great abilities*, firmly *fixed* in his throne *by descent*, served by *ministers like himself*, and rendered either *venerable* or *terrible* by the *glory of his successes*, may execute what his predecessors did not dare to attempt. *Henry* the Fourth tottered in his seat during his whole reign. *Henry* the Fifth drew the strength of that kingdom into *France*, to carry on his wars there, and left the *commons* at home, *protesting*, "that the people were not bound to serve out of the realm."

* In the year of the city 428, "Duo singularia hæc ei viro primum contigere; prorogatio imperii non ante in ullo facta et acto honore triumphus." *Liv. B.* 8. *Chap.* 23. 26.

"Had the rest of the *Roman* citizens imitated the example of *L. Quintius*, who refused to have his consulship continued to him, they had never admitted that custom of proroguing of magistrates, and then the prolongation of their commands in the army had never been introduced, *which very thing was at length the ruin of that commonwealth.*" *Machiavel's Discourses, B. 3. Chap. 24.*

† I dont know but it may be said, with a good deal of reason, that a quick rotation of ministers is very desirable in *Great Britain.* A minister there has a vast store of materials to work with. *Long Administrations* are rather favorable to the *reputation* of a people abroad, than to their *liberty.*

It is true,* that a strong spirit of liberty subsists at present in *Great-Britain*, but what reliance is to be placed in the *temper* of a people, when the prince is possessed of an unconstitutional power, our own history can sufficiently inform us. When *Charles* the Second had strengthened himself by the return of the garrison of *Tangier*, "*England* (says *Rapin*) saw on a sudden an *amazing revolution;* saw herself *stripped of all her rights and priveleges*, excepting such as the king should vouchsafe to grant her : And what is *more astonishing*, the *English* themselves *delivered up* these very rights and privileges to *Charles* the Second, which they had so *passionately*, and if I may say it, *furiously* defended against the designs of *Charles* the First." This happened only *thirty-six* years after this last prince had been beheaded.

Some persons are of opinion, that liberty is not violated, but by such *open* acts of force ; but they seem to be greatly mistaken. I could mention a period within these forty years, when almost as great a change of disposition was produced by the SECRET measures of a *long* administration, as by *Charles's* violence. Liberty, perhaps, is never exposed to so much danger, as when the people believe there is the least; for it may be subverted, and yet they not think so.

Public disgusting acts are seldom practiced by the ambitious, at the beginning of their designs. Such conduct *silences* and *discourages* the weak, and the wicked, who would otherwise have been their *advocates* or *accomplices*. It is of great consequence, to allow those who, upon any account, are inclined to favor them, something specious to *say* in their defence. Their power may be fully established, tho' it would not be safe for them to do *whatever they please*. For there are things, which, at some times, even *slaves* will not bear. *Julius Cæsar* and *Oliver Crom-*

* "Granted" in newspaper text.—*Ed.*

well, did not dare to assume the title of *king.* The *Grand Seignor* dares not lay a *new tax.* The king of *France* dares not be a *protestant.* Certain popular points may be left untouched, and yet freedom be extinguished. The commonalty of *Venice* imagine themselves free, because they are permitted to do what they ought not. But I quit a subject, that would lead me too far from my purpose.

By the late act of parliament, taxes are to be levied upon us, for "defraying the charge of the *administration of justice*—the support of *civil government*—and the expences of *defending* his Majesty's dominions in *America.*"

If [63] any man doubts what ought to be the conduct of these colonies on this occasion, I would ask him these questions.

Has not the parliament *expressly* AVOWED their INTENTION of raising money from us FOR CERTAIN PURPOSES? Is not this scheme *popular* in *Great-Britain?* Will the taxes, imposed by the late act, *answer those purposes?* If it will, must it not take an *immense sum* from us? If it will not, *is it to be expected,* that the parliament will not *fully execute* their INTENTION when it is *pleasing at home,* and *not opposed here?* Must not this be done by imposing NEW *taxes?* Will not every addition thus made to the power of the *British* legislature, *by increasing the number of officers* employed in the collection?* Will not every additional tax therefore render it *more difficult* to abrogate any of them? When a branch of revenue is once established, does it not appear to many people *invidious* and *undutiful,* to attempt to abolish it? If taxes, sufficient to *accomplish the* INTENTION of the parliament, are imposed by the parliament, *what taxes will remain* to be imposed by our assemblies? If *no material tax remains* to be .imposed by them, what must become of *them,* and the *people* they represent?

*This section is not in the newspaper text.—*Ed.*

* "If any person considers these things, and yet thinks our liberties are in no danger, I wonder at that person's security."

One other argument is to be added, which, by itself, I hope, will be sufficient to convince the most incredulous man on this continent, that the late act of parliament is *only* designed to be a PRECEDENT, whereon the future vassalage of these colonies may be established.

Every duty thereby laid on articles of *British* manufacture, is laid on some commodity, upon the exportation of which from *Great-Britain*, a *drawback* is payable. Those *drawbacks*, in most of the articles, are *exactly double* to the *duties* given by the late act. The parliament therefore might, in *half a dozen lines*, have raised MUCH MORE MONEY, only by *stopping the drawbacks* in the hands of the officers at home, on exportation to these colonies, than by this solemn imposition of taxes upon us, to be collected here. Probably, the artful contrivers of this act formed it in this manner, in order to reserve to themselves, in case of any objections being made to it, this specious pretence —"that the drawbacks are gifts to the colonies, and that the late act only lessens those gifts." But the truth is, that the drawbacks are intended for the encouragement and promotion of *British* manufactures and commerce, and are allowed on exportation to *any foreign parts*, as well as on exportation to these provinces. Besides, care has been taken to slide into the act, some articles on which there are no drawbacks.† However, the *whole duties* laid by the late act on *all* the articles therein specified are *so small*,

---

* Demosthenes's 2d Philippic.

† "*Though duties by the late act are laid on some articles, on which no drawbacks are allowed, yet the duties imposed by the act are so small, in comparison with the drawbacks that* are *allowed, that* all *the duties together will not amount to so much as the drawbacks.*" Footnote in newspaper text.—*Ed.*

that they will not amount to *as much* as the *drawbacks* which are allowed on *part* of them only. If therefore, ⌊64⌋ *the sum to be obtained by the late act,* had been the *sole object* in forming it, there would not have been any occasion for " the COMMONS of *Great-Britain,* to GIVE and GRANT to his Majesty RATES and DUTIES for *raising a revenue* IN *his Majesty's dominions in* America, for making a more certain and adequate provision for defraying the charges of the administration of justice, the support of civil government, and the expence of defending the said dominions;"— nor would there have been any occasion for an * expensive board of commissioners, and all the other new charges to which we are made liable.

Upon the whole, for my part, I regard the late act as an *experiment made of our disposition.* It is a bird sent out over the waters, to discover, whether the waves, that lately agitated this part of the world with such violence, are yet *subsided.* If *this adventurer* † gets footing here, we shall

---

* The expence of this board, I am informed, is between Four and Five Thousand Pounds Sterling a year. The establishment of officers, for collecting the revenue in *America,* amounted before to Seven Thousand Six Hundred Pounds *per annum ;* and yet, says the author of " The regulation of the colonies," "the whole remittance from *all* the taxes in the colonies, at an average of *thirty years,* has not amounted to One Thousand Nine Hundred Pounds a year, and in that sum Seven or Eight Hundred Pounds *per annum* only, have been remitted from *North America.*"

The smallness of the revenue arising from the duties in *America,* demonstrates that they were intended only as REGULATIONS OF TRADE : And can any person be so blind to truth, so dull of apprehension in a matter of unspeakable importance to his country, as to imagine, that the board of commissioners lately established at such a charge, is instituted to assist in collecting One Thousand Nine Hundred Pounds a year, or the trifling duties imposed by the late act? Surely every man on this continent must perceive, that they are established for the care of a NEW SYSTEM OF REVENUE, which is but now begun.

† In the newspaper text this letter concludes : "If *this adventurer* gets footing here, we shall quickly be convinced, that it is not a Phœnix ; for we shall soon see it followed by *others of the same kind.* We shall find it rather to be of the breed described by the poet—"—*Ed.*

quickly find it to be of the * kind described by the poet—
"*Infelix vates.*"
A direful foreteller of future calamities.

A FARMER. [65]

LETTER XII.

My Dear COUNTRYMEN,

Some states have lost their liberty by *particular accidents:* But this calamity is generally owing to the *decay of
virtue.* A *people* is travelling fast to destruction, when *individuals* consider *their* interests as distinct from *those of
the public.* Such notions are fatal to their country, and to
themselves. Yet how many are there, so *weak* and *sordid*
as to *think* they perform *all the offices of life,* if they earnestly endeavor to encrease their own *wealth, power,* and
credit, without the least regard for the society, under the
protection of which they live ; who, if they can make an
immediate profit to themselves, by lending their assistance
to those, whose projects plainly tend to the injury of their
country, rejoice in their *dexterity,* and believe themselves
entitled to the character of *able politicians.* Miserable
men ! Of whom it is hard to say, whether they ought to
be most the objects of *pity* or *contempt:* But whose
opinions are certainly as *detestable,* as their practices are
destructive.

Tho' I always reflect, with a high pleasure, on the integrity and understanding of my countrymen, which,
joined with a pure and humble devotion to the great and
gracious author of every blessing they enjoy, will, I hope,
ensure to them, and their posterity, all temporal and
eternal happiness ; yet when I consider, that in every age
and country there have been bad men, my heart, at this
threatening period, is so full of apprehension, as not to per-

* "Dira cælæno," *&c. Æneid 3.*

mit me to believe, but that there may be some on this continent, *against whom you ought to be upon your guard*— Men, who either* hold, [66] or expect to hold certain ad-

* It is not intended by these words, to throw any reflection upon gentlemen, because they are possessed of offices : For many of them are certainly men of virtue, and lovers of their country. But supposed obligations of *gratitude*, and *honor*, may induce them to be silent. Whether these obligations *ought to be* regarded or not, is not so much to be considered by others, in the judgment they form of these gentlemen, as whether *they think* they ought to be regarded. Perhaps, therefore, we shall act in the properest manner towards them, if we neither *reproach* nor *imitate* them. The persons meant in this letter, are the *base-spirited wretches*, who may endeavour to *distinguish themselves*, by their sordid zeal in defending and promoting measures, which *they know beyond all question*, to be *destructive* to the *just rights* and *true interests* of their country. It is scarcely possible to speak of *these men* with any degree of *patience*—It is scarcely possible to speak of them with any degree of *propriety*—For no words can truly describe their *guilt* and *meanness*— But every honest bosom, on their being mentioned, will *feel* what cannot be *expressed*.

If their wickedness did not blind them, they might perceive along the coast of these colonies, many men,† remarkable instances of wrecked ambition, who after *distinguishing themselves* in the support of the *Stamp-Act*, by a courageous contempt of their country, and of justice, have been left to linger out their miserable existence, without a government, collectorship, secretaryship, or any other commission, to console them *as well as it could*, for loss of virtue and reputation—while numberless offices have been bestowed in these colonies on people from *Great-Britain*, and new ones are continually invented, to be thus bestowed. As a *few great prizes* are put into a lottery to TEMPT *multitudes to lose*, so here and there an *American* has been raised to a good post.—

" Apparent rari nantes in gurgite vasto."

Mr. *Greenville*, indeed, in order to recommend the *Stamp-Act*, had the *unequalled* generosity, to pour down a golden shower of offices upon *Americans ;* and yet these *ungrateful* colonies did not thank Mr. *Greenville* for shewing his kindness to their countrymen, nor *them* for accepting it. How must that great statesman have been surprised, to find, that the unpolished colonies could not be reconciled to *infamy* by *treachery ?* Such a *bountiful* disposition toward us never appeared in any minister before him, and probably never will appear again : For it is *evident*, that *such a system* of policy is to be established on this continent, as, in a

† In the newspaper text this reads, " many skeletons of wretched ambition."—*Ed.*

vantages, by setting examples of servility to their country-men.   Men, who trained to the employment, or self taught by a natural versatility of genius, serve as decoys for draw-ing the innocent and unaware into snares.   It is not to be doubted but that such men will diligently bestir them-selves on this and every like occasion, to spread the in-fection of their meanness as far as they can.   On the plans *they* have adopted, this is *their* course.   *This* is the method to recommend themselves to their *patrons.**

From *them* we shall learn, how *pleasant* and *profitable* a thing it is, to be for our SUBMISSIVE behavior *well spoken of* at *St. James* or *St. Stephen's ;* at *Guildhall*, or the *Royal Exchange.*   Specious fallacies will be drest up with all the arts of delusion, to persuade one colony *to distinguish her-self from another*, by unbecoming condescensions, *which will serve the ambitious purposes of great men* at home, and therefore will be thought by them *to entitle their as-sistants in obtaining them* to considerable rewards.

Our fears will be excited.   Our hopes will be awakened. It will be insinuated to us, with a plausible affection of *wisdom* and *concern*, how *prudent* it is to please the *power-ful*—how *dangerous* to provoke them—and then comes in the perpetual incantation that freezes up every generous

short time, is to render it utterly unnecessary to use the least *art* in order to *conciliate* our approbation of any measures.   Some of our countrymen may be employed to *fix* chains upon us, but *they* will never be permitted to *hold* them afterwards.   So that the utmost, that any of them can ex-pect, is only a *temporary provision*, that *may* expire in their own time ; but which they may *be assured*, will preclude their children from having any consideration paid to *them*.   NATIVES of *America* must sink into total NEGLECT and CONTEMPT, the moment that THEIR COUNTRY loses the constitutional power she now possesses.   [*In the newspaper text this note continues ·* "*Most sincerely do I wish and pray, that every one of us may be convinced of this great truth—that* industry *and* integrity *are the* '*paths of pleasantness*' *which lead to happiness.*"—*Ed.*

* In the newspaper text this paragraph continues : "They act consist-ently, in a bad cause.   They run well, in a mean race."—*Ed.*

purpose of the soul in cold, inactive expectation—"that if there is any request to be made, compliance will obtain a favorable attention."

Our *vigilance* and our *union* are *success* and *safety.* Our *negligence* and our *division* are *distress* and *death.* They are *worse*—they are *shame* and *slavery.* Let us equally shun the benumbing stillness [67] of *overweening sloath,* and the feverish activity of that *ill informed zeal,* which busies itself in maintaining *little, mean,* and *narrow* opinions. Let us, with a truly wise *generosity* and *charity,* banish and discourage all *illiberal distinctions,* which may arise from differences in *situation,* forms of *government,* or modes of *religion.* Let us consider ourselves as MEN— FREEMEN—CHRISTIAN FREEMEN—*separate from the rest of the world,* and *firmly bound together* by the *same rights, interests* and *dangers.* Let *these* keep our attention inflexibly fixed on the GREAT OBJECTS, which we must CONTINUALLY REGARD, in order to *preserve those rights,* to *promote those interests,* and to *avert those dangers.*

Let these *truths* be indelibly impressed on our minds— *that we cannot be* HAPPY, *without being* FREE—that we cannot be free, *without being secure in our property*—that *we* cannot be secure in our property, *if, without our consent, others may, as by right, take it away*—that *taxes imposed on us by parliament,* do thus take it away—that *duties laid for the sole purpose of raising money,* are taxes —that *attempts* to lay such duties *should be instantly and firmly opposed*—that this opposition can never be effectual, *unless it is the united effort of these provinces*—that therefore BENEVOLENCE *of temper towards each other,* and UNANIMITY *of councils,* are essential to the welfare of the whole—and lastly, that for this reason, every man amongst us, who in any manner would encourage either *dissension, diffidence,* or *indifference,* between these colonies, is an enemy to *himself,* and to *his country.*

The belief of these truths, I verily think, my countrymen, is indispensably necessary to your happiness. I beseech you, therefore, * "teach them diligently unto your children, and talk of them when you sit in your houses, and when you walk by the way, and when you lie down, and when you rise up." What have these colonies to *ask*, while they continue free? Or what have they to *dread*, but insidious attempts to subvert their freedom? *Their prosperity* does not depend on *ministerial favors doled* out to *particular* provinces. *They* form *one* political body, of which *each colony* is a *member*. *Their happiness* is founded on *their constitution;* and is to be promoted, by preserving that constitution in unabated vigor, *throughout every part.* A spot, a speck of decay, however small the limb on which it appears, and however remote it may seem from the vitals, should be alarming. We have *all the rights* requisite for our prosperity. The *legal authority* of *Great-Britain* may indeed lay hard restrictions upon us; but, like the spear of *Telephus*, it will cure as well as wound. Her unkindness will instruct and compel us, after some time, to discover, in our *industry* or *frugality*, surprising remedies—*if our rights continue unviolated:* For as long as the *products* of our *labor*, and the [68] *rewards* of our *care*, can properly be called *our own*, so long it will be worth our while to be *industrious* and *frugal*. But if when we plow—sow—reap—gather—and thresh—we find that we plow—sow—reap—gather—and thresh *for others*, whose PLEASURE is to be the SOLE LIMITATION *how much* they shall *take*, and *how much* they shall *leave*, WHY should we repeat the unprofitable toil? *Horses* and *oxen* are content with *that portion of the fruits of their work*, which their *owners* assign them, in order to keep them strong enough to raise successive crops ; but even *these beasts* will not submit to draw for their *masters*, until they are *subdued* by *whips* and *goads*.

* Deuteron, vi. 7.

Let us take care of our *rights*, and we *therein* take care of our *prosperity*.* †"SLAVERY IS EVER PRECEDED BY SLEEP." *Individuals* may be *dependent* on ministers, if they please. STATES SHOULD SCORN IT ;—and if *you* are not wanting *to yourselves*, you will have a *proper regard* paid *you* by *those*, to whom if you are not *respectable*, you will be *contemptible*. But—if *we have already forgot* the *reasons* that urged us, with unexampled unanimity, to exert ourselves two years ago—if *our zeal* for the public good is *worn out* before the *homespun cloaths*, which it has caused us to have made—if *our resolutions* are *so faint*, as by our present conduct to *condemn* our own late *successful* example—if *we are not affected* by any reverence for the memory of our ancestors, who transmitted to us that freedom in which they had been blest—if *we are not animated* by any regard for posterity, to whom, by the most sacred obligations, we are bound to deliver down the invaluable inheritance—THEN, indeed, any *minister*— or any *tool* of a minister—or any *creature* of a tool of a minister—or any *lower* ‡ *instrument of* § *administration*, if

* In the newspaper text this is "property."—*Ed.*

† *Montesquieu's* Spirits of Laws, Book 14, Chap. 13.

‡ "Instrumenta regni." *Tacitus's* Ann. Book 12, § 66.

§ If any person shall imagine that he discovers, in these letters, [*In the newspaper text is here inserted: " in these letters the least disaffection towards our most excellent sovereign, and the parliament of Great-Britain;"—Ed.*] the least dislike of the dependence of these colonies on *Great-Britain*, I beg that such persons will not form any judgment on *particular expressions*, but will consider the *tenor of all the letters taken together.* In that case, I flatter myself, that every unprejudiced reader will be *convinced*, that the true interests of *Great-Britain* are as dear to me, as they ought to be to every good subject.

If I am an *Enthusiast* in any thing, it is in my zeal for the *perpetual dependence* of these colonies on their mother country.—A dependence founded on *mutual benefits*, the continuance of which can be secured only by *mutual affections.* Therefore it is, that with extreme apprehension I view the smallest seeds of discontent, which are unwarily scattered abroad. *Fifty* or *Sixty* years will make astonishing alterations in these

lower there be, is a *personage* whom it may be dangerous
to offend.

I shall [69] be extremely sorry, if any man mistakes my
colonies; and this consideration should render it the business of *Great-
Britain* more and more to cultivate our good dispositions toward her:
But the misfortune is, that those *great men*, who are wrestling for power
at home, think themselves very slightly interested in the prosperity of
their country *Fifty* or *Sixty* years hence, but are deeply concerned in
blowing up a popular clamour for supposed *immediate advantage*.

For my part, I regard *Great-Britain* as a Bulwark, happily fixed between these colonies and the powerful nations of *Europe*. That kingdom
remaining safe, [In the newspaper text this passage reads: " *That kingdom is our advanced post or fortification*, which remaining safe,"—*Ed.*]
we, under its protection, enjoying peace, may diffuse the blessings of religion, science, and liberty, thro' remote wildernesses. It is therefore in-
contestably our *duty*, and our *interest*, to support the strength of *Great-
Britain*. When confiding in that strength, she begins to forget from
whence it arose, it will be an easy thing to shew the source. She may
readily be reminded of the loud alarm spread among her merchants and
tradesmen, by the universal associations of these colonies, at the time of
the *Stamp-Act*, not to import any of her MANUFACTURES.

In the year 1718, the *Russians* and *Swedes* entered into an agreement,
not to suffer *Great-Britain* to export any NAVAL STORES from their dominions but in *Russian* or *Swedish* ships, and at their own prices. *Great-
Britain* was distressed. *Pitch* and *tar* rose to *Three pounds* a barrel. At
length she thought of getting these articles from the colonies; and the
attempt succeeding, they fell down to *Fifteen shillings*. In the year
1756, *Great-Britain* was threatened with an invasion. An easterly wind
blowing for six weeks, she could not MAN her fleet, and the whole nation
was thrown into the utmost consternation. The wind changed. The
American ships arrived. The fleet sailed in ten or fifteen days. There
are some other reflections on this subject, worthy of the most deliberate
attention of the *British* parliament; but they are of such a nature, that I
do not chuse to mention them publicly. I thought it my duty, in the
year 1765, while the *Stamp-Act* was in suspense, to write my sentiments
to a gentleman of great influence at home, who afterwards distinguished
himself, by espousing our cause, in the debates concerning the repeal of
that act.

[*In the newspaper text this last sentence reads:* " I thought I discharged
my duty to my country, by taking the liberty, in the year 1765, while the
Stamp-Act was in suspense, of writing my sentiments to a man of the
greatest influence at home, who afterwards distinguished himself by espousing our cause, in the debates concerning the repeal of that act."—*Ed.*]

meaning in anything I have said. Officers employed by
the crown, are, while according to the laws they conduct
themselves, entitled to legal obedience, and sincere respect. These it is a duty to render them ; and these no
good or prudent person will withhold. But when these
officers, thro' rashness or design, desire to enlarge their
authority beyond its due limits, and expect improper concessions to be made to them, from regard for the employments they bear, their attempts should be considered as
equal injuries to the crown and people, and should be courageously and constantly opposed. To suffer our ideas to
be confounded by *names* on such occasions, would certainly
be an *inexcusable weakness*, and probably an *irremediable
error*.

We have reason to believe, that several of his Majesty's
present ministers are good men, and friends to our country;
and it seems not unlikely, that by a particular concurrence
of events, we have been treated a little more severely than
they wished we should be. *They* might not think it prudent to stem a torrent. But what is the difference to *us*,
whether arbitrary acts take their rise from ministers, or
are permitted by them? Ought any point to be allowed to*
a good minister, that should be denied to a bad one? The
mortality of ministers, is a very frail mortality. A———
may succeed a *Shelburne*—A——— may succeed a *Corn-
way*.

We find a new kind of minister lately spoken of at home
—"THE MINISTER OF THE HOUSE OF COMMONS." The
term seems to have peculiar propriety when referred to
these colonies, *with a different meaning annexed to it*,
from that in which it is taken there. By the word "minister" we may understand not only a *servant of the crown*,

---

* Ubi imperium ad ignaros aut minus bonos pervenit ; *novum illud ex-
emplum*, ad dignis, & idoneis, ad indignos & non idoneos *transfertur*.
                                                    Sall. Bell. Cat. ≀ 50.

but a *man of influence* among the commons, who regard themselves as having a share in the *sovereignty* over us. The "minister OF the house" may, in a point respecting the colonies, be so strong, that the minister of the crown *in* the house, if he is a distinct person, may not choose, even where his sentiments are favorable to us, to come to a pitched battle upon our account. For tho' I have the highest opinion of the deference of the house for the King's minister, yet he may be so good natured, as not to put it to the test, except it be for the mere and immediate profit of his master or himself.

But whatever kind of *minister* he is, that attempts to innovate *a single iota* in the privileges of these colonies, him I hope you will *undauntedly oppose;* and that you will never suffer yourselves to be either *cheated* or *frightened* into any *unworthy obsequiousness.* On such emergencies you may surely, without presumption, believe, that ALMIGHTY GOD himself will look down upon your righteous contest with gracious approbation. You will be a "*band of brothers,*" cemented by the dearest ties,—and strengthened with inconceivable supplies of force and constancy, by that sympathetc ardor, which animates good men, confederated in a good cause. Your *honor* and *welfare* will be, as they now are, most intimately concerned ; and besides—*you are assigned by divine providence,* in the appointed order of things, the *protectors of unborn ages,* whose *fate* depends upon your *virtue.* Whether *they* shall arise the *generous* and *indisputable heirs* of the noblest patrimonies, or the *dastardly* and *hereditary drudges* of imperious task-masters, YOU MUST DETERMINE.

To discharge this double duty to *yourselves,* and to your *posterity,* you have nothing to do, but to call forth into use the *good sense* and *spirit* of which you are possessed. You have nothing to do, but to conduct your affairs *peaceably—prudently—firmly—jointly.* By *these means* you will support the character of *freemen*, without losing that of *faithful subjects*—a good character in any government—one of the best under a *British* government—You will *prove*, that *Americans* have that true *magnanimity* of soul, that can resent injuries, without falling into rage; and that tho' your devotion to *Great-Britain* is the most affectionate, yet you can make PROPER DISTINCTIONS, and know what you owe *to yourselves*, as well as to her—You will, at the same time that you advance your *interests*, advance your *reputation*—You will convince the world of the *justice of your demands*, and the *purity of your intentions*. —While all mankind must, with unceasing applauses, confess, [71] that YOU indeed DESERVE liberty, who so *well understand* it, so *passionately love* it, so *temperately enjoy* it, and so *wisely*, *bravely*, and *virtuously assert*, *maintain*, and *defend* it.

" *Certe ego libertatem, quæ mihi a parente meo tradita est, experiar : Verum id frustra an ob rem faciam, in vestra manu situm est, quirites.*"

For my part I am resolved to contend for the liberty delivered down to me by my ancestors ; but whether I shall do it effectually or not, depends on you, my countrymen.

" How little soever one is able to write, yet when the liberties of one's country are threatened, it is still more difficult to be silent."

A FARMER.

Is there not the strongest probability, that if the universal sense of these colonies is immediately expressed by RESOLVES of the assemblies, in support of their rights, by INSTRUCTIONS to their agents on the subject, and by PETITIONS to the crown and parliament for redress, these measures will have the same success now, that they had in the time of the *Stamp-Act.*   D.

FINIS.

AN ADDRESS

READ

AT A

MEETING OF MERCHANTS

TO CONSIDER

NON-IMPORTATION.

BY

JOHN DICKINSON.

———

APRIL 25, 1768.

NOTE.

In the third "Letter of a Farmer," in commenting upon the act "for raising a further revenue," better known as the act granting duties on paper, glass, etc., Dickinson recommended petitions to the colonial assemblies asking them to protest against that act; and that failing to obtain its repeal, then an opposition which should consist in "the prevention of the oppressors reaping advantage from their oppression," by "withholding from Great-Britain all the advantages she has been used to receive from them." The effect of this recommendation followed quickly. February 11, 1768, the Massachusetts Assembly, taking "into their serious Consideration the great Difficulties that must accrue to themselves and their Constituents by the Operation of the several acts of Parliament, imposing Duties and Taxes," by their famous circular letter to the various assemblies, which is, in truth, a paraphrase of the Farmer's letters stated that they had so petitioned the home government and "shall take it kind in your House to point out to them any Thing further which may be thought necessary." This letter was laid before the Pennsylvania Assembly, May 10th. That body had already instructed their Agent to protest against the acts, but controlled by Galloway, it paid no attention to the circular letter beyond entering it upon its minutes.

Nor was this the only discouragement to the Massachusetts extremists. At a meeting on October 28, 1767, the Boston freeholders had voted to discontinue the use of British manufactures, as well as encourage the use of American products in every possible way, and directed that these resolutions should be forwarded to the different towns in the colonies. Franklin wrote that the "resolutions about manufactures have hurt us much, and one of the Ministry in Parliament stated that but for them the obnoxious tax act would have been at once repealed." The popular party in Philadelphia, however, agreed with the Bostonians, and upon receiving the letter, called a meeting to consider what action should be taken upon it. The result, however, was disappointing to the callers of the meeting, for it was voted merely to return an expression of sympathy. Upon the receipt of this answer the Boston merchants once more wrote to Philadelphia pleading for a non-importation agreement, and stating that they would suspend all importations of goods from Great Britain during twelve months from December 31st, 1768, provided the "colonies of New-York, Pennsylvania, &c.," would do the same.

This was considered at a meeting of the Philadelphia merchants, March 26, 1768, but the proposition was unsatisfactory to the Philadelphia merchants and after a heated debate the meeting ended in no definite action. The merchants urged, that the non-importation should only extend to the articles actually taxed in the obnoxious act, and that the non-importation should be made immediate and not at so late a date as to allow the merchants to lay in a large stock of goods. Indeed, the Philadelphia merchants looked upon the proposition partly in the light of a trick, for they well knew that the New-England ports were notorious for smuggling, and that therefore a non-importation agreement would little affect New-England, while practically destroying the trade of their city, and they therefore considered such a proposition unfair.

Despairing of any united compulsory action from the merchants, the popular party then brought forward a voluntary association, not to import any goods after October 1st, 1768. To induce the merchants to sign it a meeting was called for April 28, 1868, which the popular party succeeded in having addressed by Dickinson, who, though in sympathy with Thomson, Reed, Mifflin, and the other extremists, was nevertheless respected by the leading men of the city, and therefore likely to exert more influence. Under these circumstances the following address was read. The subsequent proceedings will be found post in the note to a "Letter to a Merchant in Philadelphia," *post.*

This address of Dickinson's was printed without his name in the *Pennsylvania Journal* of April 28, 1768, and also as a broadside, with the head-lines:

The following / Address / was read at a Meeting of the Merchants, at the Lodge, in Philadelphia, on Monday, / the 25th of April, 1768. /

It was later printed in the *Prior Documents*, with the statement that it was "written by Mr. Dickinson, author of the Farmer's Letters."

EDITOR.

AN ADDRESS.

Gentlemen, Friends, and Fellow-citizens:

You are called together to give your Advice and Opinion, what Answer shall be returned to our Brethren of *Boston & New York*, who desire to know, whether we will unite with them, in stopping the Importation of Goods from *Great-Britain;* until certain Acts of Parliament are repealed, which are thought to be injurious to our Rights, as Freemen and *British* subjects.

Before you come to any Resolution it may be necessary to explain the Matter more fully.

When our Forefathers came to this Country, they considered themselves as Freemen, and that their coming and settling these Colonies did not divest them of any of the Rights inherent in Freemen ; that, therefore, what they possessed, and what they or their Posterity should acquire, was and would be so much their own, that no Power on Earth could lawfully, or of Right, deprive them of it without their Consent. The Governments, which they, with the consent of the Crown, established in the respective Colonies, they considered as political Governments, "where (as Mr. *Locke* expresses it) Men have "Property in their own Disposal." And therefore (according to the Conclusion drawn by the same Author in another Place) "No Taxes ought or could be raised on "their Property without their Consent given by them-"selves or their Deputies," or chosen Representatives.

As they were Members of one great Empire, united under one Head or Crown, they tacitly acquiesced in the superintending Authority of the Parliament of *Great-*

Britain and admitted a Power in it, to make Regulations to preserve the Connection of the whole entire. Though under Colour of this, sundry Regulations were made that bore hard on the Colonies; yet, with filial Respect and Regard for *Great-Britain* their Mother Country, the Colonies submitted to them.

It will be sufficient here just to enumerate some of the most grievous.

1. The Law against making Steel or erecting Steel Furnaces, though there are not above 5 or 6 Persons in *England* engaged in that Branch of Business, who are so far from being able to supply what is wanted, that great Quantities of Steel are yearly imported from *Germany*.

2. Against Plating and Sliting Mills and Tilt Hammers; though Iron is the Produce of our Country, and from our Manner of building, planting, and living, we are under a Necessity of using vast Quantities of Nails and Plated Iron, as Hoes, Stove-Pipes, Plates, *&c.*, all which are loaded with double Freight, Commissions, *&c.*

3. The Restraint laid on Hatters, and the Prohibition of exporting Hats.

4. The Prohibition of carrying Wool or any Kind of Woollen Goods manufactured here, from one Colony to another. A single Fleece of Wool or a Dozen of home-made Hose carried from one Colony to another is not only forfeited, but subjects the Vessel, if conveyed by Water, or the Waggon and Horses, if carried by Land, to a Seizure, and the Owner to a heavy Fine.

5. Though the *Spaniards* may cut and carry Logwood directly to what Market they please, yet the *Americans* cannot send to any foreign Market, even what the Demand in *England* cannot take off, without first carrying it to some *British* Port, and there landing and re-shipping it at a great Expence and loss of Time.

6. Obliging us to carry *Portugal* and *Spanish* Wines,

Fruit, *&c.*, to *England*, there to unload, pay a heavy Duty and re-ship them, thus subjecting us to a great Expence, and our Vessels to an unnecessary Voyage of 1000 Miles in a dangerous Sea.

7. Imposing a Duty on *Madeira* Wines, which, if re-shipped to *England*, are subject to the Payment of the full Duties there without any Drawback for what was paid here.

8. The emptying their Jails upon us and making the Colonies a Receptacle for their Rogues and Villains ; an Insult and Indignity not to be thought of, much less borne without Indignation and Resentment.

Not to mention the Restrictions attempted in the Fisheries, the Duties laid on foreign Sugar, Molasses, *&c.* I will just mention the Necessity they have laid us under of supplying ourselves wholly from *Great-Britain* with *European* and *East-India* Goods, at an Advance of 20, and as to some Articles even of 40 per Cent. higher than we might be supplied with them from other places.

But as if all these were not enough, a Party has lately arisen in *England*, who, under Colour of the superintending Authority of Parliament are labouring to erect a new Sovereignty over the Colonies with Power inconsistent with Liberty or Freedom.

The first Exertion of this Power was displayed in the odious Stamp-Act. As the Authors and Promoters of this Act were sensible of the Opposition it must necessarily meet with, from Men, who had the least Spark of Liberty remaining, they accompanied it with a Bill still more odious, wherein they attempted to empower Officers to quarter Soldiers on private Houses, with a view, no Doubt, to dragoon us into a Compliance with the former Act.

By the Interposition of the *American* Agents and of some *London* Merchants who traded to the Colonies, this Clause was dropt, but the Act was carried, wherein the Assemblies of the respective Colonies were ordered at the

Expence of the several Provinces, to furnish the Troops with a Number of Articles, some of them never allowed in *Britain*. Besides, a Power is therein granted to every Officer, upon obtaining a Warrant from any Justice, (which Warrant the Justice is thereby empowered and ordered to grant, without any previous Oath) to break into any House by Day or by Night, under Pretence (these are the Words[l] of the Act) of searching for Deserters.

By the spirited Opposition of the Colonies, the first Act was repealed; but the latter continued, which, in its Spirit differs nothing from the other. For thereby the Liberty of the Colonies is invaded and their property disposed of without their Consent, no less than by the Stamp-Act. It was rather the more dangerous of the two, as the Appearance of the Constitution was preserved, while the Spirit of it was destroyed, and thus a Tyranny introduced under the Forms of Liberty. The Assemblies were not at Liberty to refuse their Assent, but were to be forced to a litteral Compliance with the Act. Thus, because the Assembly of *New-York* hesitated to comply, their Legislative Power was immediately suspended by another Act of Parliament.

That the Repeal of the Stamp-Act might not invalidate the Claims of Sovereignty now set up, an Act was passed, asserting the Power of Parliament to bind us with their Laws in every respect whatever. And to ascertain the Extent of this Power, in the very next Session they proceeded to a direct Taxation; and in the very Words in which they dispose of their own Property, they gave and granted that of the Colonies, imposing Duties on Paper, Glass, *&c.*, imported into *America*, to be paid by the Colonists, for the Purpose of raising a Revenue.

This Revenue when raised, they ordered to be disposed of in such a Manner as to render our Assemblies or Legislative Bodies altogether useless, and to make Governors,

& Judges, who hold their Commission during Pleasure, and the whole executive Powers of Government; nay, the Defence of the Country, independant of the People, as has been fully explained in the *Farmer's Letters*.

Thus with a Consistency of Conduct, having divested us of Property, they are proceeding to erect over us a despotic Government, and to rule us as Slaves. For "a "despotical Power, says Mr. *Locke*, is over such as have "no Property at all." If, indeed, to be subject in our Lives and Property to the arbitrary Will of others, whom we have never chosen, nor ever entrusted with such a Power, be not Slavery, I wish, any Person would tell me what Slavery is.

Such then being the State of the Case, you are now, my Fellow-Citizens, to deliberate, not, whether you will tamely submit to this System of Government—That I am sure your Love of Freedom and Regard for yourselves and your Posterity will never suffer you to think of—But by what Means you may defend your Rights and Liberties, and obtain a Repeal of these Acts.

In *England*, when the Prerogative has been strained too high, or the People oppressed by the executive Power, the Parliament, who are the Guardians and Protectors of the People's Liberties, always petition for Redress of Grievances, and enforce their Petitions, by withholding Supplies until they are granted.

Our Assembly, who are the Guardians and Protectors of our Liberties, I am told, has applied for Relief from their Acts of Parliament. But having nothing left to give, they could not enforce their Application by withholding any Thing.

It is, however, in our Power, in a peaceable and constitutional Way, to add Weight, to the Remonstrance and Petition of our Representatives, by stopping the Importation of Goods from *Britain*, until we obtain Relief and Redress by a Repeal of these unconstitutional Acts.

But this, it may be said, is subjecting ourselves to present Loss and Inconvenience.

I would beg Leave to ask, whether any People in any Age or Country ever defended and preserved their Liberty from the Encroachment of Power, without suffering present Inconveniences. The *Roman* People suffered themselves to be defeated by their Enemies, rather than submit to the Tyranny of the Nobles. And even in the Midst of War, the Parliament of *England* has denied to grant Supplies, until their Grievances were redressed; well knowing that no present Loss, Suffering, or Inconvenience, could equal that of Tyranny or the Loss of Public Liberty. To cite an Example, which our own Country furnishes; you all remember that in the very Heighth of the late terrible *Indian* War, our Assembly and that of *Maryland* chose rather to let the Country suffer great Inconvenience, than immediately grant Supplies on Terms injurious to the public Privileges and to Justice.

As then we cannot enjoy Liberty without Property, both in our Lives and Estates; as we can have no Property in that which another may of Right take and dispose of as he pleases, without our Consent ; and as the late Acts of Parliament assert this Right to be in them, we cannot enjoy Freedom until this Claim is given up, and until the Acts made in Consequence of it be repealed. For so long as these Acts continue and the Claim is kept up, our Property is at their Disposal, and our Lives at their Mercy.

To conclude, as Liberty is the great and only Security of Property; as the Security of Property is the chief Spur to Industry, (it being Vain to acquire what we have not a Prospect to enjoy); and as the Stopping the Importation of Goods is the only probable Means of preserving to us and our Posterity this Liberty and Security, I hope, my Brethren, there is not a Man among us, who will not chearfully join in the Measure proposed, and with our

Brethren of *Boston* and *New-York* freely forego a Present Advantage; nay, even submit to a present Inconvenience for the Sake of Liberty, on which our Happiness, Lives, and Properties depend. Let us never forget that our Strength depends on our Union, and our Liberty on our Strength.

" *United we conquer, divided we die.*"

A SONG

FOR

AMERICAN FREEDOM.

BY

JOHN DICKINSON.

———

JULY, 1768.

NOTE.

The greatest problem in American politics for over one hundred years, was to obtain united action, and to this, nearly every American statesman gave his chief thought and labor. As early as May, 1754, Franklin printed his divided serpent, with the legend "Join or die," and from that time on, its constant republication in various forms and versions proved how pressing every American felt the question of union to be. This feeling produced the Massachusetts circular letter of February 11, 1768, pleading for united opposition to England, and when the Philadelphia Merchants quickly met to consider what action should be taken, Dickinson ended his address to them with the words: "United we conquer, divided we die." But a few weeks later, he wrote and published a song, enforcing the same idea, in which he struck the phrase:

"By uniting we stand, by dividing we fall"—

a line so epigrammatic of our crying need, that it has lived to this day, and grafted upon another song, is still sung, as our ancestors sang it, in now forgotten words and tune, one hundred and twenty-five years ago.

Dickinson sent a copy of the song to Otis, with the following letter:

PHILADELPHIA, *July* 4th, 1768.

DEAR SIR: I inclose you a song for American freedom. I have long since renounced poetry. But as indifferent songs are frequently very powerful on certain occasions, I venture to invoke the deserted muses. I hope that my good intentions will procure pardon with those I wish to please, for the boldness of my numbers.

My worthy friend, Dr. Arthur Lee, a gentleman of distinguished family, abilities and patriotism, in Virginia, composed eight lines of it.

Cardinal de Retz always inforced his political operations by songs. I wish our attempt may be useful. I shall be glad to hear from you, if you have a moment's leisure to scribble a line to, dear sir, your most affectionate, most obedient servant,   JOHN DICKINSON.

Only two days later, Dickinson again wrote Otis:

DEAR SIR: I inclosed to you the other day the copy of a song com-

(421)

posed in great haste, I think it was rather too bold, I now send a corrected copy, which I like better. If you think the bagatelle worth
publishing, I beg it may be this copy, If the first is published before
this comes to hand, I shall be much obliged to you if you will be so
good as to publish this with some little note "that this is a true copy
of the original."

In this copy I think it may be well enough to add between the fourth
and fifth stanzas, these lines:

> How sweet are the labours that freemen endure,
> That they shall enjoy all the profits secure.
> No more such sweet labours Americans know,
> If Britons shall reap what Americans sow.
> In freedom we're born, &c.

I am dear sir, with the utmost sincerity, your most affectionate and
most humble servant,   JOHN DICKINSON.

This song achieved a really marvelous success. Set to the tune of the
old English "Hearts of Oak," it was sung throughout the colonies.
The *Massachusetts Gazette* of August 18, 1768, states that at a great meeting of "persons of credit at Liberty Hall, the much admired American song
was melodiously sung" whereupon "the gentlemen set out in their char-
iots and chaises for the Greyhound Tavern in Roxbury, where an elegant
entertainment was provided. After dinner the new song was again sung,
and forty-five toasts drunk. After consecrating a tree to Liberty in Roxbury, they made an agreeable excursion round Jamaica Pond; and it is
allowed that this cavalcade surpassed all that has ever been seen in America." The *Evening-Post* of August 22, 1768, further noticed this as follows: "On Monday the 15th instant, the anniversary of the ever memorable 14th of August, was celebrated by the sons of liberty in this town, with
extraordinary festivity. At the dawn, the British flag was displayed on
the Tree of Liberty, and a discharge of fourteen cannon, ranged under the
venerable elm, saluted the joyous day. At eleven o'clock a very large
company of the principal gentlemen and respectable inhabitants of the
town, met at the hall under the tree, while the streets were crowded with
a concourse of people of all ranks, public notice have been given of the
intended celebration. The music began at high noon, performed on various instruments, joined with voices; and concluding with the universal
admired American song of liberty. The grandeur of its sentiment, and
the easy flow of its numbers, together with an exquisite harmony of

sound, afforded sublime entertainment to a numerous audience, fraught with a noble ardour in the cause of freedom : the song was closed with a discharge of cannon and a shout of joy ; at the same time the windows of the neighbouring houses, were adorned with a brilliant appearance of the fair daughters of Liberty, who testified their approbation. Which being finished, the French horns sounded ; and after another discharge of the cannon, completing the number ninety-two, the gentlemen in their carriages repaired to the Greyhound tavern iu Roxbury, where a *frugal* and *elegant* entertainment was provided. The music played during the repast: after which several partinent toasts were given out, and the repeated discharge of cannon spoke the general assent. Upon this happy occasion, the whole company, with the approbation of their brethren in Roxbury, consecrated a tree in the vicinity ; under the shade of which, on some future anniversary, they may commemorate the day, which shall liberate America from her present oppression ! Then making an agreeable excursion round Jamaica pond, in which excursion they received the salutation of a friend to the cause by the discharge of cannon, at six o'clock they returned to town ; and passing in slow and orderly procession through the principal streets, and round the statehouse, they retired to their respective dwellings. It is allowed that this cavalcade surpassed all that has ever been seen in America. The joy of the day was manly, and an uninterrupted regularity presided thro' the whole." Again, a year later, on August 14, 1769, John Adams records (*Works*, II, 218), that he "dined with three hundred and fifty sons of Liberty, at Robinson's, the sign of the Liberty tree in Dorchester . . . After dinner was over and the toasts drunk, we were diverted with Mr. Balch's mimicry . . . We had also the Liberty Song—that by the farmer, and that by Dr. Church, and the whole company joined in the chorus. This is cultivating the sensations of freedom."

No copy of the first version, which Dickinson thought "too bold " has been preserved. That here printed is from the original Philadelphia broadside edition, and is what I term the second text. The headlines were as follows:

" A New Song / To the Tune of Hearts of Oak," &c., / [Philadelphia: Hall and Sellers. 1768.] / Fol. Broadside.

It was at once reprinted from this in the *Pennsylvania Gazette* and in the *Pennsylvania Journal,* for July 7th, 1768. From one of these sources it was republished in the *New York Gazette,* for July 11, 1768, the *Boston Gazette,* for July 18, 1768) and in the *Boston Chronicle,* for September 5, 1768. Dickinson added to it his new stanza (which I te:m the third text), and sent it to the *Pennsylvania Chronicle,* where it v as printed in the issue for July 11, 1768, in this revised form, with the following note:

"Mr. Goddard. Please to insert the following Song in your next Chronicle, and you will oblige yours, &c., D."

In addition to this newspaper publication, it was printed in Boston by Mein and Fleming, as a broadside, of which I have been able to find no copy. This edition was advertised in the *Boston Chronicle* for Sept. 12, 1768, as follows:

The New and Favorite
LIBERTY SONG
Neatly engraved on COPPER-PLATE the
size of a half sheet of Paper,
Set to MUSIC for the VOICE
And to which is added,
A Set of NOTES adapted to the
German flute and Violin
Is just published and to be SOLD at the
London *Book-store King-Street,* Boston,
Price SIXPENCE LAWFUL single, and
Four SHILLINGS LAWFUL, the dozen.

The words and music were also reproduced in:

"Bickerstaff's / Boston Almanack / For the year of our Lord 1769; Being the first year after Leap Year / [Portrait of Wilkes] / Boston: Printed by Mein and Fleming, and to be sold by John / Mein, at the London Book-store, North-side of King street. / [Price seven Coppers single, and 25s Old Tenor, or 3s, 4d Lawful the Dozen.]

These words and music are here reproduced. In the preface to the almanac the compiler stated:

"Courteous Reader * * *

I have been careful to insert whatever I thought would best conduce to the Entertainment and Instruction of the Reader:—I shall only mention two Articles as Instances.—

1st. The Plate of the Favorite Liberty Song, In Freedom We're Born and in Freedom We'll Live, single Copies of which have been sold in great Numbers at Six Pence Lawful Money each."

The LIBERTY SONG. *In Freedom we're born, &c.*

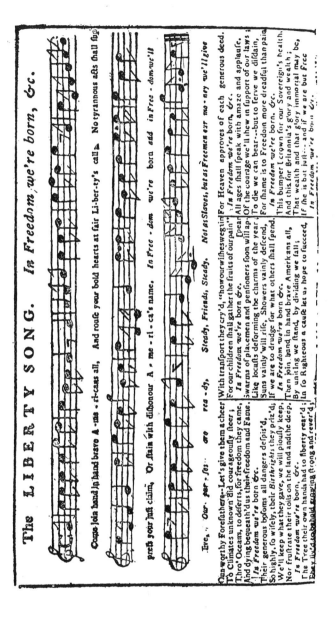

Come join hand in hand brave A‑me‑ri‑cans all, And rouse your bold hearts at fair Li‑ber‑ty's call. No tyrannous acts shall sup‑

press your just claim, Or stain with dishonour A ‑ me ‑ ri ‑ ca's name. In Free ‑ dom we're born and in Free ‑ dom we'll

live. . Our pur‑ ses are rea‑ dy. Steady, Friends, Steady. Not as Slaves, but as Freemen our mo‑ ney we'll give

Our worthy Forefathers‑‑Let's give them a cheer
To Climates unknown did courageously steer;
Thro' Oceans, to deserts, for freedom they came,
And dying bequeath'd us their freedom and Fame.
  In Freedom we're born, &c.

Their generous bosoms all dangers despis'd,
So highly, so wisely, their *Birthrights* they priz'd;
We'll keep what they gave, we will piously keep,
Nor frustrate their toils on the land and the deep.
The Tree their own hands had to liberty rear'd;
They liv'd to behold growing strong and rever'd;

With transport they cry'd, "now our wishes we gain
For our children shall gather the fruits of our pain"
  In Freedom we're born, &c.

Swarms of placemen and pensioners soon will ap‑
        [pear
Like locusts deforming the charms of the year;
Suns vainly will rise, Showers vainly will descend,
If we are to drudge for what others shall spend.
  In Freedom we're born, &c.

Then join hand in hand brave Americans all,
By uniting we stand, by dividing we fall;
In so Righteous a cause let us hope to succeed,

For Heaven approves of each generous deed.
  In Freedom we're born, &c.

All ages shall speak with amaze and applause,
Of the courage we'll shew in support of our laws;
To die we can bear‑‑but to serve we disdain,
For shame is to Freedom more dreadful than pain.
  In Freedom we're born, &c.

This bumper I crown for our Sovereign's health,
And this for Britannia's glory and wealth;
That wealth and that glory immortal may be,
If she is but just‑‑and if we are but Free
  In Freedom we're born, &c.

The song was also reprinted in Edes' and Gills' Almanac for 1770, under the title of : " A New Song, now much in vogue in North America, to the tune of the Hearts of Oak," and again, in the Virginia edition of the Letters of a Farmer.

The song was at once parodied in one entitled "The Parody," printed in *The Boston Gazette* of Sept. 26, 1768, where it was stated that, "last Tuesday the following song made an appearance from a garrett at Castle William :"

THE PARODY.

Come shake your dull noddles, ye pumpkins, and bawl,
And own that you're mad at fair Liberty's call;
No scandalous conduct can add to your shame,
Condemn'd to dishonor, inherit the fame.
   In folly you're born, and in folly you'll live,
      To madness still ready,
      And stupidly steady,
   Not as men, but as monkeys, the tokens you give.

Your grandsire, old Satan, now give him a cheer,
Would act like yourselves, and as wildly would steer :
So great an example in prospect still keep,
Whilst you are alive, Old Belza may sleep.

Such villains, such rascals, all dangers despise,
And stick not at mobbing when mischief's the prize ;
They burst thro' all barriers, and piously keep
Such chattels and goods the vile rascals can sweep.

The Tree, which the wisdom of justice hath rear'd,
Should be stout for their use, and by no means be spar'd :
When fuddled with rum the mad sots to restrain,
Sure Tyburn will sober the wretches again.

Your brats and your bunters by no means forget,
But feather your nests, for they're bare enough yet ;
From the insolent rich sure the poor knave may steal,
Who ne'er in his life knew the scent of a meal.

When in your own cellars you've quaffed a regale,
Then drive, tug and ——, the next house to assail ;
For short is your harvest, nor long shall you know
The pleasure of reaping what other men sow.

Then plunder, my lads, for when red coats appear
You'll melt like the locust when winter is near ;
Gold vainly will glow, silver vainly will shine,
But, faith, you must skulk, you no more shall purloin.

Then nod your poor numskulls, ye pumpkins, and bawl,
The de'il take such rascals, fools, whoresons and all ;
Your cursed old trade of purloining must cease,
The dread and the curse of all order and peace.

All ages shall speak with contempt and amaze,
Of the vilest banditti that swarm'd in these days ;
In defiance of halters, of whips and of chains,
The rogues would run riot,—fools for their pains.

Gulp down your last dram, for the gallows now groans,
And, over depress'd, her lost empire bemoans
While we quite transported and happy shall be,
From mobs, knaves and villains, protected and free.

This was in turn parodied by a song entitled "The Parody parodized.*
printed, with music, in Edes' and Gills' *Almanac* for 1770. This latter,
according to Lossing and Winsor, was by Mercy Warren. But they evi
dently are in error, for in the quotation from Adams' diary, already quoted
in this note, it is spoken of as written by Dr. Benjamin Church. It was
as follows :

THE PARODY PARODISED.

Come swallow your bumpers, ye tories, and roar,
That the sons of fair Freedom are hamper'd once more;
But know that no cut-throats our spirit can tame,
Nor a host of oppressors shall smother the flame.
In freedom we're born, and, like sons of the brave,
We'll never surrender,
But swear to defend her,
And scorn to survive, if unable to save.

Our grandsires, blest heroes! we'll give them a tear,
Nor sully their honors, by stooping to fear ;
Thro' deaths and thro' dangers their trophies they won,
We dare be their rivals, nor will be outdone.

Let tyrants and minions presume to despise,
Encroach on our rights, and make freedom their prize:
The fruits of their rapine they never shall keep ;
Tho' vengeance may nod, yet how short is her sleep!

The tree, which proud Haman for Mordecai rear'd,
Stands recorded, that virtue endanger'd is spar'd,
That rogues whom no bounds and no laws can restrain,
Must be stript of their honors, and humbled again.

Our wives and our babes, still protected, shall know,
Those who dare to be free, shall forever be so;
On these arms and these hearts they may safely rely,
For in freedom we'll live, or like heroes we'll die.

Ye insolent tyrants! who wish to enthrall
Ye minions, ye placemen, pimps, pensioners, all,
How short is your triumph! how feeble your trust!
Your honor must wither and nod to the dust.

When oppress'd and reproach'd, our king we implore,
Still firmly persuaded our rights he'll restore!
When our hearts beat to arms, to defend a just right,
Our monarch rules there, and forbids us to fight.

Not the glitter of arms, nor the dread of a fray,
Could make us submit to their chains for a day ·
Withheld by affection, on Britons we call,
Prevent the fierce conflict which threatens your fall!

All ages shall speak, with amaze and applause,
Of the prudence we show in support of our cause!
Assur'd of our safety, a Brunswick still reigns,
Whose free loyal subjects are strangers to chains.

Then join hand in hand, brave Americans all!
To be free is to live, to be slaves is to fall:
Has the land such a dastard, as scorns not a lord,
Who dreads not a fetter much more than a sword.
In freedom we're born, and, like sons of the brave,
    We'll never surrender,
    But swear to defend her,
And scorn to survive, if unable to save.

Editor.

A NEW SONG.

To the Tune of "Hearts of Oak, *etc.*"

COME join Hand in Hand, brave AMERICANS all,
And rouse your bold Hearts at fair LIBERTY' Call ;
No *tyrannous Acts* shall suppress your *just Claim*
Or stain with *Dishonor* AMERICA's Name—
     In FREEDOM we're BORN, and in FREEDOM we'll LIVE,
          Our Purses are ready,
          Steady, Friends, Steady,
     Not as SLAVES, but as FREEMEN our Money we'll give.

Our worthy *Forefathers*—let's give them a Cheer—
To *Climates unknown* did courageously steer ;
Thro' *Oceans* to *Deserts* for *Freeaom* they came,
And dying bequeath'd us their *Freeaom* and *Fame.*
     In FREEDOM we're BORN, *etc.*

Their generous Bosoms all Dangers despis'd,
So *highly*, so *wisely*, their BIRTH-RIGHTS they priz'd ,
We'll keep what they gave, we will piously keep,
Nor frusttate their Toils on the Land and the Deep.
     In FREEDOM we're BORN, *etc.*

The TREE their own Hands had to LIBERTY rear'd,
They liv'd to behold growing strong and rever'd ;
With Transport then cry'd, "Now our Wishes we gain,
For our Children shall gather the Fruits of our Pain."
     In FREEDOM we're BORN, *etc.**

*In the text given in the *Pennsylvania Chronicle*, the following stanza is here in-
erted :

         "How sweet are the labors that Freemen endure,
         That *they* shall enjoy all the Profit, secure—
         No more such sweet Labors AMERICANS know
         If Britons shall *reap* what Americans sow."—*Ed.*

(431)

Swarms of PLACEMEN and PENSIONERS * soon will appear
Like Locusts deforming the Charms of the Year ;
Suns vainly will rise, Showers vainly descend,
If *we* are to *drudge for* what *others* shall *spend.*
    In FREEDOM we're BORN, *etc.*

Then join Hand in Hand brave AMERICANS all,
By *uniting* We stand, by *dividing* We fall ;
IN SO RIGHTEOUS A CAUSE let us hope to succeed,
For Heaven approves of each generous Deed—
    In FREEDOM we're BORN, *etc.*

All Ages shall speak with *Amaze* and *Applause,*
Of the *Courage* we'll shew IN SUPPORT OF OUR LAWS;
To DIE we can *bear,*—but, to SERVE we *disdain*—
For SHAME is to *Freemen* more dreadful than PAIN—
    In FREEDOM we're BORN, *etc.*

This Bumper *I* crown for our SOVEREIGN'S Health.
And this for BRITANNIA'S Glory and Wealth ;
That Wealth and that Glory immortal may be,
If *She* is but *just* —and if *We* are but *Free*—
    In FREEDOM we're BORN, *etc.*

* The *Ministry* have already begun to give away in PENSIONS *the Money* THEY have *lately* taken out of OUR Pockets WITHOUT OUR CONSENT.

LETTER

TO THE

PHILADELPHIA MERCHANTS

CONCERNiNG

NON-IMPORTATION.

BY

JOHN DICKINSON.

JULY, 1768.

NOTE.

IN spite of Dickinson's arguments in his *Address to The Merchants* (*ante*) the Philadelphia voluntary association for non-importation proved inaffective by the few signatures that were given to it. Indeed the point of view of the popular party, as expressed by Arthur Lee, in the *Pennsylvania Chronicle* of May 30, 1768, was that "the spirit of liberty is lukewarm in this powerful and important city." The failure at once became a subject of newspaper controversy. Charles Thomson, over the signature of "A Freeborn American," in the *Pennsylvania Gazette* of May 12, 1768, attacked the merchants bitterly, and this was echoed by an anonymous letter in the *Gazette* for June 2nd. These were answered by Galloway, over the signature of "A Chester County Farmer," in the *Gazette* of June 24th, stating that the Philadelphia merchants had "discovered the secret intention in the New-England scheme; that it would be very disadvantageous to the Trade of this Province, and when we compare the flourishing and great increase in our Trade with the various accounts we have of their [the Boston] long declining state . . . they [Philadelphia and Boston] cannot be thought on any equal footing."

This was in turn replied to, probably by Thomson, in the *Gazette* for July 21, over the signature of "Martinus Scriblerius." Galloway continued the subject, by a set of "queries" to the Philadelphia merchants in the *Pennsylvania Chronicle* for July 25, signed "A. B.," which were replied to by "C." in the *Gazette* of Aug. 4, 1768. Nor was the controversy limited in print to the newspapers. Dickinson published a piece entitled:

A copy of a letter from a Gentleman of Virginia, / To a Merchant in Philadelphia. / Folio. Broadside.

This was answered in another sheet, signed "Pacificus," probably written by Galloway, entitled :

To the Public / Philadelphia: Printed by William Goddard. / 4to, Broadside.

A copy of Dickinson's broadside, in the Arthur Lee papers, is endorsed,

(435)

"Wrote by Mr. Dickinson, and copied by me for the printer;" making it evident that Dickinson did not wish the merchants to know that he was joining in the abuse of them.

The attempt to obtain a non-importation agreement did not end with this apparent failure. On Aug. 15, 1768, the freeholders of Boston adopted such an agreement, which was imitated by the New York merchants Aug. 25. Under the pressure of this action, the Philadelphia merchants appointed a committee to endeavor to obtain a like agreement; but though the committee met several times, they were compelled to report the measure impracticable, though the leading merchants were willing to agree not to import the articles specially taxed. Finally a public meeting was called, for Sept. 22, by the committee, but not a fourth of the merchants attended it, and nothing was accomplished, This renewed the newspaper warfare, a bitter article appearing in the *New York Journal* for Oct. 6, attacking the Philadelphia merchants, and claiming that the measure had been defeated by the refusal of only eight or ten firms. This was answered in a "narrative" in the *Pennsylvania Gazette*, which is apparently official, and is a most valuable paper. To this a reply was printed in the *New York Journal* for Nov. 3, 1768. Here the matter rested some time, the extremists having failed to force their measures, so that Galloway wrote Franklin, "Great pains have been taken in this city by some hotheaded, indiscreet men, to raise a spirit of violence against the late act of parliament, but the design was crushed in its beginnings by our friends so effectually, that I think we shall not have it renewed." In this Galloway erred, for finally, in March, 1769, the Philadelphia merchants, induced by a boycott, threats of mob violence, and other stress, united in a non-importation agreement. Under such circumstances it could hardly have been expected that it would be successfully enforced, and as early as April there were charges of violation bandying between Boston, New York, and Philadelphia, which hardly furthered "united action." How Boston cheated at the triangular game was published at the time in Mein's *State of Importations from Great Britain into the Port of Boston;* and just how far each colony lived up to its promises is shown by comparison of the actual figures of imports for four years, under unrestricted trade, and under the agreements:

	1767-8.	*1768-9.*	*1769-70.*	*1770-1.*
New England,	£419,375	£207,993	£394,451	£1,420,119
New York,	482,930	74,918	475,991	653,621
Pennsylvania,	432,107	199,909	134,881	728,744
Maryland and Virginia,	475,954	488,362	717,782	920,326
Carolina,	289,868	306,600	146,273	409,169

—bearing out Lord North's statement in Parliament that "New York has kept strictly to its agreements, but infractions of them by the people of Boston show they will come to nothing." As these facts became known, the difficulties of enforcing the agreements became greater and greater, and finally on May 15, 1770, the Philadelphia merchants partly suspended the one they had made. Two months later New York entirely receded from hers, and this marked the entire collapse of the attempt, to the relief of the whole mercantile interest, and of consumers. The popular party, especially in Boston, were greatly enraged at its failure, and were extremely bitter against New York for its "unprincipled action ;" and the charges and counter charges of various gatherings and town meetings flooded the papers till the repeal of the acts was announced, when the mutual recriminations ceased.

EDITOR.

A COPY OF A LETTER FROM A GENTLEMAN IN VIRGINIA, TO A MERCHANT IN PHILADELPHIA.

Sir:

"I Have read, with much Attention, your Apology for the Merchants of Philadelphia; and think you have great Merit, in attempting to vindicate a Conduct, which is deemed inexplicably spiritless by the Inhabitants of every other Colony.

"One would imagine there has been something very mysterious in the Behaviour of the Merchants of Boston, to have induced you to treat them with so much Contempt; if their Conduct, since the first Dispute with our Mother-Country, had not been manly, candid and ingenuous.

"You confess, that many of you opposed the *Suspension*, in Consequence of Advice received from your *particular Friends* in *London*, that prudent and pacific Measures would be most agreeable to the Ministry and Parliament; and that it was dangerous to provoke them. This, no doubt, influenced some among you—But, in my Opinion, we must look somewhere else for the real Cause of your Opposition: perhaps an Examination into the Nature and Design of the Stamp-Act, and the grevious one, to which you still bend the Knee, may discover the lurking Principle, upon which you acted.

"The Stamp-Act was intended to raise a Revenue in America: and the Produce of the several Duties were ordered to be paid into the Receipt of his Majesty's Exchequer, and there reserved, to be, from Time to Time,

(439)

disposed of by Parliament, towards defending, protecting, and securing the American Colonies and Plantations.— This Act, in your Resolutions for Suspending the Importation of Goods from Great-Britain, you, without Ceremony, declared to be UNCONSTITUTIONAL; you likewise entered into spirited Measures for obtaining a Repeal of it, which had an immediate and a desired Effect.—You observed, justly, that the Stamp-Act was *unconstitutional*—altho your Reasons, for believing it to be so, were not then explained.   Your Opinion must have been founded upon this obvious Truth, That no Power on Earth had a Right to take Money out of your Pockets without your Consent, expressly declared by yourselves or your chosen Representatives.—Not content with barely remonstrating against the Stamp-Act—You also insisted 'That the many Difficulties you then laboured under, as a trading People, were owing to the Restrictions, Prohibitions, and ill-advised Regulations made in the several *other* Acts of the Parliament of Great-Britain, lately passed to regulate the Colonies; which had encreased the Cost and Expence of many Articles of your Importation, and cut off from you all Means of supplying yourselves with Specie enough to pay the Duties imposed on you, much less, to serve as a Medium of your Trade.'

"The Acts, against which, you spoke thus freely—still remain in full Force and Virtue; and when you obtained a Repeal of the Stamp-Act, glorious as it was—you obtained but a Part of your Demand.—The Repeal of it was well worth the Pains and Trouble it cost you.—It was indeed so replete with ministerial Venom, and proved such a general and oppressive Burthen, that Judges, Lawyers, Physicians, Parsons, Merchants, Farmers, nay School-Boys and Orphans, were alike subject to its baneful influence.

"The Sufferings of all Ranks of People induced *them* to

oppose it—Business was consequently at a Stand.—The civil Courts were shut, and you could sue no Man for the Recovery of a Debt—You were therefore *obliged* to sacrifice a very considerable Interest ; and you determined to import no Goods from Great-Britain, until it was repealed. —This was *your* Virtue !—This *your* Resolution !—Your *Patriotism* and *private Interests* were so intimately connected, that you could not prostitute the one, without endangering the other : And you would have been particularly fortunate, if Great-Britain, when she repealed the Stamp-Act, had redressed all your Grievances ; and had never thought of imposing new ones—You would, *then*, have been distinguished, in the Annals of America, among her best and most virtuous Sons, for a *timely* and *resolute* Defence of her Liberties ; and the Virtues, which under the present Tax you have despised and slighted, would have been, tho' unmerited, your greatest Glory—But Charles Townshend, with an artful and penetrating Eye, saw clearly to the Bottom of your Hearts—He knew, that, the private Interests of the Merchants were the Rocks against which Greenville's favorite *Argo* had unfortunately split ; and that no Act of Parliament, for raising a Revenue in America, could be executed without *their* Consent and Approbation.

"To this Gentleman, you must attribute the Loss of your Reputation : and it was, certainly, *your* Misfortune, and the Misfortune of *all America*, that you did not know *him*, as well as he knew *you*,—He imposed Duties upon Paper, Glass, and Painter's Colours; Articles of Commerce, which will prove most grevious Taxes upon the Country in general ; but cannot affect you, as Merchants : For it is notorious, that a Merchant must have his Profit on every Article of his Trade, let the Original Cost be what it may : 'The Purchaser of any Article, very seldom reflects that 'the Seller raises his Price, so as to indemnify himself for 'the Tax he has paid. He knows that the Prices of things 'are continually fluctuating, and if he thinks about the 'Tax, he thinks at the same Time, in all probability, that 'he might have paid as much, if the Articles he buys had 'not been taxed. He gets something visible and agree- 'able for his Money ; the Tax and Price are so confounded 'together, that he cannot separate, or does not chuse to 'take the Trouble of separating them.'—Thus have the People of your Province been deceived into a Pacific Compliance with this particular Act, the Preamble of which declares it is intended to raise a Revenue in America. You did not esteem it your Duty, as Merchants nor as American Freemen, to oppose it ; BECAUSE IT DID NOT DIRECTLY AFFECT YOUR PRIVATE INTERESTS. The Parliamentary Right, of Taxing America, you thought of little Consequence, when compared with your own Ease and Safety.—You concluded, that although it was *unconstitutional*, it could not do much Harm in your Time, and, that, if your Posterity did not like it, or found it insupportable,—they might endeavour to *remove* it.—By such deceitful Reasoning, you persuaded yourselves you were discharging your Duty; when you were industriously riveting Chains upon your Descendants, who will have no great Cause of Obligation to you for such distinguished Favours.—The Merchants in the Northern Colonies, despised these inglorious Motives : They were willing to lose their *whole Trade*, rather than suffer their Country to be enslaved—and for this Reason determined to suspend the Importation of Goods from Great-Britain, until the several Acts of P——t imposing Duties on America, were repealed.—This was *their* Virtue ! This *their* Resolution !— Your Opposition to this Measure, prevented it from taking Effect, and you may thank yourselves for the blessed Consequences which are like to follow.—

"These Reflections may appear harsh and uncharitable ;

but they are the Reflections of every man, who is not tinc-
tured with the *local* Prejudices of your Province—Believe
me, your Opposition to the Proposal of the Merchants of
New-York and Boston, although it might have been
founded upon specious Arguments, has done infinite Prejudice to the American Cause; and created great Jealousies
in your Neighbours Breasts; which, nothing, but your
determined Resolution to assist in removing those heavy
Burthens, with which they and you are equally oppressed,
will effectually heal.—An Union, between the several
Colonies in Sentiment and Action, is essentially necessary
to their Preservation; and had not my Lord H——h been
informed, that we were dis-united in both—he would
never have treated the Inhabitants of the Massachusetts-
Bay with so much severity; nor the other Colonies with
such indignity. His Lordship imagined, from the Dis-
union of these Provinces, of which no Doubt he has had
faithful Intelligence, that Dragooning of *One* would intimidate and silence the *Rest;* and his Judgment was
founded upon a plausible Principle.—However, 'there are
things which at some-times even Slaves will not bear;'
and I apprehend his Lordship's Letter will prove too hard
even for you to bear. This Letter is an express Declaration, that the Ministry intend to direct and influence our
Assemblies, by threatening them with a Dissolution,
whenever they may have the Confidence, contrary to ministerial Mandates, to consult or promote the Safety, Honor
and Interest of their Constituents. I hope your Assembly
will take the first Opportunity to resent the grossest Indignity ever offered to the Representatives of a free and loyal
People, and shew no Symptoms of that Modesty of which
Mr. Pitt so justly complained in the House of Commons.—
If a B—— M——r imagines he can intimidate an American Assembly, Threats, nay Punishments, will be made
use of to execute the most slavish Maxims; and the very

Men, whom we may invest with Power to promote and
secure our Interests, will *under such Influence*, effectually
ruin us. For what Faith can we repose in our Assemblies,
when they do not esteem themselves answerable to us for
their Conduct ; *but to arbitrary Ministers*, who will always
make it their Interests to oppress and enslave us? We
had better have no Representatives, if we cannot, when
we think proper, instruct and direct them ; and, at the
same time, have a reasonable Assurance of their obeying
our Orders.   The People are to all Intents and Purposes,
Masters.—Their Representatives are their dignified Servants.—And we shall be justly chargeable with *political
Suicide*, if we are stupidly fond of an Establishment,
which, on the Principle of *ministerial Supremacy*, will destroy our Civil Existence.

"It is, certainly, a most cruel Dilemma, to be obliged to
sacrifice every Thing that is most dear and valuable
among Men, or to contend with our Mother Country.—But
let us not, in this Case, distinguish Great-Britain from
any other Power—To Freemen it must be indifferent, who
their Oppressors are—If Britons oppress us, and strive
might and main to enslave us—all pretended Ties of ancient Favours, Friendship, Duty, are destroyed : G——
B——, France, or any Power on Earth, pursuing the same
Measures, ought indiscriminately to be opposed.—I shall
conclude this Letter with an historical Fact very applicable to the present Subject.

"The Privernates had been several Times subdued by
the Romans, and had as often revolted; but their City was
at last retaken by the Consul Plautius—In these distressed
Circumstances they sent Ambassadors to Rome, to sue for
Peace—Upon a Senator's asking them what Punishment
they thought they deserved; one of them answered, 'That
which is due to Men who think themselves worthy of Liberty.'   Then the Consul asked them, whether there was

any Room to hope, that they would observe the Peace, if their Fault was pardoned? 'The peace shall be perpetual between us,' replied the Ambassador, 'and we shall faithfully observe it, if the Conditions you lay upon us are *just* and *reasonable;* but if they are *hard* and *dishonorable*, the peace will not be of long Continuance, and we shall very soon break it.'

"Though some of the Senators were offended at this Answer, yet most of them approved of it, and said that 'it was worthy of a *Man* and of a Man that was *born free:*' acknowledging therefore the Force of the Rights of human Nature, they cried out, that 'those alone deserved to be Citizens of Rome, *who esteemed nothing in comparison of Liberty.*' Thus the very Persons, who were at first threatened with Punishment, were admitted to the Rights of Citizens, and obtained the Conditions they wanted; the generous Refusal of the Privernates to comply with the Terms of a dishonourable Treaty, gained them the Privilege of being incorporated into a State, which at that Time could boast of the bravest, and most virtuous Subjects in the Universe."

A PETITION

FROM THE

ASSEMBLY OF PENNSYLVANIA

TO THE

KING.

DRAWN BY

JOHN DICKINSON.

———

MARCH 9, 1771.

NOTE.

DICKINSON'S course in opposing the petition to the King in 1764, to make Pennsylvania a royal colony, was so unpopular that it resulted in his defeat as a candidate to the Assembly in the October election of 1766 ; and from that time, till the election of 1770, the influence of Galloway was strong enough to secure his exclusion from that body. But the questions over the colonial charter became less important, while the greater questions of the relation of the colonies to the parent state became more and more vital. This change brought Dickinson once more into popular favor, and despite Galloway's opposition, he was elected to the Assembly from the City of Philadelphia, in October, 1770.

Led by Galloway, that body had hitherto taken what the extremists had deemed a very lukewarm attitude. It had paid no heed to the Massachusetts circular letter, or the Virginia resolutions of May, 1768. Indeed, Lord North, in Parliament, praised Pennsylvania for having "behaved with more moderation than the other colonies." The Assembly had indeed in 1768 voted a petition to parliament, denying to that body the right of taxation, (which was drawn by Allen with the aid Dickinson, according to *Stillé,*) but it had otherwise taken no action since the passage of the Stamp Act resolutions of 1765. Dickinson's election, however, marked a momentary change of party power, and this was quickly shown by the Assembly's transmitting, on his motion, another petition, though that sent three years before remained still unnoticed. How far the petition conformed to the draft Dickinson prepared, cannot be ascertained, as the draft was recommitted for amendment.

The history of this petition is recorded in the *Votes and Proceedings,* (VI) as follows:

Upon Motion by a Member, [Feb. 4, 1771].

That Part of the Duties imposed by a late Act of Parliament on certain Articles imported into the Colonies, remains unrepealed, and that great Danger to the rights of the *Americans* is justly apprehended

(449)

from the Continuance of such a precedent for taxing them without their Consent.

Ordered, That Mr. Fox, Mr. Dickinson, Mr. Browne, Mr. Morton, Mr. Carpenter, Mr. Swope, Mr. Montgomery and Mr. Edmonds be a Committee to prepare and bring in a Draught of a Petition to his Majesty in Council, humbly praying Relief, by his gracious Interposition with the Parliament for obtaining a Repeal of the Duty remaining on Tea &c. imported into the *American* colonies. . . .

The House resumed the Consideration of the Draught of their Petition to his Majesty, and after some Time spent therein, Objections arising to particular Paragraphs thereof, the said Draught was recommitted to the Committee that brought it in, for Alteration. . . .

The Committee to whom the Petition to his Majesty was recommitted for Amendment, reported the same with some Alterations, which were read by Order, and referred to further Consideration. . . .

The House resumed the Consideration of their intended Petition to his Majesty, and after some Time spent therein, adjourned to Three o'clock, P. M. . . .

The House proceeded in the Consideration of their Petition to the King, which being again read, and debated by Paragraphs, was ordered to be transcribed. . . .

The Petition to his Majesty being transcribed according to Order, was compared at the Table, [and] signed by the Speaker. . . .

This Petition was adopted March 9, 1771, under which date it is printed in the *Votes and Proceedings*, (VI, 299).

EDITOR.

A PETITION.

To the King's Most Excellent Majesty.

The Petition of the Representatives of the Freemen of the Province of Pennsylvania. Most humbly sheweth,

That we your Majesty's faithful Subjects, the Representatives of the Freemen of Pennsylvania, in General Assembly met, humbly ask Permission to offer to your Royal Wisdom our dutiful Supplication.

In our last Petition to your Majesty, we prayed Relief. of a Grievance, which the good People of this Province suffered, by Duties being imposed upon them by Act of Parliament, for the sole Purpose of raising a Revenue ; and though that Act has been repealed as to Part of these Taxes, yet the Duties on Tea, and other enumerated Goods, not made in Great-Britain, but from thence exported to these Colonies, are still retained with Intent, as we have great Reason to fear, of establishing thereby a Precedent for repeating such Taxations upon us hereafter.

Thus we lose Possession of Part of our Property, and the Title to the Remainder becomes extremely precarious : For as we cannot, from our Situation, be in any Manner represented in Parliament, your Royal Wisdom will perceive that we can call nothing our own, which others assume a Right to take from us, without our Consent.

The Aggrievance still continuing notwithstanding the late Repeal, our Confidence in your Majesty's transcendent Goodness, induce us to hope, that through your gracious Interposition we may yet obtain Redress.—If we attempted to promote Innovations, we might deserve Censure. We only endeavour to avoid them.—We presume not to request the Grant of any new Right in our favour, nor any

Diminution of the Royal Prerogative; but only to be restored to that which we constantly till of late enjoyed,—the invaluable exclusive Privilege of demonstrating our Affection for our Sovereign, and our Duty to his Goverment, as heretofore, by voluntary Gifts of our Property to him.

This Privilege, repeatedly recognized by your Majesty and former Kings and Parliaments, our Ancestors transmitted inviolate to us, we possessed it without Abuse, and have lost it without Offence: For we beg Leave to assure your Majesty, that none of your Subjects are or can be more affectionately and firmly attached to your Majesty's Person, Family and Government, than your faithful People, the Inhabitants of Pennsylvania.

Most gracious Sovereign,

Fully confiding, that your Majesty will always make the Preservation of the Constitutional Rights of your Subjects a principal Object of your Attention, and that your Royal Disposition delights in the Freedom and Happiness of your People, We most humbly and earnestly implore your Majesty, by your Royal Authority, Influence, and Recommendation, to procure us Relief from the Grievance now most respectfully represented.

Signed by Order of the House,

JOSEPH GALLOWAY, Speaker.

Philadelphia, March 5, 1771.

TWO LETTERS

ON THE

TEA TAX.

BY

JOHN DICKINSON.

———

NOVEMBER, 1773.

NOTE.

The first of these letters was printed in the *Pennsylvania Journal* for Wednesday, Nov. 3, 1773, with the following introduction:

Messrs. BRADFORDS

Please to insert the following Extract of a Letter to a Gentleman of this City, in your paper, and you will oblige your humble servant,

Y. Z.

The second letter was printed as a broadside, the lining of the head-lines being:

A Letter from the Country, / To a Gentleman in Philadelphia. / [signed] Rusticus. [Folio. Broadside.]

This was reprinted in New York, backed, by the "Association of the Sons of Liberty," the committee of which supplied a prefatory note, as follows:

The celebrated Pennsylvania Farmer, having been frequently called upon in public, to give his Sentiments relative to the Measures that should be adopted to Baffle the present Design of the Ministry, and the India Company to enslave America, He is, from the stile, and other Considerations, supposed to be the Author of the following Letter, published in Philadelphia, which is re-published for your information. And its material to observe, that he recommends to the Inhabitants of that City, to pursue the same Steps which have been taken here, by the Association of the Sons of Liberty, of this City; a copy of which you have on the other side. Many of the respectable Inhabitants have already signed it, and those who are disposed to give a decent and firm opposition, to the Design of enslaving the Colonies, are hereby invited to accede to it.   The Committee of the Asssociation.

New York, December 4, 1773.

This broadside was headed:

A Letter from the Country, to a Gentleman in Philadelphia: / My Dear Friend [signed] Rusticus. [Folio. Broadside.]

EDITOR.

A LETTER.

SIR,

"I RECEIVED your favor, inclosing the Act of Parliament, passed this year, to allow a drawback of the duties of customs on the exportation of Tea to any of his Majesty's colonies or plantations in America, &c.

"Can it be possible that any person of common understanding, upon reading this Act, should take up an opinion that the Tea sent to America by the East-India Company was discharged from the duty of *three pence* per pound, which the Act passed in the year 1767, for the purpose of raising a revenue in America, ordered to be paid on its being landed here. To my view, and I think I have read the Act with some attention, there is not the least foundation, on which, to ground such an opinion. This Act relates altogether to the duties of customs payable in England, and for the payment of which, the East-India Company are obliged, by sundry Acts of Parliament, to give security, under the common seal; but it has not the least reference to the duty payable here, which was laid for the purpose of taxing the Americans.

"From the recitals in this Act it appears, that by former Acts of Parliament certain duties were imposed upon all Teas imported by the East-India Company,—that the Company were obliged to give security for the payment of those duties, so soon as their Teas are sold, and were obliged to sell their goods, openly and fairly, by way of auction, or by inch of candle, within the space of three years from the importation,—that the persons, who purchased at these sales, were obliged within three days after the sale, to deposit with the Company 40s. for every tub

& chest, under certain terms and conditions,—and that upon exporting it to Ireland and America, there was granted, for a certain limited time, a drawback of three-fifth parts of the several duties of customs, which were paid upon the importation.

"Let us now review this Act, which is made expressly for the benefit and advantage of the East-India Company. In the first paragraph, instead of three-fifths, the whole of the duties payable upon the importation is to be drawn back from all Teas bought at the Company's Sales and exported to America. But lest this encouragement should increase the number of purchasers and exporters, and thereby prevent the Company from reaping the advantages of the monoply intended for them by this Act. It is provided in the next paragraph, that every buyer, instead of 40s. shall deposit *four pounds.* The third paragraph points out a way, whereby the Company, instead of exposing their Teas to sale, may be enabled to export them to any ports beyond the seas; and the paragraph following relieves them from the security given for the payment of duties, and provides, that they may *export* their Tea without paying any duty, or as the Act expresses it, 'discharged from the payment of any customs or duties whatsoever.' But no provision is made to discharge these Teas from the duty ordered to be paid upon their being *imported* into America. This is an objection never bro't into view by this Act, that the custom or duties from which the Teas are here discharg'd, are no other than those, for the payment of which, the Company were obliged to give security, appears plainly by the proviso, which immediately follows, whereby the Collector and Comptroller are authorized, upon certain conditions, to write off and discharge the quantity of Tea so exported, from the warrent of the respective ship in which such Tea was imported."

Fair-view, October 30, 1773.

My Dear Friend,

I am very sorry for the Piece of Intelligence you were pleased to communicate to me in your last. *Five Ships*, loaded with TEA, on their Way to *America*, and this with a View not only to *enforce* the *Revenue Act*, but to *establish* a *Monopoly* for the *East-India Company*, who have espoused the Cause of the Ministry; and hope to repair their broken Fortunes by the Ruin of *American* freedom and Liberty! No Wonder the Minds of the People are exasperated, as you say, to a degree of Madness. The Scripture tells us: *"Oppression will make a wise Man mad."* And when Insolence is joined with Oppression, I should deem him not far from a Fool or Idiot, who did not feel a degree of Madness. Pray have you heard, whether *they* and the *Minister* have not *made a Property of* US, and whether WE, our WIVES and CHILDREN, together, with the HARD EARNED FRUITS OF OUR LABOUR, are not *made over* to *this* almost *bankrupt Company*, to augment their Stock, and to *repair* their *ruined Fortunes?* Justice seems to have forsaken the old World. Three public Robbers in *Europe* have taken Possession of a neighbouring Kingdom, and divided among themselves as lawful Booty. The Rights of free States and Cities are swallowed up in Power. Subjects are considered as Property. If I am well informed, not longer ago than last Year, a Company of Merchants in *Spain* purchased from the King the exclusive Right of the Trade of one of the most considerable Islands in the *West Indies*, and to indemnify themselves for the Purchase Money, are now carrying on that Trade in a Manner that must ruin every Inhabitant of that Island. Are we in like Manner to be given up to the Disposal of the *East-India Company*, who have now the Assurance to step forth in Aid of the Minister, to execute his Plan of enslaving *America?* Their conduct in *Asia*, for some Years past, has given ample

Proof, how little they regard the Laws of Nations, the Rights, Liberties, or Lives of Men. They have levied War, excited Rebellions, dethroned lawful Princes, and sacrificed Millions for the Sake of Gain. The Revenues of mighty Kingdoms have centered in their Coffers. And these not being sufficient to glut their Avarice, they have, by the most unparalleled Barbarities, Extortions and Monopolies, stripped the miserable Inhabitants of their Property, and reduced whole Provinces to Indigence and Ruin. Fifteen hundred Thousand, it is said, perished by Famine in one Year, not because the Earth denied its Fruits, but this Company and its Servants engrossed all the Necessaries of Life, and set them at so high a Rate, that the Poor could not purchase them. Thus having drained the Sources of that immense Wealth, which they have for several Years past been accustomed to amass, and squander away on their Lusts, and in corrupting their Country, they now, it seems, cast their Eyes on *America*, as a new Theatre, whereon to exercise their Talents of Rapine, Oppression and Cruelty. The Monopoly of Tea, is, I dare say, but a small Part of the Plan they have formed to strip us of our Property. But thank GOD, we are not Sea Poys, nor Marattas, but *British Subjects*, who are born to Liberty, who know its Worth, and who prize it high. We are engaged in a mighty Struggle. The Cause is of the utmost Importance, and the Determination of it will fix our Condition as Slaves or Freemen. It is not the paltry Sum of Three-Pence which is now demanded, but the Principle upon which it is demanded, that we are contending against. *Before we pay any Thing, let us see whether we have any Thing we can call our own to pay.*

HITHERTO the dispute has been carried on with a Spirit, Temper, and Moderation, that must prove us worthy to enjoy that Liberty, for which we contend. And I hope and earnestly wish, that the Prudence we have hitherto exercised, may not be borne down by the Indignation which you say is so justly and universally kindled at these insolent Intruders. I am very sensible how the Spirit of a Man rises, when unworthy Agents are used to destroy him. It is something of Consolation to be overcome by a Lion, but to be devoured by Rats is intolerable.

BUT, my dear Friend, it is not only the cause, but our Manner of conducting it, that will establish our Character. The Happiness and Prosperity both of the Colonies and of *Great-Britain* depend upon an intimate Union & Connexion. This Union, it is true, depends upon Freedom. For without Freedom there can be no Confidence. Without Confidence no Affection; and without Affection, considering our Situation and Distance from *Britain*, the Union between this Country and that cannot long subsist. To preserve, therefore, that Union, and promote the Happiness and Prosperity of both Countries, let us resolve to maintain our Liberty. But in doing this, when any Difference arises, as on the present unhappy Occasion, let us act so as to leave Room for a Return of the old good Humour, Confidence and Affection, which has subsisted between *Great-Britain* and this Country, since the first settlement of the Colonies. —

I HEAR a Buz among my Neighbours, that the *East-India Company's* Tea is to be guarded by Men of War, and landed by a Military Force; that the Reason, why the General did not come to review the Troops in your City, was, lest in his Absence the Tea should arrive in *New York*, and his Presence might be necessary to land and protect it. Though I have no Doubt but this Company, hackneyed as they are in Murders, Rapine and Cruelty, would sacrifice the Lives of Thousands to preserve their Trash, and enforce their measures; yet I can hardly persuade myself that the Ministry are so mad, as to give Orders, at the Hazard of losing the Affection of the *Amer-*

icans, to preserve that, which, considering the Time it has already lain in the *East-India Company's* Ware-houses, must already be in a perishing State.

BUT should that be the Case, let us disappoint their Malice. We have yet a command of our Persons. Our Houses, Stores and Wharves are at our own Disposal. Resolve, therefore, nobly resolve and publish to the World your Resolutions, that no Man will receive the Tea, no Man will let his Stores, nor suffer the Vessel, that brings it, to moor at his Wharf, and that if any Person assists in unlading, landing or storing it, he shall ever after be deemed an Enemy to his Country, and never be employed by his Fellow Citizens. I am sure, from what I have formerly known of our PORTERS, there is not a Man among them, that will lend a Hand; and I question, whether among the whole Class of *Labourers* that ply about the Wharves, there will be found One, who would not rather go without his Dinner than, for double Wages, touch the accursed Trash. Believe me, my Friend, there is a Spirit of Liberty and a love of their Country among every Class of Men among us, which Experience will evince, and which shew them worthy the Character of free-born *Americans.*——It is a Question with me, from what I have seen among the *Troops*, whether any Thing less than the last Exertion of military Discipline will prevail on one Soldier, who has been but one Year in this Country to lend a Hand to unload or store the Tea. I am sure there is not a Recruit enlisted here, who would not rather desert, than be compelled to do an Act, which will render him odious to his Countrymen. Besides, it is not to be supposed, that a GENTLEMAN SOLDIER, will *submit* to the indignity of becoming a *Porter* to the *East-India Company*. And as to the *Commissioners*, appointed to receive this Tea, notwithstanding you tell me the Answer of one House was not satisfactory; yet from the Knowledge I have of the Gentlemen, that compose that House, I would venture my Life, they prefer the Esteem of their Fellow-Citizens above the Honour or Emolument of being Servants to that infamous Company. But should they undervalue your Esteem, be assured they will not hazard your Resentment.

CONFIDE, therefore, in each other. Be firm, be prudent, And may GOD prosper your Endeavours, and enable you to transmit to your Posterity that Freedom derived from your Ancestors.—

I DID not think Politics would have reached this Retreat I have chosen; but you have called on me for my Sentiments, and when our Country is in Danger, no Man ought to excuse himself. I have trepassed too long on your Patience. I shall therefore conclude with a Proposal that your Watchmen be instructed as they go their Rounds, to call out every night, *past Twelve o' Clock, beware of the East-India Company.*

I am, with sincere Affection, Your's,
RUSTICUS.

Fairview, Nov. 27, 1773.

LETTERS

TO THE

INHABITANTS

OF THE

BRITISH COLONIES.

BY

JOHN DICKINSON.

MAY, 1774.

NOTE.

In Charles Thomson's letter to W. H. Drayton (Stillé's *Dickinson*, 341), he stated:

"When the controversy was again renewed between Great-Britain and America in the year 1772, the merchants of Philadelphia, who first took the alarm at the attempt of introducing tea to America through the medium of the East India Company, were anxious to engage [Dickinson] in the dispute. But from this he was dissuaded by one of his most intimate friends, who seemed to be persuaded that this new attempt of the Ministry would lead to most serious consequences, and terminate in blood, and who theretore wished him to reserve himself for till matters became more serious. For this reason he was not publicly concerned in the measures taken for sending back the tea. But in the spring of 1774, as soon as the Boston Port Bill, &c., his friend, who had taken an active part in the measures for sending back the tea, immediately communicated to him the intelligence, and gave his opinion that now was the time to step forward. The measures proper to be pursued on this occasion were secretly concerted between them, and to prepare the minds of the people Mr. D. undertook to address the public in a series of letters."

Thomson also wrote to David Ramsay (*New York Historical Society Collections for* 1878, 221):

"In order to awaken the attention of the people, a series of letters were published, well calculated to raise them to a sense of their danger and point out the fatal effort and consequences of the late acts of Parliament and the plans of the British Ministry."

Even before finding these two references to this series of letters, I had been led by their style and argument to ascribe them to Dickinson's pen. They were printed in the *Pennsylvania Journal* under date of:

Letter I.	Vol. XVI. No. 1642.		May 25, 1774.
Letter II.	" " " 1643.		June 1, 1774.
Letter III.	" " " 1644.		June 8, 1774.
Letter IV.	" " " 1645.		June 15, 1774.

EDITOR.

(467)

LETTERS.

LETTER I.

To the INHABITANTS *of the* BRITISH COLONIES *in* AMERICA:

BRETHREN, Divine Providence has been pleased to place us in this age and country under such circumstances, as to be reduced to the necessity of chusing one of these conditions—either to submit to the dominion of others, holding our lives, liberties, and properties, by the *precarious tenure* of their Will—or, to exert that understanding, resolution and power, with which Heaven has favoured us, in striving to maintain our rank in the class of Freemen.

The importance of these objects is so immensely great, and the treatment of one of these Colonies so extremely alarming, as to call for your most earnest and immediate consideration.

The subject of the present dispute between Great Britain and us, is so generally understood, that to enlarge upon it is needless. We know the *extent* of her claims. We begin to feel the *enforcement* of those claims. We may foresee the consequences of them; for, reason teaching us to infer actions from principles, and events from examples, should convince us, what a perfection of servitude is to be fixed on us, and our posterity. I call it perfection—because the wit of man, it is apprehended, cannot devise a plan of domination more compleatly tending to bear down the governed into the lowest and meanest state of society, than that now meditated, avowed, and in part executed, on this Continent.

If this system becomes established, it may, with truth,

be said, of the inhabitants of these Colonies, "that they hold their lives, liberties, and properties, by the precarious tenure of the Will of others."*

Allowing the danger to be real—At the prospect of so abject and so lasting a subjection,—What must be the sentiments of judicious & virtuous Americans? They will quickly determine whether the first part of the alternative should be adopted.

Here arguments would be absurd. Not more ridiculous would be an attempt to prove, vice preferable to virtue— The climate of _St. Vincent_ more pleasant than that of _Pennsylvania_—The natives of _Indostan_, under the government of _the East-India Company_, as happy as English Freeholders—Or the inhabitants of Great Britain more loyal subjects, than those of the Colonies.

That Liberty is inestimable—and should, if possible, be preserved—you _know_. To pretend to convince you of the truth of the former proposition, or of the duty of the latter, would be to insult you.

You must be, you are resolved, to observe the properest conduct, for securing your best and dearest interests. What _that_ may be, deserves—demands—your closest attention—your calmest deliberation.

On this head I venture to submit some observations to your consideration. I am, by every tie of interest and duty, an _American;_ and, unless my heart deceives me, I am an _American_ in affection. My fortunes, hopes, and wishes are bound up in your prosperity. With my countrymen I must mourn or rejoice; and therefore, though I am perfectly sensible I cannot present to them reflections arising from great abilities, or extensive learning, and

---

* "_Non nobis nati sumus. It is for our posterity we desire to provide —that they may not be in worse case than villians. For a_ FREEMAN _to be a_ TENANT AT WILL _for his_ LIBERTY _! I will not agree to it. It is a tenure not to be found in all Littleton. Speech of Sir Edward Coke, Lord Chief Justice. Parliamentary Hist. Vol. 8. Page 61._

adorned by elegance of composition, yet I trust they will lend a careful and candid attention to plain thoughts, dictated by honest intentions, and a participation of afflictions. Aiming solely at your welfare, and not at the trifling reputation of a writer; far be from me the overweening presumption, that my opinions are free from error. Conscious of my frailties, I desire those opinions to be severely examined. The correction of them will confer a real obligation upon me, if it serves my country; and happy shall I esteem myself, if the detection of my mistakes shall open to you a clear view of the most expedient measures to be pursued.

There are some men who say, that the late act of Parliament, abolishing the privileges of the port of Boston, was occasioned by the particular imprudence of the inhabitants, and in no manner concerns the other colonies.

To form a true judgement on this point, it will be proper to take a short review of some other transactions.

Great Britain triumphant by your assistance in the late war, found at the conclusion of it, by a peace hastily bestowed on her haughty and hereditary foes, her dominions enlarged,—her fleets formidable,—her armies disciplined, —her trade flourishing—her enemies intimidated and exhausted—her colonies thriving, affectionate and dutiful.

The cup of prosperity, large and full, courted her lips. Deep she drank of the enchanted beverage, as if the vessel like the cruise of *Sarepta's* widow, could not fail. After a short, but feverish repose, she roused herself, may I say—as one of *Homer's* Giants—A race—

"By whom no statutes and no rights were known,"

to injure those who never injured her.

She had conquered her *enemies*. *That* other kingdoms had done. Should no exploits of a more transcendent energy illustrate the annals of *George* the Third? No atchievements, so shockingly great and advantageous, that even the pensioned Historians of the animated era must weep in tracing them, and blush in reciting them? Luckily for her fame—*perhaps for her profit*—the near-sighted policy, and low-spirited humanity of every state, in every period, had left untouched, for her, the novel glory of conquering *friends—Children—Flesh of her flesh*, and *bone of her bone*, unstained by any former reproach,—resting in perfect tranquility, acknowledged loyal and actual obedient to every kind of authority hitherto by her exercised over them,—perpetually pouring into her lap those fruits of her industry, which she would permit them to collect from the different parts of the world.—Proud of their connection with her,—confiding in her—loving—revering—almost adoring her—and ready and willing, as they ever had been, to spend their treasure and their blood at her request—in her cause.

* "Parcere *superbus*, and debellare *subjectos*" was a thought that had escaped the sagacity of Statesmen, and even the fancy of Poets. The subtlety of *Machiavel's* Italian brain had missed it—and no Bœotian had blundered upon it.

The temptation was too great to be resisted. The parent resolved to *seize that treasure*, and if not tamely resigned, to *spill that blood*, herself. "† O *sapiens* et *beata* regina."

The greatest ‡Ministers, who had heretofore conducted

* " *To spare the proud ; and to subdue the subject.*"

† " *O wise and happy Queen.*"

‡ "*Sir* Robert Walpole *and any other Minister to whom the project of taxing the Colonies was mentioned, rejected it.*

" *When I had the honor of serving his Majesty I availed myself of the means of information, which I derived from my office.* I speak, therefore, from knowledge. *My materials were good, I was at pains to* collect, *to* digest, *to* consider *them ; and* I will be bound to affirm, *that the profit of* Great Britain *from the trade of the Colonies, through all its branches, is* two millions a year. This *is the fund that carried you triumphantly through the last war. The estates that were rented at two thous-*

her affairs, had discovered and declared, that we were continually toiling for her benefit—that she was *sure* of receiving, in the course of commerce, all those emoluments of our labor, which reason could require—and therefore, tenderly cherished and supported us. Notions too dull! And advantages too just! to merit the slightest regard from his Majesty's enlightened and magnanimous Councellors.

"They lavish gold out of the bag, and weigh silver in "the balance—they fall down, yea, they worship (them)— "remember this and show yourselves men." Isaiah ch. 46.

P. P.

LETTER II.

To the INHABITANTS *of the* BRITISH COLONIES *in* AMERICA.

Brethren, It is not my design to travel through all the ministerial manœuvers respecting us, since the commencement of this Reign. It is not necessary. Sufficient, I trust, it will prove, to lay before you such a series of correspondent facts, as will thoroughly convince you,—that a plan has been deliberately framed, and pertinaciously adhered to, unchanged even by frequent changes of Ministers, unchecked by any intervening gleam of humanity, to sacrifice to a passion for arbitary dominion the universal pro-

---

and pounds a year three score years ago, are three thousand pounds at present. Those estates sold then from fifteen to eighteen years purchase; the same may now be sold for thirty. You owe this to America. This is the price that America pays you for her protection. *I dare not say how much higher these profits may be augmented—upon the whole I will beg leave to tell the House, what is really my opinion ; it is that the* Stamp-Act *be repealed absolutely, totally, and immediately. That the reason for the repeal be assigned, because it was founded on an* erroneous principle." *Mr.* PITT'S SPEECH.

All the most distinguished writers on the trade of Great Britain, *previous to the present Reign, held a language entirely agreeing with Mr. Pitt's sentiments. See Davenant, Child, Tucker, Beawes, Postlewaite,* &c.

perty, liberty, safety, honor, happiness and prosperity of us
unoffending, yet devoted Americans—And that every man
of us is deeply interested in the fate of our brethren of
Boston.

If such a series is not laid before you, the combined
force of which shall tear up by the roots, and throw out
of your bosoms, every lurking doubt, centure me as an
enthusiast too violently warmed by a sence of the injustice
practised against my beloved country.

The danger of a father's life once racked words from a
dumb son. Worse than death, in my view, threatens our
common mother. Pardon, therefore, a brother's imper-
fections.

Amidst a volume of institutions called Regulations—
wrong at first—corrected into other errors—again corrected
—still requiring Regulation—and remaining after all their
editions, if not like *Draco's*, codes of blood, yet codes of
plunder—confounding by the intricacy and multiplicity
of their inventions—and confiscating for having confounded*—appears the fourth of *George* the Third,
Chap. 15th, stiled "An Act for granting certain duties in
"the British Colonies and Plantations in *America*, &c."
This was the first comet of this kind, that glared over
these Colonies since their existence. Here first we find
the Commons of *Great Britain* "giving and granting"

* *"Omitting the immense increase of people, by natural population, in*
"the more northern Colonies, and the migration from every part of Eu-
"rope, I am convinced the whole commercial system of America *may be*
"altered to advantage. You have prohibited where you ought to have
"encouraged; and you have encouraged, where you ought to have pro-
"hibited. Improper restraints have been laid on the continent in favor
"of the islands. You have but two nations to trade with in America.
"Would you have twenty! Let Acts of Parliament in consequence of
"treaties remain, but let not an English Minister *become a* Custom-
"House Officer *for* Spain *or for any foreign power. Much is wrong,*
"much may be amended or for the general good of the whole. Mr.
" PITTS' *Speech.*

our money, *for the express purpose* of "raising a Revenue in *America.*"

We, busy in guiding our ploughs, felling our timber, or sailing in the circuits of traffic prescribed us, and still veering like Bees to their hive, with millions of our gains, to *Great Britain*, the center of our toils by land and sea, poor harmless Husbandmen and Traders! scarce observed the blow given us. Our hearts filled with confidence by contemplating the pleasing images of her generous distinguished virtues, from the splendor of which in our judgment, those of ancient *Greece* and *Rome* hid their diminished heads—suspicion could find no entrance. We saw, in the preamble, something of the usual forms "for extending and securing navigation and commerce," were lulled into security, nor could suppose the stroke was aimed at our vitals. An infant that had trotted along a directed walk in a garden, and loaded with flowers had presented them to a mother, would as soon have expected to be knocked down by her.—

Not long were we suffered to enjoy our tranquility. The 5th of *George* the Third, Chapter the 12th, the ever memorable Stamp-Act, quickly followed. By this, reciting the former act, the Commons of *Great Britain* "gave and granted" duties, so called, of our money on almost every piece of parchment, vellum or paper to be used in these Colonies, and declared every instrument of writing without a stamp to be void. Tax gatherers of a new kind were appointed to collect these duties. The petitions of our Assemblies previous to its passing, on notice received of the design, asserting our rights, and supplicating a respect for them, were treated with contempt. You remember the time and its distress. You behaved as you ought.*

* "*I rejoice that America has resisted. Three millions of people, so* "*dead to all the feelings of Liberty, as voluntarily to consent to be* "*Slaves, would have been fit instruments to make Slaves of the rest.* " *Mr.* PITT's *Speech.*

Convinced that a people who *wish* to be free, must *resolve* to be free, you abolished the "abominable thing"—and proceeded in your usual business without any regard to the illegal edict obtruded upon you.

Permit me to add two observations, relating to remarkable attendants on the Taxation comprised in that Act, the memory of which is perhaps grown faint, from length of time, in some minds.

By the Statutes granting stamp duties in *England* or *Great-Britain*, especial caution has been taken, that nothing more should be levied upon the subject, under any pretence whatsoever, than the duties themselves. These words run through those Acts—"That the Officers shall "receive the several duties—and stamp and mark the vel-"lum, parchment, and paper, &c., *without any other fee* "*or reward*—which stamp or mark shall be a sufficient "discharge for the respective duties, &c." And "the "Commissioners shall take care that the several parts of "the kingdom shall, from time to time, be sufficiently fur-"nished with vellum, parchment and paper, stamped and "marked as is directed, TO THE END, that the subjects, "&c. MAY HAVE IT IN THEIR ELECTION, *either to buy* the "same of the Officers and persons to be employed, &c. at "the *usual* and *most common* rates above the said duties, "or *to bring* THEIR OWN vellum, parchment, or paper to "be stamped or marked as aforesaid."*

Was the Stamp-Act for *America* like those Statutes? Judge. By this it is enacted "that the High Treasurer, "or any three or more of the Commissioners of the Treas-"ury shall once in every year SET THE PRICES, at which "all sorts of stamped vellum, parchment, and paper, shall "be sold, &c."

The stamps were kept in *England*. Ship loads of "all sorts of stamped vellum, parchment, and paper" were

---

* *5 and 6. Will. and Mar. ch. 21. 30th G 3d. ch. 19. and other statutes.*

sent over to us. We had no *choice* either to take these or to carry other vellum, parchment or paper to be stamped. We must not only have paid the certain duties imposed, but the uncertain "prices," which the Commissioners should please to "set" for the value of their "vellum, parchment, and paper;" and "penalties and forfeitures" fell upon us, every step we took, without paying these *impositions.* This surely was not only to be taxed by the Parliament, but over again for the same articles and by the Commissioners.

Here some men whose minds are strongly impressed with ideas of equity, may ask, if it is possible that even a British Parliament should so wantonly degrade us. It is as true, as that the Port of *Boston* is THIS DAY shut up.

The "forfeitures and penalties thereby imposed were to be sued for and recovered in any Court of Record, or in ANY COURT OF ADMIRALTY OR VICE ADMIRALTY, appointed or to be appointed, and having jurisdiction in the respective colony where the offence should be committed, &c."

THIS was no regulation of trade. The facts, to be tried in any dispute, must have arisen on land—within the body of a county—as remote from admiralty jurisdiction, on every constitutional principle, as a suit on a bond, or an ejectment for a freeholder. Yet thus by a few lines, was the inestimable priviledge of trial by jury, to be torn from you and your posterity. Thus the decision of the rights of property, not in controversies between man and man, on the question of "meum vel tuum," were though wrung by oppression, the wretched loser might draw a degree of consolation by reflecting that he had received some consideration for the substance taken away, or at least that a countryman gained his spoils—but in litigations found on rigid *forfeitures* and arbitrary *penalties*—was to be referred to the incorrupt tribunals of single judges—appointed from another country—filled with its prejudices—

holding their commissions during pleasure—totally independent on you—claiming fees and salaries to be paid out of your money condemned by themselves.*

* *"When the jury have delivered in their verdict, and it is recorded in* "*court, they are then discharged. And so ends the trial by jury: a trial,* "*which besides the other vast advantages which we have occasionally ob-* "*served in its progress, is also as expeditious and cheap, as it is con-* "*venient, equitable, and certain; for a commission out of chancery, or* "*the civil law courts, for examining witnesses in one cause will fre-* "*quently last as long, and of course be full as expensive, as the trial of a* "*hundred issues at* nisi prius: *and yet the fact cannot be determined by* "*such commissioners at all; no, not till the depositions are published* "*and read at the hearing of the cause in court.*

"*Upon these accounts the trial by jury ever has been, and I trust ever* "*will be, looked upon as the glory of the English law. And, if it has so* "*great an advantage over others in regulating civil property, how much* "*must that advantage be heightened, when it is applied to criminal cases!* "*But this we must refer to the ensuing book of these commentaries: only* "*observing for the present, that it is the most transcendent privilege* "*which any subject can enjoy, or wish for, that he cannot be affected* "*either in his property, his liberty, or his person, but by the unanimous* "*consent of twelve of his neighbors and equals. A constitution, that I* "*may venture to affirm has, under providence, secured the just liberties* "*of this nation for a long succession of ages. And therefore a celebrated* "*French writer,* who concludes, that because Rome, Sparta, and Car-* "*thage have lost their liberties, therefore those of England in time must* "*perish, should have recollected that Rome, Sparta, and Carthage, at the* "*time when their liberties were lost, were strangers to the trial by jury.*

"*Great as this eulogium may seem, it is no more than this admirable* "*constitution, when traced to its principles, will be found in sober reason* "*to deserve. The impartial administration of justice which secures both* "*our persons and our properties, is the great end of civil society. But if* "*that be entirely entrusted to the magistracy, a select body of men, and* "*those generally selected by the prince or such as enjoy the highest offices* "*in the state, their decisions, in spite of their own natural integrity, will* "*have frequently an involuntary biass towards those of their own rank* "*and dignity: it is not to be expected from human nature, than* the few, "*should be always attentive to the interests and good of the many. On* "*the other hand, if the power of judicature were placed at random in the* "*hands of the multitude, their decisions would be wild and capricious,* "*and a new rule of action would be every day established in our courts.*

* Montesq. Sp. L. xi. 6.

If this be "wisdom" it is not of that kind, the "ways whereof are *past finding out.*"

The act, thus revoked by you, received soon after a formal repeal in Parliament. This was done by the 6th of George the Third, Chapter the 11th. Because it was unconstitutional, as we were not and could not be represented there? No. Because it deprived "three millions" of loyal subjects of their darling privilege of trial by jury, "the best preservative of English liberty?" No. Because "the continuance of the said act would be attended with many inconveniences, and might be productive of

"*It is wisely therefore ordered, that the principles and axioms of law,*
"*which are generally propositions flowing from abstracted reason, and*
"*not accommodated to times or to men, should be deposited in the breasts*
"*of the judges, to be occasionally applied to such facts as come properly*
"*ascertained before them. For here partiality can have little scope: the*
"*law is well known, and is the same for all ranks and degrees: it fol-*
"*lows as a regular conclusion from the premises of fact pre-established.*
"*But in setting and adjusting a question of fact, when intrusted to any*
"*single magistrate, partiality and injustice have an ample field to range*
"*in ; either by boldly asserting that to be proved which is not so, or more*
"*artfully by suppressing some circumstances, stretching and warping*
"*others, and distinguishing away the remainder. Here therefore a com-*
"*petent number of sensible and upright jurymen, chosen by lot from among*
"*those of the middle rank, will be found the best investigators of truth,*
"*and the surest guardians of public justice. For the most powerful indi-*
"*vidual in the state will be cautious of committing any flagrant invasion*
"*of another's right, when he knows that the fact of his oppression must be*
"*examined and decided by twelve indifferent men ; and that, when once*
"*the fact is ascertained, the law must of course redress it. This therefore*
"*preserves in the hands of the people that share, which they ought to have*
"*in the administration of public justice, and prevents the encroachments of*
"*the more powerful and wealthy citizens. Every new tribunal, erected*
"*for the decision of facts, without the intervention of a jury, (whether*
"*composed of justices of the peace, commissioners of the revenue, judges*
"*of a court of conscience, or any other standing magistrates) is a step*
"*towards establishing aristocracy, the most oppressive of absolute govern-*
"*ments. The feodel system, which, for the sake of military subordination,*
"*pursued an aristocratical plan in all its arrangements of property, had*
"*been intolerable in times of peace, had it not been wisely counterpoised*
"*by that privilege, so universally diffused through every part of it, the*

consequences greatly detrimental to the commercial interests of" *Great Britain.*

Cool, guarded expressions! Breathing the true spirit of the modern philosophy, so prevailing among the higher ranks in that polished kingdom. How much care to avoid *inconveniences* and *detriment* to their own *commercial* interests! How sovereign a contempt for all agonies, that bowed us down to the earth, while indignation, shame, grief, affection, veneration, and gratitude combated within our hearts! They were advised to speak peace to our souls, by nobly assigning an *"erroneous principle,"* for the repeal.* No. The freedom of *America* is the *Carth-*

"trial by the feodal peers. And in every country on the continent, as the " trial by the peers has been gradually disused, so the nobles have increased "in power, till the state has been torn to pieces by rival factions, and oli- "garchy in effect has been established, though under the shadow of regal "government; unless where the miserable commons have taken shelter " under absolute monarchy, as the lighter evil of the two. And, particu- "larly, it is a circumstance well worthy an Englishman's observation, that " in Sweden the trial by jury, that bulwark of northern liberty, which con- " tinued in its full vigour so lately as the middle of the last century,† is "now fallen into disuse :‡ and there, though the regal power is in no "country so closely limited, yet the liberties of the commons are extin- "guished, and the government is degenerated into a mere aristocracy.§ It "is therefore, upon the whole, a duty which every man owes to his country, " his friends, his posterity, and himself, to maintain, to the utmost of his "power this valuable constitution in all its rights; to restore it to its an- " cient dignity, if at all impaired by the different value of property, or " otherwise deviated from its first institution ; to amend it, wherever it is " defective ; and, above all, to guard with the most jealous circumspection "against the introduction of new and arbitrary methods of trial, which, " under a variety of plausible pretences, may in time imperceptibly under- "mine this best preservative of English liberty." Blackstone's Com., 3d Vol., Page 378–381.

* *"Upon the whole, I will beg leave to tell the Houses what is realy my "opinion; it is, that the Stamp-Act be repealed, absolutely, totally, and "immediately; that the reason for the repeal be assigned,* because it was " founded on an ERRONEOUS PRINCIPLE." *Mr.* PITT'S *Speech.*

† Mod. Un. Hist., XXXIII., 22.
‡ Whitelocke of parl., 427.
§ Ibid., 17.

age of *Great Britain—delenda est.* Let us repeal the act, but never resign the principle, on which it was founded.

One *generous* step however they did take; becoming *Britons.* It demands our acknowledgments: Nor should we withhold them. Why will they not suffer us to thank them for other favours?

The repealing act spoke an indecisive language, subject to comments, that might differ on different sides of the *Atlantic.* We might have been too much agitated between hopes and apprehensions. It would have been unkind to leave us in such a state of anxiety. It would have been unworthy of a free people, who were determined to subjugate another free people. *Parmenius* may steal victories. *Alexander* scorns it.

Therefore the same day, I think, in which they repealed the Stamp-Act, in the next Chapter, however, they *candidly* explained to us their sentiments and resolutions beyond possibility of a mistake, by the "Act for the better securing the dependency of his Majesty's dominions in *America* upon the Crown and Parliament of *Great Britain.*"

"Lift up thine eyes round about: And behold, all "these gather themselves together, AND COME TO THEE : "Thou shall SURELY CLOTHE thee with them all, as with "an ornament, and BIND them on thee, as a Bride doth." Isaiah, Chapter 49.

LETTER III.

TO THE INHABITANTS OF THE BRITISH COLONIES IN AMERICA.

BRETHREN, These are the words of the declaratory act mentioned in the last letter. "Whereas several of the Houses of Representatives in his Majesty's Colonies and Plantations in *America* have of late, AGAINST LAW,

claimed to themselves, or to the general Assemblies of the
same, the SOLE and EXCLUSIVE right of imposing Duties
and TAXES upon his Majesty's SUBJECTS IN THE SAID
COLONIES AND PLANTATIONS; and have in pursuance of
such claim, passed certain votes, resolutions, and orders,
DEROGATORY TO THE LEGISLATIVE AUTHORITY OF PAR-
LIAMENT, and inconsistent with the dependency of the
said Colonies and Plantations, &c. therefore be it declared,
&c. that the said Colonies and Plantations in *America*
have been, are, and of right ought to be subordinate unto,
and dependent upon the imperial Crown and Parliament
of *Great Britain*, and that the King's Majesty by and
with the advise and consent of the Lord's spiritual and
temporal and Commons of *Great Britain*, in Parliament
assembled, had, HATH and OF RIGHT OUGHT TO HAVE,
full power and authority to make laws and statutes, of
sufficient force and validity to BIND the Colonies and
People of America, Subjects of the Crown of *Great Britain*,
IN ALL CASES WHATSOEVER."

From the croud of objects, each pressing for attention,
that present themselves to the mind of a *British American*, on reading this act, I beg leave to select and particularly mention only two.

The resolutions, &c. mentioned in this act, were those
caused by the Stamp-Act. These principal points are
firmly asserted in them—*the exclusive right of taxation*
and the *right of trial by jury*. The Parliament well
knowing how harsh and jarring it would sound in English
ears, to say, the right of trial by jury, was "*derogatory to
the Legislative authority of Parliament*, and INCONSISTENT
with the dependency of the Colonies," planted their most
direct battery against the right of taxation—common
sense and the experience of all nations, AS NOT A SINGLE
INSTANCE OCCURS TO THE CONTRARY, convincing them,
if *that* gave way, a general ruin would soon ensue, and all

the rest would follow in the train of the chief, like captive *Nobles* attending their conquered *Prince.*

However, not quite satisfyed with the slow work of exterminating them in detail, but improving upon an impartial hint, it was judged fittest upon the whole so to consolidate them, that, as if the *British Americans* had but "ONE NECK" a SINGLE *stroke* might dispatch millions —by subjecting us *at once* to the decrees of Parliament, IN ALL CASES WHATSOEVER.

Widely different was the act of the 6th of George the First, Chap. 5th, "for the better securing the dependency of the kingdom of *Ireland*, &c." By that act *Ireland* was declared "to be subordinate unto, and dependent upon the imperial CROWN * of *Great Britain.*" These words "and Parliament" are not it. It is said, indeed, that "the King with advise and consent of the Lords and Commons of *Great Britain*, in Parliament assembled, had, and of right ought to have power and authority to make laws and statutes, of sufficient force and validity, to bind the kingdom and people of *Ireland.*"

Compare the Act, and you will find the Act for *America* copied from that of *Ireland.* But in the last mentioned, the annihilating words—"IN ALL CASES WHATSOEVER" are not to be found. The people of Ireland have been for several centuries bound by *English* statutes for regulating their trade and for other purposes, and this statute, therefore, only asserted the USUAL authority over them. Their vitals, the exclusive right of taxation, and the right of

---

* "*A tax granted by the Parliament of England shall not bind those* "*of Ireland, because they are not summoned to our Parliament,*" *and* "*again,* "Ireland *hath a Parliament of its own and maketh and altereth* "*laws; and our statutes do not bind them, because they do not send Knights* "*to our Parliament: but their* persons, *are the,* King's subjects, *like as* "*the inhabitants of,* Calais, Gascoigny *and* Guienne, *while they continued* "*under the King's subjection.*" Blackstone, Vol. I., p. 101, from the year books.

trial by jury, have been preserved. If it was the intention of the British Parliament to exercise a "power and authority" over that kingdom, destructive of these rights, it is not expressed—it is not implied. Why were the unlimited words omitted in that Act? Or, why when the Lords and Commons were copying a pattern, which their fathers sent them, did they deform the transcript by such eastern flourishes?

The truth is—the fathers too much revered the English principles, for which they had been upon the point of shedding their blood, in placing their Sovereign on his Throne, so flagrantly to violate them—or, if their conduct was not directed by justice, they dared not thus to provoke the brave, generous inhabitants of that antient kingdom.

"*Are there yet the treasures of wickedness in the house, "and the scant measure, that is abominable. The rich "men thereof are full of violence.*" Micah. ch. VI.—

To P. P. *Author of the* "LETTERS *to the* INHABITANTS "*of the* BRITISH COLONIES *in* AMERICA."—

SIR,

The declaratory Act, passed by the Parliament, at the time they repealed the Stamp-Act, was such a violation of the constitution, such an assumption of new powers, so subversive of Liberty, and so destructive of property, that it deserves particular observation. That it has hitherto passed unnoticed, is owing to the gratitude and joy with which America received the Repeal of the Stamp-Act. For the same reason, the principle, on which the Repeal was founded, was suffered to pass without animadversion; and the people, who claimed the Repeal, as a point of *equity and right*, received it with gratitude as a *free gift*.

The English Constitution, whose object is Liberty, has, for the preserving that Liberty, and for the security of Property, vested peculiar powers in the different branches of the legislature, which are to be exercised for the good and safety of the subject. Salus Populi suprema Lex est. The abuse of these powers, or the attempt of one branch of the legislature to extend its peculiar powers, so as to abridge those of the others, has been the foundation of many civil wars and struggles in Britain.

From the earliest period of the English Constitution, it has been the prerogative of the Crown to grant Charters to the Subjects and terms of Capitulation to conquered countries, who were taken under the dominion of the crown. And the statute of quo warranto 18th of Edw. I. expressly declares, that "illi qui habent Charatas regales, secundum Chartas istas et earundem plenitudinem judicetur." On which statute Lord Coke observes, "in the first place, that as it was enacted, ex speciali gratia domini Regis, *it binds the King,*" and *consequently in binding the King, must also bind his Parliament;* in the second place, from the words earundem plenitudinem, that this statute is to be construed "as fully and beneficially for the Charters, as the law was taken at the time when the Charters were granted." In the third place, says he, "certainly this ancient statute was a direction to the sages of the law, for their construction of the King's Charter, as it appeareth in our books."—

On this foundation rests the declaratory act respecting Ireland. When Henry the 2d. conquered Ireland, he granted the Irish peace and annexed them to his Crown on this condition, " That the kingdom and people of Ireland should for ever be governed by the same *mild laws* as England was governed." And the statute passed in the 31 Edward 3d. confirms and renews this charter by declaring that his Majesty's subjects in Ireland, being either natives of that kingdom, or English born subjects only resident there, "sint veri Anglici, et sub eisdem degant domino et regimine et eisdem legibus utantur." And hence the act of the 6th G. 1. chap. 6, assumes no *new* power, lays no *new* restrictions upon his Majesty's good subjects of Ireland, nor claims any *new* right, but simply declares "that the King's Majesty by and with the advice and consent of the Lords spiritual and temporal and Commons of Great Britain in Parliament assembled HATH *full power and authority* to make law of sufficient force and validity to bind the kingdom and people of Ireland."

Here is no charter violated, no claim of power to deprive them of property or levy taxes on them without their consent. Their Parliament, their right of trial by jury, and of granting supplies to their King in their own way for the support of government, administration of justice, and defence of the kingdom, remain untouched. But the declaratory act passed against America 5 of G. 3, in violation of their charters, declares, that the CLAIM of the House of Reperesentatives in his Majesty's Colonies and Plantations in *America*, to the SOLE and EXCLUSIVE RIGHT of imposing duties and taxes upon his Majesty's subjects in the said Colonies and Plantations is AGAINST LAW ; that the votes, resolutions and orders passed in pursuance of such claim are DEROGATORY TO THE LEGISLATIVE AUTHORITY OF PARLIAMENT ; that the said Colonies & Plantations in *America* have been, are and OF RIGHT OUGHT TO BE subordinate unto and dependent upon the imperial Crown and PARLIAMENT of *Great-Britain*, and that the King's Majesty by and with the advise, &c. hath and OF RIGHT OUGHT TO HAVE full power and authority to make laws and statutes of sufficient force and validity to BIND the Colonies and People of *America*, Subjects of the Crown of *Great-Britain* IN ALL CASES WHATSOEVER. What is this but with the high hand of power to break down the barriers of the constitution and make us *tenants at will* of our lives, liberty and property. —

There was a time when the Crown held lands in England, "sacra patrimonia coronæ," the annual rent of which, if now resumed, would amount to near four millions sterling. These have been conveyed to subjects and are now held by virtue of Charters from the Crown. If the Chartae regales or Chartered rights of the colonies can be violated and annuled by Parliament, what security can the possessors of those lands have for the estates they enjoy? Let the Parliament try the experiment on their fellow subjects in Great Britain, and judge of the temper and disposition of the colonies, by the effect such a step will produce among themselves.

I am Sir,

A Loyal American,

A. B.

Errata in 2d Letter. *For* this kind *read* "the kind ;" *for* Alexander scorns it, *r.* "Alexanders scorn ;" *for* prosperity of us, *r.* "posterity of us ;" *for* fees and salaries, *r.* "salaries."

LETTER IV.

To the INHABITANTS of the BRITISH COLONIES IN AMERICA.

BRETHREN, The intelligence received, since the preceding letter was written, seems to render needless every attempt to prove from *former transactions*,—my first intention, if health had permitted—that a regular plan has been invaribly persued to inslave these Colonies, and that the Act of Parliament for blocking up the port of *Boston* is a part of the plan. However unprecedented and cruel that measure is, yet some persons among us might have flattered themselves, that the resentment of the Parliament is directed sorely against that town. The last advices mention two bills to be passing in Parliament ; one changing the chartered constitution of the province of *Massachusetts Bay* into a military government ; and another, empowering administration to send for and try persons in *England* for actions committed in that colony.*

By these instances we perceive, that administration has not only renounced all respect, and all appearance of respect, for the rights of these colonies, but even the plainest principles of the justice and humanity. Were the representatives of the people of *Massachusetts Bay* called upon to make satisfaction for the damage done to private property in any late tumult there? No. Yet it was known, that those representatives had made ample reparation for the injuries committed on occasion of the Stamp Act. It was known, that the like reparation had been made by the Assembly of *New-York* and *Rhode-Island*. In short, it was known, that notwithstanding the incessant pains taken by many Ministers to teaze the colonists by oppressions and insults into madness, yet they have with difficulty excited only a few tumults, for which the popular branch of the legislature in the several colonies has ever been ready to atone, upon requisitions from the crown.

* *By the first of these bills, the* Governor *is to be invested with the power of a* Justice of the Peace, *to call out the military effect, though the Minister says in his speech—"I shall always consider, that a military power acting under the authority and controul of a civil magistrate* IS A PART OF THE CONSTITUTION." *By the second*, Americans *are to be seized, confined and carried to* England, *to be tried—that is hanged, on charges for acts done in a colony. This is not all. Soldiers and others, who shall commit* any offence, *such as murdering the Colonists, under the pretence of supporting the authority of Parliament, shall be carried to England to be tried—that is—acquitted. Of the* Habeas Corpus *and* Trial by Peers "stat nominus umbra,"

That the absolute power claimed *and* exercised *in a neighboring nation, is more tolerable than that of the eastern empires is in a great measure owing to their having united the* judicial *power in their Parliaments, a body separate and distinct from both the legislative and executive, and if ever that nation recovers its former liberty, it will owe it to the efforts to those assemblies. In* Turkey, *where* EVERY THING *is centered in the* Sultan *or* his Minister, DESPOTIC POWER *is in its meridian and* WEARS A MOST DREADFUL ASPECT." I. *Blackstone* 260, 270.

Great clamour has been raised at home against Massachusetts Bay, on account of resolutions at some of their town meetings, and other writings published in that Colony ; And better it were, that many of them had been suppressed. The truth is—that people animated by an ardent and generous love of liberty saw and peculiarly felt the projects against the freedom and happiness of *America.* I know them well : and if ever a people deserved the character, they are moral, religious, quiet and loyal, affectionately attached to the welfare and honor of *Great Britain,* and dearly valuing their dependence on her. Sensible and observant, as they were, of the present and approaching evils, some of them adopted a very peaceable and justifiable method of discouraging Administration from proceeding in such alarming and dangerous measures,—that of speaking in a high tone. Words were opposed to injuries, and menaces, never designed for execution, to insults intolerable. What could they do? Their *petitions* were haughtily and contemptuously rejected. The more they *supplicated,* the more they were *abused.* By their tears, and Heaven knows many they have shed, their persecutions flourished, as trees by water poured on their roots. Their very virtue and passionate fondness for concord with their Mother-Country, occasioned this objected error. "Surely," says Solomon, "oppression maketh a wise man mad." A silly man may disregard it. Their folly shewed their wisdom. This is the true history of those futile pieces, that produced so much furious eloquence in *Great-Britain.*

Riots and weak publications, by some individuals, are sufficient reasons with Parliament to ruin many thousand inhabitants of a truly respectable town, to dissolve charters, to abolish the benefits of the writ of *habeas corpus,* *

* *Both Houses of Parliament resolved two or three years ago, that persons might be sent for from* any of the Colonies *for acts done there, and*

and extirpate American liberty—For the principle reaches
all. But in *England* the press groans with publications,
seditious, treasonable and even blasphemous. The discontented swarm over the kingdom, proclaiming their resentments. Many enormous riots have disturbed the public
peace. The sovereign has been insulted in passing from
his Palace to the Parliament-house, on the business of the
nation. Is it to be concluded from these facts, that the
BODY OF THE PEOPLE is seditious and traitorous? Can
his Majesty believe, that he is thought by his English subjects in *general* to be such a Prince, as some of them have
represented him? Will the two Houses of Parliament acknowledge what has been spoken and written and acted
against them in *England*, expresses the sentiments of the
kingdom? Or will they say, that the *People* of *England*
have forfeited their liberty, because *some of them* have run

tried in England *under the old statute of Henry the 8th—made before the
Colonies existed. The late Court at* Rhode Island *was established on
that principle. The intention of Parliament in passing the bill above
mentioned is chiefly to screen persons acting in support of their unconstitutional claims. They have declared, they have no doubt but that the 35th
of* Henry *has established a just and legal mode of cutting* American
throats.*

"*I can live, altho' another who has no right, be put to live with me;
nay, I can live altho' I pay* Excises *and* Impositions *more than I do; but
to have any* LIBERTY, *which is the* SOUL *of my* LIFE, *taken from me by*
POWER, *and to have my body pent up in a gaol, (then thrown into a ship
of war, transported three thousand miles across the ocean, to a land of bitter, selfish, furious and revengefull Enemies, there thrust in the jaws of
Dungeons,) without remedy by law, and to be so adjudged; O improvi-
dent Ancestors! O unwise Forefathers! to be so curious in providing for
the quiet possession of our Laws and liberties of Parliament, and to neglect our persons and bodies, and to let them lie in prison, and that* durante
bene placito, *remediless! If this be law, why do we talk of Liberties?
Why do we* TROUBLE *ourselves with a dispute about law, franchises, property of goods, and the like? What may any man call his own, if not the
liberty, of his person? I am weary of treading these Ways.*"

Speach of Sir Robert Philips, a member of the wise and moderate Parliament that met in the year 1627.

into licentiousness? Let a judgment be formed in *both* cases by the *same* rule. Let them condemn *those*, or acquit *us*.

Pretences and reasons are totally different. The provocations, said to be given by our sister colony, are but the PRETENCES for the exorbitant severity exercised against her. The REASONS, are these—the policy, despicable and detestable as it is, of suppressing the freedom of *America* by a military force, to be supported by money taken out of our own pockets, and the supposed convenience of opportunity for attaining this end. These REASONS are evident from the Minister's speech. The system is formed with art, but the art is discoverable. Indeed, I do not believe it was expected, we should have such early and exact intelligence of the schemes agitated against us, as we have received. Any person, who examines the multitude of invectives published in pamphlets and newspapers in *Great-Britain*, or the speeches made in either House of Parliament, will find them directed *against the Colonies in general*. The people in that kingdom have been with great cunning and labor,* inflamed *against the Colonies in general*. They are deluded into a belief, that we are in a state of rebellion and aiming directly at a state of independency; though the first is a noxious weed that never grew in our climates ; and the latter is universally regarded with the deepest execration by us—a poison we never can be compelled to touch, but as an antidote to a worse, if a worse can be—a tree of forbidden and accursed fruit, which, if any Colony on this continent should be so mad as to attempt reaching, the rest would have virtue and wisdom enough to draw their swords and hew the traitors into submission, if not into loyalty. It would be their interest and their duty, thus to guaranty the public peace.

The Minister addressing the House of Commons, uses

* *Private Letters give a further Proof of this Fact.*

several expressions relating to *all the Colonies*, and calls the stoppage of the port of *Boston* "a punishment inflicted on those, *who have disobeyed your Authority.*" Is it not extremely remarkable, after such a variety of charges affecting *all* the Colonies, that the statutes of vengence should be levelled against a *single* Colony? *New-York*, *Philadelphia* and *Charlestown* have denied freedom of Trade to ships sailing *under the protection of Acts of Parliament.* Will not the House of Commons think that the inhabitants of these places "have disobeyed their authority," and that "a punishment should be inflicted on them?" Why do we not hear of some measure pursued against those Cities? Are *they* immaculate in the eyes of Administration and Parliament? Have not each of these places done *real damage* to the *East-India* Company? Has there been even a requisition of compensation for that damage from any of them? Why is there such a *profound silence* observed with respect to them? Because they are judged by Administration and Parliament, more innocent than the Colony of *Massachusetts Bay?* No. Because Administration and Parliament do us *Americans* the honor to think, we are such very ideots, that we shall not believe ourselves interested in the fate of *Boston*, but that one Colony may be attacked and humbled after another, without shewing the sence or spirit of beasts themselves, many of which unite against a common danger.

Why were the states of Greece broken down into the tamest submission by *Philip* of *Macedon*, and afterwards by the *Romans?* Because they contended for freedom *separately*. Why were the states of *Spain* subdued by the *Carthaginians* and afterwards by the *Romans?* Because they contended for freedom *separately*. Why were the antient inhabitant of the kingdom, that now harasses us, conquered by their invaders? *Tacitus* will inform us, "Nec aliud adversus validissimas gentes pro nobis utilius,

quam quod in COMMUNE Nonconsulunt. Rarus ad pro-
pulsandum *commune periculum* conventus. Ita dum *sin-
guli* pugnant, *omnes* vincuntur. *

Why did the little *Swiss* cantons, and seven small provinces of the *Low Countries*, so successfully oppose the
tyrants, that not contented with an empire founded in humanity and mutual advantages, *unnecessarily* and arro-
gantly strove to "LAY" the faithful and affectionate
wretches "AT THEIR FEET?" Because, they wisely regarded the interest of *each* as the interest of *all*.

Our own experience furnishes a mournful additional
proof of an observation made by a great and good man,
Lord President *Forbes*. "It is a certain truth," says he,
"that all states and kingdoms, in proportion as they grow
great, wealthy and powerful, grow wanton, wicked, and
oppressive, and the history of all ages gives evidence of
the fatal catastrophe of ALL SUCH states and kingdoms, when
the cup of their iniquity is full." Another "truth" as
"certain" is—that "such states and kingdoms" never have
been, and never will be checked in the career of their "wan-
tonness, wickedness and oppression " by a people in any
degree, dependent upon them, but by the prudent, virtuous
and steady UNANIMITY of that people. To employ more
words to elucidate a point so manifest, would be the idle attempt of gilding gold. Surely you cannot doubt at this
time, my countrymen, but that the people of *Massachusetts-
Bay* are suffering in a cause † common to us all ; and there-

* "*Nor was any thing more advantageous to us against very powerful
nations, than their imprudence in not* consulting together for the interest
of the whole. *Conventions for repelling a* common danger *were rare.
Thus, while* each *state resisted* singly, all *were subdued.*"

Tacitus *in vit.* Agric.

† *The act for shutting up the port of Boston, orders, that it shall not be
opened until "peace and* obedience to the laws *shall be* so far *restored in
the said town of* Boston, *that the trade of* Great-Britain *may safely be carried on there, and his Majesty's* DUTIES DULY COLLECTED, *&c." Thus it
appears, if the inhabitants renounce the common cause of the Colonies, the
port may be* opened—*if they* adhere *to that cause, it will remain* shut.

fore, that we ought immediately to concert the most
prudent measures for their relief and our own safety.

Our interest depending on the present controversy is un-
speakably valuable. We have not the least prospect of
human assistance. The passion of despotism raging like
a plague, for about seven years past, has spread with un-
usual malignity through *Europe. Corsica, Poland*, and
Sweden, have sunk beneath it. The remaining spirit of
freedom, that lingered and languished in the Parliaments
of *France*, has lately expired, by the new moddelling their
Parliaments. What kingdom or state interposed for the
relief of their distressed fellow creatures? The contagion
has at length reached *Great-Britain*. Her Statesmen
emulate the *Nimrods* of the earth and wish to become
"mighty hunters" in the woods of *America*. What kingdom or state will interpose for our relief? The preservation of our freedom and every attendant blessing must be
wrought out, under providence, *by ourselves*. Let not this
consideration discourage us. We cannot be false to each
other, without being false to ourselves. We have firmest
foundation of Union and Fidelity—that we wish to attain
the same things—to avoid the same things. The friendship of others might be precarious, suspected, deceitful.

The infinitely great, wise, and good Being, who gave
us our existence, certainly formed us for a state of society.
He certainly designed us for such a state of society, as
would be productive of happiness. Liberty is essential to
the happiness of a society, and therefore is our right. The
father of mercies never intended men to hold UNLIMITED
authority over men. * Craft and cruelty have indeed tri-

* "To live by one Man's Will became the cause of all Men's misery."
Hooker's Eccles. Pol.

"Is not *universal misery* and *ruin* the SAME, whether it comes from
the hands of *many* or of *one*."

Bishop Hoadly's dis. on Govt.

"Of so contrary an opinion was this good man (*Hooker*) to that of

umphed over simplicity and innocence, in disobedience to his holy laws. The father of mercies never intended *us* for the slaves of *Britons.* Craft and cruelty indeed are striving to brand us with marks infamously denoting us to be their property, as absolutely as their cattle. Their pre-

some others, who can never oppose one *extreme*, without running to *another*, as bad, *if not worse;* and think they cannot enough condemn *Rebellion*, without giving the devine sanction to *tyranny* and *oppression.* This judgment ought likewise to be of the more weight, with such as profess the most profound veneration for the memory of Charles the first, and the honour of the *old Church of England:* Because this treatise, in which it is to be found, was chosen out of many others by that *Prince*, to be recommended to his *children*, as the best *instructor* they could converse with; and was had in such *estimation* by all *churchmen*, from the time of its appearance, that it may well pass not only for his own *judgment* in particular, but for the *judgment* of the whole *church* of England at that time."

Bishop Hoadly, ibid.

" Would not the *unhappiness* of this nation in particular have been the same, whether a late King *alone*, or BY A FORMAL LAW had subjected it to the religion of *Rome* and THE MAXIMS OF FRANCE? And upon supposition of such an *attempt*, would not our *late deliverance* have been as *glorious* as *great* and *justifiable;* as much wanted and as truly beneficial; as it was upon the attempt of the *king alone;* would not *the invitation of the Prince of Orange;* ̗the *election* and *meeting* of the persons, who made the *convention;* and *the consequent establishment* in the *protestant line* have been as requisite and as useful? Nay would not the ENDS OF GOVERNMENT have been more effectually answered this way, than by SUBMISSION to a TOTAL DISSOLUTION OF ALL HAPPINESS at *present* and ALL HOPES for the *future?* How can it be said that the *ends of Government* require *that* degree of *submission* upon the *one* supposition, which they were allowed not to do upon the *other;* when the *same* MISERY and DESTRUCTION *must* follow a *Submission* in *both* cases; and the *same universal* HAPPINESS *must* in *both* be the CONSEQUENCE OF A JUST and WELL MANAGED DEFENCE? Or would the *ends of Government* be destroyed, should the miserable condition of the whole people of *France*, which hath proceeded from the Kings being absolute, awaken the thoughts of the *wisest heads* among them, and move them all to exert themselves, *so as that those ends should be better answered for the time to come.*"

Bishop Hoadly, ibid.

It was resolved by the House of Commons that this Bishop, then *Mr.*

tensions to a right of such power, not only oppose constitutional principles, but even partake of impiety. The sentence of bondage against us is only issued by the frail OMNIPOTENCE* of PARLIAMENT.

"Non sic inflectere sensus
"Humanos edicta valent." †

We cannot question the *justice* of our cause. This consideration will afford comfort and encouragement to our minds.

Let us therefore, in the first place, humbling ourselves before our gracious Creator, devoutly beseech his divine Protection on us his afflicted servants, most unreasonably and cruely oppressed. Let us seriously reflect on our manifold transgressions, and by a sincere repentance, and an entire amendment of our lives, strive to recommend ourselves to divine favour.

In the next place, let us cherish and cultivate senti-

Hoadly and Rector of St. *Peter's* poor, *London*, "for having often strennously justified the PRINCIPLES, on which her *Majesty* and the *nation* proceeded in the late happy revolution, had justly merited the favour and recommendation of that House." And accordingly addressed *Queen Anne*, "that she would be graciously pleased to bestow some dignity in the church on the said Mr. *Hoadly* for his eminent services both to the *church* and state.

"Whatsoever dishonours human nature, dishonours the policy of a government, which permits it; and a free state, which does not communicate the natural right of liberty to *all* its subjects, *who have not deserved by their crimes to lose it*, hardly seems to be worthy of that honourable name."

Lord Littleton's history of Hen. 2d.

"Without *goodness*, power would be *tyranny* and *oppression*, and wisdom would degenerate into *craft*, and mischievous contrivance."

Archbishop *Tillotson's* sermons "Etiam si non sit molestus dominus; tamen est miserrimum posse, si velit."—Cicero. Even if a Sovereign does not oppress, yet it is a most miserable condition for the subjects, that he has *power*, if he has the will.

* 1. *Blackstone* 161.

† *Edicts cannot so bend the common Sense of human Creatures.*

ments of brotherly love and tenderness among us. To
whom under the cope of Heaven, can we look for help in
these days of "darkness and trouble," but one to another.

O my Countrymen! have pity one on another—Have
pity on yourselves, and your children. Let us—by every
tender tie, I implore you—let us, mutually excuse and
forgive each other our weaknesses and prejudices, (for who
is free from weakness and prejudices?)—and utterly abolishing all former dissentious distinctions, wisely and
kindly unite in one firm bond, in one common cause.

If there are any men or any bodies of men on this continent, who think that an accomidation between us and
Great-Britain, or that their own particular interest, may
be advanced by withdrawing themselves from the councils
of their countrymen, I would wish them most deliberately
to consider the consequences, that may attend such a conduct. What step can possibly be taken more directly tending to *prevent* an accomidation between us and *Great-Britain*, than supplying administration with *proofs of our intes-
tine divisions?* What do our enemies so ardently wish for,
as for these divisions? Has not the expectation of these
events encouraged the ministry to treat us with such unexampled contempt and barbarity? Will not the *certainty* of
these events excite resolutions in them to press us—to take
every advantage of a people so industriously studying and
labouring to weaken and destroy themselves? Then a minister may with reason call upon the House of Commons—
"NOW IS OUR TIME TO stand out—to *defy* them—to proceed
with *firmness* and *without fear*—to produce a conviction to
ALL *America*, that we are now in *earnest*, and that we will
proceed with firmness and rigor—until SHE SHALL BE
LAID AT OUR FEET." *

I appeal to every man of common sense, whether any
measure will be so likely to induce administration to

* *Lord North's speech.*

think of an accommodation with us, as our *unanimity*. Must not, therefore, every measure impeaching the credit and weight of this unanimity in the same degree obstruct all accommodation? Will not every such measure naturally produce *haughtiness, perseverance* and *fresh rigour* in our oppressors? Will not *these* still more enrage us, and place us farther from an accommodation? If the PROTECTION and PEACE, we wish to derive from our unanimity be taken from us, by the imprudence of our brethren, who break that unanimity or destroy all respect for it in *Great-Britain*, and thereby encourage her to seize, what she will certainly think, the lucky opportunity for pursuing her blows, what must be the consequence? We held up a shield for our defence. If our brethren have pierced it through and rendered it useless—their indiscretion will, according to the usual course of human affairs, compel us to change the mode of defence, and drive us into all the evils of civil discords.

What advantages can they gain, that can compensate to men of any understanding or virtue, for the miseries occasioned by their bad policy? Their numbers will be too small, in any manner whatever to controul the sentiments or measures of the people of *America*. Their conduct never can prevent the exertions of these Colonies in vindication of their liberty. It may, by provocations, render those exertions more rash and imprudent. But their numbers will be so extravigantly exaggerated, as all facts have been against us, on the other side of the *Atlantic* that *Great-Britain* may be *deceived* and *emboldened* into measures destructive to herself and to us. We are now strenuously endeavouring, IN A PEACEABLE MANNER, by this single *power* the force of UNANIMITY—to preserve our freedom. Those, who *lessen* that unanimity, *detract* from its force— will *prevent* its *effect*—and must be, therefore, justly chargeable with all the dreadful consequences to the Colonies.

The third important consideration, I beg leave to recommend to my countrymen, is to draw such reflections from their situation as will confirm their minds in that manly noble fortitude, so absolutely necessary, for the maintenance of those inestimable privileges, for which they are now contending. The man, who fears difficulties arising in the defence of freedom, is unworthy of freedom. God has given the right and means of asserting it. We may reasonably ask and expect his gracious assistance in the reasonable employment of those means. To look for miracles, while we abusively neglect the powers afforded us by divine goodness, is not only stupid, but criminal. We are yet free—Let us think like freemen.

In the last place I beg leave to offer some observations concerning the measures that may be most expedient in the present emergency. Other nations have contended in blood for their liberty, and have judged the jewel worth the price that was paid for it. These colonies are not reduced to the dreadful necessity. So dependent is *Great-Britain* on us for supplies, that Heaven seems to have placed in our hands means of an effectual, yet peaceable resistance, if we have sense and integrity to make a proper use of them. A general agreement between these colonies of non-importation and non-exportation faithfully observed would certainly be attended with success. But is it now proper to enter into such an agreement? Let us consider that we are contending with our ancient venerable and beloved parent-country. Let us treat her with all possible respect and reverence:* Though the Rulers there have

* *By justice* (*saith the Scripture*) *" the throne is established," and "by justice a nation shall be exalted." I resemble justice to* Nebuchadnezar's *tree, shading not only the palace of the King and the house of Nobles, but sheltering also the cottage of the poorest beggar. Therefore if now the blast of indignation hath so bruised any of the branches of this tree, that either our persons or goods or possessions have not the same shelter as before, let us not therefore* neglect the root of this great tree; *but rather*

had no compassion upon us, let us have compassion on the people of that kingdom : And if to give weight to our supplications and to obtain relief for our suffering brethren, it shall be judged necessary to lay ourselves under restrictions with regard to our imports and exports, let it be done with tenderness, so as to convince our brethren in *Great-Britain* of the importance of a connexion and harmony between them and us, and of the danger of driving us into despair. Their true interests and our own are the same ; nor should we admit any notion of a distinction, till we *know* their *resolutions* to be UNALTERABLY HOSTILE.—

In the mean time, let us pursue the most proper methods for collecting the sentiments of all the British colonies in North *America*, on the present situation of affairs—the first point, it is apprehended, to which attention should be paid. This may be affected in various ways. The assemblies that may have opportunities of meeting, may appoint deputies to attend a general congress at such time and place as shall be agreed on. Where assemblies cannot meet, such of the people as are qualified by law to vote in election of representative may meet and appoint—or may request their representatives to meet and appoint.

When the inhabitants of this extended continent observe that regular measures are prosecuted for re-establishing harmony between *Great-Britain* and these Colonies, their minds will grow more calm. Prospects of accommodation, it is hoped, will engage them patiently and peaceably to attend the results of the public councils and such applications as by the joint sense of *America* may be judged

with all our possible means, endeavours and unfeigned duties, both apply fresh and fertile mold unto it and also water it even with our tears, that so those bruised branches may be recovered and the whole tree again prosper and flourish." Mr. Creskeld's speech in the Parliament that met in 1727.

proper to be made to his Majesty and both Houses of Parliament.

"Better is a little with righteousness, than great revnues without right." Proverbs 16.—